AF478205

Rethinking Contemporary Social Theory

Rethinking Contemporary Social Theory

Roberta Garner, Black Hawk Hancock,
and Grace Budrys

Paradigm Publishers
Boulder • London

All rights reserved. No part of the publication may be transmitted or reproduced in any media or form, including electronic, mechanical, photocopy, recording, or informational storage and retrieval systems, without the express written consent of the publisher.

Copyright © 2013 by Paradigm Publishers

Published in the United States by Paradigm Publishers, 5589 Arapahoe Avenue, Boulder, CO 80303 USA.

Paradigm Publishers is the trade name of Birkenkamp & Company, LLC,
Dean Birkenkamp, President and Publisher.

Library of Congress Cataloging-in-Publication Data
Garner, Roberta.
   Rethinking contemporary social theory / Roberta Garner, Black Hawk Hancock, and Grace Budrys. — 1st Edition.
      pages cm
   Includes bibliographical references and index.
   ISBN 978-1-61205-259-5 (hbk. : alk. paper)
   1. Sociology. I. Hancock, Black Hawk, 1971– II. Budrys, Grace, 1943– III. Title.
   HM585.G37 2013
   301—dc23
                                                                    2013002222

Printed and bound in the United States of America on acid-free paper that meets the standards of the American National Standard for Permanence of Paper for Printed Library Materials.

Designed and Typeset in Adobe Garamond by Straight Creek Bookmakers.

17 16 15 14 13   1 2 3 4 5

Contents

Acknowledgments

The authors would like to thank the chapter contributors—Julie Artis, Dan Causton, Tait Runnfeldt Medina, Greg Scott, Jose Soltero, and Julian Thompson—for their vital participation in the project, which made it so much more readable and wide ranging.

Colleagues at DePaul made the book possible, and we thank them for their patience when we trapped them in the hall and shared our thoughts and enthusiasm. These conversations had the marvelous effect of encouraging us to think about the ideas from new perspectives.

The department is fortunate to have a loyal, hardworking, and very alert staff, and we would like to especially thank Jessica Chiarella, Joshua Covell, Valerie Paulson, and Kathleen Tallmadge for being ready to help us with everything, including complicated technological support.

Anonymous reviewers for Paradigm Publishers enabled us to focus the project, and Jeffrey Alexander—who does not necessarily agree with everything we say—was supportive and encouraging.

Dean Birkenkamp has been our guiding spirit throughout—supporting us and believing in the value of our inquiry, but also prodding us to improve and sharpen our formulations. Ashley Moore, Jennifer Kelland, Julie Grady, and Jennifer Top made the production process at Paradigm a pleasure.

We only wish that it were possible to thank Mayer N. Zald for his help throughout the project and especially in the writing of Chapter 8, "Political Sociology and the Analysis of Collective Action." Mayer was not always convinced by our conclusions, and it was always fun to argue with him; every encounter with Mayer sharpened one's wits and created joy in sociological inquiry. It is largely thanks to him that this chapter has a tone of cooperation and harmony, describing a community that is able to reach out to new ideas while sustaining the scholarship of past decades. Mayer offered suggestions and ideas that made the chapter come alive in fresh ways after he read it in the winter and spring of 2012. Roberta was looking forward with enthusiasm to his reaction to the finished product. She misses him so much—mentor, coauthor, friend.

Part I
Paradigms

Introduction to Part I:
The Premise and the Project

We suggest that in recent decades sociology has been deeply permeated by a new paradigm, conflict constructionism, which is characterized by several defining features: attention to the microlevel, analysis of discourses or frames and a renewed interest in signs and language, examination of the construction of difference and dominance, attention to regulation and punishment, interest in cultural hybridity and transculturation, a focus on the body, new approaches to the role of the state, and a consistent conflict perspective.

The paradigm combines elements of both social constructionist theory and conflict theories. It has deep roots in critical theory and more recent links to postmodernism. It is associated with postmodern social thought, although it is less radical and more adaptable to empirical inquiry than postmodernism. The paradigm incorporates elements of Marxist analysis but adjusts them to new global realities and eschews old orthodoxies. In the historical trajectory of many subfields of sociology, conflict constructionism emerged after an intense engagement with conflict theories in the 1970s and early 1980s, which in turn contested the structural functional paradigm of the immediate postwar period. We identify causes for this paradigm shift, which include the contributions of specific individuals, the general intellectual climate, and various social changes, such as globalization and neoliberalism. Conflict constructionism emerged to address puzzles and problems in the conflict paradigms of the 1970s. As a result, old perspectives were reevaluated, presuppositions were rethought, and new tools for social analysis emerged to confront these new conditions.

Conflict constructionism is not a single monolithic paradigm that claims to have solved all puzzles posed by the social world. Rather it is a cluster of perspectives, a loosely connected web of ideas woven together from the work of theorists who have influenced each other without forming a tightly knit community of the like-minded. For example, Erving Goffman and Michel Foucault independently seized on the treatment of the "mad" as a key to understanding power, regulation, and the construction of deviance. Yet, despite differences in their approaches, the intersections of their ideas yielded new webs of connections across disciplines, and new theoretical framings emerged to speak to multiple audiences.

The subfields of sociology differ markedly in the degree to which they have embraced this new paradigm as a whole, accepted specific elements of it, remained unaffected, or rejected its ideas. In the second part of the book, we examine differences among fields in the ways the new paradigm has been integrated. Sometimes it has come to dominate the field in areas such as the analysis of ethnoracial and gender inequality, culture in the global system, media studies, and the analysis of the self. This type of paradigm shift often reflects massive social change. In other fields, older mainstream theories coexist with the new paradigm, either in harmony or in contention with it. In yet other fields, its impact is limited or contained—and largely confined to new exploration of macro/micro linkages. In at least one field, the sociology of health, a striking reconfiguration of the uses of theory—new or old—has taken place.

Our project is to provide an overview, or map, of the multiple developments that emerged and coalesced into what we have labeled "conflict constructionism" in order to gain a better sense of our bearings within this new intellectual territory. We do not advocate for conflict constructionism; we only seek to chart it and to provoke discussion of changes in sociology.

We hope to create dialogue among different subfields of sociology, to prod sociologists into reflection on their common assumptions, their differing methods, and ways in which they may speak to each other. Whether conflict constructionism is the new paradigm of sociology or already outdated, whether one agrees with our overview or rejects the summation, we use this opportunity to open further conversations.

Part I, "Paradigms," provides an overview of conflict construction. Here we provide a model for thinking about social theory and discuss the ways changes in theory can be conceptualized. We examine how theories permeate fields of knowledge and the meaning of the term "critical" in social inquiry (Chapter 1, "Paradigms in Sociology"). Having established our model, we turn to conflict constructionism itself and address the eight elements we identify as its defining features, accompanied by empirical examples (Chapter 2, "Conflict Constructionism: Elements of the Paradigm"). Finally, we provide an overview of the key theoretical innovators who contributed to conflict constructionism, examine the intellectual and sociohistorical political and economic forces that sparked it, and explore its impact. Finally, we discuss whether new modes of thinking add up to a paradigm at all (Chapter 3, "History of a Paradigm").

Part II, "Paradigm Change in Selected Subfields," explores the impact of conflict constructionism on ten subfields of sociology. Section 1, "Deep Impact: The New Paradigm Becomes Dominant," explores the analysis of race-ethnicity and gender, culture in the era of globalization, media and information, and the self as personality and person. These fields are seen as having embraced conflict constructionism wholeheartedly, largely as a result of massive social change, and as a result have been the most revolutionized by its ideas. Section 2, "Paradigms in Play," looks at fluid and sometimes unstable and contentious relationships between old and new paradigms in the fields of political sociology and collective action, urban sociology and spatial analysis, and deviance. Here we see, rather than a full embrace of conflict constructionism, a selective engagement with various elements of the paradigm, sometimes in a harmonious mixing of mainstream and new approaches (e.g., in political sociology and the study of collective action) and sometimes in contention. Section 3, "Paradigm Limited," probes the areas of inequality, social class, and the sociology of families and traces how, in these fields, conflict constructionism has a limited impact. Mainstream approaches remain very strong, and the influence of conflict constructionism can be mainly seen in the dissection of macro/micro linkages. Section 4, "Paradigms Reconstituted in a Transdisciplinary Field," is a detailed case study of how one area of sociology has been transformed in the way that theories are deployed. Largely as a result of interdisciplinary collaboration, the field tilts toward a grounded, concept-driven approach rather than embracing any one complete theoretical framework.

The conclusion considers the impact of the new paradigm, assessing whether it contributes to progress in our understanding of society.

A summary chart follows to help the reader navigate Part I.

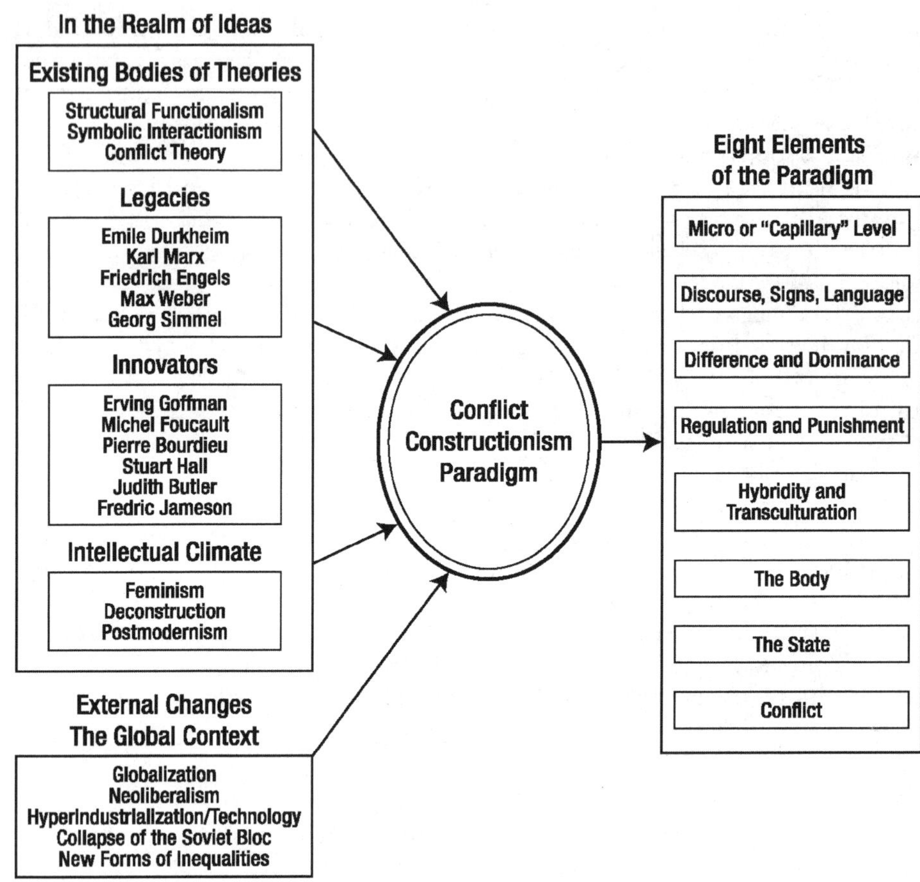

Origins and Elements of Conflict Constructionism
Source: Dan Causton.

Chapter One

Paradigms in Sociology

Introduction

In order to obtain a better grasp on the new paradigm presented here—conflict constructionism—we must step back and reflect on the notion of social theory itself. More specifically, we need to think about thinking, to reflect on the ways we go about theorizing. We should begin by asking a few simple, essential questions about theory itself: Why and how do scientific theories change? Is change in the social sciences similar to change in the natural sciences? What do we mean when we use the term "paradigm"? How does theory help us understand the world around us? How does theory change as the world changes? In order to make sense of these broad questions and to establish a vocabulary and set of concepts for discussing change in theory, we first discuss Thomas Kuhn's seminal 1962 study, *The Structure of Scientific Revolutions*.

Thomas Kuhn and *The Structure of Scientific Revolutions*

In his groundbreaking *The Structure of Scientific Revolutions*, Thomas Kuhn (1962) argued that science has moved forward not only by the steady accumulation of new empirical data and research findings but by shifts in paradigms, the large frameworks that organize thought and specify methods in fields. For example, physics moved from Ptolemy's model of the solar system to the Copernican model and then from Newtonian physics to Einstein's theory of relativity and eventually to quantum mechanics.

Sometimes the new paradigm replaces the old one; no one is likely to return to a Ptolemaic view of the cosmos. But in many other instances, older paradigms become "local" theories that pertain to a limited set of phenomena, to a specific "region of reality." For example, Newtonian mechanics is still enormously valid and useful for understanding the flight of rockets. Even if we live in a probabilistic quantum universe, we do not need to use either Einstein's theory of relativity or the paradigm of quantum mechanics to design bridges or launch the space shuttle. (In-depth discussions of this issue appear in Camilleri 2009 and Ford 2011; a decidedly maverick and provocative view of scientific "progress" can be found in Feyerabend 1975.)

Why do paradigms shift? Kuhn carefully addresses the question of why paradigm shifts occur. He argues that unsolved puzzles accrue in the field, and as researchers find increasing problems in explaining a phenomenon with existing theories and models, they eventually have to make a leap to a new framework. Paradigm trouble often starts with anomalies, small empirical findings that don't fit with theoretical predictions and with existing empirical knowledge. Such anomalies accumulate and become increasingly hard to dismiss. Eventually scholars see them as "a problem"—a finding that cannot be understood within the existing theories. The anomalies finally come to be seen as an unsolved puzzle that challenges existing ways of thinking and conducting research. For example, in physics, anomalous results such as the duality of the particle and wave characteristics of light and the puzzle posed by electron orbits within the atom contributed to the shift from classical physics to quantum physics in the early part of the twentieth century (Grometstein 1999).

But the puzzles that are unsolvable within a particular paradigm are not just given by nature; they become identified as unsolvable puzzles by the community of scientists. A social and interactive process among researchers moves toward labeling a phenomenon an unsolved and currently unsolvable puzzle. Solving it—encompassing it within a satisfactory theoretical framework—often requires not only changes in concepts and models but new methods of research as well.

Dominant or contending paradigms? Not all fields have a single dominant paradigm. As noted above, multiple paradigms may provide insights into different phenomena—for example, at different orders of scale. Quantum mechanics is not needed for routine puzzle solving on the scale of planetary phenomena. Relativity is not necessary for applied physics and engineering in the "local" environment. But a discipline can encompass multiple paradigms for other reasons as well. The existence of several paradigms and absence of a dominant one is particularly pervasive in the social and behavioral sciences. These fields are marked by contending paradigms and difficulties in getting rid of paradigms that some believe are no longer intellectually convincing. The overarching reason for the contentious situation, the uneven ripple of paradigm shifts in the field, and the existence of multiple paradigms, often with ill-defined and overlapping boundaries, is that human beings are the subject matter of the social sciences. These troublesome subjects of the social sciences are in turn associated with two major problems that hamper the establishment of dominant paradigms: the historical context of all human action and the problem of objectivity.

The social sciences are historical sciences; therefore their paradigms must change with history. This statement may shock the reader who became interested in sociology because it is about the issues of today! Yet even if we are not historical sociologists, we have to be aware of the historical changes that led up to the conditions we are studying now. The social sciences—and sociology in particular—are about historically situated phenomena. The subject matter of most of the social sciences changes with human history. Many behavioral science paradigms (those that guide psychological research) are largely or partially ahistorical, but few social scientists claim to follow theories or explanatory models of behavior without reference to history; exchange theory and rational choice theory are among the few making this claim because they posit relatively unchanging individual motivations. Many sociological theories are tightly linked to historical analysis—for example, both Marxist and Weberian theories and their offspring, such as world-systems theory, are specifically focused on historical change. Most paradigms in the social sciences include at least some reference to social change, and for this reason, social science paradigms are more fluid than those in the natural sciences.

Objectivity, knowledge, and ideology. Without exaggerating the problem of objectivity in the social sciences, one must concede that the contentious state of paradigms in these fields is partly due to the blurry boundaries between theories or paradigms and ideologies. Many social scientists believe objectivity in the pursuit of knowledge should be an ideal in the social as well as the natural sciences. But theories emerge from theorists' own experiences and social location, making objectivity more difficult. An even more serious problem with achieving objectivity is that contending theories about human action and societies—unlike theories of astrophysics or quantum phenomena—produce contending plans for practices, policies, and courses of action that impact human beings. (The reader may point out that theoretical physics contributed to the making of atomic weapons, but the contentious issue in that case was the application of the theoretical knowledge, not the objectivity of our understanding of the atom. Yet even that is not as simple as one might think; see Camilleri 2009.) For example, contention between efficient market theorists and neo-Keynesians has implications for human action and well-being. The issue of objectivity is in turn linked to disputes about methods and the larger question of whether the natural sciences provide a viable model for acquiring knowledge about human beings at all. These disputes are often built into paradigms, which are not only different explanatory frameworks but fundamentally different views of the nature of knowledge and inquiry.

Practitioners and paradigms. In addition to these two fundamental intellectual barriers to establishing a long-term dominant paradigm in the social sciences, the history and formation of social sciences disciplines is also a barrier. In a large field such as sociology, there is not one all-encompassing community of scholars but many loosely linked groups identified with subfields, such as sociology of health and illness, sociology of family life, urban sociology, and so on. In turn, the various subfields of a discipline have their own communities of scholars, which are formed in different ways and have different links to closely related fields. Subfields of sociology have different histories, and some have links to applied fields, such as criminology, social work, and public health—human disciplines in which both practitioners and those on whom they practice engage in contention over ideas and policies. The communities of scientists who constitute subfields are different and have markedly different orientations toward the available paradigms.

For these reasons, it is difficult to establish a single dominant paradigm in the social sciences. Sociology only briefly enjoyed paradigm dominance for a few years after World War II when in US universities, structural functionalism appeared to be very popular. But its dominance faded quickly, and since then the field has been contentious and organized around many paradigms.

A New Paradigm in Sociology?

Examining trends in concepts and theories over the past half century, we can discern the emergence of a paradigm, conflict constructionism, that permeates many areas of contemporary sociology. In the following pages we trace the circumstances in which this paradigm appeared and discuss the extent to which it transformed subfields of sociology. It has influenced theoretical and empirical work without emerging as the recognized dominant paradigm that commands scholarship throughout sociology. The purpose of the analysis is not to defend conflict constructionism but to argue at a metalevel that this set of overlapping premises and ideas came to constitute a paradigm that guides sociology and many of its subfields. We use Kuhn's (1962) analysis of paradigm shifts to explore how this approach can help us understand changes in the field of sociology.

The owl of Minerva flies at dusk, and sometimes it is possible to recognize a paradigm only after it has been in use for a while—perhaps when it is about to fade away or come under attack. In 1959 Kingsley Davis, a leading theorist of the post–World War II era, published "The Myth of Functional Analysis as a Special Method in Sociology and Anthropology," arguing that functional analysis was not *a* method in the social sciences but *the* method and that the dominant theoretical and explanatory paradigm of the disciplines was functionalism. This article, based on Davis's presidential address to the American Sociological Association, summed up and celebrated the fundamental paradigm of the late 1940s and 1950s, the exciting years when sociology was coming into its own as a major field in US universities. Yet, at the very moment that Davis named the paradigm, it was already losing its dominant position and becoming one of a troika of perspectives (functionalism, conflict theories, and microinteractionism). Within a few years, this troika, or triad, was in turn recognized as the new canon, now a three-paradigm configuration, to be taught in introductory sociology and undergraduate sociological theory courses and inscribed in every major textbook until the end of the century and beyond. (Sometimes it was expanded to include rational choice and exchange theories.)

But a further, or expanded, paradigm shift has been under way since then. We can retrospectively discern a major paradigm that emerged in the discipline in the last decades of the twentieth century—for which we suggest the name "conflict constructionism" because it combines elements of conflict theories and theories of social construction. It is closely linked to postmodernism and represents the application of postmodernism to empirical exploration in sociology. This paradigm is not enjoying the degree of dominance that functionalism appeared to enjoy in the post–World War II years, but its presence is visible across many fields of the discipline. It may be said to permeate rather than dominate contemporary theoretical and empirical work in sociology.

In this book we define key ideas of the paradigm, abstracting its essential features as an ideal type, and then discuss its evolution. It emerged in response to a wide spectrum of changes, ranging from transformation in the social context—the momentous changes in societies on a global scale—to shifts in the intellectual climate and interaction within the community of social theorists. We examine its uneven penetration into subfields of sociology, and using Thomas Kuhn's framework for understanding paradigm shifts, we investigate how it changed the way sociologists look at societies and human actions.

Theories, Paradigms, Permeation, and Dominance

What do we mean when we say that a paradigm has permeated subfields of sociology? In the natural sciences, a paradigm shift often is visible in a rapid shift to new terminology, research questions, methods, and scientific apparatus. In the social sciences, with their more contested shifts, paradigms may permeate without dominating a field, and new and old paradigms can exist alongside each other. When a paradigm permeates, its terms are widely used, and in some areas of sociology, they have become de rigueur—scholars can no longer write with the old vocabulary. The permeating paradigm influences and guides empirical research. It has displaced older concepts and structures our understanding of the field of sociology as a whole. The very fact that the new permeating paradigm of conflict constructionism has not yet been explicitly named (unlike microinteractionism, structural functional theory, conflict theory, and other paradigms from the middle of the twentieth century) makes it particularly powerful and difficult to challenge. It has permeated subfields of sociology unevenly, and this characteristic has also made it less visible as a dominant paradigm. We do not all think of ourselves as conflict constructionists, even if many of us talk the talk of construction, dominance, micro/macro linkages, the body, regulation and transgression, capital and fields, postmodernism and postcolonialism, discourses and practices, and frame analysis.

At this point it may be useful to remind readers of Kuhn's framework for discussing change in paradigms. Paradigms are broad theoretical frameworks. They are not specific theories to explain specific phenomena, although they may have originated as specific theories and continue to be applied to specific phenomena. Social scientists use the word theory in two radically different ways.

Empirical-explanatory theories. In one usage, theories are explanations that are extremely close to empirical research and used to understand specific situations.

They are generally disconnected from any larger philosophical considerations about the nature of knowledge or the foundations of human society. Research published in leading peer-reviewed research journals of a discipline usually conforms to this usage. Often a research project seeks to find support for one of these theories over another or to determine which theory is supported by the data. These theories are closely associated with testable hypotheses. These hypotheses are falsifiable in the sense that specific empirical data can disprove the hypothesis and thereby cast doubt on its parent theory. Theory in this sense may be deductive ("Let's see which theory is best supported by the data") or inductive ("Let's see if we can develop an explanation that makes sense of the data"). Historically these types of theories were referred to as middle-range theories, but the term is no longer used very much, perhaps because it was never clear what the theories were in the middle of; presumably they were mid-range between grand theories and statements that were specific to a research problem and very close to testable hypotheses.

Theories of crime provide an example. Sociologists have explained the occurrence of crime in terms of individual social psychological characteristics, life-course analysis, community disorganization, subcultural norms and values, constricted opportunity structures, and the anomic gap between cultural goals and legitimate means. Of course these theories complement each other, but nevertheless each cluster of scholars has foregrounded its own explanation. Each theory points to different causes and to effects measured on different units of analysis (for example, individual lawbreaking is measured on people, and community crime rates are measured on places). Each theory calls for its own research design and methodology, although studies can be designed to test the explanatory power of the theories against each other. We can argue that the theories are ultimately linked to broader paradigms for understanding human action (paradigms of rational choice, irrational individual motives, cultural frames, community and societal structure, and so on), but scholars who propose these specific theories do not always identify or appeal to the underlying foundations in social thought.

Paradigm theories. In the other usage of the term "theory," theories are large paradigms that specify what knowledge is worth having, what methodologies are effective in acquiring it, and what discourses should be produced to explain the world around us. Theory in this sense is much closer to what Kuhn means by the term "paradigm." Theories in this sense are the subject of articles in journals of theory and are often disconnected from empirical research. These large paradigm theories are not easily testable. They are not falsifiable because specific data cannot disprove them. The division between empirical-explanatory theories and paradigm theories seems to have grown larger in recent years, for reasons we discuss. Once upon a time, paradigm theories were called grand theories.

In the following pages, we look especially at paradigm theories, not empirical-explanatory theories. But the latter continue to be of great importance. They dominate empirical research, forming the basis of research questions and research designs. Some fields of sociology appear to be focused only on empirical-explanatory theories, and their practitioners have little patience with paradigm theories. Many sociologists continue to work within a paradigm of positivism, canonical research methods, and data collection. They insist that good hypotheses and their parent theories must be falsifiable by data.

Yet there is more appearance than reality in this—the tectonic plates of paradigm theory can shift gradually, behind the backs of the practitioners of empirical research and empirical-explanatory theorizing. For example, in the field of sociology of family life (the field formerly known as sociology of marriage and the family, which is now a very archaic sounding name), late-twentieth- and twenty-first-century paradigm shifts—especially feminist theory—have not dominated contemporary research. Relatively few researchers in this area would claim to be feminist theorists and to use this paradigmatic label for their work. And yet, some things that were said in the 1950s can no longer be said (for instance, that the nuclear family with a stay-at-home mom and a breadwinner dad is the most functional form for modern societies). The field has moved on in its discourses and underlying premises, even though many contemporary researchers do not explicitly refer to these changes. We explore this example of permeation and continuity in more detail in later chapters of the book.

In other fields, the paradigm shifts have been extremely dramatic. The landscape in areas such as gender studies and the study of race and ethnicity has been completely rearranged by the force of conflict constructionism and its accompanying critical theories (feminist theory, critical race theory).

Conflict Theories versus Critical Theory: What's the Difference?

At this point it may be useful to discuss the differences between conflict theories and critical theory (or theories). Most students in sociology are familiar with the term "conflict theory." Conflict theories are based on the view that all human societies contain lines of cleavage, categories of individuals with distinct and at least partially opposed interests. Many conflict theorists focus on different classes—capitalists and workers, slave owners and slaves, peasants and landowners. Conflict theorists who focus on class cleavages generally acknowledge the influence of Karl Marx and Friedrich Engels. Other conflict theorists may point to the divergent interests of men and women or to conflict among ethnoracial and cultural groups. Conflict theorists recognize that these lines of cleavage are not always clearly discerned or acted upon by the social actors, so that categories do not always act as groups with will and agency. Conflict theorists do not agree among themselves about which lines are most important or how the lines of cleavage are related to each other. They do agree that the apparent unity of cultures is illusory: despite seemingly shared values and norms, societies cannot be considered unified wholes. The task of sociologists is to understand the lines of cleavage, identify the divergent interests of whatever groups or categories exist in a society, and dig beneath the surface appearance of shared values and norms.

It is useful to keep in mind that not all conflict theorists celebrate conflict or champion specific forms of conflict. Most notably, Weberian conflict theorists recognize conflict as an ever-present force in human societies but do not take sides in these conflicts as scholars. Max Weber reminded his readers in no uncertain terms that they must remain objectively distant from partisan positions if they are to be scientists. Whatever values scientists hold in their personal and political life, they cannot carry them into scientific work. The two spheres—politics and science—must be separated. While values and politics may impel us to choose a topic or area of research, they cannot be brought into a research project in ways that might distort or confound the findings and analysis. As Weber remarked,

> The primary task of a useful teacher is to teach his students to recognize "inconvenient" facts—I mean facts that are inconvenient for their party opinions. And for every party opinion there are facts that are extremely inconvenient, for my own opinion no less than others. I believe the teacher accomplishes more than a mere intellectual task if he compels his audience to accustom itself to the existence of such facts.... If you take such and such a stand, then according to scientific experience, you have to use such and such a *means* in order to carry out your conviction practically. Now, these means are perhaps such that you believe you must reject them. Then you simply must choose between the end and the inevitable means.... The teacher can confront you with the necessity of this choice. He cannot do more as long as he wishes to remain a teacher and not become a demagogue. (1946/1958, 147)

Because the designation "conflict theorist" usually includes Weberian as well as more engaged conflict theorists, care must be taken not to confound conflict theory with advocacy, political engagement, or specific commitments.

In contrast to conflict theories, which are about society and social relationships, critical theory focuses on the terms that we use to think and talk about society. Critical theory is about theoretical discourse, not about society directly. It is critical of knowledge. It is not immediately about empirical phenomena such as institutions and inequalities.

The templates for much of conflict theory (apart from Weberian conflict theory) and critical theory are derived from the thought of Marx and Engels, who proposed a critical view of social institutions, the organization of societies, and class inequality. They exposed the contradictions between the forces of production that promise the full development of all individuals' capacities and the persistence of human misery, inequality, and exploitation that are imposed in the social relations of production. Capital and labor are necessarily in conflict. But Marx and Engels were also proposing a critical theory, a critique of the categories of thought of economics, political economy, and philosophy itself. They believed that the realities of inequality, conflict, and contradiction in society become apparent only when we discard the misleading concepts of bourgeois thought and approaches to knowledge. To understand human societies we have to free ourselves from categories of thought that lead to mistaken notions about reality and replace them with concepts that enable our ideas to more closely match how the world works.

For example, as Marx points out in his discussion of commodity fetishism, we are misled by the notion that the laws of supply and demand are natural phenomena and external to human action—akin to the laws of motion of objects in a gravitational field—and so we fail to see that the economy is a human creation constructed in the social relations of production. Marx and Engels also argue that many of our notions about human nature—such as positing greed or freedom as universal, biologically given characteristics of humans—are really based on values associated with historical formations such as capitalism.

The Marxist critique of prevailing views of the economy, human nature, universal values, and many other categories of thought set the template for other types of critical theory. The Frankfurt School theorists (who worked in Germany between World War I and the Nazis' accession to power) defined much of their work as Critical Theory (the capital letters denoting this specific theoretical school). As Marxists, they first and foremost developed a critique of culture under capitalism and its characteristic ways of thinking, but they recognized it was not enough to debunk the ideologies of the free market, individualism, and (in the days of fascism) the strong leader who claimed to help the little guy. They also formulated a critique of the social sciences (which they thought imitated the natural sciences for mistaken reasons), the forms of Marxism that they encountered in daily political life (which they found simplistically materialist and determinist), and the modern belief in instrumental reason. Ultimately, Critical Theory had to be reflexive, a practice of constantly examining the sources and political uses of one's own categories of thought.

The Frankfurt School's critical approaches to culture and ideology were the foundations of later twentieth-century social and political thought as well. Much of modern feminist theory is focused primarily not on institutions and relationships but on categories of thought that cloud our understanding of gender—for example, the notion that gender is a simple and automatic product of sex category and largely a natural rather than socially constructed phenomenon. Critical race theory offers a critique of naturalizing thinking about the category of race. Postcolonial theory is a critique of the prevailing Western or Eurocentric notions about cultural difference. Edward Said's dissection of orientalism was a groundbreaking study in this field as it identified and deconstructed the categories of thought and description that Western intellectuals used to typify Middle Eastern and North African societies.

Sociologists engaged in empirical research also make use of critical theory (in the broad sense of the term, not necessarily the Frankfurt School's version). For example, Loïc Wacquant (2009b) identifies the elimination of certain terms and concepts as one of the primary aims of his critical-reflexive approach to sociology. A term such as "underclass" obscures and obfuscates our understanding of inequality in contemporary capitalist society and prevents us from seeing correctly that capitalism generates a "precariat," a stratum of individuals who cannot find secure work at living wages. We must get rid of terms such as "underclass" in order to free our thought from categories and images that interfere with our ability to see reality.

Critical theorists' critique of prevailing terms and discourses is of course closely associated with conflict theories. Almost all critical theorists lean toward one or more types of conflict theory. Most conflict theories contain a slice of critical theory because (conflict theorists assert) we cannot see the conflicts clearly as long as we see and talk about social reality using the lenses and terms of prevailing conventional discourses. These prevailing conventional notions not only dominate in the popular media but also infest scholarly and theoretical discourses. As intellectuals, theorists should focus their energy on deconstructing these misleading ideas, and changing language may be a necessary first step toward changing reality.

The close linkage of conflict theories and critical theories makes it difficult to distinguish the two neatly. As we examine paradigm shifts in sociology, we emphasize changes in how theories encompass empirical phenomena—reality—but these shifts almost always involve critiques of prevailing terms, concepts, and discourses as well. This is especially the case when theories about society are conflict theories that insist we talk in terms of conflicts and divergent interests, rather than a holistic, unified "society," shared values, and/or "natural" bases of social arrangements. Notice how critical theorists want to place quotation marks around many words and phrases to alert us to the fact that these terms are always pulled out of specific discourses with distinct political agendas and, in most cases, are misleading guides to reality!

It's All Critical Thinking to Me! Sociology as a Critical Practice of Inquiry

We have distinguished at least two methods sociologists use to think critically: conflict theories that criticize the social order and social institutions, and critical theories that criticize concepts and theoretical frameworks of traditional, popular, and mainstream perspectives.

Apart from these two approaches, most of sociology is critical because no sociologist takes human actions, institutions, and arrangements for granted. By focusing on and asking questions about human phenomena, sociologists are implicitly, if not explicitly, taking the view that existing conditions are not natural and inevitable—that they could be otherwise. Sociologists problematize society and institutions, not in a simplistic sense by saying that all these arrangements are social problems, but in a sophisticated way—by asking the reason for their existence. Even sociologists who appear to approve of existing social arrangements, such as structural functionalists, are engaged in this more subtle form of critical-reflexive thinking. They too are asking, Why is society the way it is? Why do these arrangements exist? How did they emerge? Why do they persist? These types of questions give a foundation of critical thought to all sociological work, whether it is primarily empirical or theoretical.

Sociologists' penchant for problematizing human actions and arrangements, hence for regarding them critically, makes others uneasy about sociology and sociologists. It is not surprising that totalitarian states like Nazi Germany and the Soviet Union under Stalin promptly shut down university sociology departments and that everywhere sociologists are viewed with hostility by defenders of the status quo. (Psychologists, who focus on individual behaviors, do not create this general uneasiness about their discipline.) Even the sociologist who explains a specific practice or institution or the social order as a whole has put that institution or practice under the microscope, on the agenda for discussion, on the dissecting table for the scientific gaze. This act gives a distanced and critical tone to all sociological discourse. We need to keep this overall critical perspective in mind even as we differentiate mainstream paradigms from those that are explicitly critical, such as Marxism, feminism, critical race theory, most conflict theories, Frankfurt School Critical Theory, and critical theory in general, including deconstructionism and postmodernism.

Chapter Two

Conflict Constructionism

ELEMENTS OF THE PARADIGM

We propose to introduce a name for the direction of theory in recent decades: conflict constructionism.

Conflict constructionism emerged from existing bodies of theories (such as the triad of structural functionalism, symbolic interactionism, and conflict theories), but it is distinct from all of them. It is not a clearly defined mainstream that is sharply distinct from other currents, but a number of key ideas or elements can be identified. In this chapter, we briefly discuss eight elements of the paradigm. The list is neither exhaustive nor mutually exclusive, since many of these elements overlap and reinforce each other; nor is it a rigid, definitive, or canonical list of defining elements. It is a starting point for exploring the loose web of ideas that form the paradigm.

1. Attention to the micro-, or capillary, level. We use these terms (derived from the microinteractionists and the work of Michel Foucault) to mean that sociologists are devoting close attention to interactions and the microlevel. They link their analysis of social structure, dominance, hierarchies, inequalities, and institutions to the interactions of everyday life. This premise was already present in symbolic interactionism and other microsociologies (ethnomethodology, Erving Goffman's dramaturgical model), but it was reinforced by the theoretical innovators, especially Foucault and the feminists. While theorists by no means abandoned macroanalysis, they increasingly addressed it in terms of macro/micro linkages (e.g., Burawoy et al. 1991).

2. The discursive turn: attention to discourses, narratives, and texts; the importance of signs and language; and the connection between relations of dominance and the establishment of categories of difference. Sociologists are giving careful attention to the framing, wording, and discursive origins of what had previously been treated as structures, institutions, and inequalities. Here too the new theoretical ideas clearly aligned with existing work in symbolic interaction (e.g., labeling theory); Goffman's writing on stigma, media frames, the "looping" process in the destruction of the selves of inmates, and so on (1961, 1963a, 1963b, 1974); and long-standing Marxist interests in hegemony (Gramsci 1971; Hall 1986). However, the theoretical impact was broadened and made more pervasive by the introduction of the deconstructionist and Foucault-inspired vocabulary of "discourse," "discursive formation," "text," "narrative," and so on. This terminology influenced theories of culture, the self in society, the construction of deviance, and the imposition of racial-ethnic and gender dominance, among many others. The analysis of texts, discourses, and narratives led to more studies of the media, and one might hypothesize that the explosion of new media helped to shift attention to textuality as the whole globe appeared to be swathed in a dense, totalizing "symbolic environment" emanating from the media (Castells 1996; Gerbner 2002). Attention to discourses, a critique of prevailing and conventional terms, and emphasis on the relationship between discourse and dominance link the new paradigm in sociology to critical theories. The interest in language and the categories established through language in turn links the paradigm to deconstructionism in philosophy as well as to new directions in social psychology, such as the work of Eviatar Zerubavel (1999).

3. A constructionist and relational model of difference and dominance. Sociologists are treating inequalities and dominance as processes based in discourses of difference—in social construction of categories, in other words. Groups and their relationships are no longer seen as natural but as social products. The end of the twentieth century saw a powerful shift away from a naturalizing treatment of categories of difference and domination as ascriptive. Of course, after the defeat of the Nazis and the discrediting of racialist ideologies, few social scientists still believed race was a fixed natural category, but they often treated it as if it were, with little attention to its construction. Sex persisted as a natural distinction even more tenaciously. By the end of the century, these neat pigeonholes, with their pseudoscientific justifications, were no longer acceptable to theorists and were replaced by an extensive new vocabulary of social construction. This shift in the analysis of difference was clearly related to the rise of critical theories, especially feminist and critical race theories. The social construction of difference was generally treated as a manifestation of conflict, not as a product of either consensus or a common value system. With this new framework came changes in political sociology as well, since identities were no longer natural and given as the logical social bases of political action. Identity construction was now seen as the prime target of states, social movements, and collective action as these actors strove to form and manipulate identities that potentially can be constructed in many different ways.

4. Regimes of regulation and punishment. The idea that the core of sociology is the analysis of regimes of normative regulation and punishment originated with Emile Durkheim and is hardly a new thought in the discipline. But it returned with enormous force in recent decades after lying dormant for a long period. This reawakening of the centrality of normative regulation meant that Durkheim was now read in an altogether different way than he had been in the 1950s, when he was interpreted as the father of structural functionalism. Starting with a reading of Goffman as a radical micro-Durkheimian whose work focused on normative regulation at the microlevel, theorists turned to a new way of connecting Durkheim to interaction and micro-, as well as macro-, processes of regulation and punishment. This perspective was strongly reinforced by the impact of Michel Foucault, especially his influential *Discipline and Punish* (1979). Foucault and the feminists added a new element: the emphasis on resistance and the idea that power and resistance are always twinned and that power and the establishment of dominance meet with transgression. The new centrality of regulation and punishment utterly transformed the fields formerly known as the sociology of deviance and criminology, plunging them into contentious divisions between the new critical theories and more traditional perspectives that sought to explain individual rule breaking or high crime rates.

5. *Hybridity and transculturation.* The concepts of hybridity and transculturation, most notably associated with the contributions of Stuart Hall and Nestor Garcia Canclini, in many ways represented a global variant of the microprocesses of power and resistance. The previous generation of conflict theorists had pointed to imperialism, Western dominance, modernization (on Western, capitalist terms), colonialism, and assimilation as forces in the world-system that emerged after the European Middle Ages and became clearly visible after 1492. By 1992, a reassessment associated with new theories of culture and postcolonial critical theory had set in. The conquered and colonized were seen not only as victims but also as agents who had actively responded to their circumstances, sometimes in complicity with the politically, militarily, and economically dominant forces and always also in resistance (Wolf 1982). With this new view of a more proactive stand came an appreciation of assimilation and cultural change as a two-way street, or, more accurately, as a wide plaza with swirling, crisscrossing flows: the imperialists, colonizers, and settlers had been transformed too, becoming "transcultured" and "creolized." All cultures are hybrid cultures, formed by many influences. This analysis applies to and reflects the current globalized world of multicultural societies and increasing numbers of communities in diaspora. But it can also be read back into the past—in a revision of historical understanding—revealing, for instance, a "black Atlantic" in which people of African descent were not only at the center of the formation of societies in the Americas but had an impact on political ferment in England as well (Gilroy 1993).

6. *The body.* Sociology of earlier decades had been curiously disembodied. Structural functionalists and conflict theorists seemed to write as if people existed not as bodies but as roles, statuses, classes, groups, identities, and so on. It is perhaps not surprising that in the twentieth century, both structural functionalism and Marxism often hooked up with psychoanalysis, as if to leave the messy business of bodily drives and the experience of the body to some other type of theory. The body began to make a reappearance in Goffman's work (his attention to gestures, visible stigma, the mortification of the bodies of inmates in total institutions, and the positioning of the female body in *Gender Advertisements* [1988]), and it moved to center stage in the work of Foucault and the feminists. It is precisely because characteristics of the body are no longer taken for granted in a naturalizing perspective—no longer seen as the natural foundation of race and gender—that bodies have become the focus of analysis of the creation of categories, a site where power and dominance are enacted and expressed, and the venue for performances of gender, race, and other socially constructed categories. The phrase "inscribed on the body" has become important for understanding power, categories, identities, and action. French theorist Pierre Bourdieu developed the concept of habitus to incorporate the body with social dispositions.

7. Bringing the state (back) in. Macrolevel conflict theories, such as those derived from the work of Max Weber and Karl Marx, have a long history of analyzing the state, and the state was also included in Parsonian functionalism as the guiding mechanism of societies. Microinteractionist theories targeted the state as the institution involved in labeling and involuntary confinement of deviants. Conflict theorists in the 1970s certainly included the state in their analysis, and Marxists in particular saw it as a powerful structure of coercive and ideological apparatuses. Contemporary theory builds on these approaches but expands them with constructionist concepts.

What is new is not the idea that the state is a major societal institution and power center but the strong emphasis on the state's role in constructing difference, defining deviance, and formulating and implementing social policies. The state is a key transmission belt between the micro- and the macrolevel. The circumstances of everyday life and interactions—the micro-, or capillary, level—are highly constrained by decisions and choices made by actors in the state at the macrolevel.

The state in all modern societies has a key role in establishing categories of individuals—for example, citizens and noncitizens, legal residents and illegal aliens, those entitled to government services and those not entitled to them. This categorization of individuals does not simply, or even primarily, reflect underlying demographic cleavages but creates them in the first place. For example, the US Census defines categories of race and ethnicity (a practice not permitted for the French census), and all states define categories of legal immigrants.

One of the main categories defined by the state is that of deviance. In all states, certain acts are defined as deviant; there is considerable variation among cultures, religions, and historical periods as to which acts are criminalized. The function of defining and punishing deviance has existed as long as there have been states, but the work of Foucault and social constructionists has drawn new attention to it, a focus that has been sharpened by the high rate of incarceration in the United States.

Beyond establishing difference and generating deviance, the state has drawn theoretical attention for its role in the shift from embedded liberalism to neoliberalism (Harvey 2007), which has brought with it radically reduced and reorganized public services (Klinenberg 2002). Some observers argue that the withdrawal of the state from social services was intimately linked to its expanded police and penal functions. The atrophied social state is necessarily accompanied by a supersized and hyperactive penal state (Wacquant 2009a) to take up the slack in managing and controlling "problem" populations in the lower tier of the class structure. Theorists are devoting attention to variation in states' willingness to shift toward the neoliberal model.

These issues have contributed to the adoption of the concept of a political field (Bourdieu). The state is one element of a complex and contentious field of political and social practices and discourses. It can be unitary—controlled by a single societal force, such as the capitalist class—or a terrain of struggle. It usually includes multiple actors. Sometimes it is formed with rigid powerful apparatuses of coercion and ideological indoctrination, but in other situations it can be more fluid. The political field is closely linked to civil society as well as to the fields of the media and the economy; at their capillaries these fields extend into the microlevel of individuals and households.

The concept of the political field and treatment of the state as one element in the field contrasts with both structural-Marxist views of the state as an apparatus (Althusser 1971b) and structural functional views of the state as an institution within a larger system or as the societal-level element that fulfills the function of goal attainment (Parsons 1951).

Another contributor to new formulations of the role of the state was Michel Foucault in his exploration of surveillance and his introduction of the concept of governmentality (a composite of "government" and "mentality") to refer to manipulative practices of power for the management and control of complex modern societies. Foucault's late work included exploration of different modes of governmentality, or governmental rationality. The term refers to the practices of government or governing and not only to the formal institutions of the state. Governing is now less likely to make use of the objectifying power that turns bodies into docile objects but rather turns to subjectivitizing power that constructs individuals capable of choice and action. Governmentality is a process of turning individuals into active subjects. It is a form of rationality that seeks to align personal or individual choices with governmental goals. Through this new mode of conceptualizing and acting in the world, citizens take on an active role in their own subjectification through their own complicity. Governmental rationality therefore simultaneously totalizes and individuates. Foucault's analysis connects a particular mode of rationality to the specific modes of securing, observing, monitoring, shaping, and controlling individuals. Thus it focuses not on the state but rather on all particular practices of governing locally in multiple and local sites, such as families, schools, places of worship, and all other points of socialization as well as social regulation. For Foucault, governmentality as a set of practices has populations as its target of scrutiny, political economy as its major form of knowledge, and apparatuses of security as the central instrument of social regulation.

At the heart of Foucault's argument about governmentality are the authorities' efforts to promote security and prosperity. Rather than securing complete control, the authorities, whose mechanism of rule is governmentality, govern the population by promoting the well-being of the subjects in both political and economic life. Security and predictability are preeminent goals of these practices and the knowledge on which they rest. Foucault's work converges with Goffman's analysis of how havoc is contained to insure order and predictability (Burchell, Gordon, and Miller 1991; Goffman 1963a). This governmental rationality is individualizing and totalizing as it seeks to govern both the individuals and populations of a society.

8. Conflict. The term "social construction" has been in use for a while, but it leaves out a reference to a key element of the new paradigm: conflict. The new paradigm consistently emphasizes the contentious, conflictual, power-related aspects of construction. Construction is a process in societies structured in racial dominance (Hall) and in gender inequality. It is intimately linked to punishment. Construction is always an expression of power; as such, it is always associated with resistance as well. The state is a major actor in construction (or a major site of construction), and therefore processes of social construction are potentially always buttressed by coercion and violence. Construction of identities is both a product and a source of contentious collective action and social movements. In short, the word "conflict" must be part of the paradigm's name. The emphasis on conflict has allowed the new approaches to absorb and preserve many insights of existing conflict theories.

No One Knows What the Past May Bring: Reinterpreting the Legacy of Sociological Theory

These eight central aspects of conflict constructionism impel us to reconsider previous paradigms and theories—the entire legacy of sociological theory.

"No one knows what the past may bring," joked Hungarians during the Communist era in which the party constantly revised the narrative of the past in order to legitimate the present. But the practice of reinterpreting the past applies to paradigm shifts as well. The theories of the past are not simply discarded but reinterpreted and changed in scope and meaning in order to fit into the new paradigm. Every paradigm shift brings with it a rereading of the theoretical legacy.

Sociological theory was changed not only by new theories but also by the rereading and transformation of classical and twentieth-century theories. The new readings became part of the new paradigm as it evolved from many sources. For example, Erving Goffman reformulated Durkheim's insights, and Stuart Hall revised concepts inherited from Marx, Friedrich Engels, and Antonio Gramsci, which he then recontextualized and applied in new external circumstances. We explore a few examples in the next pages.

The Legacy of Durkheim

Durkheim is the most protean of the classical theorists, and his work encourages constant rereading and reinterpretation. Instead of reading him as a structural functionalist, we are seeing him as a theorist of normative regulation, punishment, and integrative forces in contemporary capitalism. Here are a few of the ways his legacy is being incorporated into the new paradigm.

Normative regulation and the empty self. Contemporary sociological theory focuses on regulation through discourses, frames, scripted performances, and rules governing interaction. This Durkheimian legacy marks the work of Goffman and feminist theories. Foucault's analysis of regulatory regimes has an affinity with these aspects of Durkheim's legacy. The postmodern self as a protean persona is an extension of Durkheim's "empty self" formed by social regulation. We explore the reinvention of this legacy in Chapter 7, "Sociology of the Self."

Focus on punishment, crime, and social control. A second key element of Durkheim's legacy is the emphasis on punishment, definitions of crime, the social construction of deviance, and social control as the central topic of sociology. The nature of a society is revealed in its punitive practices. Deviance and crime are products of normative regulation, not of individual dispositions and experiences. This perspective overlaps the focus on normative regulation; both are revisited in readings of Foucault. We explore it in Chapter 10, "Disruptions in the Field Formerly Known as Sociology of Deviance."

The complex integration of capitalist society. Postmodernists are returning to Durkheim's argument that capitalist society enjoys extremely powerful, noncoercive mechanisms of social cohesion and integration. Its organic composition holds it together through the interlacing of myriad economic groupings that in turn crosscut the mechanical solidarities based on religion and race-ethnicity. Far from splitting along class lines, capitalist society is held together by these multiple crosscutting ties. Durkheim's ideas connect to Foucault's concept of governmentality, theories of civil society, and postmodernist views such as Jean Baudrillard's contention that "modes of repression and integration of the simulation order are, in this regard, more comprehensive, more complete, and the prospects for liberation less optimistic" (1983, 104). We return to this reinterpretation of the legacy of Durkheim in Chapter 11, "Social Class and Socioeconomic Inequality."

The Legacy of Marx and Engels, Weber, and Simmel

These classical theorists are linked by their attention to capitalism and their understandings of the historical context of human action. Here are several ways their ideas are being reintegrated into the new paradigm.

The historical context of human action.   All four theorists insisted that human action is historically situated and that theorists must give attention to the changing social context, which now includes new forms of capitalism, neoliberal state policies, globalization, transnational migration, new media and information technologies, and new patterns of urbanization and collective action.

Analysis of capitalism and the money economy.   All four focused on capitalism; and the neoliberal shift, with its global and weakly regulated markets, demands the attention of sociologists. We can see this focus in the work of Bourdieu and Hall, as well as in new theories of inequality. The analysis of capitalism remains a major theme in virtually all areas of sociological inquiry, such as the study of global cities, examination of media impact, and attention to inequalities in health care.

Continuing analysis of inequalities.   Marx and Engels and Weber examined the key dimensions of social inequality and the conditions under which these categories of disadvantage turn into social identities and the basis of collective action. Weber and the Marxists had different views on these matters, and their contending positions continue to inform the discussion of global inequalities, classes in contemporary capitalism, and the continued force of status identities such as religion, national origin, citizenship rights, gender, and race-ethnicity.

The role of the state.   Weber and Marx and Engels focused attention on the state, and contemporary theorists remain committed to understanding the role of the state in the political field, in regimes of social control and punishment, and in the construction of categories of difference and domination. Even though the neoliberal state has withdrawn from economic regulation and social services, it has expanded social-control functions and developed new relationships with civil society. "Bringing the state back in" means rereading the classical theorists.

The conflict perspective.   Weber and the Marxists originated the conflict perspective in sociology, and although it is unwise to lump all conflict theorists together, common themes in their work challenge the concept of a unified society with shared values. The new conflict constructionist paradigm is deeply rooted in the legacy of conflict theories. Conflict theories have been revised to include a pervasive play of power and resistance, often defined locally and occurring at the micro-, or capillary, level of social interactions.

Weber's verstehen *as the dawn of the discursive turn?*   One can argue that the "discursive turn" (a surge of interest in words as foundational to actions and practices) already lurks in Weber's methodological contribution of *verstehen*. To understand the meanings that actors give to their actions, to read the texts that reveal their ideas and ideologies, is to insist on the importance of words and discourses. When Weber discerned the origins of the modern commitment to instrumental reason in the words of the Hebrew prophets, when he found the preconditions for a capitalist view of the world in the writings of Martin Luther and John Calvin, he was already engaged in the analysis of discourse and culture. For Marxists and Durkheimians, words and ideas had a secondary existence, forming a part of reality that could only be explained in terms of social structure and social action; they were a determined rather than determining element of action. For Weber they had a larger degree of autonomy and contributed to our efforts to explain social reality, a theme reiterated in the discursive turn of contemporary theories.

The legacy of interwar Marxism, cultural analysis, and critical theory. Theorists working in a Marxist vein in the early and middle parts of the twentieth century influenced the new paradigm in areas such as the construction of gender inequality, the production of whiteness and racial dominance, the production of deviance by criminal codes, the symbolic environment formed by the media, and the creation of identity narratives. Although these topics of theory are quite new, the overall method of analyzing texts, discourses, and narratives has roots in the Marxist analysis of culture proposed by Walter Benjamin and Antonio Gramsci and elaborated in post–World War II critical theory.

The Legacy of Conflict Theories and Microtheories

These two streams of theories—originally countercurrents against structural functionalism in the 1980s and 1970s—provided much of the basis of the new paradigm. The trajectories of almost every area of sociology passed through a period of conflict theories and microtheories, such as feminist approaches to family life, the theory of physician dominance in health care, critical analysis of ownership patterns and the effects of professional routines in the media, and labeling theory in sociology of deviance. These critical approaches persist even though they have been modified by the contributions of the theoretical innovators and revised to fit new social contexts. In many cases, the conflict theories have been "disaggregated" so that Marxist, Weberian, and feminist theories are not casually lumped together. On the other hand, macro- and microapproaches are better integrated with each other.

New Paradigms, Old Questions

Another way of thinking about the persistent legacies of sociological theory is to examine the themes of social thought that are still central to the new paradigm, even if the answers are framed differently than they were in the past. As a result, let us return to some enduring questions of sociology in light of the paradigm of conflict constructionism.

- *The relationship between self and society.* How does society get into the self? What is the self and how is it organized?

- *Difference, inequalities, identities, and collective action.* What are the major inequalities of our times? How are they constructed and reproduced? What is the role of the state in these processes? What is the relationship between economic inequality and status stratification? Under what conditions are inequalities transformed into identities, and when do these identities become the basis of collective action?
- *The relationship of culture and society.* What is the relationship between ideas and behaviors, between social arrangements and the way people represent these arrangements? How is culture produced and disseminated? What is the explanation for consistent misrecognitions? What role do culture and the media have in the construction and reproduction of inequalities?
- *The problem of social order and social control.* What is the basis of social order? What forces keep people interacting with each other in relatively stable and consistent ways? What prevents a "war of each against all," and when do these arrangements break down? What is the role of the state and of microprocesses in maintaining social orders? How is social control related to inequalities? How is order imposed by regimes of regulation and punishment, and how is it inscribed on the body?

Theorists are inventing new concepts (such as habitus, field, construction of difference and dominance, microphysics of power, frame analysis, and so on) to answer these questions. New circumstances, such as new media, globalization and neoliberalism, immigration and urbanization, new organizations of civil societies and their relationships to states, and new types of inequalities in the global economy, all lead to new answers to these thematic questions. But the questions and themes remain central to the field.

Conflict Constructionism as a Paradigm: Is It One?

Conflict constructionism may not be a coherent paradigm but rather consist of overlapping and converging fragments of paradigms drawn from conflict theories, the central concept of social construction, and reworked legacies of classical theories. Some of its paradigmatic nature is given in a play of opposites—it gains its paradigm status by being clearly the opposite of the structural functional paradigm, the negation of all of structural functionalism's underlying assumptions (see Table 2.1). It has this characteristic because it emerged from theoretical attacks on structural functional dominance after the 1950s by both microinteractionists and conflict theorists. The clarity and coherence of its antiparadigm character suggest that it is indeed a paradigm, if for no other reason than that it inverts the earlier dominant discourse. This inversion distills and reiterates most of the criticism of structural functionalism voiced by microsociologists and conflict theorists.

**Table 2.1 Conflict Constructionism as an
Antiparadigm to Structural Functionalism**

Structural Functionalism	*Conflict Constructionism*
Structure	Fluidity
Value consensus	Conflict, contention
Institution	Power and resistance
Stratification, supply, and demand	Construction in dominance
Overall system	Open-ended contention
Coherent personality system	Self as persona, performance, narrative
Roles associated with statuses	Roles as performance
Ascribed gender and racial status	Gender and race constructed and performed
Society as unified, organic whole	Society as a fluid process of construction

Source: Dan Causton.

Conflict constructionism is most clearly not structural functionalism, but it is also distinct from both microinteractionist and conflict theories. Its relationship to both conflict theories and microperspectives is more complicated than its relatively simple binary opposition to structural functionalism, and in many respects it is a hybrid of conflict and interactionist theories.

It dissolves many firm structural terms of conflict theory into a far more fluid interactionist view. It dances away from many conflict theorists' assertions that their object of analysis—be it class, gender, or race—is the master inequality that must be recognized as fundamental and eliminated once and for all if liberation is to be a possible prospect for the species. The new conflict constructionists are much less focused and less optimistic than the conflict theorists of the 1970s: the play of power and resistance, of conflict, discourse, and dominance, will continue forever, not necessarily along lines of class, race, and gender but certainly along some lines. The conflict constructionist paradigm is much more fluid than either structural functionalism or conflict theories. It does not identify permanent and relatively stable groups that are the contending forces in conflict, and it does not build on the assumption that such groups are always present or clearly defined. Groups themselves are always fluid; socially constructed; defined within changing boundaries, both local and global; and often complicit in the processes that construct them. Where conflict theories posit relatively long-term binary oppositions (women/men, proletarians/capitalists, whites/people of color, natives/colonizers), conflict constructionism destabilizes these binaries and puts all of them into play.

But conflict constructionism is distinct from the microinteractionist paradigm in that it has a strong focus on the macro- (and meso-) levels and devotes careful attention to the construction of dominance on a scale beyond individual interaction. While using the terminology of construction and fields, conflict constructionists do address phenomena that conflict theorists and structural functionalist theorists had termed "institutions" and "society." Conflict constructionists recognize the existence of such entities in a way that radical symbolic interactionists had not because the interactionists had viewed the terms "society" and "institution" as reifications of processes that exist only as interactions and communication. Conflict constructionists make explicit and more macro oriented the conflict assumptions that lurked in many symbolic interactionist writings and even, in Durkheimian wrappings, in Goffman's work on stigma and total institutions.

However, conflict constructionism is not just a negative antiparadigm defined by its difference from all the paradigms that went before. It has also been influenced by social thought from beyond the confines of US academic sociology. For example, European developments of the mid-twentieth century, such as structural Marxism, existential phenomenology, and deconstructionist philosophy, had an impact on and were incorporated into it. Conflict constructionism may not look like a single coherent paradigm at all but like clustered and reconstituted fragments of other theories and paradigms. It includes elements of existing theories such as conflict theories and microsociology, reworkings of classical legacies, and new ideas from philosophy and cultural studies. We explore its emergence in more detail in the next chapter.

Chapter Three
History of a Paradigm

Sources of the Paradigm

What were the sources of the conflict constructionist paradigm? What influences felt by the community of sociologists propelled them in new directions? This chapter examines three concentric circles of influence around the community of sociological theorists who adopted the paradigm: (1) individual theoretical innovators who strongly and directly influenced the emergence of conflict constructionism; (2) the intellectual climate that stimulated its emergence; and (3) the larger social context of changes in societies on a global scale that both affected sociological theory directly and influenced the intellectual climate.

Examining the sources of conflict constructionism draws the observer back to the 1960s. Conflict constructionism begins with the break from structural functionalism. As stated in the previous chapter, conflict constructionism is in many respects the antiparadigm of structural functionalism, reversing almost every one of its major axioms.

Historically conflict constructionism began to emerge as structural functionalism was challenged by two contenders, symbolic interactionist theory and conflict theories, drawing on a sometimes eclectic mix of Marxist and Weberian ideas, later to be joined by feminist theories. By the early 1970s, conflict theories appeared to be becoming the dominant discourse in sociology, sweeping across subfields from media analysis to the sociology of health and illness. Already in this period, mixes of the two antifunctionalist paradigms or traditions were gaining popularity. For example, Eliot Freidson's (1970a, 1970b) critique of physician dominance combined conflict and microinteractionist approaches, while Erving Goffman's analysis of gender combined conflict perspectives on male dominance and gender hierarchy with attention to microprocesses and interactive rituals for dominance.

Conflict constructionism emerged in response to both positive forces and problems encountered in the development of conflict theories, as we discuss below.

Who Were the Innovators? Goffman, Foucault, Bourdieu, Hall, Butler, and Jameson

One force in the emergence of conflict constructionism was the work of theorists. Among specific individuals one can single out at least the following six for a broad impact on sociology: Erving Goffman, Michel Foucault, Pierre Bourdieu, Stuart Hall, Judith Butler, and Fredric Jameson. These innovators are not individuals who had central positions in the community of sociologists, and five of them are not sociologists at all. Their peripheral or marginal location in sociology actually enabled them to suggest ideas that overturned the prevailing premises of the field.

Erving Goffman

Erving Goffman was chronologically the first of our innovators and the only one who was officially a sociologist. In his own day, he was widely read but not seen as central to the discipline because he was too popular and too hard to label. Some found him a crafter of charming vignettes drawn from fiction and memoirs more than from his own fieldwork. Many labeled him a social psychologist because of his apparent interest in the self and in mental illness, as well as his ample citations of psychological and psychiatric sources. We need to remember that in the postwar period (from the 1940s to the early 1960s), social psychology was a vital part of sociology. It was still linked to a critical practice of psychoanalysis and had a central place in structural functionalism and Parsonian theory. A close look at much of the sociology of the period (e.g., research on social movements and David Riesman, Nathan Glazer, and Reuel Denney's *The Lonely Crowd* [1961]) reveals it to be focused on individual motivations and predispositions. Much of the sociological and anthropological research of the period answered research questions about institutions, opinions, and social actions in terms of individual motivation and personality structure or prevailing types of character.

At first Goffman fit easily into this framework, but after a while his presence turned out to be subversive as he was turning away from and undermining the basic premises of social psychology—namely, that we can understand societies and institutions by examining their bedrock of individual dispositions. Instead it became increasingly clear that he was interested in shifting the Durkheimian legacy from structural functionalism to a microanalysis of normative regulation. Goffman (1988) took seriously the paradigm of the empty self developed by Emile Durkheim and extended it through the dramaturgical model. For Durkheim, the self was constituted by society, that is, group processes, the formation of the collective conscience/consciousness, and the experience of intense gatherings (collective effervescence) from which we acquire our sense of the sacred and our very categories of thought. For Goffman, the apparently real and acting self is revealed to be a performance created and judged according to aesthetic criteria. These aesthetic judgments of performance are the means of imposing normative regulation. We insist that people perform "honesty," "sincerity," "empathy," and "expertise"; our actions are regulated through the evaluation of performances as convincing displays. Goffman (1959, 1967, 1971) latched onto the emptiness of the self and gave it a new twist with his interest in performance.

A second decisive shift in Goffman's work came with frame analysis in the 1980s. This concept resolved the issues in Durkheim's concept of the collective conscience/consciousness by showing exactly where that mysterious entity is located—in frames. Thus Goffman took the discipline into the discursive turn. Goffman's work on frame analysis was foundational to the growing emphasis on frames and discourses. His reflections (1963a, 1963b, 1974) on havoc and its containment contributed to new perspectives on regulation, and *Stigma* opened the analysis of the body as a new theme in sociology.

In conclusion, we owe to Goffman many of the fundamental features of the conflict constructionist paradigm: theories about performance and the body, frame analysis and the discursive turn, and a return to Durkheim's themes of regulation, transgression, and punishment.

Michel Foucault

Foucault was a philosopher, not a social scientist, whose work has had a powerful impact on social thought (and not only sociology). Like Goffman, he elaborated an earlier French, Durkheimian legacy of absent subjects (not so much dead as irrelevant) whose words, thoughts, and gestures are shaped by a series of discursive formations. (His later work [1980] veered in other directions, such as care of the self, but had less impact on the social sciences.) Foucault (1965, 1966, 1969, 1973/1975, 1979) drew attention to the role of the human disciplines in the construction of the modern self, and this critical view of fields such as psychology, psychiatry, and social work aligned with perspectives in feminism and symbolic interactionism.

The "European Goffman" pursued questions similar to those that intrigued Goffman but worked even further outside the mainstream paradigms of American social science. Erving Goffman appeared to be interested in the mainstream concerns of his day—field research, observation of interaction, the operation of institutions, and other areas—in all of which he was really breaking with mainstream research and theory. Foucault parallels Goffman in the interest in mental illness as a limit condition in which societal response forms the template of all regulatory practices, all efforts at containment of disruption (which Goffman called havoc). Like Goffman, Foucault was interested in the body and saw it as a site of struggle, regulation, and resistance. Where Goffman looked at stigmas inscribed on the body and efforts to maintain physical boundaries at a microlevel, Foucault was particularly interested in the way the state is a major regulatory force. Like Goffman, Foucault contributed to the microshift with his ideas about "the capillaries" and the "microphysics of power." Foucault linked the regulatory theme to the state via governmentality and other strategies of rule.

Foucault insisted on the universal twinning of power and resistance, with resistance being a more generic term for the activities that Goffman in *Asylums* (1961) labeled "the underlife of the institution." And we owe to Foucault the term "discourse," which opened the door to an analysis that converges with Goffman's frame analysis.

Pierre Bourdieu

Bourdieu reshaped sociology, although his theoretical work began in anthropology. His research among the Kabyle in North Africa revealed exchanges of different types of resources and helped him to develop his ideas about different types of capital and their terms of exchange. He was certainly influenced by Karl Marx and Max Weber, but one can also discern a conversation with Durkheim in the development of his concept of habitus. Habitus is an answer to the Durkheimian puzzle of the location of the collective conscience/consciousness. The solution: it's embodied. The concept of embodied knowledge is a point of convergence with Goffman and Foucault (and Butler too, as we shall see shortly), because the embodied knowledge that forms the habitus draws the researcher's attention to the body. From this concept stems the research practice of carnal sociology—the researcher can only understand a culture by bodily experiences (Bourdieu 1990).

Important contributions of Bourdieu include his concepts of field and the different forms of capital. The concept of field is a direct response to the Marxist tendency to view institutions as apparatuses, or rigid structures of power. The term "field" turns us away from the rigid structural analogy to a more open space of contention, cooperation, alliance, and overlapping activities. The political field not only consists of the state apparatus but includes organizations and movements of civil society. The media field is rarely state controlled and includes a wide range of contending actors and stakeholders. Education may have been state based during the period of high modernism in Europe, but it can also be a much larger contested terrain. And to obtain and perpetuate power in these fields, contenders use not only the coercive force of the state but also symbolic violence, that is, discourses that control and constrain action and ostracize or nullify opponents (1989, 1993a, 1993b; Bourdieu, Wacquant, and Farage 1994).

Capital is another concept that addresses and shakes up Marxist formulations. Economic capital is not the only capital, and Bourdieu (1991) identified three other types: cultural capital, a store of socially valuable knowledge; social capital, the capacity that comes out of social connection and organization, a resource that even poor people can muster; and symbolic capital, the ability to shape the discourses that prevail in society, a type of power that in modern times takes the form of connections in the media and action in the field of media.

Bourdieu explored how the legacy of cultural capital can thwart efforts in egalitarian educational systems to use schooling to level the social-class playing field; students bring very different amounts of cultural capital into the classroom, and so no egalitarian blueprint can fully disrupt the process of social reproduction—replication of class structures—through education. Bourdieu's (1984, 1990, 1996) exploration of social inequality and cultural capital was used in *Distinction,* an analysis of taste as a marker of class difference.

Bourdieu contributed new ideas about ethnography as practice in carnal ethnography and in his call for a critical-reflexive social science (Bourdieu, Chamboredon, and Passeron 1991; Bourdieu and Wacquant 1992). The social scientist must strive to produce objective knowledge, but this accomplishment is not a matter of following technical rules of data collection. Rather it is a practice of self-discipline, of reflection on the basis of one's own knowledge and ideas, and a relentless rooting out of conventional wisdom that constantly drags one's work in the direction of stereotypes and platitudes. In the same vein, the researcher should not fear finding and writing about "misrecognitions" held by research subjects; the purpose is not to act as a mouthpiece for a community but to clarify our understanding of reality. The purpose of a critical analysis of institutions is served better by recognizing misrecognitions than by allowing them to remain unchallenged and thereby unintentionally supporting the status quo.

Bourdieu can be cited as another key theoretical innovator who helped to reestablish a number of Marxist insights in a more fluid form. Apparatus shifted to field; capital expanded to multiple capitals; false consciousness turned into the kinder, gentler concept of misrecognition. The solid forms of structural Marxism melted into related but far more open concepts.

Stuart Hall

Stuart Hall is often hailed as the father of cultural studies. Working in an explicitly Marxist framework, Hall offers a global perspective on the relation between culture and power, as well as rooting the analysis in English politics and Caribbean experience. Hall reiterates the concept of hegemony (most often associated with the writing of Antonio Gramsci, an Italian communist) and expands it in many new directions, especially analysis of the media. He argues that although major media producers generally seek to encode hegemonic messages, the audiences do not always acquiesce in decoding these messages and may absorb them only partially or reject them altogether. Hall's emphasis on the complexity of culture can be discerned in his analysis of Thatcherism as authoritarian populism, as a discourse that used elements of antielite feelings and understandings (the popular side of the equation) but intertwined them with xenophobia, racism, and uncritical support of law-and-order policies. Similarly he demonstrates the hybridity of cultures, using Caribbean culture as a template, with its multiple origins and fusion of many cultures into a single imagined community.

Hall (1980a, 1981, 1986) revolutionized the analysis of race and ethnicity, arguing that there is nothing permanent about race and ethnic identity. He proposed that race is a floating signifier, a constantly changing notion of identity that takes on different meanings and values at different times and places in history. The different categories of race and ethnicity that we map out as a society only make sense within a field of relations; that is, the identification of any one particular racial or ethnic group only has meaning insofar as it is compared to and contrasted with another (Hall 1986, 1991b, 1992).

Stuart Hall (1980a, 1980b) contributed to the growing interest in media and thus, ultimately, in discourses and texts (also an element in Foucault's impact), the recognition of hybridity in culture, and the reconceptualization of race and hegemony.

Judith Butler

Judith Butler's (1990, 1993, 2004) writing was a decisive force through its radical questioning of gender categories, emphasis on gender as performance, focus on the body and gender as "styles of the flesh," and discussion of transgression. Butler took the analysis of gender and sexualities beyond conflict theory into a radical questioning of the categories themselves, not only of the inequalities they generate.

In the 1990s, she analyzed gender as performance and proposed an increasingly radical subversion of the concept of identity. Much like Foucault's theorizing, her contributions span philosophy, textual analysis, and the social sciences in order to develop an understanding of the construction of categories of difference. Butler argues that the construction of gender is the binding together of sex, gender, and heterosexuality into a single package. This packaged identity is then inscribed on the body in a process that appears to be natural—that is, anatomy, gender, and sexuality seem to be aligned with each other in what most people choose to call a normal manner. Even gay and lesbian identities, though not normative, are expected to follow certain conventions of performance and naturalized identity.

Gender as performance is "a stylized repetition of acts." One could say that gender is an act, with all the double meaning inherent in the expression. On the one hand, gender is an embodied practice. We hold our bodies and move our limbs and torsos in a certain way, we wear certain expressions on our faces, we gesture in one way and not another, and we dress our bodies "appropriately." Gender consists of "styles of the flesh," stylized acts that are repetitively performed by bodies and inscribed on bodies (Butler 1990, 139). In this way we perform or act out gender according to rules that make a practice normative.

Gender is also an act in a second sense: it may not correspond at all to the thoughts and feelings of the actor. Butler emphasizes that the performance—the acting—of gender must be self-concealing. This concealment is important because it creates the illusion of naturalness and necessity, that one could not possibly be otherwise. If the performance draws attention to itself, it may undermine rather than enhance the impression of naturalness. A woman who wears too much perfume or very long false eyelashes may be perceived as trying too hard, as may a man who always wears camouflage combat gear. Gender performances are judged as credible or noncredible, reiterating Goffman's perspective on the self as performance, always subject to aesthetic judgments (Butler 1993, 2004; Goffman 1988).

Gender performance is linked to power differences in society (Butler 1993, 2004). The naturalization of gender—the way its correct performance conceals the performed and unnatural stylization—sustains masculine dominance and compulsory heterosexuality. When convincing gender performances make gender (and its link to sex category) taken for granted and natural, gender cannot become a topic of reflection, discussion, contestation, and possible collective action. The dualism of man/woman is sustained as natural and mapped to the pair dominant/subaltern in speech, discourses, and representations. Butler pulls the veil of naturalism off these arrangements and thereby pushes them onto the agenda of contestation.

Many conflict feminists had considered gender a stable identity and tried to raise the consciousness of women so that they would rebel against gender inequality. Although they sought to change gender relations and often celebrated women's qualities over men's, they left intact the naturalism and dualism of gender construction. Butler seeks to do away altogether with gender (and with it, heteronormativity), freeing human beings from the category of gender itself. The point is not to liberate women from men but to emancipate human beings from compulsory gender categorization.

The convergence of the theories of Goffman, Foucault, and Butler on concepts such as performance, transgression, the body, and the creation of discursive categories (or frames) is a key feature of the emergence of conflict constructionism.

Fredric Jameson

As a theorist of literature, Fredric Jameson is decisively outside the boundaries of sociology. But his influence on the analysis of culture is extremely powerful. Like Stuart Hall, Jameson (1998, 2007) defines himself as a Marxist but seeks a dialog with the ideas of postmodernism. Jameson (1990/1996) is best known as a theorist of postmodern culture, dissecting it as a form of culture that is distinct from high modernism and the cultural forms favored and disseminated by the bourgeoisie in the nineteenth century and the first part of the twentieth century. Postmodernism, as the new "cultural dominant," has core characteristics that link it to the media, the explosion of consumerism in recent decades, and transnational markets. As a Marxist, Jameson remains optimistic and pursues the development of "cognitive maps" that can help us navigate from postmodern capitalism to more fulfilling and liberating types of society. This optimism infuses his writing on science fiction as well, enabling him to portray it as an experiment in rewriting history and freeing us from the slavish enchantment that binds us to conventional views of the flow of time. As Jameson puts it, "I think everybody is able to think the idea that late capitalism is a permanent crisis: there's structural unemployment, increasing poverty, environmental disaster, and so on. Then on the other hand, they see that late capitalism is also a moment of enormous social pluralism, new opportunities and all these cultural openings.... The dialectical move would be to see these things together. I think that's why the notion of postmodernity is difficult. It's difficult to do it right, because one has to see both at once: permanent crisis and *also* new kinds of social emancipation" (2007, 164–165). And to close on another point of convergence: Jameson (1972, 1981, 1988) is intrigued by Goffman's concept of frames and finds it useful in the analysis of culture.

Paradigm Changers

All six of our innovators share interests in what we have defined as key elements of the new paradigm. Their work converges, and in many instances they give slightly different names to the same phenomenon (or cluster of related phenomena): discourses or frames; bodies, embodied knowledge, embodied performance, and habitus; the state with its mechanisms of governmentality and regulation and its role in fields and the production of ideology and identities; culture, especially hybrid cultures and new types of culture such as postmodern culture; and power, resistance, and opposition. Not all sociologists are avidly reading their work, but their concepts have seeped into the discipline, affecting theory in general and even the mid-range theories that guide empirical research. For example, in the field of social movements and collective behavior, analysis of organizational strategies of movements now interconnects with analysis of culture, discourses, the framing of identities, and the actions of the state (Meyer, Whittier, and Robnett 2002).

We have only introduced our innovators here, and each one of them will make an appearance in the chapters of Part II, so we will encounter them again.

All of these theorists contributed to a new paradigm that retained key elements of conflict theories but distilled them into critical analyses of discourses and practices. Theories were delinked from immediate struggles to change society, and theorists expressed less conviction that groups with relatively simple identities, definitions, boundaries, and interests (such as "oppressed races," "women," "the proletariat," and so on) would soon become revolutionary subjects. The terrain of struggle shifted from the streets and barricades to the field of discourse.

Changes in the Intellectual Climate: Feminism, Deconstructionism, Postmodernism

New intellectual orientations emerged, creating a climate for change in sociological theories and facilitating the growth of conflict constructionism. These orientations emerged during and after the student revolts of the 1960s when European and North American universities were rocked by demands for liberation from hierarchical, bourgeois, racist, and sexist ideologies. Questioning and protest focused not only on prevailing institutions such as militarism but also on the practices of everyday life and interpersonal interaction that perpetuated inequalities (Caute 1990). After the 1970s, these currents flowed increasingly inward, into the channels of academic thought and communities of intellectuals, turning away from public political issues. The tone of critical thinking became less direct, less confrontational, and less focused on changing society and institutions. The critical gaze was eventually turned on political activism and engagement itself and led to second thoughts about the efficacy of political action. The claims of progress and liberation that movements of the Left had made for so many decades—and at a fever pitch during the 1960s— were scrutinized and put in doubt. Liberation was not rejected as a goal, but it was no longer seen as one that was easily defined, associated with definite structural changes in institutions, carried forward by identifiable groups, and attainable within our lifetime. Claims of progress in human history were dismissed as questionable metanarratives. What remained of the bold aims of the liberation movements of the 1960s was an interest in deconstructing discourses associated with racist, sexist, and homophobic oppression. Willingness to struggle against oppressive practices in everyday life persisted. These limited traces of the movements of the 1960s had an impact on social thought at the end of the twentieth century. Three important influences on sociology from the aftermath of the 1968 upheaval were feminism, deconstructionism, and postmodernism.

Feminism

Feminism as an intellectual trend (rather than a political ideology or agenda) questioned the naturalness of the gender divide and by implication the naturalness of many other categories. Feminists challenged the timeworn traditions that emphasized the great divide between men and women. In terms of the formation of the conflict constructionist paradigm, the crucial formulation (beyond the critical perspectives offered by multiracial feminists and perspectival theorists such as D. Smith [1990]) was proposed when Judith Butler challenged the very notion of gender difference itself, arguing that it is socially constructed, naturalized in discourse, inscribed on the body, and judged as performance.

Deconstructionism

Deconstructionism was an intellectual trend that began in philosophy, especially in the work of Jacques Derrida. It is not possible to provide a summary of his thought here; suffice it to say that his ideas were translated into forms that were more accessible and applicable to the social sciences, especially in the emerging fields at the border between social inquiry and the humanities (e.g., cultural studies, communications, comparative literature, ethnic and women's studies, and media studies). Like feminist thought, deconstructionism hacked away at the process by which difference is established, categories are defined, naturalness or "bedrockness" is attributed to these categories, and, ultimately, dominance is justified. The analyst can only query contending texts about an elusive reality, seeing this reality only darkly, in the textual glass. Deconstructionism was an indirect challenge to Marxist thought, raising doubts about the premise that the mode of production is the foundation—the base—of objectively prevalent inequalities. The emergence of deconstructionism challenged themes and currents of Marxist thought but reinforced the critical-theory side of Marxism, the position that most terms and discourses of the bourgeois social sciences have to be undone in order to develop a clearer view of social reality. It also undermined structural functional analysis, already under siege by conflict theories · and microsociologies, such as symbolic interactionism and Goffman's dramaturgical model. Deconstructionism aligned well with themes in symbolic interactionist thought, especially labeling theory.

Postmodernism

Postmodernism was a more nebulous intellectual trend. In part it was fueled by deconstructionism and feminism. Like feminists, postmodernists questioned the notion of an objective observer with a godlike and universalistic gaze. All accounts of social reality are constructed narratives—texts about reality that may be more or less accurate but have only dubious claims to truth. Postmodernists deeply imbibed Friedrich Nietzsche's perspectivism, his agnostic stance toward the truth claims of scientific inquiry and historical analysis. Postmodernists remained unconvinced of Marx's thesis that the point is not to interpret the world but to change it. Given that interpretation itself turned into the production of competing texts, it seemed unlikely that the project of changing reality would yield feasible or desirable outcomes.

Marxists and postmodernists quickly squared off, each team insisting that its epistemology caught its opponent in a net that could not be escaped: For postmodernists, Marxists were just telling another story with no more claim to truth than anybody else's text. For Marxists, postmodernism was only the ideology of late capitalism, a reflection of flexible capitalism, the globalization of finance capital, the power of the capitalist-controlled media, and the discrediting of socialism (or even moderate reform) as a viable alternative to neoliberalism (Jameson 1990/1996, 1991/2005, 2007; Best and Kellner 1991).

*   *   *

Conflict constructionism represents a partial and unstable compromise between older conflict theories (chiefly Marxist) and postmodernism, a gambit of salvaging conflict paradigms while softening their hard, decisive tone and blending them with postmodernist perspectives. Conflict constructionism builds on the common ground of Marxism and postmodernist social thought, namely, the critical-theory critiques of prevailing concepts and discourses, including those of the social sciences themselves.

In this broader global, social, and intellectual climate, sociological theory as a whole was deeply affected and transformed, although in many subfields, postmodernism had little impact.

External Changes: Establishing the Global Context

By the end of the twentieth century, a series of shifts and shocks had changed the global landscape and thus the context and subject matter of the social sciences. The social sciences are different from the natural sciences in that their subject matter is historically situated. Human behaviors and, above all, human societies change in ways and on a time scale that stimulates ongoing innovation in social sciences. Changes in historical conditions precipitate changes in social thought. We refer to this process as the influence of external change because it originates outside the community of theorists and social scientists and the larger community of intellectual discourse. We identify several changes on a global scale that impacted sociological theory.

Globalization

Although this word has many meanings, a useful definition is the expanding and accelerating flow of people, capital, technology, products, ideas, media, and movements across national borders. These flows are in disjuncture with each other and do not form unified streams. They have increased in volume—more of everything is circulating—and sped up. Increases and acceleration in cross-border flows are not necessarily natural phenomena. In large part they are the results of policies of states. Globalization drew theorists' attention to multiculturalism and cultural hybridity, new forms of ethnic contention, transnational processes and problems, identity formation, and global media. Many observers saw globalization as an effect of neoliberalism (to which we turn our attention next) rather than as a primary cause of new social arrangements.

By the first decade of the twenty-first century, globalization seemed to be associated with a decline in US hegemony. In the short run, globalization had often appeared to be an imposition of Americanization in cultural and economic forms, but as the process unfolded, American economic and political dominance in the global arena came into question. The rapid industrialization of Asia, especially China, the issues of US indebtedness and the BRIC (Brazil, Russia, India, and China) nations' call for a new global monetary order, the European debt crisis and the financial crash of 2008, and the uncertain outcomes of US military engagement in Iraq and Afghanistan created doubt about US hegemony and reduced Eurocentric cultural, economic, and political preeminence. A process that had begun with the dissolution of the colonial empires after World War II was transforming the global system.

Neoliberalism

States withdrew from involvement in the economy, especially from regulation of markets and provision of social services, a process that became apparent around 1980, with clear leadership from the Margaret Thatcher and Ronald Reagan administrations in the United Kingdom and the United States, respectively. In these two countries the process moved more rapidly and extensively than in other developed economies where the state retained more regulatory and social service functions, in part because of pressure from unions and parties on the left side of the political spectrum.

An obvious effect of neoliberalism on theory was that it stimulated theory construction designed to explain its emergence. But it had a more subtle and indirect impact as well. One of the main impacts of neoliberalism on social thought and sociological theory was that it stimulated a far more fluid picture of social processes than before. Market volatility was reflected into the intellectual climate and theory construction. Theories tried to encompass more fluid social processes, less regulated by the state, less fixed, and less secure. For example, Richard Sennett (1998) directly addresses the impact of flexible capitalism on character, the work ethic, and the sense of self. But there was also a seepage of images and discourses of fluidity, instability, openness, and flexibility into the core of theory construction, a new reluctance to use the language of apparatus, system, ascription, structure, and any other terms that appeared to confer a fixed character on social phenomena.

Hyperindustrialization, New Technologies, and New Media

> *Late capitalism, far from representing a post-industrial society, thus appears as the period when all branches of the economy are fully industrialized for the first time.*
> —Mandel 1978, 191

Hyperindustrialization is the penetration of new technologies into many areas of human life that had not been previously industrial, such as information processing, management, communication, media and entertainment, education, and health care, as well as agriculture and the production of raw materials themselves. New developments in biotechnology align with the growing interest in the body as a central concept in sociological theory and social thought. The body itself can be seen as a social construct.

Although these innovations began with the Industrial Revolution, by the end of the twentieth century, electronic media, computers, the emergence of a global network society, and very sophisticated telecommunications systems amounted to a great leap forward. New information technologies changed the way we interact with others, how we perceive the world, and how we experience space and time. They have contributed to globalization because production processes can be disintegrated physically and organizationally and distributed among many countries (Reich 1991). Places that seemed very far away are now very close, and information can be conveyed instantaneously. Knowledge transfer and data access across national borders collapse space and proximity and seem to speed up time.

A dense global "media sphere" has emerged, which some observers believe forms a "total symbolic environment" on an unprecedented scale and with results for perception, cognition, and collective action that we do not yet understand very well. Some theorists (notably Castells 1996) suggest that "informationalism" is a new mode of development, linked to capitalism as a mode of production but with its own distinct technologies and social structures.

The new media had a dramatic effect on theory, creating entire new subfields of media analysis and cultural studies (on the borders between sociology and communications and the humanities) and raising the possibility that sociological theories of self and society and urban sociology would need to be radically revised.

The Collapse of the Soviet Bloc and "Really Existing Socialism"

A major development of the post-1968 period was the collapse of the Soviet bloc, which included the end of Soviet hegemony in eastern Europe, the collapse of Communist parties in that region, and eventually the disintegration of the Soviet Union itself, all within the space of a few years and strongly associated with the emergence of neoliberalism.

The impact on theory was complex. Marxist theories became defused and diffused. They were almost completely decoupled from movements for change (and were defused in that sense). Yet, at the same time, fragments of Marxism floated into many other perspectives (and hence were diffused, though in rather harmless forms because the diffused fragments were detached from the Marxist foundation of revolutionary praxis). For example, it is almost impossible to discuss contemporary phenomena such as global cities without reference to the global market economy, finance capital, and other crypto-Marxist concepts. Discussion of the causes and consequences of the changing shape of the distribution of jobs and income in the United States—the shift to an increasingly unequal "bowling-pin" or "hourglass" distribution—is another example of Marxist thought influencing sociological analysis. Fragments of Marxist theory (generally without the Marxist label) are contributing to the leading contemporary perspectives in sociology of health (Chapter 13).

As in the interwar period, Marxist thought is turning to the analysis of culture as well as new types of class inequality and the role of the state in neoliberal policy.

New Forms of Inequalities

Systems of stratification that were typical of industrial capitalism have shifted under the impact of many new trends, including the entry of women into the paid labor force; the shrinkage of the industrial working class in the older centers of industrial capitalism, coupled with its growth in China and India; the emergence of large middle classes in some newly industrializing regions; and new patterns of integration of immigrants into various levels of the class structure of developed economies and world cities. Race-ethnicity has been linked to class stratification for a long time, but structures of racial dominance such as apartheid and US-style segregation have given way to more fluid post–civil rights formations, as well as to heightened ethnic conflict in some countries. China appears to have rapidly moved up in the global structure, but with the benefits of industrialization and productivity being quite unevenly distributed. The linkages to neoliberalism and the reduction of state functions are complex. One consequence for social structure appears to be that the industrial proletariat is being replaced by a "precariat" that is not primarily engaged in industrial labor in the developed economies (Wacquant 2007, 2008, 2009a, 2009b). Coupled with new forms of gender and racial-ethnic stratification, these changes have forced new formulations for understanding the construction of difference and dominance.

Marxism versus Postmodernism—and Beyond— in the Conflict Constructionist Paradigm

In the introductory chapter, we suggested that conflict constructionism contains elements of both Marxism and postmodern theories. Neither is present in a pure form. Marxism in its orthodox forms was discredited in the collapse of the Soviet bloc, but the analysis of market societies—aka capitalism—is certainly still relevant. Postmodernist thought in its more flamboyant manifestations does not lend itself so easily to the analysis of societies and social action, but in a toned down version, it provides a framework for examining contemporary societies. In order to more fully explain the intersections of Marxism, postmodernism, and conflict constructionism, we must briefly reflect back on their historical trajectories.

It may be useful to recall that the first and leading postmodernists were mainly maverick Marxists who had second thoughts about basic premises of Marxism as it was practiced in Europe and elsewhere in the second half of the twentieth century. These maverick Marxists became critical of the Communist parties, even of the Eurocommunists who contended within the political systems of western Europe; they tried to distance themselves from the Soviet Union, and although several had flirted with Maoism, they eventually were repulsed by developments in China as well. They came to believe that the movements of the 1960s had failed and had in fact provided an unintended boost for the modernization of European capitalism, serving primarily to wipe away archaic features of the system and clearing the way for a shift in economic enterprise into a postindustrial or hyperindustrial phase (Debray 1979). Above all, they became very pessimistic about the overwhelming power of the modern media in "the society of the spectacle," and with a sort of "if you can't beat them, join them" mentality, formerly Marxist postmodernists began to display attitudes of celebration and enjoyment of the all-encompassing media world. Postmodernists questioned the narratives of progress that the Left had propounded throughout modern European history, narratives in which humanity moved from capitalism to socialism and a more humane and rational social order. Thus contemporary Marxists and postmodernists are unhappily conjoined twins, growing out of the same matrix of experience and ideas in the postwar era.

The contributions of Marxist and postmodernist theory are overlapping and competitive. For the Marxists, the postmodernists are fine specimens of capitalist ideology, with their denial of progress in human history, distrust of metanarratives, belief that the proletariat no longer exists as a class (if it ever did), emphasis on culture, sensuous embrace of the all-consuming media, and celebration of novelty. For the postmodernists, the Marxists are old-fashioned, tedious, and strident tellers of erroneous world-historical narratives, economic reductionists, and party hacks (if not for a specific party, then for political parties in general). Marxists want to explain postmodernists away as products of late-capitalist ideology. Postmodernists want to explain Marxists away as leftover ideologues of superseded movements of the nineteenth and early twentieth centuries.

But a closer reading of both orientations draws our attention to converging ideas and analysis and more compatibility than is apparent at a superficial glance. In fact, we argue that conflict constructionism emerged from the efforts to use postmodern insights to solve problems in the conflict theories—especially Marxist conflict theories—that enjoyed a brief heyday in the 1970s. And Marxism and postmodern social thought share a commitment to critical theory and the critique of prevailing, or mainstream, theories. So a synthesis of sources in Marxist conflict theory and postmodernist thought, combining elements of each and thereby creating new concepts and approaches, helps us to understand contemporary social phenomena.

Paradigm Change: 1970–2013

We suggest that in most subfields of sociology in which conflict constructionism emerged as an important or dominant new paradigm, it followed a period of domination by conflict theories. It represents one effort to address puzzles, problems, and practical difficulties encountered in conflict theories. In the movement of theory from the pre-1960 dominance of structural functionalism to various forms of conflict constructionism by the turn of the century, the trajectory almost always passes through a period of dominance of conflict paradigms.

Unsolved Problems and Puzzles: A Kuhnian Approach

Returning to our Kuhnian approach to the understanding of changes in theory, one can argue that conflict constructionism emerged to deal with specific unsolved puzzles and practical problems that became apparent in sociology in the last decades of the twentieth century:

1. It was an attempt to reconcile the increasingly divergent sociological traditions or elements of the triad (structural functionalism, symbolic or micro-interactionism, and conflict theories), providing at least a minimal coherence to the enterprise of sociology.

2. It offered a solution to the diverging poles of macro- and microanalysis, qualitative and quantitative methodologies, and agency-structure explanations (where agency refers to meaningful action and structure to limiting conditions created by past actions); it accomplished this reconciliation by creating a conceptual language that allows the poles to be reintegrated, validates research at both ends of each spectrum, and encourages a cooperative rather than a divisive approach to these different ways of doing sociology. For example, to understand domestic work in global labor markets, one could observe employer-employee interaction within a household as well as look at state policies concerning immigration (Cheng 2006), and one could analyze statistics concerning transnational employment as well as carry out ethnographic observation in one city or community.

3. It was able to integrate sociology better with what was going on in competing fields (literally competing for university resources): ethnic studies, gender studies, cultural studies, media studies, and so on. Scholars in these fields were strongly influenced by one or another variety of critical theory (feminism, critical race theory, postcolonial theory, etc.), and so

sociologists using conflict constructionist perspectives could create dialogs with these scholars—and compete with them for students and resources by offering a unified perspective on all these disparate areas of difference and contention.

4. It was a response to trends in other disciplines, especially philosophy (a sort of bedrock field that has always had an impact on sociology), and specifically deconstructionism, postmodernism, and so on.

5. It became a practical means of coping with the increasing embarrassment of a field dominated by conflict theories, a perspective that became out of touch with realities of funding and hiring after 1980.

6. It encompassed new types of institutions and behaviors associated with globalization, neoliberalism, greater gender equality, race relations in the post–civil rights era, the media explosion, identity politics, and so on. In other words, it offered promising avenues for understanding contemporary social change and was fueled by external phenomena and not only by change within the communities of theorists.

The result is a hybrid type of theory that continues to integrate large chunks of classical theory (e.g., the reinterpretation of Durkheim as a student of normative regulation and punishment rather than a functionalist), conflict theory, Marxist theories, critical theory, microinteractionist and symbolic interactionist insights, and pieces of postmodernist theory.

Conflict constructionism must be read ambiguously on the issue of whether it is universally valid as an approach to human action or constitutes a new historically situated paradigm that is particularly applicable to contemporary conditions such as globalization, neoliberalism, and post–civil rights racial and gender stratification.

To read it as a universally valid approach to the human condition is to assert that human beings have always constructed meanings and social situations in circumstances of conflict and contending discourses. That reading is a social constructionist interpretation that can be applied to all historical contexts. It says that human actions must always be understood in historical context and that categories of thought are always socially constructed and then used to establish difference and dominance.

To read conflict constructionism as a historically situated paradigm means that one believes it is the key to understanding the contemporary world and therefore supplants other paradigms that may have been valid in the past. We live in times that are specially marked by neoliberalism and globalization, by the power of the media, and by multiple contending cultures and the collapse of traditional beliefs and metanarratives that gave meaning to life. In the past, in times that were more stable and rigid, with clear boundaries around societies, dominant belief systems, and more fixed social structures, paradigms such as structural functionalism and orthodox Marxism may have been useful. In the present, we need a paradigm that can encompass fluidity and the impact of global media.

Differences in the Impact of Conflict Constructionism on Sociological Subfields

Sociology is not a simply unified field; rather, it is composed of multiple communities of theorists and empirical researchers. Each field has its own history, traditions, and current climate, and therefore the multiple communities (and subcommunities within the fields) change at different rates in different directions. By fields of sociology we mean areas of the discipline that generally have their own section in the professional association (the American Sociological Association), their own journals, and an identity in the community of scholars. Often these fields correspond to titles of courses at universities. For example, most sociologists would concur that sociology of education, criminology (or sociology of crime and punishment), urban sociology, sociology of health, sociology of stratification, sociology of race and ethnicity, sociology of gender, and political sociology are examples of fields (or subfields) within sociology as a general field.

Because sociology has many subfields with distinct histories and communities of scholars, and because paradigm dominance in sociology has never been total or uncontested, changes in theory associated with conflict constructionism did not affect all subfields of sociology equally or at the same pace. We examine the unevenness in penetration, or "seeping," of the new paradigm in the second half of the book.

What Is the Mainstream?

Analysis of how the new paradigm spread unevenly through sociology returns us to the question of what mainstream was or was not replaced by the new paradigm. As noted earlier, it is difficult to define a mainstream for the discipline as a whole. Fifty years ago one might have said that it was structural functionalism, coupled with a rather positivist empiricism as the leading research orientation. The empiricism certainly persists and has become more sophisticated and quantitative as new tools for data collection and statistical analysis have become available. The theoretical mainstream, however, had become divided and muddied by the later 1960s, and one could even argue that by the 1970s, conflict perspectives had become so popular and diffused as to constitute a new mainstream, or at least a powerful current. Today it seems fair to say that many fields have no mainstream or that mainstream work in these areas is primarily empirical. Insofar as it is theoretical, it is driven by empirical-explanatory theories, not by explicit invocation of paradigms or grand theories. Sometimes "mainstream" means using concepts developed much earlier in the history of sociology (in classical sociology or post–World War II sociology).

In some fields, scholars with a conflict constructionist orientation directly challenge the mainstream of the field or even build up a new field completely from scratch with a conflict constructionist approach. In other cases, they have tweaked theories in the field, shifting them in a conflict constructionist direction by introducing new concepts, placing more emphasis on the discursive turn, focusing on micro/macro linkages, or making other changes that allow conflict constructionism to seep into the mainstream rather than completely rechannel it.

Alternatives to a Paradigm Shift: The Varieties of Paradigm Persistence

Let us lay out the possibilities more systematically. We identify at least seven possible ways in which fields fall short of undergoing a paradigm shift. In a sense they remain centered on a mainstream, but it is not the same mainstream in all these fields, and the continued existence of a mainstream does not take a single form. These patterns are not mutually exclusive, and some subfields display several of them. We provide examples of these ways of sustaining the mainstream of a subfield, as well as examples of areas of sociology in which they can be discerned (some fields exemplify more than one of these developments).

1. Classical theories and their contemporary revised, elaborated versions form the basis of theoretical work in this subfield. For example, Marxist theory, Weberian theory, or the legacy of Durkheim continues to be essential. In this case, the mainstream remains connected to the classical fountainhead of sociology. *(Sociology of social class and socioeconomic stratification)*

2. Theoretical continuity is largely formed by the preservation and elaboration of the many theories of the post–World War II period. New research questions, new empirical data, and new methodologies contribute to revising and elaborating these theories, but they are not eliminated or replaced by a new paradigm. The mainstream continues much as it did throughout the second half of the twentieth century, with complementary perspectives from conflict constructionism often applied at the microlevel. *(Sociology of family life)*

3. Empirical-explanatory theories dominate theoretical development in the field. Theories are defined in middle-range terms and are close to empirical research. Multivariate analysis specifies key predictor variables and allows researchers to distinguish the explanatory power of different models. *(Sociology of education; sociology of family life)*

4. The new paradigm seeps in around the edges of the subfield and fails to become its mainstream. It is visible in changes in terminology, formulations of research questions, or emphasis but not recognized or named as a leading theory. For example, terms such as "frames" and "discourses" appear, attention is given to macro/micro linkages, and other signs of the conflict constructionist paradigm can be noted, but the field is not defined as undergoing a paradigm shift. *(Sociology of family life; sociology of education)*

5. There is a high degree of collaboration and conversation between the old and the new paradigms and even an effort to blend the two, but the existing mainstream does not dry up or disappear in this cooperative effort. *(Sociology of collective action)*

6. The new paradigm and the old mainstream flow on in parallel or in tandem, paying little attention to each other. For example, scholars do not review each other's work, and the communities of scholars attend separate

conferences or, at the very least, separate sessions at the same conference. An air of indifference greets mention of scholars who are not part of one's community. *(Sociology of deviance)*

7. Finally, in some fields one can also discern heated and antagonistic interaction between proponents of new and old paradigms; specific efforts are made to dispute the rival conceptualization or to falsify the other paradigm with empirical data. This situation is less common than one might think. *(Some areas of sociology of crime and deviance)*

In short, the mainstream in sociology has always been quite fluid. In many subfields, the new paradigm is absorbed or seeps into research and theory without explicit acknowledgment of a shift.

Barriers to the Adoption of a New Paradigm

We have discussed facilitators of the adoption of the new paradigm, including intellectual trends that affected sociology and changes in the real world that led theorists to seek new paradigms. Other forces that operated within specific subfields of the discipline acted as barriers to the new paradigm and, in some cases, reduced interest in theory altogether. We discuss a few examples of such deterrents or barriers, a topic to which we return in the chapters on specific fields.

Partnerships with Practitioners in Applied Fields

One of the most important barriers appeared in fields where sociologists were carrying out applied work or building partnerships with applied researchers and policy makers. Researchers in applied and policy-oriented fields are often wary of theories, and when partnerships are formed with these fields, theory may be deemphasized or introduced in ways that do not threaten interdisciplinary research. For example, sociology of health is partnered with public health, urban sociology with urban planning, sociology of deviance and crime with criminal justice and corrections, and sociology of families with family and child policy. In Part II of the book, we examine how applied and interdisciplinary work affected the integration of the new paradigm into fields such as sociology of health and sociology of deviance and public safety. Theoretical concepts such as inequality may be of value in these fields, but scholars avoid connections to grand theories and references to Marxism, Weber, or social construction.

In order to create a common discourse about the subject with colleagues in related fields, sociologists in these areas have come to avoid theoretical labels (especially those that indicate critical and conflict approaches), to avoid critical theoretical concepts, or to use softer, less contentious terms. A very telling sign of this avoidance is the substitution of "disparities" for the harsher and more theoretical term "inequalities." Yet a deeper examination of these apparently atheoretical approaches reveals shared understandings and ways of thinking that are in effect theoretical.

We examine this apparent paradox of the emerging deep structure of theory in a superficially weakly theorized field when we discuss the sociology of health.

Multivariate Models and Theories

Sophisticated methodologies with multivariate analysis of large data sets also discourage theoretical formulations, and complex multilevel models are seen as the best formulation of theoretical reasoning. When large amounts of quantitative data are available in a field, as they are for epidemiological studies of population health and illness, educational attainment and academic achievement, patterns of crime, and many other areas, there is a strong incentive to develop quantitative models rather than formulate theoretical concepts.

In fact, a sophisticated multivariate model can encompass several theories and even assign relative weights to their explanatory value! For example, to return to the example of crime and theories of crime, we could develop a model that would include variables associated with different theories—individual life-course variables, community disorganization variables, local opportunity structures (defined, for example, by labor market characteristics), neighborhood and city demographic characteristics, police behavior, and cultural attitudes. We could see how much each of these variables contributed to explaining variations in outcomes such as community crime rates, individual involvement in criminal activities, or incarceration. (Many of our readers will be familiar with statistical terms such as "R^2" and "hierarchical linear model," which point to the effort to distinguish the complex interplay of different types of explanatory variables.) These models, based on similar quantitative work in economics, are now popular in sociology. Does the model replace theory? Does it help us to sort out the most useful of the empirical-explanatory theories and dump the rest? Does it have anything to say about the underlying or foundational paradigms to which the empirical-explanatory theories are often linked?

While there is no fundamental reason why theorists and quantitative researchers should be opposed to each other's work—indeed, the spirit of Durkheim would want us to recognize these as mutually supportive projects—areas that are highly quantified tend to be resistant to new paradigms. Scholars in these areas often see the multivariate model as the embodiment of theory, and they lean toward empirical-explanatory theories and away from the broader paradigm theories. The multivariate analysis is closely linked to a focused explanatory theory expressed by identifying significant predictor variables in the model.

The Uneven Impact of Conflict Construction on Sociology

From this point forward, we will examine the extent of penetration of contemporary theory into various areas and subfields of sociology, providing a sociology-of-knowledge perspective on why paradigms do or don't shift within a discipline.

The unevenness of the impact and the complicated ways different subfields were impacted by conflict constructionism are the topics of the second part of the book. The impact ranges from a deep impact—in which fields are entirely constructed or thoroughly reconstructed around the new paradigm—to more limited, blended, and contested situations.

In the remaining chapters we discuss reasons for this uneven penetration of conflict constructionism into sociological subfields. We look at both facilitators, such as dramatic social changes that make new theories imperative, and barriers, such as partnerships with policy fields (e.g., public health, criminal justice) and the use of vast quantities of data and sophisticated statistical analysis, which promotes the development of empirical-explanatory models in place of conceptual paradigm theories.

The reader must be forewarned. The subfields of sociology do not have identical histories. They have developed along different trajectories, have different relationships with other disciplines, and are guided by different types of research questions. For this reason, the chapters are not entirely uniform. In each chapter we trace the trajectory of the subfield, identify current theories and theoretically driven research questions that guide the subfield, and discuss the extent and forms of penetration of conflict constructionism into the subfield.

Part II

Paradigm Change in Selected Subfields

Introduction to Part II

A paradigm shift to conflict construction has affected subfields and areas of sociology unevenly. As noted in Part I, sociology has been permeated—affected slowly and often only partially—by the new paradigm. Composed of many elements to begin with, the new paradigm has not consistently appeared as a clear shift across the entire discipline. Rather it may be thought of as a cluster of elements that point in a similar direction, that are derived from postmodernist thought, feminist theories, Marxist and non-Marxist conflict theories, critical race theory, microperspectives on normative regulation, and other contemporary theories (as well as reconstituted legacies), but that add up to something that is not identical to any one of these progenitors. Some fields have been transformed or even newly created through this new framework, while others resist these theoretical elements and frameworks or veer away from theory altogether. This part offers an analytic overview of, and effort to explain, the variation among the subfields.

We examine the impact of the new paradigm, or at least elements of it, on various areas and subfields of sociology, summarizing theoretical development in these areas and offering explanations for why paradigms do or don't shift within areas of a discipline. Instead of treating the transition to contemporary theory as the work of a few individuals—the innovators—here we treat the transition more impersonally, as response and resistance within areas of the field.

In the following pages we explore change in theory and in the overarching paradigm in a sample of ten subfields of sociology. Subfields and areas are typically defined by research journals, sections at the professional association meetings, and rubrics in comprehensive and review journals of the larger discipline. These areas were selected because they are major, central areas of the field of sociology and illustrate the impact of changing theories in intriguing and diverse ways.

Deep Impact

In Section 1, "Deep Impact: The New Paradigm Becomes Dominant," we can see strong effects of the new conflict construction paradigm and even situations in which a whole area evolved together with the new paradigm. This set of chapters begins with the construction of racial-ethnic categories and gender; the link between construction of difference and imposition of dominance has transformed analysis of race-ethnicity and gender. This area of inquiry has undergone so much change that the new paradigm can be said to have transformed it, and it provides a template for the new paradigm as a whole. A second area of profound change is the analysis of culture in the global system—an area in which dramatic changes in recent decades have forced major new turns in theoretical development. Work carried out in this area—for example, Stuart Hall's writing on hybridity—has contributed essential elements of the new conflict construction paradigm. Finally, one should not forget that the discourses of these two areas (culture in the global system and the production of difference and dominance) have been transformed because the communities of theorists themselves have changed. Without resorting to any simple reductionist model of how theory is developed, one can nevertheless venture the assertion that as women, people of color, and individuals from postcolonial regions enter the community of scholars, the discourses of these communities must change, and the new paradigm reflects these changes as well as changes in the larger social landscape.

Another obvious "deep impact" area is the study of the media because the media explosion of the latter half of the twentieth century has transformed—indeed created—the subject matter of the field.

Our fourth "deep impact" area is the sociology of the self. We can see a strong impact of the elements of the new paradigm, such as construction; the role of framing; self-processes as texts, narratives, and performance; and the primacy of the body. These concepts are applied to the analysis of the self in all times and places, but some theorists argue that the postmodern self in the era of advanced capitalism is qualitatively different from previous selves.

Paradigms in Play

In Section 2, "Paradigms in Play," we examine situations in which older paradigms and contemporary theories coexist, sometimes in contestation and sometimes with a peaceful division of the terrain. These mixed situations can be detected in political sociology, spatial analysis and urban sociology, and the subfield formerly known as criminology and the sociology of deviance. In political sociology and the analysis of collective action, the new and the old are blending harmoniously. Political sociology has been strongly affected by Pierre Bourdieu's concept of the political field, and the sociology of collective action has incorporated new insights on states, civil society, and identities and culture in social movements.

Urban sociology persists in its traditional forms, but a lively new area—the analysis of space—has emerged alongside, in part stimulated by new metropolitan patterns, the growth of new global cities, and urbanization in developing regions. Old and new approaches to the city move along on parallel tracks, but they must all respond to changes in urbanization and urban form at a global level.

The areas of criminology and the study of deviance responded to Michel Foucault's theoretical assault but still include older theories as well as new links to public health research and criminal justice perspectives. The analysis of "deviance" (the quotation marks signal problems in the very definition of the field), crime, social control, and punishment is a highly volatile area, marked by contradictory and antagonistic approaches, theories "talking by" one another, new connections to fields such as public health and the analysis of high risk behavior, and many other lines of division. Everyday pressures from the applied field of criminal justice and law enforcement produce major splits between practice-oriented scholars and scholars whose approaches are shaped by the work of Foucault, radical criminology, critical race theory, and other critical theories. This area can be described as churning in that new critical perspectives compete with existing ones.

Paradigm Limited

In Section 3, "Paradigm Limited," we examine two areas where existing paradigms remain extremely powerful, although social conditions have changed. These areas are the analysis of class and socioeconomic inequality and the sociology of family life. In the analysis of inequality and social class, distinct perspectives persist, many of them extensions of classical theories derived from Karl Marx and Friedrich Engels, Max Weber, and Emile Durkheim but now tweaked or stretched into postmodern and late-capitalist formulations (Wright 2006). Although elements of a conflict constructionist paradigm appear—for example, in more attention to macro/micro linkages in the formation of socioeconomic inequalities—these newer elements have not displaced the three powerful and contending classical paradigms.

Another instance of limited impact of the new paradigm is sociology of the family. It has maintained many of the earlier paradigms, with radical feminist theory (and its Foucaultian and Butlerian underpinnings) being somewhat isolated from mainstream work in this area; microlevel research is congruent with the mainstream but has hardly displaced it. Here, as in the study of socioeconomic disparities, quantitative analysis is a major element of the mainstream paradigm, serving as a barrier to constructionist approaches. The presence of demographic data is central to the field, and many researchers are drawn to examining these data rather than to the microlevel studies and qualitative research that typically provide the empirical basis of the conflict construction paradigm.

Paradigms Reconstituted

A special case is presented in Section 4, "Paradigms Reconstituted in a Transdisciplinary Field," which features the sociology of health, a field that appears to have once been extensively theorized and now to have turned away from theory. Initially we labeled this development as "theory lost" because sociology of health, illness, and medical practice has moved from structural functional theory to conflict theory to a growingly atheoretical discourse, even as researchers dissect contentious and potentially theoretical areas such as the effects of inequality on population health. The communities of scholars working in this field are reluctant to foreground theory, but theories such as Marxist or Weberian perspectives on class persist in a shadowy, spectral, or trace form visible in the use of concepts such as inequalities and disparities. Yet this apparently atheoretical and even antitheoretical approach veils a strong effort to redeploy existing theoretical concepts like inequality and to reintegrate them into a new perspective that encompasses several disciplines and very large issues in human well-being.

In short, we examine the causes of the uneven impact of theory and the conflict constructionist paradigm (or specific elements of it). Our analysis requires special attention to the partnership with policy fields (e.g., public health, criminal justice) that has impacted several fields, as well as the effects of vast quantities of data and tools for sophisticated statistical analysis that have appeared across most fields of sociology.

We begin the discussion of each area with an overview that identifies the main themes associated with contemporary theories. The next section, "Trajectory," traces the development of these themes from the legacies of classical theory through the structural functional period and the ascendancy of conflict and interactionist theories to the present. We reflect on external influences from the real world, identify facilitators and barriers to the adoption of new theories, and provide examples of theories and applications.

Barriers and Facilitators of Paradigm Shifts

Several forces affected theorizing in the subfields and the extent to which new frameworks, and specifically the conflict constructionist paradigm, had an impact. Some of these forces are facilitators that encourage sociologists to adopt new approaches, and others are barriers.

Facilitators: Forces That Led to Adoption of New Theories

These forces were discussed in detail in Part I, in the chapter on sources of the new paradigm, so here they are only reviewed briefly.

1. Change in the external or real world: Changes such as urbanization, transnational migration, freer transnational markets and neoliberal policies, the growth of enormous transnational corporations, and the formation of multicultural societies forced sociologists to revise their ideas about social reality. For example, the field of medical sociology had to encompass the rise of HMOs and the entry of profit-making organizations into health care.

Urban sociology had to address the fact that half of the globe's population is now urban and that previously agrarian developing nations contain many of the world's poorest and fastest-growing cities. Sociology of crime and deviance had to include an analysis of the soaring rates of incarceration in the United States.

2. Intellectual trends: The subfields are impacted by shifts in the larger and grander theories and fashions in social thought. These theories are incorporated into middle-range theory in the subfields. For example, deconstructionism in philosophy was appropriated by the social sciences and incorporated into social constructionist theories that emphasized the creation through discourse of categories such as race, sex and gender, and deviance and normality.

3. Internal dynamics of the field: Overall sociological theory and perspectives shifted from the dominance of structural functionalism and social psychology in the decade after World War II to a much more contentious state of affairs with the proliferation of conflict theories in the 1960s and 1970s. By the 1960s, interactionist and conflict theories had become popular, and in the following decade, conflict theories in particular seemed to be at the exciting new frontiers of sociology. Variants of Marxism and feminism defined the cutting edge of areas such as urban sociology, sociology of the media, and sociology of medicine. For instance, Marxist theories guided the analysis of the urban growth machine (developers and their political allies) and grassroots urban activism. Conflict theories in medical sociology criticized professional dominance and the power of physicians. Theories of corporate monopolies and hegemonic processes of news construction guided research on the media. By the 1980s and 1990s, conflict theories were being refined, toned down, and combined with constructionist approaches. Many scholars throughout the subfields of sociology followed these trends, and the overall movement of sociological theory was an impetus for shifts within the subfields.

Barriers to Paradigm Shifts: Conditions That Made Scholars in a Field Less Likely to Shift toward the New Paradigm

Three barriers to a shift toward the new paradigm include the following:

1. Partnerships with applied and policy fields: Researchers in applied and policy-oriented fields are often wary of theories, and when partnerships are formed with these fields, theory may be deemphasized or theoretical terms transplanted into apparently nontheoretical research projects. For example, sociology of health is partnered with public health, urban sociology with urban planning, sociology of deviance and crime with criminal justice and corrections, and sociology of families with family and child policy. Public policy makers are not thrilled by theories with a negative critical spin, like

Marxism, feminism, critical theory in general, and, by extension, conflict constructionism, which shares the critical and conflict-oriented premises of these theories. These premises make partnerships with colleagues in applied fields more difficult and are not an asset in applying for funding or developing pragmatic policies. Consequently, partnerships with applied fields lead to more muted or deeply buried theoretical perspectives and even to a generally atheoretical stance and the avoidance of any broad critical theoretical labels, such as "Marxist" or "Weberian." Theoretical terms may be replaced by softer, less contentious terms. A very telling sign of this avoidance is the substitution of "disparities" for the harsher and more theoretical term "inequalities." These terms remain as traces of critical theories and conflict perspectives, but scholars avoid self-labeling with conflict labels or recognized theoretical labels in general.

2. Multivariate analysis as the theory: Quantitative analysis has a complicated relationship to theories; on the one hand, ever since Auguste Comte and Emile Durkheim, sociologists have based theories on the premise that societies have discernible, stable patterns and that careful empirical data collection and quantitative analysis enable us to recognize the patterns.

   But the amassing of very large and sophisticated data sets combined with multivariate analysis, the development of highly refined, intricate, and multilevel linear and logistic regression models, has revolutionized the process of not only discerning patterns but identifying causal chains as well. For some sociologists, theory now lies in identifying significant predictor variables for outcomes in complex multilevel models. If we can identify these variables while we control for possible confounding variables, we have established an explanatory and causal model. Complex models are a satisfactory substitute for theoretical paradigms because they demonstrate that we understand causal pathways. When these types of data are available in a field, as they are for epidemiological studies of population health and illness, educational attainment and academic achievement, patterns of crime, and many other areas, there is a strong incentive to develop the quantitative models rather than theoretical constructs. While there is no fundamental reason why theorists and quantitative researchers should be opposed to each other's work—indeed, the spirit of Durkheim would want us to recognize these as mutually supportive projects—areas that are highly quantified tend to be resistant to theory. Quantitative analysis has become the mainstream way of "doing sociology" in some subfields and dominates several of the leading journals in the field. It is also a major component of much empirical-explanatory theorizing and of theory development at a middle range, within subfields rather than for the discipline as a whole. Quantitative analysis has become a way of reaching conclusions without making claims about paradigms.

3. Paradigm persistence: A third reason why some subfields and areas have resisted contemporary theories is that the preexisting paradigms seem

perfectly serviceable, and scholars do not feel impelled to introduce new paradigms, or they do so only to address very specific questions (often those that address micro/macro linkages) and not to reconfigure the field as a whole. The troublesome puzzles that motivate paradigm shifts have not been discerned.

Chapter Organization

In this part, variation among the subfields makes it hard to impose a single rigid format for chapter organization. Each chapter places an overview of new ideas in the context of the trajectory of the field, that is, its history of theoretical change. In some cases, theories need to be traced back to the classical period in order to understand the present situation, whereas in other fields, we begin with the post–World War II dominance of structural functionalism. Most of the fields passed through a phase of prominence (if not dominance) of conflict theories in the 1970s, and it is from this matrix that conflict constructionism emerged by the end of the twentieth century. In the rest of the chapter, we review examples of theoretical work with a conflict constructionist perspective and assess its relationship to the mainstream (if a mainstream can be identified at all).

SECTION 1

Deep Impact: The New Paradigm Becomes Dominant

Chapter Four

Constructing Difference and Dominance

Race-Ethnicity and Gender

Why do we see so many disparities among racial and ethnic groups in health, education, income and wealth, incarceration rates, and life expectancy—even though racial discrimination is against the law? Why do women earn lower incomes than men, even in comparable occupations, despite the fact that women now outnumber men in college attendance? Why does television present so many stereotypical and degrading images of women and minorities? What caused a growing fear of and hostility toward immigrants in recent years—a wave of xenophobia? Have you or your friends or family ever been racially profiled? And how will life in the United States be different by the mid-twenty-first century when erstwhile minorities become the new majority?

These kinds of questions are not new in the United States, but sociologists are thinking about race, ethnicity, and gender very differently than they did in the mid-twentieth century. This chapter focuses on race-ethnicity and gender, the two categories of inequality and *difference* whose analysis has been most extensively revised in a conflict constructionist direction. Although sociologists certainly expressed concern about racial-ethnic and gender disparities throughout the twentieth century, they tended to treat the differences themselves rather casually, even as natural (a term itself loaded with many assumptions about nature). In the decades since the civil rights and women's movements, however, increasing attention has been focused on the social *construction* of differences.

To provide an integrated overview of the chapter, we begin with several broad reflections.

First, differences of gender and ethnicity (by which we mean language, history, shared norms and values, and a sense of group identity) have been part of human life for a long time. How are we to think about them?

A strong tendency to naturalize these differences appears in many cultures and societies. By "naturalize" we mean that they are construed as fixed, immutable, and formed in a way that is prior and external to social relationships. In premodern times, this naturalized quality was expressed in religious terms—for example, in the creation of Adam and Eve and in the story of God's destruction of the Tower of Babel and the scattering of humanity into groups with different languages. In modern times, with the growth of science and the rise of colonial empires, difference came to be explained in biologistic terms, culminating in the approach that is labeled "scientific racism," now a pejorative term for what has come to be seen as a pseudoscience. From the perspective of scientific racism, in the late nineteenth and early twentieth centuries, differences among societies and cultures were explained as the result of fixed, innate traits of different races.

Gender and ethnoracial difference are bases of inequality and relations of dominance. Both Max Weber and the Marxists considered these types of inequalities examples of status inequality. The Marxists tended to believe that their significance would decline as class inequalities became the major dimension of inequality in capitalist society, but Weber thought they would persist and continue to form one of the bases of party, a term he used to mean collective action.

After the mid-twentieth century (following the abuses of racially based eugenics, the horrors of Nazi genocide, and the contributions of improved scientific research), social scientists moved away from biologistic views of the naturalness of these inequalities, but in the period of structural functionalism, they were still often taken for granted. By the 1960s and 1970s, conflict theorists associated with the successes of movements against colonialism, for civil rights, and for women's equality focused on these inequalities. The scholar-activists not only called for an end to gender and ethnoracial inequalities but also saw the oppressed groups as historical subjects—just as much so as the proletariat in Marxist theory—who could lead human beings toward a more egalitarian and just social order.

Conflict constructionism, however, stretched the conflict position further, explicitly attacking the fundamental naturalness of these divisions, showing the differences (and associated dominance) to be socially constructed categories that emerge from social relationships, discourses, and practices, including state policies.

The treatment of gender and ethnoracial difference follows a unified trajectory in the period from World War II to the present:

- In the postwar period, the notion of scientific naturalization was abandoned, and both gender and race-ethnicity were rather casually treated as ascribed differences.
- Conflict theorists, linked to movements, called for equality and even reversed the valence of the categories (women and people of color being seen positively and white males negatively), but they did not fully question the categories themselves.
- Conflict constructionists took an explicitly antinaturalistic stand, examining—and thus deconstructing—the construction of these categories. Key

concepts in this analysis included discourses; practices, including state policies; the inscription of categories on the body (or the body as the site where these categories are constructed, giving them a biological appearance); the relational model (the categories exist only in relationship to each other, not as immutable properties of individuals); and structuration in dominance.

Returning to the Kuhnian logic of paradigms, we can see how this interpretive shift has forced a rethinking of all categories at play, especially those of the body and its relation to race-ethnicity and gender-sexuality. It is here that conflict constructionism has found its most fertile ground.

Trajectory: Facilitators and Barriers

One major facilitator of the shift to conflict constructionism was the force of the movements that decisively rejected the notion that inequalities are natural phenomena, destinies set by biology or by functionality. But beyond this point, scholars had to turn from a straightforward challenge of inequalities to a more nuanced analysis of why these inequalities persisted, even when the movements were able to claim victories. Scholars and activists began to look at ways the media perpetuated stereotypes and how *whiteness* and masculinity were silent and taken-for-granted categories of dominance. These insights were closely linked to the discursive turn in theory, placing emphasis on discourses and representations.

Another facilitator of new theories was increased immigration, which complicated the racial hierarchy of the United States and created multiethnic societies in Europe. It suggested to theorists that racial and ethnic identities and stratification systems are fluid and that the state, as the defining agent of citizenship and identity, has a very powerful role in the social construction of identity. Similarly, as states shifted from being simply agents of male domination toward becoming terrains of contention between movements and countermovements on the question of women's rights, the state was recognized for its role in constructing gender as well as race, ethnicity, and citizenship.

If these forces—movements, media, immigration, and the role of the state—impelled sociologists to reconceptualize race, ethnicity, and gender, there were also barriers against the shift to a paradigm anchored in both conflict and construction. One of the most powerful barriers was simply a pragmatic one: analysis of quantitative data and the large available data sets could not linger on navel-gazing concerns about "What is race?" and "What is gender?" Increasingly sophisticated quantitative analysis rested on relatively unproblematic understandings of the categories in which survey data and biomedical data were collected and tended to force research back into simpler ascriptive frameworks. There continues to be soul-searching among biomedical and epidemiological researchers about race, but it is not a central concern in the mainstream (Navarro and Muntaner 2004).

Similarly, policy pressures turned social scientists away from deeper exploration of the discursive turn, apart from yet another round of tweaking the ethnic and racial categories of the US Census.

Race and Ethnicity

Overview

The analysis of race and ethnicity has changed drastically from the mid-twentieth century to the present, moving from a taken-for-granted naturalization of racial categories toward various versions of social constructionism. These perspectives include the following:

- Attention to the formation of categories of discourse that establish racial-ethnic differences and dominance
- Attention to the role of the state in establishing and perpetuating difference and dominance, including the role of apparently race-neutral or "color-blind" policies
- A focus on the *historical invention of race as a concept* and specifically the formation and expansion of *whiteness* as a category of identity and its relationship to white supremacy
- Continued interest in the relationship between class stratification and racial-ethnic stratification
- Analysis of how racial dominance is perpetuated in the United States in the post–civil rights period and globally in the postapartheid era, when discrimination is no longer legal
- Controversy around the question of how much variation in racial stratification exists among nations and whether or not their trajectories of racial dominance are convergent

Trajectory: From Ascription to Construction

Classical Approaches

The analysis of racial-ethnic dominance has roots in both Marxism and Weberian sociology. Karl Marx and Friedrich Engels associated the rise of capitalism with the conquest and enslavement of Africans and Indians. Weber treated the matter rather more abstractly by posing the general problem of the relationship between class stratification and status ranking; ethnic and cultural groups are ranked into status stratification systems. W. E. B. DuBois showed the interconnection of class and race in his studies of the condition of African Americans in the United States and pioneered contemporary approaches to race by focusing attention on the formation of an ideology of whiteness during the slave trade and colonialism. Emile Durkheim explicitly and systematically challenged prevailing notions of race by showing that supposed racial differences were very poor predictors of differences in behavior. Despite efforts by anthropologists such as Franz Boas, notions of race as a meaningful category of biological difference persisted well into the twentieth century.

After World War II

The use of race as a biologically based concept was discredited during the World War II period amid the horrors associated with Nazi ideology of the ethnoracial *essentialist* doctrine of the *Volk,* racial hierarchy, and racial supremacy. Developments in biology and physical anthropology showed that race as a folk category had no relationship to population genetics. Nevertheless, most postwar social scientists were comfortable using race as a commonsense category that described ascriptive, essentially fixed characteristics of individuals. As social scientists and public intellectuals, they generally challenged the legalized racial stratification and segregation system that still prevailed in the United States before the civil rights movement. They certainly saw it as both dysfunctional and morally pernicious. But they did not much question the category of race itself, and much of the research of the mid-twentieth century focused either on the South as a retrograde region or on individual sources of prejudice.

From Conflict Theories to Constructionism

The sociology of race and ethnic relations has moved decisively from seeing race and ethnicity as ascribed characteristics of individuals to analyzing how these categories of difference are constructed and from attention to individual sources of prejudice to a focus on the construction of dominance. The first shifts in this direction came with conflict theorists who wanted to analyze the enormous economic disparities that persisted after the civil rights movement. These disparities were in part a result of historic discrimination and constricted opportunities and in part a result of dominance inscribed into discourses, practices, and relationships on an ongoing basis. The Marxist premises of conflict theory led to interest in intersections of class and race and to elaboration of the idea that African Americans (as well as Latinos in the southwestern United States and Indians throughout the Americas) were an internal colony, oppressed and exploited in much the same way as indigenous peoples in colonies (Leggett 1968; Georgakis 1998; Blauner 1972). Parallels were drawn between anticolonial insurgencies and the militant Black Power movements that followed the civil rights movement.

Theories were beginning to move in a constructionist direction, and so the last decades of the twentieth century saw a variety of such theories, which developed the general concept of social construction, attention to historical origins of white supremacy and whiteness, and the elaboration of a relational model of race-ethnicity.

The Social Construction of Race

Contemporary theories focus on the discourses that constitute difference, on the naturalization or normalization of difference and dominance, and on the historical processes that underlie the discourses. These theories dissect the meanings attached to the way people look—the stories, myths, ideas, stereotypes, and ways of thinking and talking by which we come to believe that physical differences are associated with other differences.

The constructionist paradigm argues that race and ethnicity are the products of systems of classifications: people are assigned to particular positions or categories based on physical appearance (in the case of race) and language or national origin (in the case of ethnicity). Associated attributes and characteristics are *essentialized*; that is, they are believed to be tied to those traits and thus inherent in the person being categorized that way. Ethnicity is frequently linked to race, and in the popular imaginary of difference, both are seen in essentialist terms. These racial classifications appear as natural and inevitable; we act on them as stereotypes, as presumed understandings of what those groups are like. The power of classification lies in its leading us to think that these characteristics are natural.

Following the work of Stuart Hall, who argues that there is nothing permanent about race and ethnic identity, conflict constructionist theorists propose that *race is a floating signifier,* a constantly changing notion of identity that takes on different meanings and values at different times and places in history. The different categories of race and ethnicity that we map out as a society only make sense within a field of relations; that is, any one particular racial or ethnic group only has meaning insofar as it is compared and contrasted with another. The most powerful example for understanding this process is the dominant racial comparison in the United States—that of black and white. This difference is defined *relationally*: to be black has traditionally meant all that is not white, and vice versa. Sociologists and social theorists such as Michael Omi and Howard Winant (1994) refer to this process of the formation and transformation of racial groups using the language of *racial formation and racialization* by which categories are created, transformed, and destroyed. For example, the ethnic and racial categories of the US Census can be deconstructed; they change with each successive census, but the larger project of racial classification of the population persists (Yanow 2003).

The process of racial and ethnic categorization is not arbitrary or neutral but always part of the creation and perpetuation of racial and ethnic inequality. Classification serves as a mechanism of power. As noted in the discussion of Michel Foucault, the first step in the exercise of power is differentiation. Power generates meaning and hierarchies and shapes the social world through categorizations, which in turn are linked to the organization of racial and ethnic groups in terms of domination and subordination. Once a system of classification is put in place, the maintenance of that order is crucial to keeping society structured in dominance. Thus classification is always a process of social struggle: to keep the boundaries in place, to stabilize them, to maintain the hierarchy, and to keep the positive and negative attributes in place.

Another important aspect of the social construction of race is the collapsing and *conflation of categories* of race-ethnicity and national origin into simplistic labels often associated with visible physical differences such as skin color, eye shape, hair texture, and so on. British sociologist Paul Gilroy (1994), in his study of the African diaspora, argues that conflating all dark-skinned peoples in the United Kingdom into the category "black" obscures the crucial cultural, national, and historical experiences of diverse groups with backgrounds in Africa, the Caribbean, and South Asia. Similar lumpings in the United States have created the "Asian" and "white" categories. "Hispanics" is also a lumped category, eliding differences of national origin and culture into a term based on regional origin (Latin America).

Analysis of the Historical Invention of Race

Although many societies have noted differences in language and culture (ethnicity), these differences became part of a sweeping concept of race during the development of Western modernity. Race as a major classification system linked visible physical characteristics and ethnic differences and placed them together in a master category believed to be inherited and immutable.

Ethnicity-race became the construct that had a defining role in shaping life chances and formulating government policies in the colonial world and the new nations organized by European settlers in the Americas and elsewhere. These states were explicitly organized according to racial dominance, with the power and freedom of some (white settlers) contingent on the enslavement and displacement of others (Foner 1999). The emergence of race and ethnicity as categories of dominance must be seen not as an issue isolated or separate from the formation of settler societies and all states in the New World (as Europeans called it) but rather as intertwined with these nations' political and economic development.

Ethnoracial categories were used to define opportunities, authority, place of residence, and job access. They organized the schema of social control and defined relations of economic dominance and the exploitation of labor; both Marxist and Foucault-based perspectives are relevant here. In perspectives influenced by Marxism, racial ideology followed and justified the establishment of European control over resources and labor power (Fields 1990). An early template of ethnic dominance was formed by English policies in Ireland and other regions with Celtic populations, as well as by European states' variable ways of "managing" Roma communities (Ladanyi and Szelenyi 2006). Extreme forms of racial systems of dominance were apparent in slavery in the Americas and the displacement and attempted extermination of Indians in state policies such as the expulsion of Indians from the southeastern United States (known as the Trail of Tears), the Indian Wars in the United States in the 1870s and 1880s, the "caste war" of the Yucatan, the deportation of the Yaqui, and the genocidal "desert war" conducted by General Roca in Argentina.

Scholars such as Noel Ignatiev (1996) have explained how this process, in which racial categories hardened and the concept of white identity came into consciousness in relation to other racial and ethnic groups, helped justify to ordinary whites their own special social identity as distinguished from all other groups. As racial identity, the social order, and the American nation melded into one dominant ideology, the racial organization of society began to crystallize and the United States to become institutionalized as a nation that belonged to whites. Ethnic groups such as Jews, Italians, Irish, and Arabs, whose whiteness had not been evident initially, made efforts to define themselves as whites in the course of the later nineteenth and early twentieth centuries (Takaki 1994; Cankar 2006; Yanow 2003).

We see from these examples that once authority and power are institutionalized, normalized, and legitimized as a natural state of affairs through numerous mechanisms and discourses, a certain set of corresponding social arrangements and racial relations is put in place and normalized as eternal and unchanging. Thus are the principles of racial and ethnic division put beyond the scope of history—that is, outside the temporal process of historical development and social construction—making these differences ever present and reified.

The historical analysis of the invention of race pointed to three important theoretical lessons: (1) the intertwining of racial and ethnic classifications with economics, politics, and policies of national states; (2) the link between classification and material consequences, including rights, privileges, and freedoms; and (3) the role of racial classification in the founding of all New World and settler societies and the persistent—though certainly contested—construction of these societies in racial dominance.

By unveiling the dynamics of power that define racial and ethnic groups for what they are, constructionist theory showed that they are contingent and arbitrary products of history, that there is nothing natural about them, and that an understanding of history is indispensable for pragmatic interventions in present-day life contexts. The next step in the new paradigm of race was to examine racial dominance in recent decades, especially the role of the state in its persistence.

The Relational Model and the Role of the State

The relational model examines not only how societies become structured in racial dominance but how racial dominance is built into the very fabric of everyday life and is reproduced on everyday levels, often at a level below people's awareness (Hall 1986). Whereas prejudice and discrimination models offered psychological explanations for the way that race and ethnicity generate racial inequality, the new model of *societies structured in racial dominance* bypasses individual attitudes in order to highlight the everyday, ordinary ways that racial and ethnic inequality are reproduced, regardless of the intentions, attitudes, or behaviors of people in everyday life.

Racial dominance was furthered by state policies, sometimes intentionally and sometimes not. Ira Katznelson, in his trenchantly titled *When Affirmative Action Was White* (2006), dissects a number of policies that originated in the New Deal and continued throughout the postwar decades and that favored white people in the distribution of government benefits and services. The state also permitted practices that had profound accelerating effects on urban segregation—for example, bank redlining, in which entire communities in the inner city were denied mortgage loans.

Government officials in both the United States and France allowed public housing to become segregated. Mass incarceration in the United States has become a policy of controlling young, uneducated African American men; though formally color-blind, the practices and policies involve regulating a specific race-class category by punitive means, with the consequences of extending racial isolation and exclusion (Wacquant 2004, 2009a, 2009b).

In addition to examining the role of the state, theorists focus on resources and institutions such as the distribution of power (legal, legislative, and political power, the ability to mobilize voters), money (bank loans, credit cards, cash, savings accounts, and, above all, assets and wealth), and resources (college degrees and social networks, cultural capital). This model emphasizes structural relations, both in terms of the different positions of racial and ethnic groups relative to each other and in terms of the power, money, and resource relations that are reproduced.

The Analysis of Whiteness

The new models associated with the conflict constructionist paradigm focused increasingly on the construction of whiteness, just as feminist theories began to focus on the construction of masculinity.

At the center of recent developments of racial and ethnic theory is the concept of whiteness. Rather than begin with minority groups and their assimilation to whiteness, new theories of race start at the center of power—with what is invisible, normative, unspoken, commonsense—in order to understand our tacit assumptions about the normal workings of race and ethnicity in everyday life (Hartigan 1999). For some theorists this necessitates a paradigm shift from whiteness conceptualized as white supremacy (agents acting in conscious coalition toward maintaining racial supremacy and hierarchy) to whiteness as the invisible, underlying, normalized operation of the racial organization of society. (But not all theorists are quite so ready to give up the term "white supremacy" [Roediger 1999; Allen 1997].)

Whiteness is not an individual phenomenon, to be examined on an individual level (as theorists of prejudice and discrimination are wont to do). Instead whiteness is theorized as the defining principle of social organization by which white values, ideas, aesthetics, and preferences are made to appear normal and the basis of the social order. In shifting the focus of the study of race and ethnicity to whiteness, sociologists understand how these specific social dynamics are institutionalized and naturalized and explore how such social organization becomes invisible even to whites themselves. In this way whiteness is an embedded system of norms, aesthetics, and orientations and the institutional modes of operation that emerge out of this social organization of resources and opportunities. Whiteness need not be overt, explicit, direct, or conspiratorial—the normalized racial operations of society sustain white dominance, and nonwhites can easily slip into supporting these ideas as well. And finally, whiteness as a mode of social/racial domination is a world we are born into, one that is already constructed and in which racial meanings are already in play and taken for granted. The ideology of whiteness seems seamless and invisible in everyday life. As a result, our perpetuation of these ideologies is never apparent because our everyday participation in them goes unnoticed. Finally, there is a crucial distinction between whiteness as a system of social organization that structures society in racial dominance and white people as racialized actors within that system.

Transnational Issues in the New Paradigms of Race-Ethnicity

Theoretical discussion focuses on the extent and reasons for variation among nations in the definition of ethnoracial categories and the construction of racial dominance. For example, the French government does not permit any collection of data about race and ethnicity, while these categories are an obsession in the United States. There is controversy about whether US models of racial categorization and dominance are being exported, for example, to Brazil.

US ideologies of race relations are being erroneously projected into discussions of events in other countries, such as the car burnings in the peripheries of French cities. Loïc Wacquant (2009b) and Hugues Lagrange and Marco Oberti (2006) argue that defining the November 2005 riots in France as manifestations of "Islamic identity politics" is to mistakenly project a US model of ethnic relations into France, when the French disturbances should be interpreted as a demand for economic opportunities and integration. Meanwhile, Eduardo Bonilla-Silva and Karen Glover (2004) argue that the United States is moving toward a Latin American–style racial hierarchy, with whites at the top, followed by Asians and European-looking Latinos, and dark-complexioned Latinos and blacks at the bottom of the hierarchy; not all observers agree.

The situation is further complicated by transnational immigration and the formation of new patterns of ethnoracial dominance, often with state complicity in the definition of some migrants as more racially congenial than others, thus contributing to the intertwining of immigrant status with occupations and race. For example, Shu-Ju Ada Cheng (2007) contrasts the racialized treatment and state classification of Filipino domestic workers and caregivers in Taiwan with that accorded ex-pats from wealthier and "whiter" countries in professional and managerial occupations.

Race as Performance, Embodied Knowledge, and an Inscription on the Body

A final new twist in constructionist models of race and ethnicity is the use of theory derived from the work of Pierre Bourdieu to redefine race (and ethnicity) as elements of habitus, as embodied knowledge, inscribed on the body and acted out physically. We are not white or black or people of color simply because of a few phenotypical characteristics; we enter these categories as we act out and expect others to act out a racial performance. This position, it must be said, is easier to propose half a century after the integration of public facilities in the United States and after the election of an African American president who disrupts stereotypical preconceptions about the performance of race. (Yet one might consider that even in the days of unchallenged de jure segregation of key American institutions in the 1930s, major-league ball players recruited from Cuba were conveniently thought of as "not Negroes" as long as their phenotypical characteristics were ambiguous.)

In this vein, a leading study is Black Hawk Hancock's analysis of steppin', an African American dance form closely related to the Lindy, jitterbug, and swing. Recounting how the appearance of the researcher (a white man) and his dance partner (a white woman) on the dance floor of steppin' establishments disrupted the assumptions underlying race as embodied performance, Hancock explores how the construction of race is based on discourses about performance, the body, embodied skills, and what Bourdieu terms "habitus." Hancock performed a breaching experiment (to return to a term and method used by ethnomethodological researchers in the late 1960s and 1970s), disrupting what most people treat not as an embodied skill but as an essential difference that constructs race: white men can't dance (Hancock 2005).

Gender and Feminist Theories

Overview

The theorizing of gender closely paralleled the theorizing of race-ethnicity.

- Theories of gender moved in a constructionist direction with a strong impetus from Foucault and, more directly, from Judith Butler.
- Attention is being given to the role of the state in defining gender and heightening gender differences.
- Theorists agree that gender must be studied in the context of ethnoracial dominance and class inequalities as well as *state policies.*
- Theorists of gender focus increasingly on the construction of masculinity, paralleling the focus on the construction of whiteness. Conflict constructionist theorists place emphasis on the social construction of the dominant category in a category system that distinguishes the dominant and the subaltern. Previously the dominant category was treated as normative, and its very existence was taken for granted. Conflict theorists of the 1970s had focused on the social construction of women but not of men, which now became the center of attention.

Trajectory: Feminist Theory in the Period of Conflict Theory

Functionalist theorists of the postwar period tended to treat sex and gender as natural differences and took gender roles of the period for granted, even justifying them as intrinsic to the family and societal division of labor. This position was abruptly overturned with the rise of the women's movement, the entry of women into sociology (as well as the labor force as a whole throughout the economically developed world), and the rise of feminist theory. The growth of contemporary feminist theory was associated with the entry of large numbers of women into the paid labor force in most developed economies. Feminist theory progressed rapidly from 1970 on, becoming a major force in cultural and social inquiry.

Different types of feminist theory emerged, some aligned with liberal feminist movements calling for gender equality within the institutions of modern capitalism. Others aligned with Marxist analysis and focused on the intertwining of gender hierarchy with capitalist class structure. Black feminist scholars in the United States such as Angela Davis (1984/1990), Audre Lorde (2004), Deborah King (1988), Patricia Hill Collins (2000), and bell hooks (1990) (see also Baca Zinn and Dill [1990]) pointed out that white liberal feminists were insensitive to the persistence of racism and white supremacy and failed to address the multiple jeopardies that women of color faced. This political position was eventually developed into a comprehensive theoretical analysis of intersectionality and how the construction of gender is closely tied to other processes of social construction, such as racial hierarchies, heterosexual dominance, immigration laws and citizenship rights, the role of religious traditions in family law, and class relationships that are produced and reinforced in labor markets.

Feminist theorists analyzed gender hierarchies and inequalities, but many of them were also critical theorists who challenged the categories of thought and discourses associated with hierarchy and inequality. They argued that these categories and assumptions pervaded not only popular discourse and opinion but scholarly discourse as well. Feminist theory as critical theory was a major force in propelling the analysis of gender in the directions of a conflict constructionist paradigm.

Enter Judith Butler

Finally, by the 1990s, postmodernist theory and the influence of Judith Butler's work began to add yet another layer to *gender construction* theory, a growing emphasis on gender as performance and an increasingly radical subversion of the concept of identity. Much like Foucault's theorizing, her contributions span philosophy, textual analysis, and the social sciences. Butler argues that the construction of gender is the binding together of sex category, gender, and heterosexuality into a single package. This packaged identity is then inscribed on the body in a process that appears to be natural. We expect anatomy, gender, and sexual orientation to be aligned with each other and each component to be "normal." Even gay and lesbian identities, though not normative, are expected to follow certain conventions of performance and naturalized identity. As Foucault pointed out in his history of sexuality and John D'Emilio (1983) elaborates in his discussion of gay identity in capitalist society, gay and lesbian identity has not always been a coherent and stable category of self and identity.

Gender is an act. This assertion has several implications for thinking about gender. First of all, gender is performed. Butler says that it is a stylized repetition of acts. We perform gender with our gestures, movements, and facial expressions. Gender is styles of the flesh, inscribed on our bodies and repetitively performed with masks that are glued to our faces. We costume ourselves to meet the expectations of our audience for a convincing performance of our gender.

Gender is also an act in the sense of putting on an act because sometimes the performance of gender does not does not match the thoughts, feelings, and self-image of the actor. But we must never show any slippage between the performed gendered self and the interior self. Any incongruity is deemed to reveal the individual's inadequacy or abnormality.

The performance of gender has to be not only flawless but also self-concealing. When we perform gender, we must convince viewers that the gender display is natural and that we could not possibly look and act otherwise. It must be an effortless performance that does not draw attention to itself or signal that we are trying too hard—as might be revealed by a woman's consistent use of heavy makeup and a babyish, breathy voice or by a man's persistent wearing of soldier-of-fortune gear. Inflexible and exaggerated *gender performance* and costuming can undermine the intended message of effortless and natural femininity or masculinity.

The reader might note that in modern Western capitalist societies the rules governing gender performance are especially restrictive for men. It is acceptable for a woman to act or dress like a man, to a certain extent—in any case, it is acceptable not to act in a completely feminine manner—but it is seen as unsettling if a man acts out of character for a man, and his performance may be sanctioned with abuse or even violence. On the other hand, in other cultures, gender performance for women is also narrowly defined, and women who do not keep their hair, ankles, and wrists covered, or who violate restrictive clothing rules, may be beaten or assaulted if they venture into public spaces. Punishments may also be meted out to men who fail to grow beards, and this norm is even more oppressive than the dress codes for women because it is so intensely and physically connected to the body.

As in Erving Goffman's dramaturgical model of the self, gender performance is judged as credible or noncredible. Noncredible performances include a large range of transgressive acts, such as wearing drag, behaving tomboyishly, and displaying stereotypical homosexual mannerisms. These acts are seen as unnatural, and they fail (or refuse) to seamlessly lock together sex category, gender, and sexual orientation. They disrupt the links that are supposed to exist among these components of the performance. *Transgression* involves rendering incredible that which is supposed to be credible; the ludicrous, unsettling, and mismatched acts put the entire understanding of gender as natural into question. Sometimes transgression may be recuperated by placing these acts into the category of the carnivalesque. For Halloween or Mardi Gras, it is okay for a man to wear a dress—in fact, his funny appearance reaffirms that this style is not appropriate for men. At what point does transgression become really transgressive, going beyond play and carnival performance?

At the microlevel sociologists observe gender performance, but these stylized, repetitive performances are linked to macro power differences, to the dominance of men and the subaltern condition of women, and to compulsory heterosexuality. The insistence that gender is natural, that it must be performed well at all times, and that only a narrow range of performances is deemed correct and convincing is part of a process that takes gender inequality off the agenda of public scrutiny and discussion. The man/woman dualism, with its attendant power differences, is constantly re-created and reproduced in speech, discourses, thought, practices, and performances.

Butler calls attention to these naturalized gender differences in order to show that gender is not a natural and stable identity at all. The purpose of her analysis is not to heighten the value of women and reduce the value of men or to raise the consciousness and self-esteem of women; she aims to undermine the foundation of difference and free all individuals from compulsory and constant categorization that limits and constrains us. The point is not to emancipate women from men but to emancipate human beings from compulsory gender identity and *heteronormativity.*

Examples of Feminist Theories of Gender Construction

Macro/Micro Linkages and the Role of the State

By the beginning of the twenty-first century, feminist theorists offered a sophisticated and highly contextualized understanding of gender inequality, with close attention to its ongoing construction and reinforcement in other institutions and multiple processes of dominance and subordination. An excellent example of this type of theoretical analysis with a firm basis in empirical research is Shu-Ju Ada Cheng's (2006) study of Filipina domestics in Taiwan. She uses qualitative methods to show how inequality is established in multiple sites, not only in the household between Filipina domestics and their Taiwanese employers but also in state regulation of immigration and the growing transnational market in care work, as well as in state surveillance of the personal and sexual behaviors of immigrant workers. Furthermore, both individual employers and the Taiwanese media and state add a racialized construction of subordination, typifying Filipinas by racial images and stereotypes and applying restrictions to them that are not applied to immigrants of more favored nationalities and occupations. These multiple-channel and state-sanctioned processes of constructing inequality are, of course, not unique to Taiwan but are taking place across the globe in situations of immigration from poorer to wealthier regions. In . fact, Cheng extended her analysis of the transnational construction of intertwined inequalities to Canadian immigration law, Filipina domestic workers in Singapore and Korea, Polish domestic workers in the United States, and, most recently, mail-order brides from Russia.

Microlevel Theories of Gender Performance and Gender Rituals

A different, though ultimately interconnected, theoretical tack was taken by the theorists who analyzed gender construction at a microlevel with a focus on border work and performance. These theorists were often inspired by the work of Butler, Foucault, and Goffman. An excellent example of this type of analysis is Barrie Thorne's (1993) writing on border work and *gender rituals* among children. The situation of relative gender equality and low differentiation prevailing among young children is transformed, with a large amount of intervention by parents and school authorities, into a situation of sharp boundaries between girls and boys in elementary school and beyond. Thorne provides close observation of the establishment of these borders, their imposition on youngsters who are unwilling to fall into line, and the role of adults in initiating and reinforcing these rituals of differentiation.

This line of theorizing involves the extension of Goffman's work into the analysis of gender (a direction he had already initiated in his 1988 *Gender Advertisements,* with a focus on how visual advertisements perpetuate gender imagery and stereotypes). In this view, drawn from Goffman (and ultimately linked to new interpretations of Durkheim as a constructionist theorist of collective regulation), the category of gender is a social construction that is constantly produced and reinforced in interaction and both expressed and perpetuated in rituals and scripted performances. Contrary to 1950s structural functionalism with its uncritical acceptance of the belief that we are simply men and women, social constructionist theory looks at the ways we learn to play the roles of men and women.

An example of empirical research strongly influenced by these views of gender as performance is the work of Janice Boddy (1990), a Canadian anthropologist, who studied gender in a community of Arabic-speaking Sudanese. Very strict norms govern gender behavior in this community, and the practices of male circumcision and female infibulation (excision of the clitoris and the labia and partial sewing shut of the genital opening) heighten gender differentiation. Women are identified with closure (by the partial sewing up of their genitalia, by their location inside the home, and by cousin-marriage rules that keep them within the extended family), but in a spirit-possession ritual they perform other identities. Their performances as wise male elders, prostitutes, cannibal sorcerers, and other roles deeply prohibited to them in their everyday life both transgress and reinforce their prescribed performance as modest and "closed" women of the community. Like all carnivalesque performances, such as that of drag queens and outrageous Halloween masquerades, this transgressive performance of gender is ambiguous, both undercutting the naturalness of conventional roles and also reaffirming them. A similar analysis of gender as performance can be carried out in many activities that are more familiar to readers in industrialized nations, such as stripping and exotic dancing, dating rituals, sports, and interaction in bars.

The Construction of Masculinity

Although feminists first focused on women, who seemed more obviously pressed to perform gender according to conventional scripts of femininity and subordination, the perspective encompasses men. Men are expected to follow scripts of normative masculinity that call for displays of bravado, machismo, and violence. Indeed, in many societies, the enactment of masculine scripts seems even narrower and more inescapable than the performance of feminine gender.

Just as theorists of race-ethnicity, beginning with DuBois in "Souls of White Folk," turned to analysis of the formation of whiteness as the dominant or hegemonic position, feminists increasingly examined the formation of masculinity. The puzzle to be solved was not only how some people (women) were forced into subaltern positions but how others (men) became dominant. The near universality of this hierarchy presented a major challenge to theorists who opposed biological *essentialism.*

Was the clue to this condition to be found in historical processes linked to class, the mode of production, and state formation? This answer had been suggested by Engels in *The Origin of the Family, Private Property, and the State* (1884/1970). As a surplus was amassed and unequally distributed along class lines, men in the emerging economically dominant classes restricted the sexual freedom of women in order to insure their own sons' inheritance of property and power. State structures emerged to preserve property rights both directly, by policing class, and indirectly, by policing gender—that is, by controlling women and inheritance. In a similar vein, though focused more on production technologies, materialist anthropologists and sociologists linked escalating levels of gender inequality to the historical transformation from hunting and gathering and small-scale agriculture to plow-based, intensive agriculture. Property rights shifted decisively to patrilineal inheritance, households became patrilocal (women had to move to their husbands' homes), and power shifted in a patriarchal direction. These patterns began to reverse only with the advanced industrial modes of production that helped to equalize the productive powers of men and women. Once industrial and military technologies reduced the premium on heavy fieldwork and hand-to-hand combat, gender hierarchy diminished. In contrast to this historical and economically oriented analysis, David Gilmore (1991) argues that male dominance is a sort of reward offered to men in all societies to induce them to take risks; in terms of procreation, "sperm is cheap" while "eggs are dear," and so it is reproductively advantageous to have men assume the burden of taking physical risks, even though they are just as prudent and afraid of pain as women. Aggression and risk taking are therefore encouraged in men. Gilmore's analysis of male dominance has the advantage of explaining its omnipresence in human societies without recourse to any argument about hormones or biological propensities—and without blaming men for their dominance, a moral judgment that was an undercurrent in earlier feminist theories.

Other theorists of masculinity focus more on the contemporary construction of masculinity and on its consequences, such as the much higher crime rate among men, as a by-product of the rewards for violence, aggression, and risk taking (Messerschmidt 1993). Another key topic in this area involves variants of masculinity and the differences in its construction in different cultures and milieus (Duneier 1994; Connell 1995).

Sociology of Sexualities

The Critique of Heteronormativity

A critique of heteronormativity, not only of conventional gender roles, is inherent in these theories of gender as script, text, and performance. Generally the correct performance of gender is a highly heterosexual one. Transgression is associated with a same-sex sexual orientation, and, conversely, same-sex sexual behaviors are the leading form of gender transgression in most Western societies. The situation in comparative perspective is a bit more complicated, as historians and ethnographers are quick to point out; for instance, Gilbert Herdt (1987) found that homosexual relations are a prescribed part of Sambia coming of age in Papua New Guinea, the berdache is an accepted role among Plains Indians, bisexuality was common among ancient Greek men and among Japanese youth prior to the period of the shogunate, and so on. In many cultures outside the highly restrictive Abrahamic traditions (Judaism, Christianity, and Islam), same-sex sexual relations and/or ambiguous performance of gender roles is either prescribed for part of the life cycle or accepted for some individuals.

The understanding of heteronormativity strongly veered away from any simple conclusions about the naturalness of sexualities or the fixed character of sexual identities. For this reason, scholars have increasingly turned to the term "sexualities" rather than "sexual orientation." Foucault's contribution to this conversation is fundamental. He insisted that the bedrock of sexuality is the body and its pleasures, not a system of categories of natural and unnatural or moral and immoral—or any other classification, for that matter. In this view, the heterosexual/homosexual dichotomy is the result of discursive practices imposed on pleasure, a position closely related to Foucault's refusal to identify himself as "gay." This line of analysis was developed, with a strong historical grounding, in the work of John D'Emilio (1983), who argued that the concept of gayness and formation of a gay community are products of modern capitalism. A specific identity and a community with identifiable borders are products of a specific historical context, closely related to modern wage labor, the individual as the unit of the economic system, new forms of residence, and perhaps, in recent decades, democratic and libertarian ideologies of twentieth- and twenty-first-century capitalist societies.

Conclusion: Difference and Dominance

The analysis of differences—race-ethnicity and gender-sexuality—that were formerly treated as ascribed individual characteristics (and, in the case of race and gender, even assumed to be biologically based) has moved to a completely new paradigm of relational and performative construction of difference and dominance.

In the area of both race-ethnicity and gender-sexuality, contemporary theories create a major shift from individual-based models of ascription and attitudes that are associated with fixed demographic categories to a more fluid paradigm that emphasizes the way these categories are established and turned into practices of dominance. Attention focuses on both microprocesses and the role of the state in these constructions. These perspectives have roots in Durkheim's radical sociological position that individual actions are always to be understood as products of normative regulation and the force of collective gatherings, as well as in Weber's and DuBois's work on status and class. While chronologically following and apparently building on conflict theories of the 1970s, the new conflict constructionist paradigm reworks both the classical legacy and the earlier conflict theories. It reconfigures them by introducing the emphasis on discourse and frames and by focusing on the social creation of differences and identities.

Practically all theoretical writing and most qualitative research is now influenced by conflict constructionism; yet a substantial amount of empirical quantitative research still treats gender and race-ethnicity as relatively unproblematized characteristics of individuals—as conceptual categories that can be turned into operational variables in a relatively straightforward way.

Chapter Five

Culture in an Era of Globalization

José Soltero

How many of the products you use today and the clothes in your closet are manufactured in the country in which you live? How many of your family members and friends (including your Facebook friends) were born in the same country in which you were born—and is that the country in which you live today? Do you listen to music, watch movies, go to websites, or eat foods that originated in many different regions of the globe? Was there ever such a thing as a "100 percent American" way of life, or have all cultures influenced each other for as long as there have been human beings? In this chapter we explore ways of thinking about the rapid globalization that is taking place now—and we revisit and revise older theories of culture contact and cultural diffusion.

Overview

Theories of culture were deeply affected by globalization in recent decades. This area of theory shifted in response to changes in the real world in the latter twentieth century: the end of colonial empires, new streams of migration, the rise of global media networks, and the rapid economic development of some regions while others experienced growing poverty. Before summarizing the work of a sample of theorists, we identify themes and ideas that appear frequently in the new perspectives on culture in an era of globalization.

- Tracing *global cultural flows* is a recurrent theme, and cultural flows are often associated with *commodity circulation*. Products, ideas, information, and cultural artifacts as diverse as capital, coffee, and soap operas move throughout the global system, usually in the form of commodities, and have an impact on cultures.
- Attention focuses on inequalities in the global system, the formation of new types of class structures, and the cultural impact of these inequalities. Analysis focuses on the relationship between *cultural domination* and global socioeconomic inequalities that have persisted into the postcolonial era.
- Theorists explore and celebrate *hybridity* (a concept associated with Stuart Hall's work), rejecting the notion that cultures ever are or were pure; this perspective leads to the reexamination of earlier theories of modernization, westernization, and cultural imperialism and to interest in two-way cultural flows in which bearers of the apparently dominant culture are also influenced by indigenous and subaltern cultures.
- *Borders* are conceptualized as key locations of cultural flows and the creation of hybrid cultures.
- Theorists give attention to the position of the observer, critical analysis of ethnography and ethnographic writing, and development of a reflexive methodology.

Trajectory: From Evolutionary Theories of Modernization to Complex Cultural Flows

Evolutionary Models

Prior to the end of the twentieth century, many theories of culture had an evolutionary orientation. Certainly in the nineteenth century, an evolutionary sequence was posited in which smaller band-level societies were seen as "earlier forms" than complex state-level societies. State-level societies and their cultures—especially Western or westernized culture—were defined as the highest and most evolved forms. Classical sociological theorists developed more refined and critical versions of this model that were less celebratory of the modern, but nevertheless they still posited an irreversible traditional-to-modern sequence that first emerged in the West.

Marxist theorists interpreted this sequence in a more critical vein than other evolutionary theorists. They perceived it dialectically and did not share the view that the capitalist nation-state and bourgeois culture represented the pinnacle of societal evolution; instead, capitalist society was seen as an evolutionary way station on the road to socialism and communism. Nevertheless, their analysis of human history was strongly evolutionary.

Even as late as the immediate post–World War II period, modernization theorists believed that a general shift to "the modern" was likely and that successful nation-states would undergo some version of this process. "The modern" meant the formation of a viable nation-state that unified diverse communities and ethnic groups, creation of a market economy and participation in global markets, and (on a hopeful note) development of pluralist cultures and political institutions that met the criteria of Western democracy.

Modernization theory was closely entwined with structural functionalist theories. Much functionalist analysis focused on the shared values of a society as a major element of culture, with a little bit of attention given to subcultures of ethnic minorities, deviant groups, youth, and other social "sublevels." In transnational analysis, the dominant theme in the postwar period was as yet one of contrasting Western and modern cultures with traditional cultures and societies found in other regions (Lerner 1958). Evolutionary assumptions about a relatively uniform movement from traditional to modern, agrarian to industrial, and hierarchical to democratic structured the analysis, which was often entangled with Cold War aims of encouraging postcolonial and unaligned nations to move toward western European and North American models.

Postcolonial and Conflict Theories

As new nations emerged in the regions of the former colonial empires and global markets offered new opportunities for economic dynamism in some of these regions, new themes appeared in theories of culture by the later decades of the twentieth century. They were often associated with postcolonial theory and with conflict theories.

These themes included a more positive view of indigenous cultures, which were no longer seen as backward, passive receivers of modernization carried to them by Westerners. A second theme was an increasingly negative view of the West as a force that distorted the potential for independent development of other regions. Whereas traditional Marxists tended to see Western domination as a necessary stage in which a proletariat would be formed, a secular culture established, and the basis created for socialist movements, the new theorists of globalization were less convinced that this type of transformation was either possible or desirable. Postcolonial theorists focused critically on the way Western modernization and modernist discourses had framed regions, nations, peoples, and cultures outside the West, with the aim of deconstructing these frames. One pioneering work was Edward Said's *Orientalism* (1979), analyzing how Western writers had described Middle Eastern and Islamic societies as exotic and mysterious and contributed to stereotypes of these cultures.

A different critical line was developed in world-systems theory at more or less the same time (the 1970s to the end of the century). This type of theory emerged from traditional Marxist views of the global system, and like other Marxist theories, it emphasized the role of capitalism. But unlike traditional Marxists, world-systems theorists were not firmly convinced that the peripheral regions of the global system would develop industry, proletarian classes, and widely diffused modern, secular worldviews—the stuff that fuels class consciousness and socialist movements.

The overall trend toward conflict and interactionist theories also affected the discussion of cultures in the global system. One of the main efforts of conflict and interactionist theory was to recenter this conversation with far more celebratory attention to the "sub" cultures and a much more critical view of mainstream, dominant, or hegemonic culture. Theorists questioned the evolutionary premises that had influenced theories of culture. Many conflict theorists welcomed movements in the Third World to disengage from the Western capitalist sphere and strike out in directions that attempted to combine socialist models with indigenous cultural forms. The conversation opened further as it included not only reinterpretations of classic works of theory by Karl Marx and Friedrich Engels, Emile Durkheim, and Max Weber but also the twentieth-century legacy of Antonio Gramsci (Marxist theories of hegemony), Louis Althusser (structural Marxism and the analysis of ideological apparatuses), and Immanuel Wallerstein (world-systems theory).

New Directions: Globalization and Postmodernity

By the end of the twentieth century, the divergent paths of new nations and rapid globalization with complex new interconnections among economies and states led theorists to feel increasing doubt about all evolutionary models, whether they celebrated the modern (as did those of modernization theorists) or treated it dialectically as a necessary stage toward socialism and communism (as did the Marxists' models). Any evolutionary and unidirectional model, whether celebratory or critical, came under fire. Postmodernists attacked all evolutionary narratives of human history.

This convergent work, now infused with a critical spirit of questioning the supremacy of Western values, has given rise to a large body of theories about cultural flows in the global system. World-systems theory, postcolonial critical theory, and influences of postmodernism have generated new themes in the analysis of culture in the global system. More attention is being given to the active involvement of the subaltern (the indigenous, colonized, enslaved, exploited, displaced, and/or marginalized) in the creation of culture. They are not seen as simply passive, as either the fortunate receivers of westernization in postwar modernization theories nor alternatively as the unfortunate oppressed victims of it (in theories of imperialism). Rather they are seen as agents who resist, fight back, make choices about adoption and rejection of elements of culture, and are capable of complicity as well as resistance and opposition. Following directly from this premise, theorists insist that global cultural change is not simply a one-way flow of influence. More attention is given to the discursive and representational side of global inequalities, to framing and the creation of images of the global, and to the popular imaginary of resistance. The role of the state and the force of markets are by no means neglected, but a strong emphasis is placed on cultural contention and complexity.

The study of culture is also being transformed by the critical analysis of ethnography itself. These critical and reflexive approaches include attention to the position, feelings, beliefs, interactions, choices, and position of the ethnographic observer, whose external and objective perspective can no longer be taken for granted (Rosaldo 2004); deconstruction of the ethnographic text as a narrative (Crapanzano 2004, 596); feminist critiques (Smith 1990); and experimentation with carnal or embodied ethnographic projects in which the physical experience of the ethnographer as a participant becomes a tool for refining theoretical constructs (Wacquant 2004, 2009b). Some of these approaches to the study of culture are reflections of postmodernist and deconstructionist thought. Certainly, postmodernist theorists and standpoint feminist scholars cast doubt on the very notion that observers should or even can be separate from the actions they observe. For instance, the postmodernist position on interviewing—a basic act in the study of culture—is that the interview data are generated in a dialog between interviewer and respondent in a specific social context (Alvesson 2002). Analysis of life narratives, another basic element of many ethnographies, was recast as the analysis of formulas and frames of narrative construction and no longer seen as the recovery of facts about life course and culture; this thrust of deconstructive readings began with Norman Denzin's (1993) work on the stories told by participants in Alcoholics Anonymous. Adler and Adler (2008), writing about styles of ethnographic writing, identify "postmodern ethnography" as a currently popular form in which the focus is on the experience of the ethnographer and his or her construction of an ethnographic narrative. The postmodernist and deconstructionist positions in reading and writing ethnographies have led to the extensive use of quotation marks in all writing; our terms are "merely" words and frames in a discourse, not a direct apprehension of reality (or "reality").

The carnal sociologists influenced by Pierre Bourdieu's concept of habitus and embodied knowledge would absolutely reject the charge that they write primarily about their own experience as full participants in the embodied life of a cultural community; they argue that their own embodied experience is necessary for understanding embodied knowledge. Ultimately they use the experience to develop an external and objective understanding of culture (Wacquant 2009b; Widick 2003). Yet they too have contributed to a much more critical and reflexive view of what happens in ethnographic research.

Facilitators and Barriers

In the study of global culture, the enormous changes that have taken place in global society since the middle of the twentieth century probably constitute the main facilitator in changing paradigms of culture. The most important single change was the end of colonial empires and the formation of new sovereign nation-states. Ultimately decolonization means the creation of a formally level cultural playing field and therefore the end of the notion that the West represents a necessary and desirable endpoint of an evolutionary sequence. Once the colonial empires were a thing of the past, new players could enter the global economy, and a number of them became extremely successful, exemplified by Korea and the other, smaller "Asian tigers" in the last two to three decades of the twentieth century and, by the end of the century, the emergence of China and India as new economic powerhouses. Neoliberal opening of markets and fostering of transnational flows of capital and commodities aided this reshaping of economic power in the global system and, with it, a reassessment of culture.

A second major real-world facilitator was the transnational flow of migrants, first accelerated by US immigration-law reform in the 1960s and then speeded up by push factors of Third World poverty amid growing aspirations to greater well-being and living standards comparable to those of "First World" capitalist societies. Few societies could completely shut out flows of migrants, whether they were Mexicans and Central Americans in the United States; North and West Africans in France, Italy, and Spain; Mozambicans in South Africa; or Poles in Ireland. With the flows of migrants came not only xenophobia and new forms of racism but also exposure to a much larger range of cultures and the formation of cultural communities in diaspora.

In the face of these momentous changes in the global cultural and economic system, there were few barriers to change in theoretical perspectives. Yet not all previous theories were so easily jettisoned, and several approaches from both the postwar period and the conflict models persisted with modifications and updated research questions. Marxism and related theories of global inequalities were able to persist because economic inequality was not only persistent but even increasing in some respects; but Marxist theories also addressed new questions, as we will see in a number of examples.

The postwar modernization theories faded away in some respects but resurfaced as theories of democratic transition applied to the Soviet bloc, the southern cone of South America, South Africa, and, most recently, the Arab world. The subtext in the analysis of democratic transitions remains that all of these regions not only can, but should, adopt Western political institutions of representative democracy and multiparty competition, whatever their cultures may be. It remains to be seen if this will happen. Thus the unevenness of the paradigm shift was less a matter of barriers to new theories of culture in the global system and more a matter of older theories persisting as they were adapted to new conditions and challenges.

Examples of New Theories and Old Theories with New Twists

The remainder of the chapter reviews the ideas of a few leading contemporary theorists of culture and identifies key concepts and frameworks. This discussion is organized loosely into three distinct conversations: The first involves a resurfacing and refreshing of traditional Marxist theories and their application to trends in the global system. The second (while not completely disconnected from Marxist concepts) focuses primarily on the cultural flows themselves. The third conversation is about the nature of ethnography, the act of writing about culture, and the standpoint or point of view of the observer of culture.

Conversation One: Marxism Refreshed

Our first conversation about global culture is among scholars who acknowledge a large debt to Marxist theory while adapting it to new developments in the global capitalist system, such as neoliberalism and *postmodern culture,* focusing it on changes in cultures and using it to reinterpret earlier historical periods and processes.

David Harvey: Neoliberalism and Culture

The global economic context of cultural change is addressed by David Harvey, a geographer deeply influenced by Marxism. He charts the role of neoliberal capitalism in providing a base for cultural change (1990, 2007; see also G. Williams 2002). Neoliberalism has had at least two major cultural effects. First, it is linked to transnational flows of capital, and these carry with them globalized cultural products and state policies. Second, it is associated with flexible capitalism, a new form of capitalist production accompanied by cultural fragmentation and the undermining of class and national identities, geographic dispersal of industry from high-wage to low-wage countries, low wages and insecurity of employment for increasing numbers of workers, cutbacks in public services, and privatization of collective needs. Postmodernism as a cultural form is linked to flexible capitalism. It has accentuated the "volatility and ephemerality of fashions, products, production techniques, labor processes, ideas and ideologies, values and established practices" (Harvey 1990, 280). In this way postmodernism encourages the disposability and transitory nature of all relationships. (We return to the theme of the ephemeral in postmodern culture in our discussion of theories of the self in Chapter 7.)

Eric Wolf: Colonialism, Global Trade Networks, and the Creation of the Peasant

Eric Wolf confronted the tendency of anthropologists to examine "small living cultures" as if villages and remote ethnic communities were self-contained. Inspired by Karl Marx and, more recently, Immanuel Wallerstein (1974) and Andre Gunder Frank (1971), Wolf shifted the study of culture to the consideration of the impact of general processes, such as world capitalism, on the microlevel of local cultures. The cultures of the periphery, semiperiphery, developing regions, and the Third World have developed interactively with the cultures of the core capitalist regions for a very long time. Trade networks in which gold, furs, sugar, ivory, and slaves were exported to Europe and regions of European settlement predated actual colonization, and these interactions between Europeans and "others" had utterly transformed many societies, from the Iroquois to the West African kingdoms, by the nineteenth century. The "others" were not passive victims, but active, though unequal, participants in these transformations. Later, the introduction of the capitalist mode of production into colonial areas and those subject to economic imperialism changed rural populations into *peasants,* migrant laborers, serfs, and bandits. This penetration of capitalism created the preconditions for the great revolutions of the twentieth century in Mexico, Russia, China, Vietnam, Algeria, and Cuba, especially as institutions such as the state, the legal system, the hacienda/plantation system, and the church reinforced the emerging class structure of capitalism in the periphery (Wolf 1990/1999). Wolf challenged anthropologists to shift their focus from local communities and systems of meaning to understanding how people cope with material and organizational problems that have been produced by the global capitalist system over the course of centuries.

Michael Taussig, Culture, and Commodity Fetishism

Like Wolf, Michael Taussig (1985) seeks to understand the impact of capitalism on the societies and cultures on which it was imposed. Capitalism has impinged on the cultures of societies that have been penetrated by the profit motive, a process permeated by conflict. Cultural struggle between the new culture of capitalism and the former precapitalist representations has been an integral part of class struggle. The core of the cultural struggles is the imposition of commodity fetishism, the attribution of a natural and overriding power to production based on the purchase of human labor by entrepreneurs and capitalists. Human relations are established on the basis of relations of commodity exchange and are not based on human needs or use value. Indigenous and African American populations in Latin America represented their own resistance to this externally imposed culture in terms of the magical power of the devil or beliefs drawn from *syncretic* and populist forms of Catholicism. Taussig thus seeks to understand how class conflict and ethnic resistance are represented in societies in which capitalism appears as neither natural nor benign in contrast to the positive image that came to be hegemonic in economically developed Western societies. The apparently magical power of capitalism—its commodity fetishism, in which the relations of production are experienced as a force that is external to human relationships and human needs and money takes on a life of its own—is countered in oppressed and exploited communities by the development of magical faith in the devil as an ally against the capitalists, as exemplified in the beliefs of the Afro-Colombian peasantry and the Bolivian miners' cult of the devil, whom they call "Tio," meaning uncle.

Fredric Jameson, Postmodernism, and Late Capitalism

(Having discussed Jameson as one of the six innovators in Part I, and as we will be returning to his work in the discussion of the media, we only provide a few illustrative themes in his writing on postmodern culture here.)

Fredric Jameson is struggling to understand the relationship between culture and capitalism in its late or advanced phase. Late capitalism is characterized by a new international division of labor, free flows of capital, new forms of media and transportation systems, computers and automation, shifts in production to formerly nonindustrialized regions and countries, and concomitant shifts in class structure. These changes in the base produce marked changes in the cultural superstructure, which include commodification of all art forms, blurring of the lines between high culture and popular culture, and the dominance of the media, themselves corporate enterprises. This new form of culture is taking hold on a global scale, and unlike the cultures associated with capitalism in the past, it is less clearly Eurocentric and elite, though it still can be interpreted as "the internal and superstructural expression of a whole new wave of American military and economic domination throughout the world" (Jameson 1991/2005, 5). Jameson gives relatively little attention to classes as coherent purposive social actors. The *cultural dominant* that he seeks to understand is a pattern of representation that appears across different media and art forms as an indirect reflection of the underlying mode of production and social conditions; it is not the same concept as the dominant culture imposed by a class-conscious dominant class. Just as Taussig found that the devil became the image that Bolivian miners used to represent their opposition to exploitive mine owners, so Jameson sees a refraction of capitalist relations of production into works of the imagination, especially visual arts and architecture, such as the mirrored surfaces of the Bonaventure Hotel in Los Angeles. Postmodern forms of culture are (ultimately, like all culture) not a simple, direct reflection of a mode of production and its class structure into the realm of representations. Postmodern culture is characterized by surface intensities rather than a claim to express deep feelings, a fragmented and schizoid sense of self and other, and an amnesiac flattening of history into a celebration of retro style. Jameson's analysis has been extremely influential; it is an effort (from the Marxist side of the aisle) to grasp, rather than dismiss, the meaning of the postmodern.

Conversation Two: Culture Is Not a One-Way Flow

In this conversation we can group together innovative scholars of culture in the global system who emphasize new ways of thinking about culture: *creolization, transculturation,* and *hybridity*; "two-way flows of culture" in which a powerful stream of ideas and practices runs from the colonized, enslaved, and subaltern to the dominant; and the emergence of communities in diaspora. Stuart Hall provides an important voice in this conversation, and we suggest to the reader a review of our description of his work in Chapter 3, in the section titled "Who Were the Innovators? Goffman, Foucault, Bourdieu, Hall, Butler, and Jameson."

Ulf Hannerz and Markets of Culture

Ulf Hannerz (1992) conceives of culture as a system of meanings developed by social groups; he suggests four frameworks to study this flow of meaning in complex societies: form of life, market, state, and social movement. The first of these tends to be small-scale, domestic, and habitual or enduring. In the market framework, cultural commodities are moved, carrying with them symbolic meanings. The state is an organizational form with publicly acknowledged power in a territory, including power over meanings and cultural flows. Social movements seek to transform meanings.

These frameworks are active within a global structure. Globalization has affected the distribution of cultures and subcultures around the world by a structure of asymmetrical center/periphery/semiperiphery relationships. The trajectory of this structure is not necessarily a homogenization of culture. The market framework favors *cultural dumping* from the center to the periphery and the semiperiphery, since the "cost of taking old Western movies, soap serials, or skin flicks (choosing only examples from the screen) to their final resting place in the Third World is so low that whatever income they generate is almost pure profit.... The periphery here is treated to leftovers" (Hannerz 1992, 235). The state framework, on the other hand, mediates between the transnational and the nation and takes an interest in cultural welfare, opposes cultural dumping, attempts to constrain transnational cultural flows, and resists cultural imperialism.

As cultural flows move through the global system, the end product is the creolization of cultures. "Creole cultures, like creole languages, are intrinsically of mixed origin, the confluence of two or more widely separated historical currents which interact in what is basically a center/periphery relationship" (Hannerz 1992, 254). But the current does not have a one-way flow; peripheral cultures can flow to the center, and bearers of dominant cultures can be profoundly influenced by the cultures of the subaltern. Here we can see a strong convergence with Hall's concept of hybridity, with Latin American writers' notion of *mestizaje* and transculturation, and ultimately with theoretical ancestry in W. E. B. DuBois's bold view that all Americans are culturally African American as well as European American. There is agency in the process of creole transnationalization of cultures, often associated with networks of frequent travelers, including intellectuals, city dwellers, and the wealthy and powerful, since cultural flows are entangled with class as well as with center/periphery power relations.

Nestor Garcia Canclini, Cultural Globalization, and the Developing World

The analysis of global flows of culture has become a hospitable terrain for intellectuals whose heritage lies in Latin America and postcolonial societies. Nestor Garcia Canclini, a Latin American anthropologist, focuses on the meaning of cultural modernity and the process of cultural modernization in Latin America. He takes the position that cultures of the Third World are more resilient and autonomous than had been assumed.

While acknowledging the economic dependency of much of Latin America and the periphery in general, Garcia Canclini argues that culture in these regions proved to be vital and autonomous. Well into the middle of the twentieth century, modernization was slowed by the lack of democracy and literacy, low enrollment in universities, and an oppressive Eurocentric elite hegemony. Despite this strategy of elitist exclusion and the effort to marginalize popular and indigenous cultures, a process of *mestizaje,* syncretism, or cultural hybridization has taken place in Latin America and is ever more recognized and celebrated. Garcia Canclini uses the example of the embrace by the bourgeoisie and intellectuals in Santiago, Lima, Bogota, and Mexico City of both multilingual libraries and indigenous crafts, modern telecommunications and colonial furniture, financial speculation and centuries-old familial and religious rituals. He suggests that now to be modern includes knowing how to incorporate the avant-garde in art and literature and technological innovations into traditional modes of thought and action. Furthermore, in contrast to those scholars who posit the idea of the hegemonic core culture that slowly but surely destroys peripheral or semiperipheral cultures, Garcia Canclini advances the thesis that Latin American cultures, like all other cultures of the developing world, are more resilient and capable of elaborating hybrid cultural responses to the cultures of the centers.

Garcia Canclini (2003) examines the changing role of the state in forming cultural policy, paying special attention to Mexico. He argues that the role of the state in shaping Mexican cultural policy changed throughout the twentieth century. First, after the 1910–1923 Mexican Revolution, the state promoted a cultural policy of integration between the traditional and the modern, the cultured and the popular; then, during the 1940s, starting with the period of President Miguel Aleman, the popular utopia gave way to modernization and industrial planning. During this period, the state applied a different cultural policy for different social classes: the National Institute for Fine Arts was created to give impulse to high culture; on the other hand, the state created the National Museum of Popular Crafts and Industries and the National Indigenous Institute to support crafts and indigenous ethnic groups in Mexico. From the 1940s to mid-1970s in Mexico, both the state and private entrepreneurs played an important role as sponsors of artistic activities; in fact, artistic activities were less dependent on the market than in other countries, such as Colombia, Venezuela, Brazil, and Argentina. Garcia Canclini analyzes the way policies of the Mexican state attempted to integrate the traditional and the modern, the cultured and the popular, and the indigenous and the Western. These *cultural policies of the state* were developed from the 1920s to the 1980s, creating museums, supporting artists, and encouraging indigenous crafts. Generally the Mexican state had a more energetic view of its role and was less inclined to accept a market-driven model of culture than other Latin American states. However, during the transformation of Mexico after the economic crisis of 1982, all important sectors of the economy were transferred to the market, based on the role of private corporations as promoters of culture at all levels. For example, Televisa, the Mexican mass-media giant, came to have a dominant role in television, radio, documentary production, and even museums of high and popular art.

Although cultural hybridization occurs everywhere—in the cities, the rural areas, the museums, the public avenues, and the monuments—one geographic area is particularly prone to show this phenomenon: the US-Mexico border cities and towns. At the border populations are bilingual and bicultural and live in a condition of ambiguity and historical oscillation in national sovereignty and border policies. Therefore the inhabitants of border areas, such as the US-Mexican border, have greater knowledge of and an expanded capacity for communication, even though they have lost some of their autonomy and their sense of an exclusive connection to the territory.

Paul Gilroy and the Black Atlantic

These reflections on hybridity and border cultures not only parallel Hall's analysis but also underline that cultural globalization and fluid cultural borders are not a new phenomenon. The external experiences of hybridity and fluid cultural borders of our own times provoke a reinterpretation of the past. Like time travelers, contemporary intellectuals revisit a past that had been viewed as a history of imposition of Euro-centric culture and suddenly see that this imposition was never a perfected, total, one-way, and unresisted project. On the contrary, not only had cultures of indigenous, enslaved, or displaced peoples been highly resilient and able to incorporate European elements judiciously and ingeniously, but they had also profoundly transformed the supposedly dominant culture. An excellent example of this recentering of cultural histories is provided by Paul Gilroy's (1993) Atlantic-centered analysis of the role of Africans and the African diaspora not only in the making of New World cultures but in the making of European political cultures—and not only in the twentieth century but as far back as insurgent activism in eighteenth-century England.

Arjun Appadurai and the "Scapes"

Arjun Appadurai (1993) is contributing similar analyses of global cultural flows and their role in collective action. He identifies five such flows, which he refers to with the suffix *-scapes*: ethnoscapes are flows of people; technoscapes, of technology; finanscapes, of capital; ideoscapes, of ideologies such as democracy and national-ism; and mediascapes, of mediated images and representations. These flows are not coordinated with one another but are in *disjuncture*; historically their pace of diffu-sion has been uneven, and states have often resisted one or the other of them. In the neoliberal era, for example, flows of capital move easily, while states channel and restrict migration. Like most of the theorists in this area, Appadurai insists that these flows are not all from a single Western or Americanized center to the periphery; nor are they imposed in a one-way process. There are counterflows from periphery to center, as well as from regional and local centers, that may be as troubling to locals as the distant global powers; for the people of Irian Jaya (western New Guinea), Indonesian rule is more of an issue than US imperialism.

The scapes produce *deterritorialization,* a feature of the new global system that also appears in the analysis of world cities and spaces. Connections among people in the same family or ethnic community become transnational, and just as there are global webs of production in the neoliberal economy, so there are global networks of political and cultural affiliation. Some of them support violent activism in the home country. Thus Appadurai, like many theorists in this area, acknowledges the pioneer-ing formulations of Immanuel Wallerstein and the world-systems school but explores how the center/semiperiphery/periphery model needs to be revised and made more fluid in the analysis of culture. In keeping with Appadurai's thinking, in recent years the dynamism of China and other formerly underdeveloped nations is challenging earlier models of one-way flows of influence from the Western capitalist nations.

Synthetic Traditions: Eric Hobsbawm and Terence Ranger

Finally, not only are all cultures complicated hybrids, but they are often synthetic. In a thoroughly deconstructionist move, veteran Marxist historian Eric Hobsbawm and Terence Ranger, in *The Invention of Tradition* (1992), showed how many "venerable traditions" are really recent inventions created by elites as an ideological gambit to produce "instant history" in situations where the past carries an aura of authenticity and moral authority. New institutions can be cloaked in trappings that appear archaic in order to gain popular legitimacy. The most amusing examples in the volume of collected articles are the sartorial inventions of the British empire, such as kilts and tartans, as phony in their use in imperial uniforms as are the "native potentates" whom British colonialists dreamed up to place on thrones as the figureheads of indirect rule.

Conversation Three: Writing about Ethnography

Renato Rosaldo, Vincent Crapanzano, and Pierre Bourdieu are examples of scholars who engaged in a reinterpretation of culture through the critique of ethnographic research and the call for a critical-reflexive orientation to research.

Changes in the understanding of culture focused on the act of writing about culture, on ethnography itself. Changes included a sharp critique of objectivism, of the widely held perspective that the ethnographic researcher can stand outside the action and view it in an accurate, detached, systematic, and unbiased way. Renato Rosaldo (2004) explains how the death of his wife (and research partner) in an accident during research in the Philippines in 1981 transformed his understanding of the practices of the Ilongot, who express their rage and sorrow at the death of a loved one by cutting off and tossing away the head of a stranger. He was no longer able to dissect these practices in a detached manner using exchange theory as his mainstream perspective. His personal loss, grief, and rage over the senselessness of her death led him to a radical critique of ethnography and rejection of the notion that it could be a pursuit of detached, scientific, and absolute truth. Here we can see a parallel with Dorothy Smith's feminist critique of social science as a detached, objective, and external position (1990).

Vincent Crapanzano (2004) also criticizes anthropologists (specifically Clifford Geertz) for creating texts about cultures that purport to establish the anthropologist's superior ability to interpret them. These texts establish a hierarchical relationship between the anthropologist, who discovers, understands, and interprets the culture of the native, and the native whose culture is interpreted by the anthropologist. Here we can see a thread of postmodernist thought, the emphasis on the textuality of our thought, the way understanding of the world is necessarily constructed as a text, as a narrative, and in this case as one that a relatively powerful individual (the anthropologist) imposes as the privileged representation of reality.

Pierre Bourdieu continues to affirm the possibility of an external and objective analysis of culture; yet, at the same time, he calls for a break from any simple version of the dichotomy of subjectivity and objectivity. The researcher, as much as the native, is caught up in misrecognitions of social relationships and the tendency to view these existing relationships as natural. Rigorous attention to theory, as well as self-scrutiny of one's own preconceptions and biases, is necessary to avoid falling into the twin traps of accepting the native's misrecognitions and assimilating observations into simplistic scientific schema that are based on uncritical and antitheoretical empirical observation and a passion for positivist measurement. Bourdieu uses the term "critical-reflexive orientation" to refer to this constant effort to examine the unconscious, embedded, and embodied misrecognitions that both the native and the researcher bring to the understanding of culture. Lived experience is not enough; it is not an accurate and complete source on which to base our representations of the reality of the social world. We need to understand regularities—structures, laws, systems of relationships—that are independent of the individual's consciousness and will. This understanding requires theory and a rejection of commonsense ideas about the world because they inevitably lead to accepting the natural and taken-for-granted character of what we see.

Conclusion: Linked Conversations

The postcolonial, neoliberal era has ushered in a completely new way of looking at culture on a global scale. Of the many exciting discussions taking place, we have focused on three overlapping ones: an effort to refresh Marxist theories of culture by removing evolutionary assumptions without dumping historical perspectives and by recognizing the multiple circuits through which culture and commodities flow; a conversation about cultural flows, their links to commodity flows, and their connections to states and power differences in the global system, as well as to the formation of hybrid cultural forms; and a conversation about ethnographic writing itself that examines the construction of ethnographic texts and seeks to develop a more sophisticated, critical, reflexive, and integrated understanding of objectivity and subjectivity in the analysis of culture. Although we have discussed these theorists as belonging to three conversations, their work is really overlapping and not hermetically sealed from each other's contributions.

Contemporary studies of culture in the era of globalization owe a major debt to Marxist theories, especially as these are filtered through Marxist theories of culture (based on the work of Antonio Gramsci, Walter Benjamin, and Stuart Hall) as well as postcolonial critical theory. They also draw on dependency theory and world-systems theory, both formulated in the era of conflict paradigms. Thus concepts such as hegemony, center and periphery, commodification of culture, and domination and marginalization all persist, and the reader can certainly still discern the influence of conflict theories of culture. But the more recent work explores more complex flows and counterflows of culture than previous work. Any simple models of modern versus traditional culture, bourgeois and Eurocentric dominance, and cultural imperialism are being revised in light of the concepts of hybridity, creolization, multiple disjunctive flows, power and resistance, and postmodern cultural fragmentation—and of course, the rise of dynamic new economic actors in South and East Asia. So powerful is the impact of current cultural flows that the past is itself being reread to reveal a centuries-old story of hybridity and two-way cultural influences.

In the study of culture in the global system, theories are necessarily influenced by powerful external forces—the dynamic of global economic and political relationships. The paradigm must shift as these forces themselves change. As the global order shifted from colonial to postcolonial in the second half of the twentieth century, and as Asian nations—especially China—became leaders in global markets, the theories themselves had to reflect new realities. Many of these new theories can be interpreted as affiliated with conflict constructionism, sharing its elements of emphasis on representation, contention, open-endedness, hybridity, and the role of the state as a field of frames and discourses.

Chapter Six

Media in the Information Age

SURFACE INTENSITIES AND TOTAL SYMBOLIC ENVIRONMENTS

How much of your day is spent consuming and using media—watching TV and movies, downloading and listening to music, surfing the web, looking at your favorite sites, meeting people in social media, and communicating with friends? How does your media use compare to your parents' and grandparents' media habits? Do you think that the intensity and extent of media consumption have changed not only our use of time but our fundamental ways of thinking and feeling—and if so, how?

The analysis of the media is an area of sociology in which scholars are strongly attuned to contemporary developments. They must address the media explosion that began with radio and recorded music in the early twentieth century, gathered intensity with television, and reached its present level with computers and the Internet. The new situation calls for new paradigms. The paradigms must be new because the empirical phenomena themselves are new. The subfield is also influenced by its academic competitors, disciplines such as media studies and communications.

Overview

New theories of the media impact reflect profound changes in the media themselves.

- This area is highly influenced by external developments—the emergence, ownership patterns, and globalization of television, computers, and telecommunications.

90

- Many of the theories focus on the formation of an alternative irreality—a total symbolic environment, a *society of the spectacle,* a world of make-believe, of images and representations.
- Theorists differ in their view of the political implications of this total symbolic environment. Some see it entirely as a *colonization* of thought processes while others believe that new media—especially the Internet and digital film—contain possibilities for restoring creativity and autonomy.
- A definite split between Marxist and postmodernist views is discernible; the former are more critical, the latter more accepting and even celebratory of the media explosion. These theoretical differences somewhat crosscut the debate between those who emphasize the totalitarian force of the new media and those who see potential for autonomy and creativity.
- Theories of media impact link sociology to communications and cultural studies; they spill across traditional boundaries of disciplines.

Trajectory

Before Television

Critical sociological analysis of the media began with Karl Marx and Friedrich Engels's view that the *ruling ideas of an age are the ideas of the ruling class* and that those who own the means of material production also command the *means of mental production.* In the first half of the twentieth century, new media—film, radio, the recording industry, mass-circulation magazines, and pulp fiction—drew the attention of Walter Benjamin and the Frankfurt School theorists, who began a debate that continues to the present (Adorno 2001). Are new media and information systems primarily a mechanism for strengthening the control of elites over the perception of the masses, or could they become a source of creativity, global awareness, and challenges to domination? Although most of the Frankfurt theorists believed the media contributed to the colonization of minds by the ideas of the dominant class, Walter Benjamin (1968) thought that the mechanical reproduction of works of art—the assembling of films and musical recordings and the reproduction of works of visual art—stripped art of its *aura,* the special, authentic, and one-of-a-kind quality often associated with the mystique of the individual genius. Mechanical reproduction revealed art to be a product, an object assembled by a team of workers under capitalist conditions of labor in order to realize exchange value—for profit. This demystification of art had a revolutionary potential.

After World War II, the critical analysis of media production was continued by Hortense Powdermaker (1950) in her anthropological study of Hollywood as a dream factory, but many sociologists embarked on more neutrally framed research on the *two-step communication process* by tracing media's indirect impact on individuals through the influence of opinion leaders in unions and professional associations (E. Katz 1957; Katz and Lazarsfeldt 2005).

Expanding Media

After the 1960s and the mass diffusion of television across the globe, theorists began to doubt that the media impact could be contained in existing social structures, personal networks, and institutions. The transition from the two-step communication model of the media to theories of an encompassing media environment with a direct impact began with three major theorists in the 1960s: Marshall McLuhan (1964) in Canada, Guy Debord (1967/1995) in France, and Erving Goffman (1974), a Canadian working in the United States. These three theorists began to formulate parallel views of the media as purveyors of fantasy worlds—the society of the spectacle, as Debord termed it.

McLuhan emphasized the global impact of the media, coining the vivid term *global village,* which captures the ability of TV to create a shared experience, linking everyone on the planet in transnational networks of gossip and information. As a Canadian, he was keenly aware of both the power of the United States as the world's leading media producer and the power of the media to alter the established patterns of national and regional identities. McLuhan believed that ways of thinking were closely linked to the technology of the media, that television would create a different mentality from the mentalities associated with oral communication and print. The new structure of television-mediated thought was associated with the *icon,* the powerful, condensed visual image, and the *mosaic,* pieced-together fragments of images and messages.

Guy Debord took a more critical position on the media. Influenced by Marxism and surrealism, he began to examine how capitalism separates artists from the rest of society as their work becomes specialized and commodified, at the same time that the creativity of everyone else is stifled. Debord reiterated Georg Simmel's insight that as culture expands, the individual human being is diminished. He asserted that "man is more and more, and ever more powerfully, the producer of every detail of his world. The closer his life comes to being his own creation, the more drastically he is cut off from that life" (1967/1995, 24).

In 1967, Debord published *The Society of the Spectacle.* Spectacle is the complete alienation of experience. In modern capitalist society, representations of reality are created and manipulated by dominant classes. The main purpose of these representations is the formation of a pseudoworld that justifies the present system and maintains dominance and hierarchy. The spectacle includes media and political propaganda, spectator sports, and escapist fantasy; beyond the media, spectacle in capitalist society is the entire set of social relationships projected into and mediated by images. Although spectacle was also present in traditional societies with religious ideologies and in the Soviet Union, with its "real socialism," spectacle is perfected in its fully commodified form in capitalist society. "The spectacle is a permanent opium war waged to make it impossible to distinguish goods from commodities" (Debord 1967/1995, 30).

The third theorist to suggest new ways of looking at the media was Erving Goffman, who introduced the concepts of *frames* and hyperritualization. Goffman adapted his early work in the presentation of self to the growing sphere of the media by tailoring the concepts of frames and frame analysis to chart the impact of media—especially advertising—on our thought processes. The frame—the particular wording of statements or composition of visual images—forces us to think in a particular way and keeps us from thinking in other ways. The frame is a box in which we must think our thoughts.

Goffman was especially interested in how gender is conveyed and reproduced by framing practices in advertisements. In *Gender Advertisements,* he collected and displayed hundreds of ads that define, frame, and constrain the meaning of gender. Goffman argues that advertisements are displays of gender rituals that guide and shape our perceptions and interpretations of reality. They are conventionalized representations of gender—concentrated mirrors of gender displays in everyday social life. However, they are not direct representations since they are abstractions of what they depict. Thus, they emphasize some aspects of gender and deemphasize others. As a result, our understandings of gender (or any other aspect of identity that advertisements depict to us) are partial and distorted. Advertisements present social life as "commercial realism," in a highly stylized form, condensing *stereotypes* into ideals and presenting these stylized images as if they were copies of real people and real behaviors (Goffman 1988, 15). Through commercial realism social life is cast into projections of an ideal that displays and may ultimately create a hyperritualization of behavior and interaction. Goffman asks,

> What is the difference between the scenes depicted in advertisements and scenes from actual life? One answer might be "hyperritualization." The standardization, exaggeration, and simplification that characterize rituals in general are in commercial posing found to an exaggerated degree, often rekeyed as babyishness, mockery, and other forms of unseriousness…. By and large, advertisers do not create the ritualized expressions they employ; they seem to draw upon the same corpus of displays, the same ritual idiom…. Advertisers conventionalize our conventions, stylize what is already a stylization, make frivolous use of what is already something considerably cut off from contextual controls. Their hype is hyperritualization. (1988, 84)

For Goffman, advertising edits out the normality and unevenness of everyday life and displays only the polished ideal without defects or flaws. As these displays are mass mediated and become the basis of social interaction, they mediate the ritualized interaction orders of society. What appears real is not real at all, and we may never know the difference since it is face work that holds society together.

Goffman's orientation was less sweeping and critical than Debord's, but in his usual deadpan and meticulous way, he was charting the impact of the media—especially advertising—on our thought processes. By the end of the century, after a period when conflict approaches focused on ownership and control of the media, sociologists had begun to place frames and framing practices at the center of their analysis.

The Era of Engaged Media Criticism: Conflict Theory Approaches

From the later 1960s to the 1980s, conflict theorists became increasingly interested in media impact. The opening sally in North American sociology was C. Wright Mills's (1954/1963) charge that the media were becoming distant from ordinary people in sharp contrast to the era of locally owned newspapers; national newspaper chains and the emerging television industry created an enormous gap between *receivers and senders of opinion* or information, making it virtually impossible for citizens to "talk back" to the media.

Themes of ownership and control of the media, the media as purveyors of propaganda for the dominant classes, and the ideological effects of the routines of news and entertainment production appeared in powerful, theoretically driven empirical studies of this period. Some of these theorists explicitly used a Marxist framework. Others developed a critical view of the media but utilized a broader conflict approach with non-Marxian concepts.

Stuart Hall's establishment of cultural studies in England was the most comprehensive of these critical frameworks. Because of its long-term theoretical impact on the field, its close association with the formulation of a new paradigm, and the vital influence it has on current work, we examine it in more detail below. Among dissections of ownership and control of the media and the impact on public opinion we can list the following: Michael Parenti's (1986) Marxist analysis of the media as part of the capitalist system designed to reflect ruling-class interests; Ben Bagdikian's (1983) discussion of the *media monopoly*; Mark Hertsgaard's (1989) critical view of the supine position of the media vis-à-vis the Reagan administration; and Edward Herman and Noam Chomsky's (1988) influential effort as public intellectuals to focus on the manufacture of consent to US foreign policy.

Other critical media studies, such as those of Warren Breed (1954), Herbert Gans (2005), and Gaye Tuchman (1980), focused on the routines and interactions through which journalists constructed the news—that is, the micro- and mesoprocesses of construction rather than the macrocontext of capitalist ownership. The norms and professional self-identities of reporters and editors appeared to favor autonomy; yet these norms were highly constrained by the economic and ideological context. Most journalists learned to engage in *self-censorship* and conform to the larger forces of news production in ways that they could justify within their professional codes of competence and ethics. Michael Schudson (1981) added a historical perspective to the analysis of news reporting by tracing changes from journals of opinion in the early years of the United States to the emergence of the penny press, whose blander news coverage bolstered mass circulation, then the period of the sensationalist press in the later years of the nineteenth century, and eventually the emergence of the code of *objectivity* as the hallmark of modern reporting. Objectivity and balanced coverage had become a formula that protected journalists against the more blatant forms of government propaganda and corporate press releases, yet functioned subtly in favor of the status quo.

A similar analysis of the subtle injection of ideology into entertainment was offered by Todd Gitlin in his *Inside Prime Time* (1983). Like Schudson, Gitlin pointed to the deep *encoding* of ideological hegemony in the messages conveyed by the whole range of popular TV shows, from cop shows to sports, sitcoms, and soaps. The emphasis throughout is on the value of competition, law and order, and violent or private solutions to public issues. While the perspective of the shows is increasingly liberal on social issues, with occasional nods to rebellious dreams, it never oversteps the bounds of capitalism. Gitlin's (2003) earlier study of the role of television in coverage of the war in Vietnam and the antiwar movement had hinted at the media as a possible terrain of struggle, but the *prime-time* content analysis was more pessimistic and located firmly in the theoretical analysis of hegemony inspired by the work of Antonio Gramsci.

Advertising also drew the attention of theorists with a conflict perspective and reiterated the theme that the media create an alternative irreality, a make-believe world of increasing power. Schudson (1986) called ads "images of *capitalist realism*," comparing them to Soviet socialist realist propaganda, which depicted only positive images of socialism, such as happy collective farmworkers with new tractors and the realization of large industrial projects. Schudson argues that ads are the images of capitalist realism, its idealized representation of itself as a world of strong, beautiful people happily fulfilling their lives and solving their problems through the purchase of intensely wonderful objects—the commodities (products) of consumer capitalism. The viewer is induced by constant repetition to believe in the existence, beauty, and attainability of this magical, make-believe world of objects. It functions ideologically to valorize a political and economic system and to induce individuals to perform their roles in the system. Stuart and Elizabeth Ewen (1982) offer a similar probe of the ways in which popular aspirations, desires, and identities are shaped by and sucked into the dream world of consumer goods and name brands, especially among women and immigrants.

In short, throughout the conflict phase of media analysis, which extended from the late 1960s into the 1980s, both theorists and empirical researchers took a critical stand toward the media whether or not they labeled themselves as Marxists.

Criticism and Celebration: Contemporary Theories and the Media World of Make-Believe

As computers, information technologies, telecommunications, and global networks expanded rapidly in recent decades, sociological theories of the media continued to focus on the nature of the new encompassing symbolic reality and returned to the questions raised in the work of McLuhan, Debord, and Goffman. Although there is a considerable amount of agreement among theorists in identifying this total symbolic world as a stunning new force in human cultures, differences between Marxist and postmodernist perspectives can be discerned in their answers to questions about matters such as the power of the media pseudoworlds, the extent to which hegemonic encoding can be resisted by counterhegemonic *decoding,* the effectiveness of local resistance to global media, and whether the media shape or merely reflect worldviews. Can the media, including the Internet and the new social media, be a resource for opposition, or are oppositional messages always *recuperated* by elites?

Critical and Marxist-influenced theorists are more likely to see growing global media monopolies and the pseudoworld of the media in negative terms, while, at the other end of the scale, postmodernists such as Jean Baudrillard tend to believe that the media explosion is irreversible and have a celebratory attitude toward it, reveling in its exuberant and magical qualities. But postmodernists and Marxists are divided among themselves as well on the question of how all-consuming the media are and the extent to which local and oppositional decodings are possible. A few examples of this vital area of theory will give the reader a sense of the new concepts and perspectives.

Stuart Hall

Media have an established fundamental hegemonic role in the cultural sphere, whereby the production, circulation, and consumption of social knowledge in societies depends on modern forms of mass communication. People live their social relations, and these are then reflected back to them through the mass media, which provide images, ideas, meanings, values, practices, and representations of groups. In this way the media provide the images and representations through which the social totality, even as fragmented and disjointed, can be conceptually grasped as a whole. Hall argues that the machineries and regimes of representation play an active and constitutive role in culture and are not merely reflexive. This places representation in a formative, not just expressive, place in the constitution of social life. Therefore Hall argues for a "politics of the image." The politics of representation are not detached from empirical reality; for Hall, the politics of representation are the struggle over the ability to define the conditions, limits, and modalities of meaning.

Media also bring together and organize what has been fragmented, selectively represented, and selectively classified. There is a simultaneous process of fragmenting social reality and making it integrated and cohesive. An imaginary unity is constructed and organized into an acknowledged, stabilized order. One important operation is to present power, domination, and exploitation through a language of neutrality. Consensus and consent work through the interplay of free opinions freely given and exchanged. Consensus shaping, unification, and consolidation are part of . the media's ideological work. At the surface, the outlets of media appear pluralistic, multiple, and contradictory; yet below this surface, they are structured to produce consensus and legitimacy.

By establishing the parameters of interpretation and representation of what is legitimate and what is not, the field of media serves as an effective means of hege-monic reproduction.

Media also serve to mark and define different types of cultures, styles, and forms of social knowledge that are classified, ranked, ordered, preferred, or marginalized so as to make a map of the social reality through which these forms of knowledge are objectified. Here the social knowledges produced and circulated come with normative and value-added classifications in which there are preferred meanings and interpretations.

For Hall, this classification of knowledge is not a top-down hierarchical or simple class-based model of media control. Although in general the knowledge of the economically dominant class and institutions of the state is privileged over local knowledge of subaltern groups, the media can also marginalize knowledge by labeling it as "elitist." Hall's analysis of authoritarian populism as the ideological mechanism underlying Margaret Thatcher's mass appeal pointed to the folksy and populist representations of her program and the celebration of "good old English traditions" with undercurrents of xenophobia. The media emphasize that they are open and diverse so that their ideological functions are not readily apparent.

Hall argues that there are ideological practices at work in privileging or discounting and excluding certain activities, forms of knowledge, and practices. It is here that the struggle over the dominant and dominated or preferred and excluded meanings is contested as images themselves become ideological signs open to a plurality of significations. Signs contend in the arena of hegemonic ideological struggle.

Many images and discourses are organized around dominant and preferred codes that appear to be natural explanations; these are the most readily acceptable and serve as templates to cast events and ideas into the dominant ideology. They are made to appear as the only forms available. These modes of interpretation become taken for granted and thus generate invisible commonsense understandings. Hall elaborates Gramsci's contributions to the concept of hegemony; Gramsci believed that hegemony is most perfected and powerful when a dominant ideology is transformed into common sense so that it seeps into every pore of everyday life and can no longer easily be spotted as ideology. Here we remind the reader of our discussion of Michael Taussig's work and the naturalization of capitalist relationships.

Meaning is both produced and consumed through the process of encoding and decoding. Encoding is the process by which the dominant definitions structure and accent events and images in a way that reproduces the ideological structures. The dominant encoding of an image works to win the consent of the audience not through the bias of interpreting events but through the legitimacy and range of limits within which encoding operates—which makes the dominant mores of reading events the point of identification through which the receiver decodes the message. But it is not necessary that the audience decodes the images through the preferred encodings, since, as Hall argues, there are spaces within which peoples and groups situate themselves and incorporate alternative readings, or decodings different from the preferred hegemonic decodings.

Manuel Castells and the New Symbolic Environment

Manuel Castells's (1996) analysis of the media is one element of his grand theoretical overview of the emergence of the information age. Castells argues that in the 1970s capitalism entered a new phase of *informationalism,* characterized by new technologies of computerization, communication networks, biotechnology, and multimedia systems. Using concepts derived from Marxist theory and from Daniel Bell's (1973) writing on postindustrial society, Castells makes clear that he considers informationalism a new mode of development, while capitalism remains the prevailing mode of production. Capitalist relations of production shape the form and use of technological innovations, but informationalism has a logic of its own that produces change in social relations and institutions. The media impact is a key facet of this larger transformation of society and contributes to changes in economic activities, occupations, and global flows of products, technologies, and capital.

Writing thirty years after Debord, Castells takes a more neutral tone but shares Debord's large-scale vision of a society transformed by an encompassing *new symbolic environment.* Castells believes that this new symbolic environment is absorbing traditional cultures on a global basis. Global virtual culture irreversibly penetrates and changes local cultures. There is indeed a degree of diversification and segmentation of the television audience on a global scale, but television has become more "commercialized and oligopolistic" (Castells 1996, 341). Therefore, diversity, the plethora of choices, and cultural and local differences among viewer responses are in fact superficial and mask an underlying increase in uniformity and centralization. In Castells's words, "While the media have become indeed globally interconnected, and programs and messages circulate in the global network, *we are not living in a global village, but in customized cottages globally produced* and locally distributed" (1996, 341; italics in original). He examines the impact of new information media and the pervasiveness of symbolic, mediated experience. He concludes, "What is then a communication system that, in contrast to earlier historical experiences, generates *real virtuality? It is a system in which reality itself (that is, people's material/symbolic existence) is entirely captured, fully immersed in a virtual image setting, in the world of make believe, in which appearances are not just on the screen through which experience is communicated, but they become the experience*" (1996, 373; emphasis in original).

This view is a direct challenge to Hall's theory that viewers can decode media messages in complex, ambiguous ways and sometimes ascribe oppositional meanings to messages that media industries have produced with hegemonic intentions. Castells is also challenging the position of fellow media analyst Ien Ang (1996) that globally disseminated media products are given *local interpretations* by local audiences. She gives as one example the way viewers in the Netherlands interpreted broadcasts of the First Gulf War quite differently from US viewers—the Dutch lost interest and deliberately disengaged from coverage that they saw as a form of propaganda and ideological colonization. Castells appears to discount the local meanings and sees these local processes as relatively weak and, in the long run, unable to remain autonomous from the global media systems and messages.

Castells suggests that information and media technology will absorb and transform existing cultures, not vice versa. He proposes four hypotheses about the social and cultural impact of informationalism and new media.

- There will be widespread social and cultural differentiation and fragmentation of audiences, a proposition that directly challenges the thesis of massification of message content and tastes.
- There will be an increase in social stratification (akin, but not identical, to the digital divide) in which only a few are adept at extracting, interpreting, and using information. Just as mere literacy did not make people powerful, neither will being online guarantee political efficacy.
- Messages will be increasingly integrated into common cognitive patterns so that, although social and cultural differentiation and segmentation take place in content, thought processes will become more standardized and homogeneous, dictated by the practices of the new media.
- The long-term impact of the information revolution and its accompanying media is the creation of a new symbolic environment.

George Gerbner: The Cultural Environment and "the Mean World"

Empirical support for the concept of an all-encompassing symbolic environment comes from the research of George Gerbner (2002), who was dean of the Annenberg School for Communication for twenty-five years and launched the Cultural Indicators Research Project, which collected and analyzed thousands of television programs. Gerbner was certainly not a Marxist but a critical voice from a mainstream progressive position that only government regulation can ensure the presence of values of diversity, pluralism, balance, democracy, and civic responsibility in the media. Gerbner's early work in critical scholarship examined how the state—government—could become a force for diversity and pluralism in the media. He saw that government authority was required to ensure that "the marketplace of ideas" really contained many different voices and orientations, but the state gave up this regulatory power in many countries during the neoliberal era.

Gerbner uses the term "cultural environment" rather than "symbolic environment," but his conclusion converged with Castells's. The media are expanding in influence, our understanding of most of the world is increasingly based on the media, and this space of images, news, and stories is increasingly monopolized by a small number of extremely powerful companies, or "conglomerates" as Gerbner termed them. This analysis is congruent with earlier work on media monopolies proposed during the heyday of conflict theories, but Gerbner focuses on the discursive and cognitive impact rather than on the structures of ownership and control. The media are particularly powerful in socializing children. Human beings live by stories, and children learn through stories, but the media have replaced parents, elders, religious leaders, schools, and books as storytellers. In a frequently quoted phrase, Gerbner remarked that the media conglomerates "have nothing to tell, but a great deal to sell."

His second conclusion, often called the *mean-world syndrome,* has grave political implications. The world of television is an insecure and terrifying one. The stories told are about violence and brutality. The most immediate effect of this violent pseudoworld is to make viewers (especially children) not significantly more violent themselves but more fearful. The empirical data strongly suggested that a high volume of television viewing is related to fearful attitudes and a perception of the world as a much more violent place than it really is. Gerbner believed that this effect has broad political consequences. He commented that "fearful people are more dependent, more easily manipulated and controlled, more susceptible to deceptively simple, strong tough measures and hard-line postures.... They may accept and even welcome repression if it promises to relieve their insecurities" (Gerbner 1981). Gerbner thus provided empirical support for theoretical insights first formulated by the Frankfurt School: the concept of a total media environment, the brutality and violence of that environment, and the possible link between media exposure and the formation of what Theodor Adorno called an authoritarian personality, a character type that was most dangerous not as a violent person (though he or she might well be violent) but as an insecure and frightened individual who would accept repressive policies to assuage unmanageable fears (Adorno, Frenkel-Brunswik, and Daniel Levinson 1993; also see Chapter 7, "Sociology of the Self").

Note that Gerbner's "mean world" of violence, brutality, uncertainty, disaster, and tragedy is the flip side of Schudson's ideal world of capitalist realism. The two worlds are twinned aspects of the media pseudoworld. Commercials, sitcoms, and sports are places where all problems are solved and everything is under control, while news and action shows depict a violent and terrifying world.

Paul Willis and Common Culture

In contrast to Castells, Gerbner, and many postmodernists who point to the all-encompassing and totalizing character of contemporary media, Paul Willis is one of a number of theorists who emphasize the relative autonomy and agency of audiences. Audiences do not passively absorb a pseudoworld that standardizes and homogenizes their thinking. On the contrary, they respond actively and critically. Local, class, and cultural interests shape these responses, which are often skeptical and humorous. We have already encountered this view in Stuart Hall's analysis of coding and decoding. Willis (1990) is a Marxist, but like Michel Foucault he sees resistance not primarily in organized movements but in everyday life and *common culture.* There is a constant and pervasive play of cultural domination and resistance, which usually has ambiguous outcomes.

Willis takes the hopeful position that culture is not a top-down imposition monopolized by elites or a dominant class; nor is it a seamless web of hegemonic meaning that hopelessly entraps the masses. Ordinary people constantly create culture themselves, often by mocking, reworking, cutting up, and twisting strands of hegemonic culture. Willis takes a more optimistic view than Mills and many traditional Marxists. Symbolic activity is not monopolized by the corporate media but continues to be an activity of ordinary and rebellious people. Willis and his research team document these new cultural forms with interviews and observations of working-class English youth from many ethnoracial backgrounds; their findings support the thesis that young people are involved in new forms of oppositional culture detached from direct confrontations on the factory floor. Although a traditional Marxist might scoff at the notion that the proletarian vanguard consists of young people mocking the "telly" and shopping in flea markets, Willis suggests that these new forms of symbolic activity can be part of a vital opposition to capitalism. They create new meanings, undermine both consumption and production as central values of capitalism, and preview a postcapitalist culture. We can recognize convergence with Benjamin's optimistic analysis of new media as potential tools for deconstructing capitalist hegemony. In a similar vein of celebrating the inventive edge of youth subcultures, Dick Hebdige (1981) charts the emergence of punk as the British industrial sector wound down and rebellious youths fashioned a subculture influenced by Caribbean immigration as well as earlier English working-class styles, such as Mod and Rocker. Hebdige's work in turn expands observations of hipsters, delinquents, and rebels in the 1950s and 1960s (e.g., Matza 1961; Goodman 1962).

Fredric Jameson: Media and Postmodern Culture

Jameson, a professor of literature at Duke University, offers a Marxist-influenced analysis of postmodern culture, including media, art, literature, and architecture. While retaining core premises and values of Marxist theory, he transforms many of its concepts and analytic tools to handle new realities in media and culture, specifically the content and form of the emerging global culture, which is characterized by *surface intensities,* the loss of the past, and dissociated, fragmented states of feeling and patterns of consciousness.

In Jameson's analysis, postmodernism is the form of culture associated with late capitalism. Capitalism itself has distinct phases; currently we are in a phase of extended commodity production (the consumer society), high-tech (or electronic) technology, multinationalism (or globalization), and media penetration of our unconsciousness as well as our consciousness. This phase of capitalism shapes postmodern culture.

Jameson believes that distinct phases of the mode of production have distinct "cultural dominants," or forms of culture. The cultural dominant is not the same as the dominant culture, that is, the culture of economically and politically dominant classes; Jameson gives relatively little attention to classes as coherent purposive social actors. Rather, the cultural dominant is a pattern of representation that appears across different media and art forms. It is an indirect reflection of the underlying mode of production and social conditions, not the product of a class-conscious dominant class.

Jameson begins his analysis with aesthetic populism, the blurring or even complete collapse of the boundary between high culture (the arts) and popular culture. This blurring is a product of modern media. It carries further the process already observed by Benjamin when he hypothesized that film and radio would obliterate the ideological notion that a work of art is the product of the individual genius. Mechanical production of cultural work would replace art with skillfully assembled and mechanically reproduced media objects disseminated to mass markets in an instantaneous process that annihilates space and destroys the aura of the authentic, one-of-a-kind artistic treasure or great performance.

Messages and representations are flattened, with surface intensities emphasized at the expense of "deep meaning." The concept of surface intensity is based on the experience of seeing images on television and monitor screens. The screens glow and shimmer with images in brilliant colors. The real world appears dull and grey compared to the world on the screens.

Jameson uses the telling example of the contrast between Vincent Van Gogh's late-nineteenth-century modernist painting of peasant shoes and Andy Warhol's *Diamond Dust Shoes.* The former depicts a pair of worn, broken work boots, refers to a life of toil, and implicitly calls for change in the social order; the latter delights in a brilliant, hyperreal representation of party pumps that demands nothing from the viewer except pleasure in viewing the object. In postmodern culture there is only the text (words or images) and no exploration of, let alone outrage over, a reality outside the text. This textuality of postmodernism is heightened by cyberspace and virtual reality; attractive websites do not mean that there is anything, let alone anything attractive, really there. They form a *simulacrum,* a perfect copy of a nonexistent original (Baudrillard 1969/2000). The collective and individual past is lost and replaced by nostalgia, pastiches of cannibalized, decontextualized fragments of the past, and a playful invention of "retro" styles that displace memory and history. The media contribute to the immersion in "the perpetual present which is daily life under postmodernism and late capitalism" (Jameson 1990/1996, 231).

A waning of affect takes place; the search for true feelings disappears. Just as the search for a more just social order is jettisoned, so is the quest for a truer, unalienated inner self. The belief in the inner self had been expressed in paintings like Edvard Münch's *The Scream* (the expressionistic painting of a distorted man standing on a pier screaming) and in the Freudian project of recovering repressed, unconscious desires. Postmodernism ends the faith that these true selves exist at all, as discussed Chapter 7 on new theories of the self. Contemporary media contribute to the formation of a protean, shifting persona in place of a "deep self."

As a Marxist, Jameson insists that these cultural forms are connected to social conditions and social relations of late capitalism. Culture is not a free-floating fantasy embodied in texts, media, and artworks. It is part of a new configuration of production, markets, and social relationships. At the same time, Jameson recognizes that there is no going back to an earlier, serious radical social critique; the new forms of capitalism and capitalist culture must be challenged through new forms of political culture adapted to the postmodern situation, but he does not provide a clear picture of how to create this new oppositional consciousness.

Conclusion

The media are an area in which innovations in the real world are giving rise to new concepts and new debates, deeply influenced by contemporary theoretical paradigms. Some theories contain traces of Marxism, but they are being applied to such startling new circumstances that they are quite transformed and live in an uneasy relationship with postmodernism—intertwined with it, sometimes opposing its celebratory tone and sometimes converging with it in the analysis of the long-term impact of new media on human thought, action, and possibilities.

Chapter Seven

Sociology of the Self

From Personality to Persona

What is the self? What do we experience when we are aware of ourselves? Do we have an *unconscious,* and if so, what is stored in it? Where is the self when we sleep or dream? How is the self related to the body? Is the self-feeling always in our heads, behind our faces, even when we are experiencing a great orgasm or an ingrown toenail? Do we have multiple selves or one single self that remains the same in every situation? Is the self a deep, stable structure or a shifting persona? Are selves basically the same in all societies and historical periods, or are they very different?

As Eviatar Zerubavel (1999) points out, at one level all human beings have the same brain structures and are fundamentally alike, while at another level each one of us is a unique individual. Sociologists are interested in what happens "between" the generically human and the uniquely individual, in the differences in cognition, thought processes, and self-formation that are shaped by social and cultural forces. While few sociologists would completely dismiss exploration of genetic variation, they are more intrigued by the way that culture and social interaction affect the formation of selves and can be used to explain variation among human beings. This underlying orientation provides an opening to the discursive and constructionist turn.

In this chapter we suggest that contemporary sociologists' writing on the self is deeply influenced by the conflict constructionist paradigm. While one can hardly claim that "the self" is a new phenomenon in human history (in contrast to television, computers, the Internet, and global markets in derivatives), sociologists' ways of thinking about the self have changed very rapidly in recent decades. The self is an area in which theorists have extended a strong welcome to many elements of conflict constructionism, such as attention to the body, the *self as text* and performance, and the discursive construction of the self, as well as emphasis on the fluidity of self-construction and interest in the way the media produce distinct types of selves. Indeed, while the human self is not new, sociologists are intrigued by the new ways selves are being constructed in the age of the media and *flexible capitalism.*

Overview

In the contemporary period, theories of the self have the following characteristics:

- Increasing emphasis on a self that exists as a text, a performance, or a narrative
- Views of the self as fleeting, changeable, fragmented, protean, destabilized, and shifting rather than as a permanent structure
- Renewed attention to historically situated and contingent selves, especially in terms of how selves are changing in response to flexible capitalism, globalization, the Internet and virtual realities, and expanding markets
- An effort to integrate psychoanalytic insights with the analysis of culture and texts

Trajectory

The sociology of the self is an area that has changed rapidly and been open to contemporary theories. Although traces of earlier concepts of the self persist, they have been strongly influenced by new theories. Nevertheless, to understand contemporary approaches to the self among sociologists, it is useful to start early in the history of the social sciences, at the beginning of the twentieth century.

Four Classical Paradigms of Self and Society

During the formative period of sociology and other social sciences, four basic perspectives on the self emerged. The earliest perspective, that of the "empty self," insists that social theory must reject all psychological explanations. The self is only an empty space defined by social control, normative regulations, and social forces. This radical position is most clearly associated with Emile Durkheim among the classical theorists. A second view, that of the "historical self," holds that the most important characteristics of the self are shaped by changing social forces lodged in larger, macrolevel structures. The selves of people in modern, capitalist societies are fundamentally different from the selves of people in traditional societies. The *historically contingent self* is shaped by changing social conditions but is not as blank and agency-less as Durkheim's empty self. This position can be found in the theories of Karl Marx and Friedrich Engels, Max Weber, and Georg Simmel. A third view of the self, the "interactive self," was developed a little later by the social behaviorists (especially Cooley [1983] and Mead [1932]); this self is seen as constantly formed and produced in social interaction and communication, and it was conceptualized as largely conscious, coping, sociable, and pragmatic. Finally, a fourth view of the self that has influenced sociological theory is the "psychoanalytic, unconsciously driven self" proposed by Sigmund Freud (1920/1966, 1958, 1960).

Searching for a Hookup: The Early Twentieth Century

In the years following these early fundamental formulations, sociologists experimented with a wide range of hookups between sociology and theories of the self. The matchups were often quite surprising. A few examples will give the reader the flavor of how theories of the self were related to other bodies of sociological theory. Symbolic interactionists leaned toward social behaviorist views of the self. Structural functionalists not only made use of Durkheim's empty self but were also intrigued by psychoanalytic perspectives. While orthodox Marxists rejected it, *psychoanalysis* strongly influenced critical theory and the Marxist perspectives of the Frankfurt School and Walter Benjamin (Jay 1996). For example, Theodor Adorno's study of the *authoritarian personality* (Adorno, Frenkel-Brunswik, and Levinson 1993), the individual with propensities toward fascism, racism, ethnocentrism, punitive behavior toward others, and docile submission to strong leaders, looked to psychoanalysis for clues about how deep impulses, rage, aggression, infantile drives, and childish wishes could be manipulated by leaders such as Hitler and Mussolini or channeled into escapist fantasies, cynicism, and political quiescence through mass media.

Structural Functionalism: Choosing between Psychoanalysis and Durkheim's Empty Self

Psychoanalysis was a popular theoretical hookup for structural functional theories in the post–World War II period. Offhand, this matchup seems strange, but it was powerfully propelled by the fashion of psychoanalysis in popular culture and intellectual life of the period, as well the influence of two groups of theorists: the Parsonians, on the one hand, and on the other, the Frankfurt School theorists who came to the United States as refugees from the Nazis and brought with them an understanding of psychoanalysis as a practice of social criticism, clearly exemplified in Adorno's analysis of the authoritarian personality and Herbert Marcuse's efforts to synthesize a Hegelian Marxist perspective with Freud's contribution (Adorno, Frenkel-Brunswik, and Levinson 1993; Marcuse 1955).

Nevertheless, many structural functionalists gravitated more toward the empty self of Durkheim's rigorously antipsychological view of society. Durkheimians saw the self as a product of social norms, molded by the external force of society. Structural functionalists were generally interested in large-scale patterns, institutions, and structures that operated regardless of the motivations (let alone happiness) of individuals. In practice, this Durkheimian antiself perspective was expressed through increasingly sophisticated analysis of data to identify large-scale patterns. Although the opinions, attitudes, and accounts of behavior of individuals constituted the data, the analysis was statistical and focused on the aggregated patterns, not on interpretations of individual ideas.

Yet, despite the unmistakable impact of the Durkheimian admonition to avoid psychological-level analysis, sociology in the postwar period contained a vast domain of social psychology. It was not merely linked to social psychology—much of it was social psychology. It is hard for us now in the twenty-first century to grasp the extent to which sociology was focused on the individual. This focus was visible across the spectrum of political engagement and included a critical wing of social psychology that proffered radical perspectives on social institutions, which were seen as both creating and reflecting individual malaise and even pathology. The social psychological tilt of sociology was paralleled by the culture and personality studies in anthropology and actualized by survey research that produced data on individuals' attitudes, predispositions, and orientations, characteristics that were interpreted as fundamental to their actions and roles. As noted above, the social psychological perspectives were often drawn from, or at least compatible with, psychoanalysis. It is striking how many references to social psychology and psychiatry (specifically the work of Henry S. Sullivan) Erving Goffman introduces into his early writing. Central works of the period, such as William H. Whyte's *The Organization Man* (2002) and David Riesman, Nathan Glazer, and Reuel Denney's *The Lonely Crowd* (1961), linked the critique of social institutions to the analysis of individual character or personality. Despite their critical charge, these studies were not defined as conflict theory studies but appeared to be close to the structural functional mainstream. One unintended consequence of conflict theory's rise to prominence in the latter 1960s was a turn away from social psychology—seen as too focused on intra-individual processes and hence insufficiently politically engaged, although some conflict theorists continued to read psychoanalysis—and a turning away of social psychology from sociology, now seen as too contentious and politicized to be hospitable to psychologists who defined themselves by ever more positivist research practices.

Transitions to Contemporary Theories of the Self

Conflict Theorists and the Self

Theories that emerged in the 1960s and 1970s continued to draw eclectically on the classical theories of the self. Symbolic interactionists continued to elaborate the legacy of the social behaviorists (Cooley [1983] and Mead [1932]) and the work of Simmel (Lindesmith and Strauss 1956). They were also attracted by the Weberian method of *verstehen,* or understanding, that is the interpretation of ideas, be they found in texts or in the words of respondents.

Conflict theorists were more inclined to explore the historically contingent self, drawing especially on Marx's writing on *alienation* and his analysis of how capitalism (and other class societies) distorts and stunts the fundamental human capacity for labor, broadly understood as the ability to create our world. In capitalist society, this great creative potential is consistently linked to production for profit, thereby dulling the spirit, reducing human beings to machine-tending drudges, and alienating workers from their own labor and the products they create.

But conflict theorists also turned to psychoanalytic views of the self. We have already noted how the Frankfurt School brought critical and radical portions of Freud's legacy to the United States and opposed the powerful efforts of US therapists and media figures to "Americanize" Freud by turning him into a theorist and practitioner of adjustment to society, when his entire emphasis was on the pain and loss provoked by the repression of infantile drives (Freud 1920/1966, 1958; Jacoby 1986).

Feminists Salvage Freud!

Feminists' rediscovery and rehabilitation of Freud as a protofeminist was a surprising development in view of his patriarchal and misogynist veneer. For many feminists, Freud was a misogynist who supported patriarchal authority. Both his central European environment and his Jewish cultural heritage seemed to impel him toward conventional stereotypes of women as mysterious, capricious, seductive, and emotional. He even referred to women as "the dark continent." Feminists were repelled by Freud's insistence that most memories of childhood sexual abuse—or seduction, as he jauntily termed it—were fantasies and in fact projections of the child's own desires onto adult males.

Yet a number of more daring feminists decided that elements of Freud's theories could not only be recuperated for feminist thought but held the key to a central question of feminist theory: How are human beings genderized, why is this such a powerful and universal differentiation, and how is it linked to the acquisition of language? Freud had pointed to exciting ways of thinking about these processes within the self, the universal differentiation and asymmetry of gender, and the complex connection of real childhood experiences to imagination and self-construction. Feminists needed only to strip away his consistent veneer of patriarchal condescension to see the important contributions psychoanalytic theory could make to the study of gender construction.

Furthermore, Freud had a remarkably open attitude toward sexual minorities, especially homosexuals. Contrary to popular misunderstanding, he did not consider "perversions" to be neuroses, let alone illnesses. On the contrary, he argued that all human beings experience these feelings in childhood, but a majority of adults repress them. Because of a combination of genetic factors (which Freud called "constitutional dispositions") and childhood experiences, these feelings and impulses remain very powerful in some individuals. When also subjected to powerful unconscious repression, they become "fixated" and eventually produce neurotic symptoms. Unconscious repression and denial of homosexual desires produces neurosis, and their conscious recognition, acceptance, and integration into the self is in fact the only way to dispel neurotic despair and its associated symptoms.

Feminists reread Freud to gain an understanding of gender construction and heteronormativity (Mitchell 1975). Nancy Chodorow provides an outstanding example of Freudian feminist theory in her influential *Feminism and Psychoanalytic Theory* (1989). She uses Freudian theory to account for the construction of gender and the socialization of children into *gender identities,* each with asymmetric expectations and relationships with parents, as boys separate from their mothers while girls are expected to become like them. Boys thus undergo an abrupt, even traumatic break with feminine aspects of gender identity and in their relations with women, while also sensing rivalry with their father for the attention of their mother; girls experience continuity and closeness, and the mother-daughter rivalry is not as intense as that between fathers and sons. These asymmetrical relations and expectations produce fundamentally different types of people with considerable uniformity across cultures, even if details of child raising differ.

Louis Althusser: Rereading Freud—from Sexual to Textual

Finally, apparently the strangest hookup of all was that between structural Marxism and psychoanalysis, as elaborated by French theorist Louis Althusser (1971a). This link is of special note for a history of contemporary theory because it marks the discursive turn in theories of the self, the transformation of self into text. And it appears in a very unexpected venue—a work of structural Marxism, which should have been unwelcoming to what one might erroneously define as an individually oriented perspective on human action (psychoanalysis), although we will see that psychoanalysis is reformulated in textual and structural terms. When Althusser read Freud, he looked for structural properties of the text inscribed on the unconscious by the transition from infancy to childhood.

Althusser is usually put in the category of structural Marxist, but, as with almost all French social theorists, we can discern similarities to Durkheim (and to Auguste Comte as a distant ancestor) in his rejection of individual agency as an explanation of social phenomena. He insists that the freely willing and choosing subject or actor is an ideological illusion used to mask the reality of social-structural determinism. But this Marxist appropriation of the empty self—the illusory subject—did not stop Althusser from engaging with Freudian psychoanalysis. If the subject is dead and the self is formed by the external force of society, it is imperative to ask how society gets into the individual. Althusser developed an intense interest in Freud and in the work of Jacques Lacan, a French psychoanalytic theorist. Althusser and Lacan reinterpret Freud's paradigm as a theory of a special type of language in the unconscious. In Althusser's thought we can see a "braiding" or "swirling" of Durkheim's empty self, Marxism, linguistic theory, and Freudian psychoanalysis.

Althusser reinterprets Freud's work on the unconscious as a theory of language. Psychoanalysis is the science of the unconscious and the systematic and rigorous charting of the language of the unconscious. This language has its own rules and logic, a strange sort of grammar that uses displacement (metonymy) and condensation (metaphor) to create a fantasy narrative about experiences of self. The unconscious is a text with its own narrative logic. Its reconstruction of infantile experience is not literally true (and this insight of Freud's got his theory into trouble with psychologists and feminists, who insist that accounts of childhood sexual abuse are generally true—a controversy that continues to bubble). The fantasy narratives of the unconscious are not true stories but fantastical, distorted representations of each individual's forced march from infancy into childhood and then into adulthood and manhood or womanhood. As Althusser says, the text of the unconscious tells us how human beings cross the divide from "bio-nature into history and culture, from infancy into childhood, from being infants to being masculine or feminine subjects" (1971a, 206). From "mammiferous larvae" we are forced to turn into human children, and the narrative of this metamorphosis is preserved in the unconscious. Every human being who reaches adulthood has made this transition, and while it is not identical in all cultures, many of its basic elements are universal. One is the transition to language itself: human beings speak. Another is the acquisition of a gender identity. Children are forced to leave the unity of mother and child and to situate themselves in the world of adults. This transition into culture is imagined by the child as a threatening intervention by a castrating phallic father. The *Oedipus complex* is a text in the mind of the child—a fantasy narrative—about the transition.

Whatever one may think of this interpretation of the Oedipus complex, Althusser has to be recognized for making a bold advance along the road to reconceptualizing the self as a text. Freud and Frankfurt School theorists have used psychoanalysis to interpret texts and works of art and to explain the motives for writing them or the appeal they had for mass audiences. But Althusser moves in the opposite direction along this path. Instead of using the concept of the unconscious to analyze texts, he treats the *unconscious as a text* to be read and interpreted. This method was of course already present in Freud's theories as he insisted that free association and interpretation of dreams, supremely language-based methods, are the only entry points into the unconscious. Looking at the unconscious as a text like a poem or novel that recounts an imagined experience of growing up is congruent with Freud's view that stories of castration threats and incest are not usually literally true memories. But it is the timing of Althusser's textual approach that is especially important for our history of the theory of the self, because it coincides with growing interest in discourse and texts. In the last half of the chapter, we see that this perspective—treatment of the *self as a narrative*—has become a leading paradigm in social thought.

This Althusserian rereading of Freud, though not widely echoed in the sociological journals of the period or taught in most North American departments of sociology (let alone psychology!), is one of the early warning signs of the great slide into the narrative, performative, textual self, along with the work of Erving Goffman and Michel Foucault, both of whom used a Durkheimian path rather than a Freudian one to reach the endpoint of seeing the self as textual and performed.

Symbolic Interactionists

By emphasizing the symbolic and interactive context of the formation of the self, symbolic interactionists had a major role in opening discourse to the constructionist paradigm. Indeed, in retrospect some might argue that they went too far, that they construed states such as *mental disorder* and addiction to be largely the products of interactions and symbolic processes, when we now are more inclined to give the nod to physiological causes that may be triggered, exacerbated, or sustained in interaction. Similarly labeling theory placed a very large weight on the role of labels in the onset of deviant careers. Contemporary modified labeling theory has tempered this initial position in the understanding of mental illness; modified labeling theorists do not claim that stigma and stereotyping can produce mental illness, only that they serve to isolate the patient and increase the burden of the condition. Despite later modification of their sweeping claims, the new theoretical symbolic interactionist approaches had an enormous impact on the emergence of the social constructionist paradigm in the United States.

New Views of the Self: Goffman, Foucault, and Bourdieu

We briefly review how three of the theoretical innovators who launched many elements of the new conflict constructionist paradigm conceptualize the self and laid the groundwork for contemporary perspectives. All three innovators contributed to a break between sociology and social psychology by rejecting the perspective that individual motives and personalities hold the clues to explaining social arrangements.

While Marxists and feminists experimented with Freudian ideas, Goffman reawakened a Durkheimian view of the self as a product of normative regulation in "gatherings" ranging from asylums to families; this neo-Durkheimian paradigm of the self as a product of social forces and as a performance enacted for a gathering or audience was proposed in a masked form that many mistook for a variant of symbolic interactionist theory. Meanwhile, in Europe, the analysis of discourses, the philosophy of deconstructionism, and an interest in theories of language injected these perspectives into the sociology of the self, themes that became associated with Michel Foucault. Another French theorist, Pierre Bourdieu, developed the concept of *habitus* to explain how society and social class get into the self.

Toward the end of the twentieth century, all of these hookups of sociological and psychological theories of the self took a decisive turn away from any type of stable self system (and the associated concept of the personality) toward a much more fluid, shifting, fragmented view of the self as persona, narrated and performed in constant play. This move from stable and deeply rooted interior personalities to shifting personae, constituted in discourses and performed for gatherings, extended from the conclusions of these three theoretical innovators.

It is tempting to explain this movement in theory as a product of neoliberalism, transnational migration, expanding markets, and a global capitalism that destabilized fixed identities and made "everything solid melt into air," as Marx and Engels put it so felicitously in *The Communist Manifesto*. Traces of earlier theories, like psychoanalysis and social behaviorism, remained but were reworked to fit into the melting play of masks and storytelling.

Goffman: Performing the absent subject. We have already introduced Goffman as an innovator and commented on his initial interest in social psychological orientations followed by a shift into Durkheimian perspectives on regulation. He was strongly influenced by Durkheim but pursued Durkheimian analysis with a microperspective rather than through the analysis of macrostructures or statistical patterns. But in other ways, he anticipated contemporary analysis of the self in which the self is represented as a fleeting, unstable, performed persona rather than a fixed, deep, and permanent personality.

On the surface, the dramaturgical self appears to have a high level of agency, but a closer reading of Goffman reveals that although the self does indeed pursue self-interest, in order to attain its goals it must follow a script. It must adhere to the rules of discourse and performance, and these rules create a large amount of constraint in its ability to act. The more deviant or self-interested it is, the more closely its performance must meet the largely aesthetic criteria that make for a convincing show.

Note how Goffman imposed the Durkheimian view of the self as a product of society, bound to follow its rules, on interactionist ideas—it is in interaction, in performance, that the rules of society are most clearly visible. Far from being a free agent in interaction, the self is constrained to play by the rules or have its performance discredited. The self is performed. It has little or no depth, only a dim, reptilian definition of self-interest and an awareness of rules of performance and self-presentation.

Foucault: End of the subject. Foucault shared with Durkheim and Althusser a view that attacks the notion that the self is the basic unit, or atom, of society. For Foucault (in keeping with the French tradition), the self is not "there" as a driving force with will and agency. Society cannot be explained as the net outcome of purposive actions by many contending selves. The self is constituted by historically changing discourses, increasingly the discourses of the human sciences. Althusser had warned that the appeal to a self with will and agency is an ideological illusion. He called it an "interpellation," a term that refers to a police officer stopping and interrogating a suspect. We are called upon to account for ourselves—forced to play the part of an agent or subject with responsibility for our actions, but responsibility is only an ideological illusion. Foucault agrees with this radical view of Althusser's even though he does not share Althusser's Marxist analysis that the personal responsibility of the self is a figment of bourgeois ideology. Instead Foucault associates the illusion of self-responsibility with increasing self-surveillance demanded by professions such as medicine, psychology and psychiatry, social work, education, and criminal justice.

Foucault's view of the self led him into a debate with Freud's ghost. Freud appeared to have believed in a repressed, hidden self and a truth about the organization of each individual's sexual drives, but Foucault dismissed these claims. Very primitive, incoherent impulses for pleasure are organized differently under the regulatory frameworks of different discursive formations of different epochs, so that in one age people perceive themselves to be bisexual (as did men in ancient Greece), in another they are led to feel that these impulses are sinful and immoral, and in yet another that they are deemed deviant or sick. (Althusser's reading of Freud's reading of the unconscious as a fantasy text actually blurs the apparent opposition of Freud and Foucault and shows that they have common ground in discursive analysis.)

Foucault's view that subjects are constituted by discourses is compatible with Althusser's textual analysis as well as with earlier structuralist themes in Durkheim. The self is not "there" as a driving force with agency but is constituted by historically changing discourses—increasingly by discourses of the human sciences—and is experienced as an interpellation (à la Althusser), a call for self-surveillance. As pointed out earlier, there is strong convergence with Goffman's theories of the self as well—not surprising since Goffman saw himself as a neo-Durkheimian for whom the self is monitored, regulated, and even constituted in interaction (Verhoeven 1993). But late in life, in his work on care of the self, Foucault edged away from the full implications of the empty self.

Bourdieu and habitus. Durkheim left a puzzle for future generations of sociologists: How is society implanted in the empty spaces of the self? His concept of collective conscience/consciousness leaves this question unanswered, and it is probable that he did not want to answer it at all. The collective conscience/consciousness can be touched or apprehended in objects and acts such as law codes, the sacred books of world religions, ritual objects such as sacred flutes or medicine bundles, postings of the Ten Commandments, chants and public punishments, and so on, but these tangible forms are only a small part of the great power of the collective conscience/consciousness and do not provide a complete understanding of how ideas, feelings, and the very structure of thought itself gets into people's heads as well as their bodies.

Pierre Bourdieu (1993b) proposed a solution by suggesting the concept of habitus. Habitus is the shared mode of perception, judgment, and behavioral dispositions of a category of people, especially a class within a social formation. It is embodied knowledge (Wacquant 2004), and both conscious and unconscious. It is a frame of mind or mentality, but it is also inscribed on bodies and includes the way people move, wear their clothes, dance, and jump (or fail to dance or jump). It is habitus that solves the mystery of why people in Northern Ireland can generally tell who is Catholic and who is Protestant, although there is no "racial" difference, no genetically inherited visible difference between the two groups. It is habitus that makes the children of professors adept at academic careers and produces generations of jewelers, furriers, tile layers, and other skilled artisans. It is largely, but not entirely, a mechanism of social reproduction. There is room for invention and change within habitus, but generally only within certain limits because habitus affects the ways situations are defined and perceived and thereby reduces our capacity and willingness to make changes in ourselves and our actions.

The concept of habitus allows Bourdieu to answer a number of questions that Durkheim had not answered clearly: How are social structure and the collective conscience/consciousness transferred into the individual? How is society embodied in individuals? Why are inequalities reproduced from generation to generation, even if opportunities, resources, and expectations appear to have become more equally distributed?

Contemporary Theories of the Self: From Personality as System to the Fragmented, Protean, Narrative Persona

Althusser, Goffman, Foucault, and Bourdieu set the stage for contemporary understandings of the self in terms of narratives, texts, performances, fleeting personae and masks, and unstable constructs. Postmodernist theorists assert that the self in all societies has always been a performed and narrated construct; Marxist-influenced theorists argue that this elusive and multiple self is a new phenomenon associated with flexible capitalism, globalization, multicultural societies, the Internet, and a historical social formation in which, as Marx and Engels said, "all that is solid melts into air." We review and provide examples of theories of the self as performance and narrative, the metaphor of the contemporary self as schizoid, and theories of the self that emphasize the effects of flexible capitalism.

The Narrative and Performed Self

Self-narrative; self as text. Empirical work in sociology was strongly influenced by the concepts of textuality and narrative. These new concepts fused rather well with existing themes in symbolic interaction, and the result was ingenious analysis of selves as narratives, texts, or constructions created by *identity talk.*

By the latter decades of the twentieth century, the concept of a self-narrative, or a narrated self, had become very popular in sociological research and theory. In many respects it had begun with Norman Denzin's (1993) analysis of Alcoholics Anonymous (AA). Denzin showed how the members of AA learn to tell a certain type of story about themselves. This story may or may not be literally true. Just as in Freud's dismissal of most accounts of childhood seduction, the literal truth of the story does not matter; what is important is that the self is constructed, displayed, performed, and often even freed from addiction by the repeated recounting of and social support for the story of being an alcoholic. We can see linkages to Goffman's observations.

Once this basic observation was made, microsociologists and social psychologists found instances of self-narratives and identity talk throughout everyday life. Self-narratives, self-construction, and identity talk can be linked to macrodevelopments like the formation of multicultural societies, changing norms of gender and sexual identity, and the immigrant experience.

The concept of the narrative self was applied to many situations of everyday life in empirical studies. For example, David Snow and Leon Anderson (1993) observed the fictive storytelling of homeless men in which the men construct an identity that counters demeaning and stigmatized views of the homeless by elaborating stories about their past successes and future hopes. Douglas Mason-Schrock (1996) follows Denzin's lead in the analysis of Alcoholics Anonymous, tracing the stories of male-to-female transsexuals and charting how their stories are not literally true but rather narratives of self-discovery that are learned from others, follow a coherent formula, and represent a sex change as the logical outcome of the story.

A similar life narrative with organizational support was observed by Leslie Irvine (2000) in a study of participants in Co-Dependents Anonymous, an organization for individuals who have experienced problems in relationships and then learned to make sense of their situation by telling a story that follows a formula about abusive families, hitting bottom, and recovery. (See Vaughan 1990 and Loseke 1992 for more on narrative construction.)

The idea that the self is constructed in narratives dovetails well with the postmodern emphasis on social construction and textual analysis. The self is a special type of text, a story that is told and can also be inscribed on the body. One of the most dramatic ways of performing the self is making the costume and mask a permanent part of the body, as in tattooing and piercing (as well as sex-change operations). These *body modifications* tell vivid and often very public stories about the self (Pitts 2003).

The narrative self as resistance. Theorists took the process a step further. Not only are self-narratives learned and negotiated, but they are also a form of opposition, or at least resistance, to capitalism, racism, and gender hierarchy. Goffman had already shown that the performed self is at risk of being unconvincing and often of being actively discredited. Sociologists observed this contention over the constructed and narrated self. For example, Snow and Anderson observed homeless people telling stories that challenge their stigmatized and discredited status. Kathryn Fox (2001) showed how incarcerated people contest the stories they are supposed to tell about their actions and experiences. Shu-Ju Ada Cheng's (2007) ethnographic study of Filipinas working as domestics and care workers in Taiwan documented how the women resist the racial, gender, and national labeling and construction of them as inferior, submissive, and unskilled by countering with their own self-narratives of pride and competence. This analysis of narratives of resistance provides many concrete examples of what Foucault had theorized about the micropolitics of power and resistance, and the empirical studies reflect his view that this resistance is ongoing and pervasive, not simply led and implemented by a movement or party that claimed to be the historical subject.

Markets, Virtual Reality, and Flexible Capitalism: New Perspectives on Historically Situated Selves

An impact of neoliberalism on social theories of the self was renewed interest in the historically contingent self. Neoliberal, global, flexible capitalism and the Internet may be creating different types of selves from those that appeared in previous eras. Even if the self is a text or narrative, it is likely that these narratives and constructs have changed markedly in recent decades. How are theorists conceptualizing the self situated in the contemporary world?

Fragmented and multiple selves: The metaphor of schizoid disorders as postmodern selves. One approach to understanding the postmodern self was to describe it as fragmented, multiple, or schizoid. Each epoch has its characteristic forms of *mental disorder and madness* (Hacking 2002, 2003), and what are considered the normal selves of the period are socially acceptable versions of these disordered selves.

Schizophrenia and split or multiple selves were a fascinating topic for psychiatry and pop culture, but it was probably David Riesman (Riesman, Glazer, and Denney 1961) who first suggested that the self in advanced modern societies had dissolved and lost its stable core. The *other-directed* character type that Riesman believed was becoming prevalent obtains clues from peers and the media by a radar-like mechanism of perception and adjustment. They lack a stable core of character but have a protean ability and desire to shift their persona in accord with the environment as if they had multiple personalities. Riesman thought of the extreme end of the spectrum of the other direction as similar to the apathetic and thoroughly compliant cases of traumatized veterans in psychiatric wards (Riesman, Glazer, and Denney 1961, 244–245).

This metaphor of the multiple, fragmented, unstable self was more recently elaborated by Kenneth Gergen (1991) in his metaphor of the "saturated self" at risk of dissolution. Gergen uses the term "multiphrenia" to suggest an overpopulated self formed by contradictory social expectations, media that offer conflicting messages, and excessive expansion of options and opportunities.

Fredric Jameson offers a broader and deeper version of this metaphor in his groundbreaking *Postmodernism, or The Cultural Logic of Late Capitalism* (1991/2005). Jameson argues that the self of high modernity (in the late nineteenth and twentieth centuries) was neurotic in the psychoanalytic sense of experiencing tension between inner feeling and external norms, between acknowledgment and repression of desires. For Jameson, the disturbed little humanoid of Edvard Münch's famous picture, *The Scream,* represents this painful internal conflict and the associated suffering of isolation, loneliness, and alienation.

In contrast Jameson uses the term "schizoid" or "schizophrenic" to characterize the disordered and dissociated experiences of the postmodern era. These states are characterized by a waning of affect as feeling is replaced by surface intensities—sudden, short-lived bursts of euphoria and perhaps terror, which flash across the empty spaces where the self once dwelled. He makes a chilling statement about this new liberation from anxiety: "As for expression and feelings or emotions, the liberation, in contemporary society, from the older *anomie* of the centered subject may also mean, not merely a liberation from anxiety, but a liberation from every other kind of feeling as well, since there is no longer a self present to do the feeling" (Jameson 1991/2005, 15).

So the mentally disordered self can be seen as an extreme or heightened form of the types of selves that are prevalent among the normal. Disorder and normality are historically situated constructs (Hacking 2002, 2003).

Virtual selves. Information technologies, media, and the Internet contribute the idea that the self is protean and elusive. The *virtual self,* or cyberself, is a special and extreme form of the presentation of self; it is the self that is projected and presented online. For example, individuals create a profile for Facebook and MySpace and represent themselves in fanciful ways in chat rooms and online games. These projected selves range from profiles that are relatively close to the real self, to fantasy images in games and on websites, to outright misrepresentations for purposes of fraud or seduction. The Internet offers many opportunities to manipulate and create multiple selves that are situation and interaction specific and to fabricate selves that are patently false (a word that is rapidly becoming meaningless) (Turkle 1997). But beyond these flagrantly false selves, there are many instances in which individuals are playing with the multiplicity of their real selves, projecting one or another aspect of the self, including those that may be secret or taboo in face-to-face situations. In this respect, the Internet is an extension of the metropolis that Simmel observed a hundred years ago; it liberates individuals from the identities and labels they cannot escape in the small town. Manuel Castells (1996) refers to the expansion of a world of make-believe in which mediated experiences and virtual images have become a larger and larger part of reality itself.

Richard Sennett: Flexible capitalism and character—new perspectives on the historically contingent self. A major work that applies the historical perspective on the self to the character in the age of neoliberalism is Richard Sennett's *The Corrosion of Character: The Personal Consequences of Work in the New Capitalism* (1998), which focuses on how the self in flexible capitalism is different from previous selves. The analysis problematizes and explains the atomism that *rational choice theory* naturalizes. Sennett links Marxist theories of capitalism as a social formation to the question of how the self is formed and constructed. Sennett bridges micro-, self, social psychological, and historical theories. As Riesman did in the study of the other-directed, he shows how character is historically situated and how self-formation depends on the underlying form of society and economy.

In *The Corrosion of Character,* Sennett intertwines several of the threads we have been following throughout the chapter. He finds that in the world of flexible capitalism the self is destabilized. The routines of work—dull as they often were—had created fixed frameworks within which people had to live their lives. The home-job alternation, the routines of office work or assembly-line jobs, and the big bureaucratic company were sources of both drudgery and security. The new flexible capitalism, with its entirely market-oriented behaviors, risk taking, down-sized organization, and high-tech innovation, has brought a sense of failure, transience, and insecurity to many people—other than the carefree rich who find risk exhilarating. Lower down the economic ladder, risk is often depressing and disorienting. Most people affected by risk are encouraged to blame themselves for failures such as unemployment, business closings, and foreclosures and for being insufficiently entrepreneurial or technologically up-to-date, or they blame shadowy forces—the "them" of conspiracy theories and ethnic disgruntlement. The technology of most jobs has become so complex that few people can cope with breakdowns by themselves; they feel dependent on outside forces and not in control of their situation.

One result of these trends is that many people prefer to quit their jobs rather than confront problems in the workplace. Another is the high premium placed on youth, a belief that older workers are deadwood, and an associated demeaning of the past, all of which in turn lead to a loss of self-worth over the life cycle. Hard skills related to knowing how to do a job have given way to soft skills, like fitting into a team and being able to work with a series of bosses who come and go. Once the economy, the job, and the workplace were all-too-solid foundations for life, providing a grounding in routines, expectations, and even exploitation; the solid foundation has melted into air, giving way to multiple fragmented and disconnected risks, impulses, and opportunities, which are experienced as transient jobs, everlasting uncertainties, and a sense of being disposable and homeless. These disintegrating processes that Sennett groups together as the *corrosion of character* have gone furthest in the United States; in western Europe, traces of embedded liberalism, the political economy of capitalism before the neoliberal shift, persist and support more stable character types. Although Sennett works within the tradition of the historically contingent self (favored by Marx, Weber, and Simmel), he links it to the analysis of self-narratives, arguing that we have entered an age in which it is difficult to construct a satisfying, self-affirmative life narrative, to tell a story of one's life that is meaningful and fulfilling.

Sennett, like Jameson, argues that the fragmented contemporary self is actually a new form of self associated with flexible capitalism. The flexible, fragmented, constantly reconstructed self mirrors a new historical reality. The self has been shattered, and not only is its shimmering, blurry quality in the eye of the beholder (the postmodernist theorist), but it is a product of a new organization of work and a more flexible, marketized economy.

These insights into the self as a historically situated product are reiterated in a recent ethnography, Karen Ho's *Liquidated: An Ethnography of Wall Street* (2009). Ho writes as a student of culture and institutions with less of a social psychological and philosophical attention to character than Sennett, but their conclusions are strongly convergent. On Wall Street she finds analysts who believe themselves to be supremely intelligent ("smart") and who think that the entire globe should be remade in their own image: working long hours at moving money around, focusing single-mindedly on making money, taking risks, and comfortable with complete job insecurity. They are convinced that their smartness justifies their seeking to impose their way of life on humanity as a whole, as the apogee of the human spirit and the realization of a utopia of risk taking and money making in its purest form. Ho traces the formation of this mentality to their Ivy League education and the firms' recruitment practices as well as to attachment to the myth of shareholder value as the guiding light of the occupation, a myth that Ho reveals as a misrecognition of the history of the market. Ho's work (like Widick's [2003] carnal sociology of trading) goes beyond occupational studies to dissect the types of selves that are forming at the advanced edge of contemporary life.

These various views of the self include Marxist as well as postmodernist orientations. Some of their theorists draw inspiration from Durkheim, some from Freud, some from theories of the self as historically contingent, and a few from the pragmatism of the social behaviorists. Yet all of them share a typically postmodern understanding of the self as fluid, performed, and unstable. They all use elements of the conflict constructionist paradigm, such as discourse and framing as processes that constitute selves, attention to the body and embodied performance, and a preference for fluidity over stability as a way of conceptualizing self and society.

The Postmodern Self: A Summary of Characteristics

We find the following characteristics ascribed to the self in contemporary theories. Have selves always been fluid, unstable, fragmented, and textual—and we only realized it in the postmodern era? Or are these characteristics genuinely new ones produced in contemporary capitalist societies that had not been present before?

- Fragmentation takes place, creating a self that is not fully integrated and is in fact comfortable with multiple component selves.
- Surface intensities replace deep feelings.
- A schizoid, dissociative character becomes widely prevalent, both as the typical form of disorder and as a tendency among normal individuals.
- Multicultural societies produce multiple selves—the dialog of the I and the me can easily turn into a shouting match among multiple mes. Deterritorialization of identity takes place so that people feel at home—or like strangers—in many societies and places (Appadurai 1993; Sassen 2001).
- A disruption of the sense of place (both spatially and in terms of knowing one's place) occurs.
- Identity politics and fundamentalism can be interpreted as a last-ditch effort to reduce the multiplicity of identities and the fragmentation of the self; they are desperate attempts to restore order, stability, and fixity in the face of postmodern disintegration of the self.

Conclusion

In the contemporary period, we are left with our initial four classical positions on the self, but they have been adapted to postmodern positions, as follows:

- The empty self is seen as discursively constructed.
- The interactively formed self is increasingly shaped by media, advertising, unstable situations of work and family, and multicultural encounters that create situations in which the self defines itself through choices, performances, and identity talk.
- A historically contingent self is formed by flexible capitalism and globally expanding markets.
- A psychoanalytic self is reinterpreted as the adult performance of a fantasy text about the experiences of infancy and childhood.

Postmodernists argue that the self is and always has been text and performance, and it is only now that we fully understand this phenomenon. On the other hand, Marxists are more inclined to assert that the performed, textual, and fleeting quality of the self is a result of shifts in the society and economy—flexible capitalism, intensified markets, globalization, and the Internet and other information technologies.

Either way, self theories increasingly emphasize fluidity, performance, and an ephemeral quality to the self. It is seen more as a performed persona than as a stable and abiding personality. It is lodged in narratives, performances, identity talk, and rapidly shifting choices in markets, not in lifetime dispositions or firm character structures.

SECTION 2

Paradigms in Play

Chapter Eight

Political Sociology and the Analysis of Collective Action

Old and New in Harmony

Since the 1970s, about eighty-five "popular" revolts have taken place, most recently the multiple uprisings of the Arab Spring. What causes these popular revolts, and how can we explain why some succeed in producing peaceful democratic outcomes while others fade, end in disorder, or slide back into authoritarian rule? Meanwhile, has politics in the United States become divisive and polarized? Are people more or less committed to *civic engagement* than in the past—or are they equally committed but taking part in different types of organizations than they did in your grandparents' day? How do people decide to get involved in political actions and social movements?

In this chapter we group political sociology with the sociology of social movements and *collective action,* a somewhat tight squeeze of two closely related fields into a single discussion. But the two fields share theoretical foundations and have overlapping communities of scholars.

In this area of sociology, a relatively harmonious and pluralistic relationship exists between new and old paradigms. The borders between new and old theories are relatively open. A mainstream that draws on organizational and institutional analysis (and many concepts ultimately derived from Weberian conflict theories) is open to new concepts such as fields and *frames,* so that elements of the conflict constructionist paradigm are absorbed readily into existing theoretical approaches.

The authors would like to remember Mayer Zald for his feedback on an early draft of this chapter and thank Roberta Garner's social movements class at DePaul University for participating in a review of current periodical literature.

Overview

This active area of sociology includes the following developments:

- Pierre Bourdieu's concepts of the political *field* and its *political practices and practices of power* have been widely adopted. These concepts made both Marxist and mainstream analyses of power and institutions more fluid than the older concepts of *apparatus* and structure, and have meshed very readily with concepts already present in the sociology of collective action, such as multiorganizational fields.
- Michel Foucault's concept of *governmentality* has impacted institutional analysis.
- Studies of the *state and civil society* by theorists such as Theda Skocpol, Saskia Sassen, and Jeffrey Alexander forge links between existing institutional theories and new interest in the role of the state and collective action.
- New approaches to collective action that link states, identities, and *cultures* have broadened the mainstream of collective action theory, yet still incorporate twentieth-century concepts such as resource mobilization and political opportunity structure. By the 1990s, perspectives based on the discursive turn and the concept of frames were smoothly and gently brought together with the existing organizational and institutional analysis (for an example, see McAdam, McCarthy, and Zald 1996).
- Identity formation is linked to the role of the state and to the analysis of how difference and dominance are socially and discursively constructed (the focus of Chapter 4).

All of these perspectives share an emphasis on bringing the state back in. They address questions initially posed by Marxists and Weberians, but in fresh ways, with a new fluidity that replaces rigid structural concepts of institutions and apparatuses with new terms such as "framing," "fields," "practices," and "construction of identities." Structural and organizational analysis is expanded with the inclusion of research into framing and *discourses*.

Trajectory

Classical Theories

Karl Marx, Friedrich Engels, and Max Weber laid out basic concepts and questions in political sociology: the definition and functions of the state; the relationship of the state to civil society; the role of *ideology*, authority, and legitimacy in constructing the consent of the governed; and the role of class and status in propelling individuals and groups into parties, that is, into political organization.

Marxists tended to see political actions and the state as part of the superstructure of society, and many of them proposed a critical functionalist argument—that the state emerged as an institution or set of apparatuses to protect and promote the interests of the economically dominant class, turning it into a ruling class. Drawing on the writings of Antonio Gramsci (an Italian communist who wrote in the 1920s and 1930s and died after being imprisoned by the Fascists), new generations of Marxists focused on concepts such as civil society and hegemony. Civil society is not an exclusively Marxist concept; as we shall see, its use is shared by contemporary non-Marxist theorists of the relationship between the state—a coercive institution—and the realm of private and voluntary association. Hegemony is a concept that refers to the process by which an economically dominant class converts its power into a legitimated and consensual right to rule as its worldview penetrates the thinking of subaltern classes and even organizes their common sense, that is, their basic understanding of how the world works in everyday terms. Hegemony as a Marxist concept is a twin of the Weberian interest in legitimacy and authority. We can see how the growing attention to and reworking of Gramsci's concept in the last decades of the twentieth century (most notably by Stuart Hall) signaled a discursive turn within Marxism itself.

Reviewing classical theories of political action, one can emphasize the differences between Marxists and Weberians or their similarities—their common interests in conflict, the role of the state in society, the construction of legitimate/hegemonic power, and the creation of organizations as political actors using instrumental rationality to pursue their ends, whatever these ends may be.

Functionalist Views and the Social Psychological Perspective

During the heyday of Parsonian structural functionalism, the state was seen as an institution that fulfills the system imperative of goal attainment—in other words, as one able to define goals for a society and initiate action to achieve them. Durkheimians were interested in the role of voluntary associations in forming a transmission belt and buffer between the state and its citizens.

Many empirical studies of the post–World War II period focused on individual attitudes and political behaviors. The powerful role of social psychological approaches was certainly visible in the analysis of social movements, an area generally defined as part of the field of "collective behavior," a label that tied the study of movements to fads, fashions, crowds, panics, and mobs (Garner 1996). This coupling underlined the irrationality of movements. The repugnance many scholars felt for the major movements of the mid-twentieth century—fascism, Nazism, Stalinism, McCarthyism, and so on—was an external force that propelled them into an emphasis on individual irrational motivation. For example, at the left end of the spectrum of political scholarship, Theodor Adorno developed the concept of the authoritarian personality (Adorno, Frenkel-Brunswik, and Levinson 1993), an individual whose character structure drew him to fascism, a paranoid political style, conspiracy theories, obsession with racial and sexual purity, and a borderline sadomasochistic propensity to both command and obey. But a similar emphasis on individual-level explanation and attention to irrational motives prevailed not only on the left but throughout the field, for instance, in political scientist Harold Lasswell's influential view of politics as the public pursuit of private goals.

Conflict Theories and the Analysis of States, Movements, and Other Political Actors

Functionalist views of the state and social psychological perspectives on movements were the direct targets of critiques by conflict theorists, many of whom were personally inspired by the tumultuous events of the 1960s: the formation of new nations, the civil rights movement in the United States, opposition to the war in Vietnam, socialist *revolutions* in the Third World, student-worker movements in western Europe, the Prague Spring, and the Cultural Revolution in China. The spirit of the activist 1960s refreshed Marxist scholarship and led to a new turn in the mainstream as well. Movements came to be seen in a more positive light, emphasis shifted to structural causes of political action, and attention focused on organizations and institutions.

Events and movements led to rereadings of Marx, Engels, and Lenin that defined the state in terms of class struggle. The state represents the interests of the economically dominant class, and only if it is captured in a revolution and thoroughly remade can it become the expression of an insurgent class's interests. Marxists saw the state in terms of powerful apparatuses, all serving class interests and carrying out this function by coercive and ideological means. The armed forces, police, security agencies, and criminal justice system were parts of the coercive apparatus; in France, where Louis Althusser (1971b) was writing, the public school system seemed a good example of an ideological state apparatus, though in other countries, ideological functions were more diffuse and lodged primarily in private entities of civil society, such as the media and religion.

In the mainstream a major shift took place toward a neo-Weberian perspective on political action and especially on social movements, an area that was now radically decoupled from the study of individual psychodynamics and returned to institutional and structural analysis. The turn was signaled (maybe precipitated) by two key works: Neil Smelser's (1963) value-added structural analysis of collective behavior in which he identified a sequence of conditions for collective behavior to emerge and succeed in attaining the goals of the participants and Mayer Zald and Roberta Ash's (1966) seminal essay on social movement organizations and their trajectories, an article that defined social movements in terms of organizational characteristics and actions. These key works of theory were soon followed by the influential development of resource mobilization theory (Zald and McCarthy 1977), which went even further in viewing movements as rational actors.

The next major contribution to the new mainstream was the introduction of the term "political opportunity structure," a concept already foreshadowed in Smelser's work, but now fully elaborated by Sidney Tarrow (1998) and many others. Charles Tilly (1978, 1992; Tilly, Tilly, and Tilly 1975) pioneered the analysis of movement events in a broad time perspective, looking at the conditions and circumstances in which collective action events take place and the repertoires of action that are available to participants. Although the term "structure" has a structural functional ring to it, in fact this new attention to structure was much closer to Weber's analysis of the state and his premise that conflict is an open-ended, ongoing reality than it was to any kind of functional analysis.

All in all, this turn in political analysis in the 1960s and 1970s might be described as a return to Marxist and Weberian roots, an emphasis on the state and political organization, and the decline of social psychological explanations. A focus on political behavior gave way to attention to political action, to agency (if not always rational choice) or at least a mix of agency and determining structures.

Toward Contemporary Paradigms: New Concepts in Political Sociology

By the last decades of the twentieth century, Marxist and class-based movements had ebbed and faced competition from other kinds of movements, such as the *new social movements* (movements with a leftward tilt that did not have a class base—for example, the environmental movement, the peace movement, and the gay rights movement). The states of "really existing socialism" finally collapsed. Religious identity became a strong force in movements. Progressive scholars' enthusiasm for movements was dampened by the emergence of countermovements and single-issue movements, as well as fundamentalist and ultranationalist movements. In these conditions the boldly pro-movement and conflict-theory based approaches of the 1960s and 1970s were revised but not revoked.

The Rise and Fall of New Social Movement Theory

During the 1980s, new social movement theory seemed a promising way of understanding the emerging multiplicity of identities and collective action. It developed in a new climate for social movements. Class-based movements and organizations, such as socialist parties and unions, seemed weakened and no longer were seen as the "historical subject" that could transform or end capitalism. Movements based on race-ethnicity and gender were of rising importance, and identity politics seemed to preempt class-based sources of collective action.

A host of newer movements appeared, especially in Europe, and many of these movements seemed detached from any demographic or pseudodemographic and ascribed social bases. These new social movements included peace activists organizing against nuclear weapons stationing in Europe, environmental activists, housing rights activists, and many community-based groups. Theorists felt sympathy with this wide range of activism, which they saw as vital and progressive; some of them defined the new social movements as a vanguard formation, overcoming class-race-gender divisions, eschewing essentialism, avoiding the illusions of revolutionary rhetoric and inappropriate Marxist-Leninist models, and drawing strength from their very multiplicity and fragmentation (Melucci 1989; Kriesi 1996).

But after a burst of enthusiasm, the new social movements (and with them, new social movement theory) ebbed in the face of Soviet collapse, neoliberal market expansion, and a rightward shift in US and British polities that some saw as a return to pre–World War II policies favoring the wealthy and the financial sector (Kerr 2001). By the end of the twentieth century, conservative religious movements had become a powerful counterforce to globalization, neoliberalism, and cultures based on Enlightenment values. Movements espousing fundamentalism, integralism (the fusion of state, society, and religion), and patriarchal values became militant and dynamic ways of expressing discontent that for several decades appeared to supersede left-wing and class-based challenges to neoliberalism (Riesebrodt 1993/1998; Marty and Appleby 1992; M. Davis 2004).

These real-world shifts in the last decades of the twentieth century led to revision of the conflict analysis of states and politics. The discursive turn set the new direction as scholars took renewed interest in examining culture, ideology, and identity, as well as everyday microprocesses of resistance in which weak and subaltern groups (such as peasants, women, or ethnoracial minorities) expressed subtle opposition to an oppressive order (Scott 1987). Researchers and theorists examined the play of movements and states, as movements both courted and opposed states—being both with and against the state, as Manisha Desai (2002) phrased it in her study of women's movements in India. The ambiguous relationship between states and other political actors set the tone for analysis of political action.

The Influence of Foucault on the Study of Power and the State

While the state remained a major focus in political sociology and social movement theory, it came to be theorized in new ways, beyond its conceptualization as a coercive institution, the repository of legitimated violence in a society. Theorists began to examine new forms of political dominance using Foucault's concept of governmentality: the emphasis on self-regulation and choices, the shift from state services to multiple partnerships between the state and organizations of civil society, and the penetration of discourses of community, responsibility, and localism. These discourses and associated practices have an ambiguous character and can function either as a model of self-directed, democratic civic engagement or, more likely, as support mechanisms for neoliberalism and manipulated, consensual forms of dominance (Bennett 2006).

The ambiguities of the microphysics of power, the capillary processes, and the play of power and resistance—all concepts introduced by Foucault—altered the analysis of movement outcomes. In earlier analysis, institutionalization and co-optation of movements had meant their effective demise; the new paradigm leaves open the possibility that movement practices and goals will "seep into the capillaries" and succeed in changing the social order without a major sudden "jump" in institutional arrangements. As Steven Buechler put it, "When confronting centralized power, institutionalization usually means becoming subordinate to that power. When challenging the micro-physics of power associated with social politics, institutionalization implies that forms of resistance and challenge become interwoven with the fabric of power itself" (2000, 181). Yet the capillary, or micro-physics-of-power, analysis also pointed to ways existing institutionalized power holders can manipulate and buffer apparent movement victories.

Pierre Bourdieu's Concept of Political Field

Pierre Bourdieu replaced terms inherited from the period of structural Marxist analysis without dumping Marxist insights about conflict and contention. In place of the rigid concept of apparatus (as in the public education system and the military as apparatuses of the state), he suggested the term "field" (not a new term in US sociology but refreshed by Bourdieu's usage). The image is of an open expanse dotted with various institutions that include organizations of the state as well as of the private sector and civil society. These elements can move around, change, connect to each other, or become more distant. For example, the field of education can contain public schools but also private academies, religious institutions, textbook publishers, parents' associations, social movements, community-based organizations, and parts of the media. In some ways, "field" is akin to Talcott Parsons's concept of function. The parts that carry out educational functions are not single institutions, structures, or apparatuses but multiple organizations and practices. In this new geography of fields, social movements also form fields of their own and appear within other fields—for example, when activists seek to make changes in school curricula. These fluid fields are captured in social movement theory by terms such as "multiorganizational field," "social movement community," and "social movement sector" or "social movement industry."

Bourdieu's political field is a terrain of actors and practices rather than institutions and apparatuses, in contrast to the more fixed concepts of structural functionalists and structural Marxists. The political field is organized by the logic of power and domination. It includes the formation of parties and social movements, socialization and political comportment, and the production of political products such as policies, events, and mobilizations. The capture of state power can be the aim of practice. The political field overlaps in actors and practices with fields such as the media, culture and education, and the economy. It has its own types of capital—especially social capital formed by networks of political actors, but other kinds of capital, such as money and the symbolic capital of media influence, also circulate.

Bourdieu's concept of the political field dissolves political science into sociology by defining politics as one type of social practice. Key terms of political philosophy, such as "legitimacy," "authority," "sovereignty," "citizenship," and even "politics," are transformed by sociological analysis based on empirical study that is informed by a theory of the social world and practice. For Bourdieu, practices in the political field are what Emile Durkheim termed "social facts" and part of the subject matter of sociology. The concept of political field helps us to avoid the reduction of political analysis to economic causation (exemplified by the simplistic explanation of the Iraq War as only about oil—though oil is obviously part of the equation of power and global dominance).

The State and Civil Society

The last decades of the twentieth century saw a return to democracy in areas that had experienced military rule (in Latin America), in South Africa with the end of the apartheid regime, and in the USSR and eastern and central Europe with the collapse of one-party systems (Przeworski 1991). Yet the end of authoritarian and repressive states did not necessarily bring a deepening of democracy (Roberts 1999). Civil rights and multiparty elections did not automatically bring with them civic and political participation. Elites found new methods of manipulating, limiting, and narrowing political engagement, related to Foucault's governmentality.

These issues encouraged theorists to look at civil society and civic engagement, drawing on the legacies of Durkheim, Weber, Marx, Engels, and Gramsci, as well as more recent conflict theories and the perspectives of Bourdieu and Foucault.

Theda Skocpol on States, Movements, and Political Engagement

Theda Skocpol is a major contributor to these discussions. Her early achievements were in the study of revolutions, first the analysis of the French, Russian, and Chinese revolutions (Skocpol 1979) and later of Third World revolutions (Goodwin and Skocpol 1989). Her explanations centered on characteristics of the political systems in contrast to other theoretical options, such as an emphasis on revolutionary organization or on class structure as an automatic determining cause. The great historical revolutions took place when the old-regime states failed to meet international challenges, and the precondition for the Third World revolutions was an exclusionary regime.

Skocpol's next major set of studies focused on the formation of welfare systems in the United States in contrast to European nations. In the United States, until the Great Depression and Franklin Delano Roosevelt's New Deal, welfare was only awarded to mothers and Civil War veterans (and later, to veterans in general). Most benefits, available only to these two "deserving" categories, were supported by popular mobilization and civic engagement.

Civil Society and Civic Engagement:
Controversy over Bowling Alone

The return to democracy stimulated theorizing about civil society, but so did the slackening of civic participation, especially in the United States. Robert Putnam analyzed this shift in his widely hailed *Bowling Alone: The Collapse and Revival of American Community* (2001), arguing that there has been a sharp decline in membership and participation in large cross-class civic organizations and voluntary associations, such as the Masons and the Parent-Teacher Association. With this decline, American communities are experiencing a loss of social capital. People's everyday lives are privatized and focused only on friends and family, volunteer effort is diminished, and communities and the nation as a whole no longer enjoy the benefits of collective effort and commitment.

Skocpol offered a different interpretation of these observations; the slackening of civic engagement is the result of elites' efforts to remove issues from political contestation. For example, organizations such as unions had been able to represent members' interests to political parties and governments, but they lost ground when primaries and other institutional efforts to open the political process actually undermined the two-step role of organizations and made the process more susceptible to media imagery, TV ads, and campaign fund-raising. The older-style organizations had effectively mobilized across class lines (though many had excluded women and minorities) and brought working people into politics. The new style of national politics replaces mass participation with advocacy-professionals' management of media campaigns and fund-raising. Meanwhile, civic engagement is channeled into local and largely depoliticized causes. Republicans and conservatives have been more successful in mobilizing remaining voluntary associations such as the National Rifle Association and evangelical churches and connecting their mass base to professionally managed advocacy groups. Skocpol (2004) argues that *bowling alone* is not a politically neutral process that cuts across political party lines and the conservative-liberal divide; rather, it has contributed to the conservative tilt in recent political life in the United States.

Skocpol's analysis of the changing nature of civic engagement continues in her observation that 9/11 did not increase citizens' participation in civic life, unlike many previous instances of armed conflict. Skocpol argues that this response—a weak level of *civic engagement*—is a result of both the new nature of antiterrorist warfare and the professional management of civic organizations in the United States. "There is … little evidence that 9/11 and its martial aftermath led to any immediate upsurge in collective voluntary activities at all comparable to the upsurge associated with historic wars. This twenty-first-century conflict has different requirements, and Americans live in a very different governmental and civic universe than their forebears—a changed public world in which political authorities and nonprofit organizations rely on professional management and media messages rather than on organized popular participation" (2002, 540).

The Tea Party

Skocpol's most recent work about the Tea Party brings together an analysis of the social base in demographic terms, the ideology of participants, the role of right-wing funding sources, and support in the media (Skocpol and Williamson 2012). Thus the analysis is an excellent example of the leading mainstream paradigm in political sociology and social movement theory, interweaving characteristics of the movement's organization, external opportunity structure, ideology (and framing), and mobilization of distinct social bases. The social categories that are disproportionately mobilized are older white Americans, often small-business owners or other middle strata, who share very conservative ideologies. As Rebecca Klatch (2002) already found in her study of the Young Americans for Freedom in the 1960s, traditionalists (social conservatives) have a somewhat uneasy relationship with libertarians in this movement. What makes the Tea Party very different from movements on the left fringes of the Democratic Party are its wealthy supporters and the important role of the media—notably Fox News—in its successes. Although not surprising in its findings, the study is a satisfying and readable example of the mainstream paradigm applied to a current example of collective action.

Alternative Globalization and Global Civil Society

Another view of civil society and social movement activity is offered in the analysis of *alternative globalization* movements, such as the World Social Forum, and a host of loosely networked community-based organizations. Some of these movements have a clear class basis, such as the transnational Shack Dwellers Federation, a network of local organizations in Africa and South Asia that represent residents of poor communities with substandard housing and contested land rights. Others may be formed by a broader interclass cross section of community dwellers, by coalitions of middle-class intellectuals and poor people, and by activists in a spectrum of nongovernmental organizations. Yet others may have an ethnic base in indigenous communities that are opposing environmental degradation or incursions of settlers, for instance, in the Amazon, the Niger Delta, and India, where ethnic and environmental justice issues are inextricably linked. In keeping with Desai's findings, these movements have complicated relationships to states, opposing state policies yet remaining open to reform and even co-optation.

Ultimately these kinds of movements have led theorists to suggest that we are seeing the emergence of a *global civil society* (Sassen 2000), a loosely textured web of small organizations and community-based movements that does not reject the global and the modern but hopes to create alternative forms of it that are more humane, democratic, and sustainable. These forms will emerge by oozing around and through the states, using state policies only to a certain point and substituting citizen initiatives as needed. The model of change is no longer a revolutionary assault on the state apparatus.

Similarly, the work of Jeffrey Alexander (2006) affirms the ongoing strength and openness of civil society and the key self-correcting role that social movements have in it; so do the ethnographies of power and resistance compiled by Michael Burawoy and his students from a Marxist-influenced perspective (Burawoy et al. 1991). Though emerging from different theoretical foundations, both theorists see vitality in civil society, with movements playing a key role. These optimistic perspectives are in distinct contrast to the concept of governmentality with its implication of manipulation and cryptototalitarian control and mind colonization. The debate coincides with disagreement about the totalitarian or liberating potential of the media that we discussed in Chapter 6.

The Leading Paradigm of Collective Action: The Happy Marriage of the Discursive Turn to Organizational and Structural Analysis

A major step in revising and defining the mainstream paradigm was taken by Doug McAdam, John McCarthy, and Mayer Zald in *Comparative Perspectives on Social Movements* (1996). It is notable for its smooth integration of the discursive turn and the concept of framing into existing approaches that focused on movement organization, mobilization, and political opportunity structures. It drew extensively from perspectives of the resource mobilization, rational action, and conflict theory period of the 1960s to the 1980s, using concepts such as organizations and political opportunity structures and synthesizing them with concepts from the period of the discursive turn, specifically framing, a concept that originated with Erving Goffman (1974) and was introduced into social movement theory by David Snow and Robert Benford (1988). Overall one could say that the ancestor spirit of this volume was Max Weber: in the final analysis, framing is not incompatible with Weber's guiding principle of *verstehen,* or understanding of the meanings and purposes that actors assign to their situations and actions.

McAdam, McCarthy, and Zald suggest that social movement theory should be used to understand movement emergence, development, and outcomes. These are the dependent variables in the analysis. Three main concepts are proposed and linked together to explain the course of movements: (1) political opportunities, including the presence of elite allies, the state's capacity and propensity for repression, and the openness or closure of the institutionalized political system (McAdam, McCarthy, and Zald 1996, 10); (2) mobilizing structures, which include characteristics of the movement and the strategies of movement organizations, including disruption; and (3) framing, defined as "conscious strategic efforts by groups to fashion shared understandings of the world and themselves that legitimate and motivate collective actors" (1996, 6) and can be used to sustain morale, generate media coverage, mobilize bystander publics, constrain social-control options, and shape public policy and state action.

The importance of this volume lies in its opening of the organizational and structural paradigm to framing (and the cultural and ideological dimension), thereby creating a very broad and powerful overall approach to the analysis of movements, one that has essentially dominated the field since the 1990s. A brief perusal of social movement research after the turn of the century shows no end in sight to the paradigm.

The paradigm was elaborated in David Meyer, Nancy Whittier, and Belinda Robnett's key collected volume *Social Movements: Identity, Culture, and the State* (2002). Here a number of authors went beyond framing in general to focus more on the construction of identities and the broader notion of culture. In the analysis of political opportunity structures, many of the researchers emphasized the role of the state. In short, the collection provided an elaboration of the leading paradigm and many interesting examples of its use in empirical analysis; overall it reinforced rather than challenged the paradigm.

Collective Action and Identity Construction

Attention to identity in the analysis of social movements and political action links this field to the analysis of difference and dominance, discussed in Chapter 4. Many see class, race-ethnicity, gender, and sexuality as the leading dimensions of inequality and identity, and these dimensions (along with religion and nationality) are closely linked to political action and mobilization. Mobilization often attempts to make salient or even to create identities. Here we explore the construction of identity and collective action further and look at new complexities in their analysis, especially growing attention to the role of both movements and the state.

Two examples of identity construction and collective action. Two examples help to illustrate how new theoretical perspectives are being used to understand situations of *identity construction, identity formation,* and collective action.

Car burnings and identity politics in France. Issues of identity formation, the meaning of ethnicity and culture, demands for economic integration, and the role of the state can also be discerned in the debates over the meaning of the November 2005 car burnings in French suburban areas (Lagrange and Oberti 2006). Were the young descendants of immigrants involved in these actions demonstrating for better jobs and integration into French society or asserting a separate Muslim identity? Most French observers believe it was the former, but these debates themselves are part of a contentious process of constructing identities.

The debates in France are further complicated by the French policy of not defining people in ethnic or religious categories in any official data or study. Individuals are counted as native or foreign-born, classified by citizenship status, and enumerated in occupational categories that can be used for the analysis of class. Since many of the young people involved in the disturbances are native French citizens, as well as children or grandchildren of immigrants, it is extremely difficult to ascertain their ethnicity and religion. Surnames characteristic of specific national origins and religious identities provide clues, as do addresses, since many minorities live in the housing projects in the urban periphery. The data, however, offer an uncertain basis for sociological analysis. Some observers believe that many participants were children of recent immigrants from African nations south of the Sahara, such as Cameroun and Guinea, and not from the Maghreb, since the more recent immigrants are particularly disadvantaged.

The analysis of disadvantage and collective action can be refined by the inclusion of gender differences as well as national origin. Young women of immigrant descent are often more at ease in the French school system and perform better academically than their male counterparts. Young men are more likely to be shunted into dead-end vocational tracks on the basis of stereotypes and actual performance. Some observers (e.g., Kakpo 2007) believe that attraction to fundamentalist Islamic groups among young men reflects discomfort with rapid changes in gender hierarchy and the hope that they can revalorize their status as men, because young women are more likely to succeed and young men to fail in the educational system. The fundamentalist movements appear to have goals and strategies that are rather different from the feelings behind the November 2005 disturbances.

Sexuality and the formation of identity. Sexuality offers another example for analyzing how difference can be converted into identity and collective action in many ways. Buechler (2000) argues that sexual difference (as well as gender and race) is a set of categories that are present in the social organization of society. But difference does not always manifest itself as a basis of self-identity and collective action, and not all individuals move from a nascent sense of identity to a collective identity to oppositional consciousness (for any type of category of difference).

The process becomes even more complex when the individuals involved hope to gain civil rights and eventually do away with discrimination and stigma; under these conditions, the heightening of difference and the move to identity politics is a "strategic essentialism"—a step toward emphasizing difference, not to bring about a permanent outcome of separatism but in hopes of eventually establishing inclusion and the end to dominance, that is, of lessening discrimination based on difference. Strategic essentialism thus enters into a dialog with queer theory (in the case of sexuality), a discourse of deconstructing fixed categories of sexual difference. This example of the interplay among identity politics, deconstruction of categories, and strategic essentialism is also elaborated by Mary Bernstein (2002) in the analysis of organizing among gays and lesbians in Vermont who found themselves simultaneously heightening sexuality as a basis of identity in order to mobilize support, striving to impact state policies and to gain civil rights (thus reducing the role of sexuality as a category of social organization), and seeking to deconstruct rigid fixed categories of sexuality.

*   *   *

These examples illustrate themes that characterize contemporary theories about identity and political action.

- Complex interlacing of status categories, such as race-ethnicity, gender, religion, sexuality, and national origin with class, resulting in linkages of class and status issues. The analysis goes well beyond the race-class-gender triad to recognize a multiplicity of status categories and the many possibilities for intersectionality.
- The decisive but inconsistent role of the state in defining status, constructing ethnicity and citizenship, and policing boundaries, as well as the consequent action of movements both with and against the state (Desai 2002; M. Bernstein 2002)

- The participation of collective actors and movements in constructing identities in a conflictual process so that there is no underlying community but rather multiple competing claims of community
- The increasing transnationalization of identity construction (Appadurai 1993)
- The delicate balance of three elements in these forms of collective action: strategic essentialism; the goal of integration, inclusion, and civil rights; and deconstruction of categories of dominance

Identity Construction: Association and Imagined Communities

A major contribution to constructionist explanations of identity and the creation of collectivities was made by a theorist who was not working on class-race-gender. Benedict Anderson's *Imagined Communities* (1983) shows how nationalism was not an automatic product of shared culture and experience, an obvious and easily recognized peoplehood, but a construction of literate elites. Anderson's analysis is congruent with the work of a wide spectrum of movement theorists who explored the construction of collective identities, including Sidney Tarrow (1998) on the historical role of print and cycles of movement activism.

The nation is not automatically given by a sense of peoplehood, common language, and shared history. These are not simple facts but constructed insights that are created and brought to public awareness by intellectuals whose literacy makes them take note of the shared language. The maps and schooling imposed by colonial authorities backfire, creating an oppositional consciousness of the colonized against the colonizers. While peasants and laborers may experience brutality and exploitation, they are less likely to abstract these encounters to imagine an oppressed nation. The imagined community is the creation of literate intellectuals in a broad sense—journalists, schoolteachers, clerks, and business owners. These strata constructed the lines of identity and action for anticolonial movements from the American Revolution in 1776 to the Vietnamese movement of independence that attained victory in 1975, as well as for central European movements of disengagement from the Soviet bloc that succeeded by 1989. In the years in between, the imagined community of the nation inspired activists in Latin America, central Europe, Asia, and Africa, generating several waves of nationalism, anticolonial movements, and the building of new nations. Anderson's theoretical contribution is the analysis of these major historical forces in terms of construction of shared texts and narratives, maps and history books; he also deconstructs nationalism as a natural basis of human action.

In a similar vein, Sidney Tarrow (1998) argued that print as a medium made modern movements and revolutions possible by the latter eighteenth century, beginning with the French and American revolutions. The use of print enabled activists to create oppositional networks across a large territory and to propagate a vision for society in explicit defiance of prevailing ideology. It enabled activists to package discontents beyond the local level. As in Anderson's analysis, literate elites became a key force in rallying the masses because they could disseminate stories across the entire territory and knew how to tell compellingly unifying ones.

The Role of the State in Movements and Identity Formation

The state is not only the target of reform or revolution but a vital player in collective action (Meyer, Whittier, and Robnett 2002).

The forms that social movements took in the late twentieth century and early twenty-first century stimulated new approaches in social movement theory, focused on the interplay of state policies, identity construction, and culture. The new *state-identity-culture* paradigm of movements and collective action has not displaced resource mobilization theories (and related theories based on rational choice and organizational analysis), the dominant paradigm from the late 1960s into the 1980s, but it has made the perspective deeper and more complex. State policies help to create or dissipate identities that might lead to collective action. Sometimes the effects of these policies are unintended, as Jo Freeman (1982) showed in her pioneering analysis of how initiatives of the US federal government contributed to second-wave feminism and a renewed interest in women's movements in the 1960s. States and movements may play elaborate games with each other, with states and established political parties attempting to co-opt movement activists, while activists seek to influence state policies and create favorable environments for recruitment, growth, and influence. Movements not only try to influence policy but can use policies as recruiting tools. Oppositional consciousness is a construct, not an automatic response to conditions (Mansbridge and Morris 2001). Passage of new legislation produces situations in which demands are legitimated, and organization for fulfilling these demands can be a rallying point for recruitment, mobilization, and identity construction. For example, Desai (2002) examined the complex relationship between the Indian state and women's movements, which both challenged government and relied on it for support and implementation of reforms.

The theoretical contributions being made by North American movement theorists are exemplified by the work of Meyer, Whittier, and Robnett (2002) and their collaborators, who are developing an analysis of linkages among cultures, identities, and states. States, on the one hand, can foster or discourage the formation of certain identities. A state that recognizes gay marriages or same-sex civil unions contributes to the formation of gay identities and communities. Movements can also pressure states and shift policies.

Cultures, Frames, and Ideologies in the Construction of Identity

Cultures support the development of certain identities and stifle others. Yet a single set of discourses—for instance, a single sacred text—can have multiple interpretations, as Rhys Williams (2002) shows in an analysis of two readings of the Bible: the beloved-community interpretation of the civil rights movement and liberal theologians in contrast to the conservative family-values reading. This analysis draws on postmodern approaches to texts and the concept of reader response, as well as Stuart Hall's work on decoding. Collective action establishes identity rather than simply drawing on existing, relatively fixed identities. Combined with interest in the unfolding of movements in time, event analysis, and the concept of the hinge (a key decision point for movement activists), the approach has added more dynamic elements to social movement theory.

Refreshing the Mainstream

A couple of additional examples help us to understand how elements of a conflict constructionist paradigm can be harmoniously introduced into the existing paradigm, almost by an unconscious seepage of these ideas into the sociological mainstream rather than by explicit adoption.

Putting "Movement" Back in Social Movement Theory: The Dynamics of Contention

At the beginning of the twenty-first century, McAdam, Tarrow, and Tilly (2001/2003), three leading theorists in the social movement and collective action field, joined forces to develop an analysis of contentious politics, building on their earlier work on episodes of contention. The new model accomplished a number of objectives. One was to group social movements together with a wide range of phe-nomena—revolutions, industrial conflict, war, interest group politics, nationalism, and democratization. They suggested that separating social movements and other noninstitutionalized contention from institutionalized forms creates an artificial boundary between related forms of action. In their view, social movements have a "complex relationship" to institutionalized politics (2001/2003, 6). Their preference was to introduce a different line of demarcation among these forms of action—the contained and the transgressive. In this argument we can discern a position similar to Bourdieu's concept of the political field as a wide and fluid stream of actions (although Bourdieu makes no appearance in their book).

The emphasis on fluidity as a necessary counterpoint to structural analysis is also apparent in the central theme of the book: the need to examine movement in action, in episodes and trajectories of contention. Almost appearing to borrow ideas from chaos theory, McAdam, Tarrow, and Tilly point out that to understand outcomes one must look at initial conditions, combinations of forces, and sequences of actions and counteractions. They contend that the existing repertoire of concepts in social movement theory (political opportunity structure, mobilization structures of social movement organizations and networks, collective action frames, and repertoires of contention) is too static to encompass what is most important about movements and other contentious forms of politics—their trajectories, the movement toward an outcome with its multiple determinations and its unpredictability in terms of the initial structural and cultural settings. In this analysis we see the loosening of the structural framework; this loosening of structural concepts is a hallmark of the conflict constructionist paradigm.

Finally, the volume introduces the concept of the constitution of actors through the establishment of identities during the unfolding of the episode. Contention itself contributes to polarization, and brokers (interested organizations and stakeholders) can take actions and put forth threat-and-opportunity interpretations in order to amplify polarization. In this process the authors see category formation as a key element of identity constitution and polarization. In other words, as contention becomes polarized, individuals are induced to pick from their multiple possible identities and define themselves in terms of the polarized categories—for example, as "Muslims" and "Christians" in Maluku, Indonesia; "Hutu" and "Tutsi" in Rwanda; and "aristocrats" and "the people" in revolutionary France.

In this contribution to social movement theory and to political sociology broadly speaking (because the authors do not want their analysis limited to social movements), we can see a parallel development of many of the features visible in conflict constructionism—fluidity rather than structure (or in addition to structure), attention to category and identity formation, and a playing with scale in the examination of the links between local contention and larger national and geopolitical contention and outcomes. The authors do not refer to a paradigm of conflict constructionism (nor do they cite its innovators), but one could argue that a parallel drift or seepage of ideas is at work here, producing a similar and converging attention to fluidity, category construction, and macro/micro (and meso) linkages.

Mayer Zald's Work on Innovations in Institutions, Organizations, and Fields

Another recent example of the harmonious way political sociology and the sociology of social movements are absorbing elements of conflict constructionism is Mayer Zald's new work on social movements in organizations and institutional settings. He examines three social innovations: the hospice movement, the spread of nouvelle cuisine in French restaurant cooking, and the growing attraction of alternative dispute resolution in the judicial context. Zald describes his theory of movement-related social change in institutional settings as "a marriage between institutional theory and social movement theory" (2009, 1), but this is really a ménage à trois because Zald brings in Bourdieu's field theory and the concept of habitus to understand how habitus and institutional beliefs and practices are changed in specific contexts. Movements create new collective identities and can thereby change organizations. He observes the role of the state and social-control agents in these processes; analysis of the state bridges existing political opportunity structure theories and conflict constructionist interest in the role of the state. Zald's analysis of these three markedly different innovations—hospices, nouvelle cuisine, and dispute resolution—reveals underlying similarities in the process of change and illustrates openness to blending new paradigm elements (fields, identities, habitus) with existing theories of institutional and organizational behavior, opportunity structures, and resource mobilization.

Conclusion

Political sociology and the study of collective action are areas of intense activity and paradigm change. Scholars have opened the analysis of institutions, organizations, state apparatuses, and the demographic bases of political attitudes and activism—terms that once denoted relatively stable structures—and are incorporating fluid concepts such as political field, identity construction, and state practices. Bourdieu's concept of the political field (and all of its related terms) is of great importance, and Foucault's *governmentality* is influential for understanding the control and management of formally democratic market societies. Current approaches link the role of the state to culture, identity formation, and processes in civil society. Identity formation, polarized identities, the constitution of actors, the framing of threats and opportunities, and the fluidity of the entire field of political sociology and collective action all are contemporary concepts that attest to convergence with the ideas of conflict construction, if not an explicit adoption of the paradigm. While there is no dominant paradigm, these new perspectives and the refreshed Weberian and Marxist legacies on which they draw have indirectly been made at least somewhat compatible with each other. As in many other fields, quantitative analysis (e.g., event analysis of hundreds of episodes of contention) has made an appearance, but it has not displaced the more historically contextualized and theoretical perspectives.

External changes have had a strong role in theoretical change. An ambiguous return to democracy in a wide range of formerly repressive regimes, the waning of class-based movements despite enormous social inequalities, the rise of religious movements, and the emergence of terrorist networks have been an impetus to reconceptualizing relationships between state and civil society as well as links among states, movements, and identity construction.

As a whole, the field has moved forward gradually and harmoniously, as scholars refresh their approaches with new concepts and expand mainstream paradigms by including elements of the conflict constructionist paradigm.

Chapter Nine

Urban Sociology and Spatial Analysis

Paradigms in Coexistence

Do you live in a city, suburb, small town, or rural area? Where did your parents and grandparents live, and how would you explain their migrations and changes in residence? If your family has lived in cities for many generations, how have these cities changed? Over half of the world's population now lives in cities and metropolitan areas. Why have people moved to cities, and who are the new city dwellers? Some cities and city neighborhoods are exciting, wonderful, enjoyable places to live; others are nightmarish places of poverty, crime, unemployment, and ethnic violence. What accounts for the differences? How are city dwellers responding to the challenges of city growth, disparities in well-being, and environmental problems?

Urban sociology and the analysis of space is an intensely active area experiencing a powerful impetus from external changes on a global scale. Yet these changes have not brought about a complete paradigm shift to conflict constructionism. Elements of the new paradigm certainly have been incorporated into urban sociology, but previous traditions of understanding city form and city life persist. Changes in the urban landscape are dramatic but not at the level of an explosion, like the emergence of new media and global networks; for this reason, urban sociology itself has not had to create an entirely new set of theories.

Overview

- Long-standing themes of inequalities in cities, the patterning of ethnic diversity, and the city as the cosmopolitan seat of the money economy all persist but are reinterpreted to match new situations of globalization and neoliberal economies.
- Dramatic external developments include the urbanization of half the planet's population, the key role of cities in the globalization of neoliberalism and financial services, the transformation of cities into nodes in global flows, the downs and ups of the central city, the transformation of suburban and peripheral areas, the formation of *megacities,* changing ethnic compositions, the rise of cities as entertainment machines, severe environmental problems, and a tendency toward a *bowling-pin or hourglass shape of income distribution* in *global cities.*
- The state is seen as a major player in these transformations, and variation in government policies is one reason for variation among societies in the spatial distribution of activities and populations.

In this chapter we see that urban sociology is an area in which the insights of nineteenth- and early-twentieth-century social theorists continue to be of value. But the insights of classical sociologists and their perspectives on cities must be modified to encompass new urban economic functions, class structures, and spatial distributions of people and activities. Scholars use many paradigms to understand these complicated trends. These paradigms are linked but not fused into a single mainstream.

Trajectory

Classical Theories of the Urban

Urban sociology and *spatial analysis* have formed an important area of sociology since its nineteenth-century origins, so our discussion begins at that point. Cities are a long-standing feature of the human landscape; the first cities emerged in Egypt and Asia more than 4,000 years ago. But urbanization accelerated with the Industrial Revolution, and rapidly growing proportions of the world's population became city dwellers in the nineteenth century. During the first years of the Industrial Revolution, people were drawn to industrial enterprises originally located in small towns or even in the countryside in England, northern Europe, and North America. Industrial districts, with their "dark Satanic mills" (a line in a poem by William Blake, often interpreted as a reference to factories) became the nucleus of new industrial cities. Industries were also launched within older cities, in centers of government and culture such as London, Paris, and Tokyo, so that these world cities also took on an industrial character, even if manufacturing was not their main function. From the outset, the sociology of cities has been linked to the analysis of economic and technological change.

Analysis of Urban Class Structure: One Thread of the Marxist Tradition

Sociologists began to study urban life and the distribution of people and activities in the dense new city spaces. Friedrich Engels, Karl Marx's coauthor, produced a landmark study, *The Condition of the Working Class in England* (1968), which contains a chapter about the "Great Towns," such as London, Glasgow, Liverpool, and Manchester. He devotes many pages to careful observations of living conditions in Manchester, one of the new factory towns. He details the dreadful condition of buildings, unhealthy sanitary conditions worsened by flooding along the river, and the particularly miserable living arrangements of Irish immigrants, the most disadvantaged segment of the working class. Engels's writing was theoretically informed, constituting part of the general Marxist analysis of the condition of the proletariat. Other nineteenth-century writers, such as Henry Mayhew and Charles Booth, also wrote vivid accounts of the London poor and conditions of life in the great English capital, but their work was less integrated into an overall theoretical and political perspective.

The City as a Center of Finance, Commerce, and Consumption

At the end of the nineteenth century, Georg Simmel used the dynamic city of Berlin as the centerpiece of his perspective on the metropolis and mental life. Like the Marxists, he viewed the metropolis as the seat of the capitalist money economy, and he was particularly fascinated by the outlook and habits of mind that accompanied life in a gigantic center of capitalism. He identified a number of traits that accompany urban life and are closely connected to capitalism and the division of labor as well, such as a blasé attitude, an effort to screen out the dizzying sensations of the streets, rational calculation, a quantified turn of mind related to money and the focus on exchange value, punctuality, freedom from small-town constraints, and the desire to stand out and define oneself quickly while protecting and enjoying one's anonymity. Small-town dwellers care about each other—perhaps they often care too much! City dwellers feel themselves to be freer, even though this freedom comes at the price of uncaring coldness toward others. All of the classical theorists were interested in this mentality: Marx and Engels saw it as part of capitalism, Max Weber associated it with the general historical trend of disenchantment and the growing power of instrumental reason, and Emile Durkheim saw it as having both a positive side (more individuation and a less-constraining, less-primitive collective consciousness) and a negative side (growing anomie and isolation). Of the classical theorists, Simmel was the most explicitly concerned with linking these new mentalities to a specific environment, to the space of the great metropolis.

Simmel's approach to the city was reiterated by Walter Benjamin, the great theorist of modern media and culture who wrote in the 1920s and 1930s. One of

Benjamin's projects, the *Arcades Project,* sought to gain an understanding of modern culture through a reflection on the Parisian arcades (Buck-Morss 1989; Benjamin 2002). These arcades, or passages, were structures of nineteenth-century Paris that offered a startling preview of the modern shopping mall. Many of them are still visible. They are long passageways that run through the interior of a city block and eerily combine interior and exterior features. They were built of glass and iron; their light is derived from both overhead skylights and interior lamps. Shops and display windows open into the passageway as if it were a street. Outdoor cafes and restaurants are located in the passageway. It is both a private and a public place. Strongly influenced by the Napoleonic conquest of Egypt and European colonial expansion, the designers of the passageways often used orientalist elements and decorations, referencing the souks and covered passageways of Middle Eastern bazaars. Both rich and poor flocked to the passageways, the rich to buy luxury goods, the poor to gape at them longingly. For Benjamin, the arcades represented the onset of consumer capitalism, a mutation of capitalism away from its ascetic productionist origins toward a new mentality of pleasure in acquiring commodities, in harnessing dreams of happiness to the purchase of objects.

These insights were affirmed by Siegfried Kracauer, another Marxist associated with the Frankfurt School, who emphasized the excitement and diversity of street life and its close association with shopping and commodification, including the commercialization of sex: "All classes of the population received a common and uniform education in the streets ... their real education" (quoted in E. Wilson 1992, 95). The streets and cafes of large European cities were among the first environments in which women—and not only prostitutes—could mingle fairly freely with men and move about on their own.

Understanding these early-twentieth-century perspectives on the city is essential for understanding contemporary perspectives; the earlier work already broaches themes that have again become central in postmodern and contemporary Marxist theories, such as the role of cities in culture and consumption rather than production.

The Chicago School and Human Ecology

The *Chicago School* of the 1920s to 1930s was also strongly interested in city life but backed off from some of the far-reaching conclusions of Simmel, Benjamin, and the Marxists about the role of cities in advanced capitalist societies. In the North American context, they saw the city as a mosaic of immigrant communities, of ethnic enclaves in which immigrants attempted to recreate the village life of southern and eastern Europe while employed in industries. African Americans were compelled to create segregated communities when they arrived in the "great migration" from the South to the industrial centers of the North. The modern city grew out of the clash of many cultures and village lifeways with the imperatives of modern industry, the capitalist economy, and the political and cultural dominance of white Anglo-Saxon Protestant elites. The Chicago School saw a fragmented city, a diversity of cultures and lifestyles, and a mosaic of changing neighborhoods.

The Chicago School sociologists observed spatial distributions, and in addition to their studies of neighborhoods, they developed an overall theory of urban structure—the *concentric zone theory* (Park and Burgess 1925). Based on observations of Chicago and of market-driven urban development in North America generally, they created a model of growth and inequalities in cities. In this model the central business district, or downtown, is ringed by a *zone of transition,* a sketchy zone of light industry, warehouses, brothels, bars, and cheap rooming houses, then farther out by districts of tenements in which workers live. The farther from the center the residential areas are located, the newer and more attractive the housing and the more affluent the residents. The central city is encircled by bedroom communities of beautiful single-family homes with wealthy residents, from which men commute to the central city to their jobs as managers and entrepreneurs.

In truth, this concentric zone pattern did not precisely describe Chicago, let alone other cities. Chicago, in fact, had (and continues to have) a broad sectoral or wedge pattern of development, in which heavy industry such as steel mills and meatpacking moved southward in the city, while the north shore of Lake Michigan attracted the finest housing and the most affluent residents. The Black Belt, the ghettoized African American community, was confined along a southward axis, and with less deliberate exclusion, so were many European working-class ethnic communities.

North American development was heavily driven by the *real estate market* and the cultural value placed on new housing, which led to devalorization of the inner city. In other countries, elites were more attached to the historical centers of cities, and working-class housing tended to be built in the outskirts. In Paris and many other European cities, peripheral zones were areas where workers and poor people lived. There too, city patterns were in reality often more sectoral than concentric. For instance, Paris had its "red belt"—working-class districts that extended north and east from the city center into the suburbs, where voters consistently supported the Communist Party.

Well into the mid-twentieth century, urban sociology continued to be centered on a *human ecology* approach that tracked the spatial distribution of activities such as industry, retailing, residential use, and so on, and that mapped the distribution of cultures and classes.

The Period of Conflict Theories: The City as Growth Machine

Building on radical work of the earlier part of the twentieth century, especially the Lynds' Middletown studies of social class in Muncie, Indiana, urban sociologists in the heyday of conflict theory emphasized inequality, power, and political struggles in US cities (as well as European ones). They were drawing on these radical (and often Marxist) approaches as well as responding to a host of new realities of city life: white flight into the suburbs (which added a racialized twist to the process of outward movement already noted by Robert Park and Ernest Burgess), urban renewal and urban development, expressway construction through the heart of central-city neighborhoods, and siting of public housing projects. These trends became the focal points of studies of power elites, decision-making processes, and urban political contention between neighborhoods and elites. As the processes themselves unfolded and the paradigm grew, the theorists often wrote in terms of an urban growth machine formed by business elites and their allies in state, federal, and local government. They dissected the class and racial impact of these policies. Among examples of this conflict-oriented body of theoretical and empirical work, one can mention John Mollenkopf's *The Contested City* (1983), writing by William Domhoff and John Logan, and Harvey Molotch's introduction of the term *city as growth machine.* Insofar as these growth coalitions were efforts to deal with the economic base of postindustrial cities, political economy was the central theme of the analysis.

Contemporary Perspectives

Much of this original structure of the field remains, but the contents have shifted dramatically with globalization, immigration, *deindustrialization,* and the *revalorization of the inner city* in a process some refer to as the *revanchist city* (N. Smith 1996). Furthermore, urbanization is taking place very rapidly in regions of the globe that have not passed through an industrial revolution, giving rise to huge agglomerations without an industrial base in regions such as Africa and parts of Latin America and South and West Asia.

So the new urban theories (proposed by social geographers as well as sociologists) encompass the changing distribution of activities and social inequalities in urban regions, the impact of immigration, *deindustrialization* of Western economies (and the new industrialization of economies in East and Southeast Asia), globalization, and volatile *real estate markets.* A few examples show the major themes of this new work.

The LA School and Edward Soja: Postmodern Urbanization and the Six Restructurings of Los Angeles

The Park and Burgess concentric zone model of urban form not only reflected the unique characteristics of Chicago but claimed to represent a general pattern of urban form of industrial cities. As cities deindustrialized or developed around economic activities that were increasingly advanced industrial or postindustrial, their form did not conform to the concentric zone model. As early as 1945, C. D. Harris and E. Ullman proposed a *multiple-nuclei model* as closer to the reality of most cities. The clearest challenge came from the *LA School,* which included in its ranks not only sociologists but geographers and architects (Dear 2002; Soja 1996).

The LA School posited a sharp contrast between the Chicago and LA models. The Chicago model was modernist in both its conceptualization and the underlying economic structure of the Chicago metropolitan region. Early industrial development, based on large-scale manufacturing, set in motion the unfolding of the concentric zone pattern and the emergence of a coherent regional system. The model was not only based on the empirical observation of modernist industrial growth but modernist in its underlying intellectual premises—that trends are generally linear, that individual choices in markets and political structures produce social patterns, and that one can write of coherent systems. The LA School obviously observed a markedly different empirical situation in the LA area with its weak downtown and suburbanization without a center. But it also suggested that the premises of the Chicago paradigm—not merely its empirical conclusions—were subject to dispute. The scholars of the LA School saw urban change as processes in a "random field of opportunities" rather than as one systemic and linear process of industrial growth and market responses (Dear 2002). Whereas the Chicago School had generally seen industry—production—as the driving force of change, the LA School theorists were intrigued by the effects of consumption; they picked up this thread from the early-twentieth-century theorists of the city as a consumption and entertainment venue. And like these earlier theorists, they emphasized the gap between the rich and the poor rather than the more continuous class spectrum that figured in the analysis of the industrial city. The LA School proposed a centerless and fragmented urbanism, driven not by industry (though that had not disappeared from the city) but by consumption and other new or postmodern economic activities.

The work of Edward Soja provides an excellent example of the contributions of the LA School. It is important to note that the LA School is not merely a call to think about a larger range of urban forms than posited by the Chicago School; on the contrary, it represents a shift in the understanding of cultural and social forces associated with the emergence of new urban geographies. The paradigm shift may help us understand not only what is happening in Los Angeles (and Chicago) but also in São Paulo and Rio de Janeiro, Lagos and Dubai, Hong Kong and the Pearl River Delta, and the cities of the US-Mexican border.

Soja's (1996) powerful contribution to the new urban theory is his six *geographies of urban restructuring,* based on the transformation of Los Angeles from 1965 to 1992 but in large measure visible in most North American cities and many cities throughout the formerly industrialized world. Soja chooses as his starting and ending dates two riots that expressed the anger of African Americans at their treatment in the city: the 1968 Watts riot and the riot that took place after the beating of Rodney King by Los Angeles Police Department officers. Although the exclusion of African Americans from the life of the city persisted throughout the period, the city they were excluded from had substantially changed.

Soja identifies the following six restructurings as paradigmatic of urban change throughout the world in the neoliberal era:

- A shift in the economic base from large-scale unionized industries to flexible production; high-tech and information-based enterprises; low-skill, labor-intensive small enterprises; and an expanded entertainment industry and *FIRE sector* (financial services, insurance, and real estate)
- The globalization of LA, which includes transnational flows of capital and people. Over one-third of Los Angeles County's residents are foreign-born,

immigrants from a myriad of countries who include exploited proletarians as well as successful entrepreneurs and professionals.

- The transformation of urban spatial form producing suburbs with industries, urban problems, ethnic diversity, and in some instances racial isolation, as well as the formation of edge cities (outlying areas of retail, commercial, and financial activity) and satellite cities
- A complicated transformation of urban class structure and social inequality tending toward a bowling-pin configuration, with a small top level of professionals, managers, and entrepreneurs; a larger, more rapidly growing lower tier of low-wage workers in flexible production and personal service; and a growing group of homeless people, chronically unemployed, and superexploited "new slaves" in household service (Soja 1996, 133); although the structure is extensively racialized, with white people in the upper tier and people of color in the lower tier, in a somewhat contradictory trend ethnic groups are increasingly spread out across the class spectrum.
- The formation of a *carceral city,* a term derived from Michel Foucault and also utilized by Mike Davis (1992) that refers to efforts to contain and control the "dangerous classes" produced at the bottom of the neoliberal economy; these efforts include a wide range of practices, from erection of gated communities to sweeps to remove the homeless from public spaces, as well as policies of mass incarceration that take the place of social services.
- The transformation of the *urban imaginary* through development of a public relations city, a city of images, tourist attractions, entertainment, real estate booms, and swindles

Soja uses the term *postmodern urbanization* to describe the overall transformation of Los Angeles. His six restructurings offer a broad sweep of changes, and Soja implies that LA is a preview of the future of many cities, a template for postmodern urban life that we will see replicated throughout the developed world and in many developing nations as well. Other theorists focus on specific elements of this overall transformation.

Saskia Sassen: Global Cities and Their Emerging Bowling-Pin Class Structure

Saskia Sassen (2000, 2001) is examining how global cities emerged and what form they are taking. While large world cities such as Paris, London, Tokyo, and New York have been around for a long time, the global city is a new formation linked to the changing economy and global flows of people, capital, goods, media, information, and ideas. Although globalization is a new phenomenon, concepts from theorists throughout this volume may provide insights into what is happening in cities. Sassen's work is in conversation with the ideas of Marx and Engels, world-systems theories proposed by Immanuel Wallerstein, and the general project of classical theory to explore and understand irreversible transformations in societies.

In Sassen's perspective, large inequalities persist in the global system, but they are no longer as geographically based as they were during earlier phases of capitalism, when the core, semiperiphery, and periphery occupied distinct zones of the planet. Now the local and the global are intertwined in urban regions. Global cities are increasingly disconnected from their own *hinterlands*. Within the global city, there are strata of wealth and power as well as disadvantaged and exploited populations, many of them migrants or immigrants. Sassen's exploration of city form can be linked to David Harvey's (2007) analysis of neoliberalism as a global economic transformation because the deregulation of transnational markets, especially capital markets, has accelerated the formation of global cities.

Global cities are a place where inequalities become visible, including those between the global North and South; between cities and their national hinterlands; and between the advantaged and the disadvantaged within the city (Friedman 2002). Global cities are the seat of the money economy (to use Simmel's phrase), financial services, advanced corporate services such as accounting and marketing, legal services, research and development, higher education, state-of-the art health care, and entertainment, tourism, and cultural production.

Global and globalizing cities are nodes of *global communication and transportation networks,* and so they are often detached from their hinterlands, which remain poorer, culturally isolated, and even difficult to reach. Elites are more in touch with their counterparts in other global cities than they are with conationals in the rural hinterland (Castells 1996; Reich 1991).

Within global cities, there are strong tendencies toward highly unequal social structures, often described as "hourglass" or "bowling-pin" configurations. Glitzy, lucrative advanced corporate services and other cutting-edge globalized economic activities require the labor of large numbers of low-wage workers. For state-of-the-art hospitals there are hospital orderlies, for retail malls there are sweatshop garment workers, and for corporate towers there are cafeteria workers, janitors, and bicycle messengers. When the 9/11 terrorists struck the Twin Towers, they killed not only global financiers but busboys and secretaries. The lower occupations of the hourglass are disproportionately filled by immigrants, often undocumented, and people who are seen as ethnically or racially distinct from the higher strata. Many of the lowest-paid workers are women. Engels had already noted in his study of Manchester, one of the major industrial cities of England, that Irish immigrants lived in the harshest conditions, in the most exploited jobs and squalid housing. As in the early period of capitalism, ethnicity and class position are linked, but the links are complex, and many immigrants are very successful as entrepreneurs or professionals.

Although Sassen focuses mostly on immigrants as a source of low-paid labor globally, other processes also contribute to a growing lower tier in many of the world's cities. Due to *deindustrialization* in some large cities in formerly industrial regions, the children of factory workers in the sector of large industry face unemployment and downward mobility unless they have the cultural and financial capital to attain a university degree (Wilson 1997).

Also, in many large cities in economically developing regions, the numbers of the poor are growing rapidly because people are leaving rural areas and even neighboring countries where they can no longer make a living. Many of the planet's fastest-growing cities are huge urban agglomerations in poor countries, such as Dacca, Bangladesh, and Lagos, Nigeria. Social critic Mike Davis (2004) uses the term "planet of slums" to describe this form of urban growth with its accompanying absolute poverty and harsh living conditions.

Migrants and immigrants, as well as those displaced from industry, often end up in the informal sector, which includes both legitimate microenterprises and illegal activities. Sassen claims that the growth of the informal sector is a characteristic of global cities and a product of their polarized or dual social structure.

Sassen notes that the disadvantaged are not only a definite presence in global cities but a political force, forming a new global civil society as they make claims for a better life. Signs of this new civil society can be observed in many actions and events, such as the alternative globalization movement; claims for economic integration made by young people burning cars in housing projects in the peripheries of French cities; protests against toxic-waste dumping in Abidjan, Ivory Coast, and other communities threatened by pollution and environmental degradation; and mass demonstrations in US cities against criminalization of illegal immigration. These are only a few instances of the type of civic action Sassen believes might signal a new global civil society taking shape, a less violent and more progressive alternative to terrorism as a form of collective action against the oppressive aspects of globalization. But the dispossessed in global cities face great economic and political obstacles in their struggle for citizenship in the fullest sense of the term.

Manuel Castells: Megacities and Global Flows

In his sweeping three-volume study of the emerging society of the information age, Manuel Castells (1996) gives special attention to new urban spatial forms, especially the megacity. The megacity is a huge agglomeration, more properly thought of as a special type of region than as a city in any historical or conventional sense. These megacities cover a lot of territory, include tens of millions of people, contain specialized subregions, and are key nodes of the global economy. As Castells traces out the flows that lace together the global economy in the information age, he gives special attention to the cities where the flows come together in the form of financial centers; transportation nodes of airports, rail systems, and port facilities; and centers of research, entertainment, and culture.

Castells's example of a megacity is the Pearl River Delta agglomeration, which encompasses a host of well-known cities such as Hong Kong, Macau, and Guangzhou (Canton), as well as small towns and port facilities in the delta. There are five airports and five new container port facilities within this urbanized region. Open space and farming communities are also located there. These linked cities, communities, and industrial and port facilities together have a population of 40 to 50 million. Similar configurations can be seen in the New York City area, the agglomeration in Southern California that extends from the Mexican border to Santa Barbara, and the Kansai region of Japan with its vast port and industrial facilities, hypermodern airport, green spaces, bustling urban node of Osaka, and destinations of cultural, religious, and tourist importance such as Nara and Kyoto.

Some of these agglomerations, especially those in less developed countries, are disconnected from their own hinterlands yet connected to the global economy. Megacities contain segregation and segmentation within the region—for example, communities of workers in manufacturing and port facilities, rural zones, urban and suburban slum communities, and environmentally hazardous sites, as well as playgrounds of the wealthy.

Mike Davis: The Carceral City and the Planet of Slums

One of Mike Davis's best-known works, *City of Quartz* (1992), describes the political and policy decisions in Los Angeles that contributed to the restructurings observed by Soja. In the vein of Marxist theory, Davis argues that political and business interests reshaped the downtown, displaced manufacturing, attracted international capital, and organized a ferocious police presence that treated communities of color like occupied territories. This process preceded the 1992 riot, precipitated by police brutality, and then continued to move forward at an even faster pace thereafter (a period not covered in his book but in later writing). The result is a city in which the African American working class is unemployed and marginalized, Latinos are exploited as workers, ethnic groups are divided from one another socially and spatially, and the overall pattern is one of market-driven development with little attention to disparities or the general quality of life. Davis's analysis links to the new paradigm in the understanding of difference and dominance, as well as to approaches to the study of deviance, crime, and punishment.

More recently Davis published "Planet of Slums" (2004), a devastating summary of the atrocious living conditions in which a large proportion of humanity lives. Half the globe's population is now urban, and in developing and less developed nations—the former Third World—their living conditions are often wretched. Davis argues that structural adjustment programs—policies imposed by the World Bank and International Monetary Fund on debtor nations—have hastened a rural exodus. Conditions for landless rural workers and peasants with very small farms have always been hard, but in recent years prices for their commodities dropped, and government subsidies were eliminated. In some countries, these economic pressures were exacerbated by regional conflict and ethnic cleansing that forced hundreds of thousands to become refugees. As streams of impoverished people moved from the countryside to cities in the Third World, housing, sanitation, and employment could not keep up with need. Consequently, cities such as Dacca (Bangladesh), Lagos (Nigeria), Djakarta (Indonesia), Nairobi (Kenya), and Kinshasa (Congo) have high densities and many neighborhoods of shantytowns with high infant-mortality rates, problems with diseases and environmental hazards, and high rates of organized crime. Governments are unable or unwilling to provide even minimal social services, sanitation and utilities, education, and health care.

Theorists of Segregation and Exclusion

Urban sociologists have long been interested in the characteristics and experiences of the excluded, segregated, and marginalized, beginning with Engels's observations of the conditions of Irish immigrants living in filthy, flood-prone cellars along the Irk River. The intertwined stratification systems of class and ethnoracial status were already clearly visible in the spatial distribution and experiences of the residents of England's new industrial capitalist cities. Studies of Chicago's Black Belt also emphasized segregation and racial isolation.

As movements of national liberation stirred in European colonies after World War II, Frantz Fanon (1965) pointed to the segregated character of the new cities of these regions. Patterns of segregation justified by ideologies of racism appeared in colonial areas where the open, clean, spacious city of the settlers contrasted with the cities of the natives—ancient, mazelike cities in Asia and North Africa and shantytowns and townships throughout the colonized world, characterized as "teeming" or "warren-like." In apartheid South Africa displacement of nonwhites from central locations was an assiduously implemented state policy, like the destruction and rebuilding of Jewish neighborhoods during the Nazi period, most notably in Berlin (Jaskot 2000).

Ultimately colonialism triggered a flow of immigrants from the colonies, ex-colonies, and regions of dependent development to the "motherland" in search of better wages and opportunities for their children. They streamed from the Maghreb and West Africa into Paris, from South Asia and the Caribbean into London and other English cities, and from Puerto Rico, the Dominican Republic, Mexico, and Central America into US cities. In the 1950s and 1960s, at the outset of this immigration flow, there were still many opportunities in industry for immigrants. As the economies of the developed nations deindustrialized and shifted to a new economic base, these jobs in manufacturing declined as a proportion of the labor force and were replaced in smaller numbers by two diverging types of employment: high-end jobs that required postsecondary education and poorly paid jobs in personal services and small-scale factories. Immigrants were able to obtain high-end jobs, but many ended up in the precarious low-wage tier so that both the immigrant and native populations were split into an hourglass class structure, further complicating both class and identity politics.

These changing occupational, class, and ethnoracial systems of inequality were reflected in the spatial distribution of people in metropolitan areas in part because the lower incomes of minorities allowed them fewer options in housing markets and in part because racism hemmed them into ethnic neighborhoods. The patterns differed somewhat in the United States and Europe. In the United States, immigrants generally fared better than African Americans, who were still subjected to hypersegregation, so clearly documented by Douglas Massey and Mary Denton

(1993) in the 1980s and 1990s, reconfirmed by John Iceland and Rima Wilkes (2006) in 2004 and 2005, and cited by Janet Abu-Lughod (2000) as a major barrier to Chicago's potential as a global city (also see Garner, Hancock, and Kim 2007; Sampson 2011). In Europe, it was primarily the immigrants and their children who found themselves excluded from jobs, good schools, and housing opportunities.

Loïc Wacquant's (2005, 2007) analysis of *segregation and exclusion* in Paris and Chicago sorts out the similarities and differences in the two societies, and this comparative approach leads to a theoretical grounding of the empirical observations. Wacquant (a student of Pierre Bourdieu) is able to use cultural difference to explain variation because the two countries have markedly different ideas about race, citizenship, and mobility; he can also point to the role of public policy and the state in amplifying or reducing exclusion. On the one hand, Wacquant finds many similarities in the situation of African Americans in the United States and the second generation of Maghrebiens and West Africans in Paris: confinement in deteriorating public housing and decaying neighborhoods, increased hopelessness about employment, exclusion from job markets, problems in obtaining a quality education, a profound sense of stigma, and a consequent "social atomism, community 'disorganization' and cultural anomie" (2005, 151). But he concludes that there are also major differences and rejects the term "ghetto" as a description of these neighborhoods and peripheral areas (*banlieues*) in France. Racism and hypersegregation in the United States became an enduring social reality with deep historical roots; they were reinforced by public policies that are not evident in France. Most importantly, the French ideology of egalitarian citizenship legitimates the demands of young minorities for inclusion while American ideologies of racism and individualism work against African Americans who demand opportunities available to other citizens. Although there is a certain degree of convergence in the two countries, ultimately they remain far apart in the prospects for residential, economic, and cultural inclusion. This analysis is reiterated in Hugues Lagrange and Marco Oberti's (2006) study of the November 2005 car burnings and riots in the peripheral communities of French cities; the authors conclude that these disturbances were not a manifestation of a separatist ethnic and Muslim religious identity but a call for inclusion in the structures of job markets, education, and housing.

Aggressive Gentrification and the Revanchist City: The Revalorization of Central Cities

Historically exclusion and segregation of minorities and poor people meant their confinement in central areas of the city, especially near the sketchy zone of transition identified by Chicago School sociologists in North American cities and visible in parts of European cities as well. But this distribution changed by the end of the twentieth century. In Europe, elite preferences for central-city living had already produced projects in the nineteenth and early twentieth centuries to clear out the poor and minorities and force them into peripheral areas. For example, in Paris and Edinburgh, nineteenth-century planners and developers moved poor people out of their "unsanitary, unhygenic, and teeming warren-like neighborhoods" in the old parts of the city, razed the tenements, and built modern boulevards and apartment buildings for the middle class. In Italy a similar process took place during the Fascist regime of the 1920s and 1930s, when historic central-city neighborhoods of the urban poor in Rome and Turin were leveled to make room for large boulevards, public buildings, and splendid shopping areas such as Turin's Via Roma. In Nazi-era Berlin, architect Albert Speer created a plan for public buildings to replace a Jewish neighborhood once its residents were deported to concentration camps.

The end of the twentieth century and the beginning of the twenty-first saw a new wave of aggressive *gentrification* of central cities. Neil Smith (1996) coined the term "revanchist city," and the process became visible in many cities throughout the world. Older historic areas near city centers were revalorized in booming real estate markets. Their buildings were in some cases restored and in other cases simply razed to make way for new construction. The wrecker's ball hit not only old dilapidated buildings but also public housing projects built during the period of embedded liberalism (aka "the welfare state") that preceded neoliberal policies. Chicago provides an excellent example of aggressive gentrification. The large, deteriorated public housing projects were torn down and their predominantly African American residents thrown into a private housing market that offers little *affordable housing* (Venkatesh 2002). The federal government is cutting back on housing vouchers that subsidize the rents of lower-income city people, so the displaced public housing residents can expect little support as they search for new homes. Many families are moving into older housing in peripheral areas of Chicago, the poorest southern suburbs, and small towns in the Midwest and often have to double up with kinfolk.

Meanwhile housing for the middle and upper middle classes has been built throughout the areas surrounding the central business district, including rehabbed older structures and new, small gated communities of townhouses and larger apartment blocks. In Turin, the old central-city neighborhood near the Roman city wall has undergone extensive rehab into luxury apartments. In Paris, Belleville and other historic working-class districts lying to the east of the center are being "invaded" by the urban middle class, led by its usual pioneering vanguard of artists and bohemians. In Beijing and Shanghai, old city neighborhoods, some of them of great historic value and interest, are cleared to make way for new high-rise business centers and entertainment districts. Old structures may then be preserved or rebuilt, but often not according to their original plans and strictly as tourist attractions.

Changing tastes and demographics spur market processes of transformation. Young, educated professionals are eager to live in the city, a more exciting environment than the garden suburbs to which their parents and grandparents fled in the post–World War II period. Smaller family sizes enable them to make this move: many of them are childless or have only one or two children, whom they are prepared to place in private schools if they are not pleased by the prospect of the local public school system. Aggressive gentrification is accompanied by aggressive school choices, with information-savvy parents seeking out the best schools and making assertive, well-informed efforts to get their children into them. Urban sociologists from Chicago to Athens are charting these new dynamics of urban gentrification, school choice, and the increasing pressure forcing lower-income and minority populations into urban peripheries (Maloutas 2007). In a more abstract theoretical perspective, this dismantling of public services can be interpreted as an element of governmentality, of new forms of managing social order.

The City and the Commodity: Urban Sociology Meets Postmodern Theory

While some sociologists are observing these processes of revalorization of the center, soaring real estate markets, and a crisis of affordable housing, others are looking at the transformation of activities as well as residents in the central cities and, above all, at the transformation of cities into zones of tourism and entertainment. The analysis of this transformation is closely aligned with theories of globalization, the analysis of neoliberalism, and theories of the postmodern (Garner 2006). The literally down-to-earth analysis of demographic transformation and land-use patterns is paired with the heady imagery of postmodernism. The revalorized central-city neighborhoods become the sites of the urban imaginary and the imaginary city—zones of restaurants, bars, theaters, sports stadiums, and lavishly landscaped parks. Once again, Chicago provides a quintessential, though hardly unique, example with its Millennium Park, a $450 million extravaganza that contains a huge outdoor concert hall designed by architect Frank Gehry, as well as eye-catching sculptures, fountains, and gardens. In Spain's Basque region, Bilbao, a grimy, ethnically divided industrial city with a smelly waterway, was transformed into a showcase of modern architecture, from art nouveau to the Gehry-designed Guggenheim museum. Budapest's old neighborhoods, surrounding the Pest city center, are undergoing rapid real estate speculation as deteriorated courtyard buildings are restored, and the city is transformed into a major tourist center of central Europe.

In other regions, for instance, the Arab gulf states, essentially new cities such as Dubai become shopping and recreational magnets for an entire region. Las Vegas represents a new paradigm of the city, with its simulacra of ancient Egypt, Venice, Mandalay, and the fabled capitals of Europe. Here, rather than building on unique features of the historical city, the city has reinvented itself as a depository of imagined versions of real historical cities. Las Vegas repeats on the scale of a large city the strange dreams that Benjamin observed in the orientalist fantasies of the Paris arcades—the use of historic realities to create intense, condensed, commodified, and hyperreal spaces of the imagination. Many North American cities have placed large amounts of taxpayer money into the development of sports facilities (Spirou and Bennett 2003), and these too, with their gigantic video images, exploding scoreboards, skyboxes, and relentless vending, offer a total and rather expensive experience well beyond watching a game. In short, city development is tied to themes, and the purpose of the city is to attract tourists, sell commodities in shopping malls, capture tourist dollars for the oxymoronically termed hospitality industry, and excite the imagination of the consumer to the utmost.

Sharon Zukin (1991) charts the development of specially themed entertainment- and tourism-oriented cities such as Orlando, Florida, as well as the new tourism, culture, and entertainment activities in city centers. Like Sassen, she notes the bifurcated social structure that accompanies these new centers of entertainment, where the restaurateur as entrepreneur and the clientele of professionals and corporate managers depend on large numbers of poorly paid service workers.

The dedication of postmodern cities to consumption has given rise to an extensive literature describing shopping malls, entertainment zones, and themed tourist environments (Clark 2004; Zukin 1991). Like Benjamin's Parisian passages, these spaces are public only in a limited sense. Compared to the Parisian passages, these pseudopublic spaces are now larger and more fortresslike. In contrast to the truly public space of the street, they are highly defensible against "undesirable elements," such as homeless people, picketing union members, and political demonstrators. Mike Davis uses the term "panopticon" to describe these monitored and exclusionary spaces. Shopping malls, theme parks, and specially *themed urban spaces* and tourist zones of city centers exemplify postmodernist concepts of nostalgia, retro, and exoticism, offering the public extremely safe, clean, and perfect replicas (some would say simulacra) of exciting but possibly dangerous and unpredictable places such as frontier towns, Mexican villages, South Asian bazaars, European cities, and Chinatowns. Ethnic communities and neighborhoods have reacted to these themings with ambivalence (Bennett 2006; Rangaswamy 2006b) since a small dose of commercialization of ethnic traditions can generate tourist dollars, safer streets, and a spirit of cultural diversity, while a higher level may feel voyeuristic and inauthentic. (See the work of Malcolm Miles [2007] for further examples of cities and the production of culture and that of Susan Fainstein [1999, 2001] for tourist-led urban development.)

David Harvey and Eric Klinenberg: The Neoliberal Impact

While urban sociologists trace demographic change and postmodernists thrill to the urban imaginary, other sociologists contextualize these changes in the overall shift to a neoliberal economy. We have already seen how Castells relates the growth of megacities to globalization and the global information economy, but these new flows have become possible only because of the opening of the transnational economy and the withdrawal of states from regulating capital flows. Similarly the burgeoning markets in city real estate, the soaring of housing prices in major cities, and the tendency for prices of hotel rooms, restaurant meals, luxury goods, and apartments to converge (at high levels) throughout the world are results of the neoliberal shift. So is expanded immigration because professionals in fields such as software design and health care move to developed economies, while low-wage workers (often from the middle strata in their country of origin) move to expanding markets in countries with labor shortages in personal services such as domestic employment, care giving, and restaurant and hotel work. These economic changes and demographic flows have set the stage for global changes in lifestyles and stratification systems. These shifts were discussed in Chapters 1 and 5, and here we merely reiterate that David Harvey has made a key contribution in providing an overview of the transition.

In addition, the state has changed its role in the provision of social services. In part, it has simply withdrawn from offering social services at all, and this withdrawal is associated with the decline and closing down of public housing in the United States, in turn closely tied to displacement of low-income residents from the central city. In part, government has privatized these services and introduced market mechanisms even into the services that it still provides. For example, many city administrations throughout the world have moved from providing the local neighborhood public school to offering a bewildering array of quasi-marketized options under the heading of "school choice." These new options address the needs of middle-class parents to find schools for their children that will ensure reproduction of their class advantage, and middle-class parents are particularly adept at finding the information needed to make the right choices (Oberti 2005; Maloutas 2007; Lipman 2006). Klinenberg (2002), in his analysis of mortality rates in the Chicago heat wave of 1995, argues that the smart-consumer model of social services led to elderly, confused, and exceedingly vulnerable citizens being deprived of the services they needed; the plethora of agencies and nonprofits, the difficulties in contacting providers, and the welter of confusing options and messages meant that they could not find help before or during the crisis. *Consumer choice and the marketization of public services* have made life more complicated for individuals and families with little access to information and transportation. Thus the neoliberal shift has changed the terms of city life, making it more pleasant and attractive for those with private resources and more chaotic and insecure for those without them. In short, urban life is closely tied to the emerging globalized capitalist stratification system. And so we can still benefit from classical concepts of urban life, such as Engels's analysis of ethnic and class distributions in capitalist cities and Simmel's identification of cities as the spaces of the money economy.

Conclusion

In recent years, theory and research have focused on the expansion and multiplication of cities, especially in regions of the planet that are not economically developed and have little history of industrialization. Although looking at cities as sites of both heterogeneity and inequality is a long-standing tradition in the social sciences, the explosive growth of urbanization, coupled with new tools of spatial analysis, has greatly expanded this approach. Cities are the places where the new global economy and postmodern cultures are becoming readily visible. Some theorists hail cities as the places where a new global civil society can emerge and celebrate their vitality, while others emphasize their seemingly unmanageable problems of housing, pollution, inadequate social services, and concentrated poverty among vulnerable populations.

Chapter Ten

Disruptions in the Field Formerly Known as Sociology of Deviance

Greg Scott and Julian Thompson

Why does the United States have exceptionally high rates of crime and especially of incarceration, with more than 2 million people behind bars (over 1 percent of the adult population)? Why did incarceration rates climb so steeply in recent decades? Why are minorities disproportionately among the incarcerated? Have we moved from an ideal of rehabilitation to a goal of punishment, and if so, why? What are the relationships, if any, among crime, drugs, poverty, racism, and family dysfunction? Should we study these problems at the level of individuals or communities? Are drugs and violence—especially gun violence—*public health* issues? Why have drug cartels and gangs developed such a strong hold in entire countries? Is the perception of their power accurate or merely the result of media sensationalism? And if it is really true, how did it happen? Did corporate fraud and misconduct precipitate the financial crash of 2008 (and the so-called Great Recession), and should market behaviors be more strictly regulated and violations more harshly punished? These new concerns have contributed to intense controversies in the fields once known as sociology of deviance, criminology, and criminal justice.

Overview

The area of sociology formerly known as sociology of crime and deviance has turned into a whirlpool of contradictory perspectives with open frontiers with other fields.

No dominant paradigm has emerged, and communities of scholars propose dramatically different approaches and even disagree about the definition and boundaries of the field. The traditional subject matter of the field, "deviance," must now itself be put into quotes as a contested concept.

- The field is deeply divided among several currents: traditional theories of crime and delinquency, often closely linked to the applied field of criminal justice, persistent conflict approaches, and contemporary perspectives influenced by Michel Foucault and ultimately derived from the radical side of Emile Durkheim's legacy.
- The reframing of deviant behavior as a form of risk taking has generated new sections of the subfield associated with public health as an allied field.
- Dramatic external changes, such as increases in transnational organized crime, growing corporate misconduct in an era of deregulation, and the soaring rate of incarceration (and especially the relationship between *race and incarceration*) in the United States, affect theory construction, and so does the availability of large databases of crime statistics.
- Facilitators of a version of the conflict constructionist paradigm include forces external to the discipline—forces in the real world—especially the surge in US incarceration, the connection between punishment and racial dominance, and the impact of movements to abolish the death penalty and prison itself.
- Barriers to new theories include the persistence of long-standing theories —powerful mainstream theories such as community disorganization and individual-level explanation—as well as practical problems of policing. Theories have to be congruent with the goals of criminal justice programs and applied criminology; the new conflict constructionist theories are not a good fit with these applied programs.

Trajectory

The analysis of deviance begins with Durkheim, who left a complex legacy that has been interpreted differently in different periods. Currently many sociologists have returned to its radical side, but earlier readings favored by functionalists persist.

Durkheim: The Centrality of Normative Regulation and Punishment

As we noted in Chapter 2, "Conflict Constructionism: Elements of the Paradigm," the centrality of deviance is a hallmark of contemporary theories. These theories return to Durkheim's position that the study of deviance is not only a fascinating and perennially popular area of sociology but its very heart. For Durkheim (as read in our day, not in the 1950s) "society" is an ongoing process of normative regulation and punishment. There is ultimately not much else to it, only the formulation of norms, their imposition at macro-, meso-, and microlevels, and the punishment of transgressors. Norms, surveillance systems, and punishments are not historically uniform, and analysis of this variation is at the center of sociology. Foucault took up and elaborated this Durkheimian model with its absent, empty self defined by punitive regimes and its endless procession of the condemned marching to the gallows, the electric chair, the principal's office, the insane asylum, the reformatory, Siberia, Devil's Island, the Soviet gulag, and US prisons.

The Structural Functional Interpretation of Durkheim

In the era of structural functionalism, the concept of deviance implied a fairly stable and socially consensual set of norms and regulations; deviant behavior entailed the violation of these norms, and society responded with a range of sanctions designed to bring the deviant back into compliance. This view was a conservative reading of Durkheim's legacy, which turned away from his radical position that all of sociology is about normative regulation and punishment. The functionalist interpretation of Durkheim separated the analysis of deviance, crime, and punishment from the analysis of society as a whole. Functionalists were ready to concede that inequalities in society precipitated deviant behavior; for example, Robert Merton's (1938) well-known article "Social Structure and Anomie" clearly stated that the gap between American goals of material success and the structurally available means is a source of anomie, crime, and retreatist forms of deviance. But the functionalist reworking of Durkheim's vision to turn it into a critique of dysfunctional institutions diminished its original scope; Durkheim had intended the study of deviance to be a foundational theory of societies as structures generated by regulatory regimes. The mid-twentieth-century structural functional perspectives on deviance were thoroughly disrupted in subsequent decades.

Emergence of Radical Perspectives: Conflict Theories and Interactionist Approaches

The era of the theoretical triad (structural functionalism, conflict theories, and symbolic interactionism) brought two major types of challenge to structural and functional views of crime and deviance. Opportunity structure theories drew on conflict perspectives on inequality as a generating milieu of crime and elaborated Merton's pioneering work while giving more detailed attention to processes at the community level (Cloward and Ohlin 1961). A grander and more explicit challenge to functionalist views of crime and deviance came directly from conflict theories, generally Marxist or influenced by Marxism; these theories identified the capitalist system as the fundamental cause of crime in modern society and showed how class and racial inequalities are intertwined with unequal treatment in the criminal justice system and a lack of opportunities as sources of crime. A radical and Marxist school of criminology emerged in the 1970s (Quinney 1974).

The second challenge came from interactionists and microtheorists who focused on labeling processes, the construction of deviance, and the symbolic meanings of deviant behavior for those who engage in it (H. Becker 1963; Lindesmith and Strauss 1956). Erving Goffman's work on asylums, stigma, havoc, and mental illness made major contributions to this perspective.

These two critical perspectives overlapped. For example, William Chambliss's (1973) well-known study of the Saints and the Roughnecks showed how labels were applied quite differently to working-class and middle-class youths who committed delinquent acts. Howard Becker (1967) not only studied the experience of marijuana users but explicitly raised broader questions about the supposed neutrality of sociology. In 1967 his presidential address to the Society for the Study of Social Problems, titled "Whose Side Are We On?" argued that sociologists must challenge and disrupt the hierarchy of credibility that favored the perspectives of those with the highest social rank. In other words, sociologists must stand up for the deviant and the marginalized. A few years later, Donald Black (1976) studied the criminal justice system from the alleged offender's viewpoint and showed it to be a disjointed, fragmented, and inconsistent set of enterprises designed to perpetuate themselves above all else. Seeing the world through the eyes of the deviant created new perspectives on law as well as crime.

External Forces

A number of trends in the era of neoliberalism and globalization exacerbated the enormous tension in the field between theorists close to law enforcement and the emergent range of critical perspectives. These trends have further divided the communities of scholars working on deviance and have not impelled the whole field to move to a new synthesis. Examples of external issues are the growth of transnational organized crime, increasing concern about sophisticated white-collar crime, and the wave of mass incarceration in the United States.

Transnational Organized Crime

One major trend was the proliferation of drug gangs in the United States and, more generally, organized crime on a global scale. Drugs had been international commodities for a long time, but with globalization of trade patterns and wars in Southeast Asia and Afghanistan, the commodity circuits for illegal drugs sped up and expanded. Criminal organizations also became active in prostitution and smuggling undocumented immigrants. Stolen goods, ranging from automobiles to archaeological treasures and pirated intellectual property, entered global networks.

Corporate and White-Collar Crime and Criminal Negligence

White-collar crime became pervasive as deregulation loosened government controls over financial transactions, often on a global scale and with far-reaching consequences, such as the effects of unregulated and outright fraudulent expansion of subprime mortgage lending in the United States. These acts of deviance went well beyond individual fraud and embezzlement and demonstrated the complicity of CEOs and other top-level officials in bilking the public, shareholders, employees, and government. In the neoliberal climate of market enthusiasm, existing regulation was set aside or not enforced. Cybercrime became increasingly possible through the Internet. Environmental damage also became an area in which norm breaking was evident, revealed in a series of incidents such as the chemical pollution of Love Canal, the *Exxon Valdez* oil spill in Alaska, and the deaths of 4,000 people (and blinding and injury of many more) in a Union Carbide accident in Bhopal, India. A detailed study of the 1986 *Challenger* shuttle disaster revealed *routinization of deviance* within the organizations responsible for the assembly and launch (Vaughan 1996) or, in an alternative view, failure to stand up to pressures from the Reagan administration (Perrow 1999). More recently, criminal charges in the BP oil spill in the Gulf of Mexico and the coal mine disaster in West Virginia have contributed to the analysis of accidents as the results of deviance.

These developments in recent decades fueled critical approaches to deviant practices and cultures within organizations and contributed to the expansion of conflict perspectives on organizational misconduct, such as Edwin Sutherland's (1949) early admonition to sociologists to study white-collar crime using the lens of class analysis. Critical theorists called for more analysis of "crime in the suites" and less punitive approaches to "crime in the streets." The growing interest in white-collar crime has connected the field to the study of power and inequalities—to the analysis of the political field, to use Pierre Bourdieu's term.

The Surge of Incarceration in the United States

Probably the most powerful external force that impelled sociologists to develop new perspectives and also enlarged the gaps between new types of critical theory and more traditional approaches to deviance was the surge in incarceration in the United States, which came to enjoy the dubious distinction of having more people behind bars than any other economically developed nation—probably more than any nation period. This surge was fueled by the ideology of the war on drugs, and its impact was most devastating in communities of color, especially among African Americans. Because we devote a section of this chapter to this issue, we will not discuss theoretical approaches here.

The Clash of Contemporary Perspectives

The Impact of Foucault

Throughout sociology, the growth of conflict and microtheories created a positive climate for the incorporation of Foucault's work, and the sociology of deviance was no exception. Foucault's *Discipline and Punish* (1979) changed the face of critical criminology, infusing the field with previously unconsidered insights into the embedding of power and control in the everyday lives of humans in society. "This book is intended as a correlative history of the modern soul and of a new power to judge" (Foucault 1979, 23): this quotation synopsizes Foucault's project. Societal reactions to lawbreaking behavior shifted over time from grievous punishments applied publicly to the offender's body to the establishment of interlaced (though not usually harmoniously interlinked) regulatory microsystems designed to effect change in the offender's soul. The book opens with a detailed description of the public dismemberment of Damiens, who had attempted to kill a French king, and then switches abruptly to the regimen of a nineteenth-century reformatory, a place of segregation and rigid discipline. Foucault seeks to jolt the reader with the seismic shift in forms of social control—from public to hidden away, from torture to constraint, from a spectacle of punishment to an attempt to transform the offender. According to Foucault, the definition and management of deviance became the purview of a diverse phalanx of "technicians of discipline," such as psychiatrists, prison wardens, clergy, schoolteachers, social service caseworkers, and the like. The modern system of disciplinary power spread, became less public, and grew roots in establishments theretofore nonexistent or only minimally concerned with the enactment of punishment.

Foucault's history of the soul is also a critical concept in this area. The modern disciplinary regime attempts to rectify and reform the sullied soul. "Is it surprising that prisons resemble factories, schools, barracks, hospitals, which all resemble prisons?" (Foucault 1979, 228). A central point of Foucault's carceral system is that control is not contained within prison walls but interlaced with the society that surrounds them. The machinery of control, examination, and classification operates within a wide variety of social institutions. "Prisons resemble these other institutions not just because they have similar architecture, but because they all fulfill similar functions" (Foucault 1979). Thus Foucault returns to the Durkheimian insight that the study of society is the study of regulation and punishment.

Currents of the Mainstream

Community-Based Studies

A very different approach that emerged by the 1980s was a shift of focus away from individual lawbreakers to communities and neighborhood effects. This focus had, of course, appeared earlier, especially in Chicago School studies of crime and gangs, but it reappeared during the last decades of the twentieth century when drug gangs were spreading in many US cities. Community-oriented approaches coincided with efforts to control drug gangs and with law enforcement ideologies of *broken windows* and zero tolerance that tried to reorient policing into crime prevention and community engagement. Broken windows is the view that small signs of incivility and deterioration in a neighborhood need to be quickly addressed as a crime-prevention strategy (Kelling and Wilson 1982). It is also associated with the community policing movement that seeks to involve residents in a proactive way in crime prevention. By the 1980s, police-driven research and theorizing in criminal justice began to focus attention away from both institutions and individual lawbreakers. The community-focused view of crime continued into the 1990s. For example, Robert Sampson and Stephen Raudenbush (1999) developed the notion of collective efficacy; their lens examines specific neighborhood conditions that are propitious to criminality. When residents of a neighborhood do not agree about what constitutes norm breaking and lack shared ideas of what to do about transgressions, crime will flourish. This idea borrows heavily from structural functionalist theories derived from Durkheim's work and also Merton's adaptation of Durkheim in his development of strain theory.

Emerging from a series of studies conducted by the Chicago School in the mid-twentieth century—when the ecological approach to studying urban settings was the hallmark of its sociological enterprise—the community-based approach essentially rests on the notion of social organization and disorganization. The underlying premise is that neighborhoods experiencing residential instability, social isolation and exclusion, and a high concentration of poverty are socially disorganized and, consequently, conducive to higher rates of crime. This particular perspective regained strong traction with the introduction of William Julius Wilson's *The Truly Disadvantaged* (1987) and was later expanded by both Sampson (2011) and Wilson (1997) and Sudhir Venkatesh's (2002, 2006) work on the American ghetto. It is built on the idea that neighborhoods marked by extreme poverty and relative isolation from the mainstream will develop avenues for revenue generation because of the breakdown in informal social controls and the increased submersion in a cultural milieu compatible with criminality. This explanation of crime was an extension of strain, social-control, and opportunity structure theories to community-level consequences of neoliberal economic restructuring. Increasing numbers of communities were falling into these conditions as *deindustrialization* and relocation of industries beset cities in North America and Europe. Venkatesh combines opportunity theory and social-control theory but applies their key components to communities rather than individuals.

The analysis of crime and deviance at the community level sparked further controversy. Some scholars saw these studies as calling attention to communities in difficulty in order to foster policies to increase economic opportunities for residents of these areas. Others interpreted the community focus as supporting government initiatives related to the war on drugs, get-tough-on-crime policies, broken-windows and community-policing perspectives, and initiatives such as DARE and gang-loitering ordinances. Prevention became a major theme of law enforcement, but sometimes community analysis overemphasized racial differences beyond what a more individually oriented analysis might have supported because entire communities were identified as suffering high rates of HIV and crime, visible signs of deterioration and disorganization, and the challenge of reintegrating formerly incarcerated residents.

It is worth noting that the community approach with its *community-level studies of crime and deviance* remains a strong theoretical tradition in the field. Its proponents are able to show strong correlations between neighborhood disadvantage and crime rates and argue for the value of the concept of "contextual effects"—spatially structured forces that can be used to explain crime causation beyond individual-level factors. Hence, community-oriented researchers continue to utilize this approach for macrostructural explanations of crime. Although social disorganization itself is an old concept that many researchers find problematic, the approach has garnered much attention among social scientists and reentry practitioners concerned with recidivism and reintegration, as many released prisoners return to the same communities they leave behind upon incarceration (Travis and Visher 2005; Petersilia 2003; Kubrin and Stewart 2006).

Other Persistent Theories with Traditional Vestiges

Like the community-oriented approaches to unmasking deviant linkages, several other theoretical perspectives have old roots with new leaves and branches. Many of these approaches were founded in an earlier school and diverged into distinct schools, while others accumulated additions over the years and continue incorporating elements of various theories. For example, social disorganization theory gave birth to social-control theory, despite their apparent incompatibility. In this section, however, we focus on two vibrant perspectives that have grown in popularity and continue to display strong correlates to indicators of deviance. They also enjoy an affinity with commonsense understandings of crime by the public and by interventionists. These two perspectives are learning theories (also known as differential association, social learning, and subcultural perspectives) and the developmental/life-course perspective. The distinct difference between these perspectives and other theoretical approaches is that they overlap quite easily with other disciplines, such as psychology and social psychology, and emphasize the role of learning deviant behavior. As a result, they have proven quite resistant to criticism.

Social learning theories. Social learning theories have a fairly robust core of proponents who explore deviance from the idea that, like any other behavior, deviance is learned. This concept highlights the modes and means of inculcating deviant definitions and values on the part of environments and peers who exhibit a propensity for delinquency. Simply stated, if socialization is a process of learning and inculcating various values, norms, ideas, customs, practices, and cognitive schemas that affect behavior, then deviance is also part of a socialization process. Almost all theories incorporate the element of learning into the study of deviance; yet social learning theories' focus on association with deviant peers, adoption of deviant definitions, the role of delinquent milieus, and the inculcation of values conducive to deviance differentiates it from others. While other theories may either include social learning as a feature of deviant identity or mention it in passing, social learning theorists believe that these learning processes are the causal mechanisms and regard them as the primary factors that propel criminality.

For example, early in the development of social learning theories Edwin Sutherland postulated that criminal behavior emerges from the intimate relationships formed among delinquent peers and that delinquent definitions held by these groups foster and reinforce deviance through the ongoing attachment maintained among them (Warr 2001). Factors such as class, race, and broken homes only increase the likelihood of having close relationships with delinquent groups. The theoretical name for this perspective is differential association, and it is one of the most enduring theories among researchers and scholars today.

Though expanded on since Sutherland, social learning theories gave birth to subcultural perspectives that have both microlevel and macrolevel components. The infamous subculture-of-violence thesis of Marvin Wolfgang and Franco Ferracuti (1967) has been one of the most controversial and contested social learning theories around. Studying homicide rates and other forms of violence in African American communities in Philadelphia, Wolfgang and Ferracuti found that rates of homicide and other forms of violence were highest among lower-class, young, African American males. Out of this finding emerged the subculture-of-violence thesis that attitudes and definitions related to solving interpersonal conflicts were built on the belief that violence was not only a necessary and appropriate means of resolution but also that it was a learned response to dealing with personal (often trivial) issues. This response is acquired through interaction with others and takes the form of value transmission.

While the subculture-of-violence thesis has diminished in appeal and is now less favored among scholars of crime and deviance, it nonetheless influenced Elijah Anderson's *Code of the Street* (1999), which addresses a strong and continually growing phenomenon linked to street crime and violence among inner-city youth of color. Anderson's project identifies a certain code that youths (and certain kinds of families) organize their lives around and adopt as a means for interacting with the community and other social actors. This code functions as an unwritten and unspoken set of rules for acting and conducting oneself in an otherwise hostile environment. It is a subcultural value, but it is not adopted by all members of the disadvantaged community. Anderson's thesis accentuates that poor black youth in inner cities are most vulnerable to the code and that in many cases the code requires them, when confronted with violence or challenges to their masculinity and identity, not to take such disrespect lightly. Violence then is the response, and it is normalized as a part of everyday life, even when it is not a preferred resolution.

Like all theories, social learning theories have not persisted without criticism and debate. These theories have been attacked for their strict adherence to measuring deviant behaviors by association with other deviant peers and the definitions and culture formed from these relationships; for overestimating the causal role that learning plays in various deviant behaviors over the life course; for the lack of structural analyses that have larger social and political implications with regard to policy and community interventions; and for the implication that communities where crime is prevalent espouse antisocial values. The latter criticism has been wielded against subcultural theories, such as that outlined in Anderson's *Code of the Street,* charging them with blaming the victim and subscribing to what some believe to be a reconstruction of the culture-of-poverty thesis.

Nonetheless, research conducted under the paradigm of social learning theories continues to demonstrate predictive power and is useful for understanding how deviance, crime, and delinquency are formed. In fact, differential association is still one of the primary theories of youth offending, and because of this application, it is likely to continue to be a part of the theoretical landscape.

Developmental/life-course perspective. Developmental and life-course approaches do not have a long history in sociology but have their earliest rumblings in several major control theories. However, within psychology, developmental perspectives are central to understanding continuity and change in coming of age and aging—whether as a child, adolescent, young adult, or elderly adult. These theories make up the bedrock on which psychological understandings of deviance and crime are built and have been around for some time. Sociologically, they first cropped up, though indirectly, in Travis Hirschi's *Causes of Delinquency* (1969/2002). Although Hirschi's work established one of the strongest control theories at the time, he and Michael Gottfredson later expounded this perspective with the introduction of their *A General Theory of Crime* (1990). This later work sought to reconcile Hirschi's original postulate that social bonding played an important role in delinquency by examining how self-control or the lack thereof is formed by parenting practices and attachments to parents (social bonds). Because they accentuated self-control as the determining factor as to whether one deviates or not over the life course, this perspective engendered many implications for developmental theories. Gottfredson and Hirschi ultimately believed that developing low self-control early in the development process determined a life of maladjustment, deviance, and risk-taking behavior. To them, low self-control was an incorrigible trait that individuals could not change once developed; this led not only to deviance and crime but also to poor marriages and relationships, unstable employment, reckless and risky behaviors, and other problems not necessarily related to crime.

As suggested in Gottfredson and Hirschi's formulation, the primary factors that distinguish developmental and life-course approaches from other theories are the impact of family structure and dynamics on the development of children and adolescents over the life course and the centrality of charting deviance from childhood through adulthood. In essence, the developmental/life-course approach realizes not only that deviance and crime are age related—which sociologists and criminologists have long understood—but also that trajectories of continuity and change vary depending on factors that occur over the life course.

An example of this is Robert Sampson and John Laub's major work, *Crime in the Making: Pathways and Turning Points through Life* (1995). Though considered to employ a control and life-course approach, their research set the field for revealing developmental stages in deviance and for charting early pathways and turning points that spoke to persistence and desistence patterns of offending. Social bonds—or control factors—and attachments to other normative structures and institutions in society allowed for increased social capital and informal social control at various stages, which predicted offending behavior over the life course. At any point within the developmental process, these elements can change and shift. This framework promotes a dynamic understanding of crime and deviance.

Their "age-graded theory of informal social control," as they called it, addressed some of the historical blind spots in the criminological and sociological literature: that is, the reasons why youths have a higher propensity for committing crime and adults seem to age out and stop offending as they get older. These changes are due to social bonds and informal social controls, such as direct and indirect parenting (social-control factors), institutional attachments (education, employment, etc.), and important social relationships (marriage, children, etc.). All of these factors can change or develop over the life course and consequently play a major part in the process of entering or leaving deviant and criminal activity.

Moreover, in other disciplinary formulations of the developmental/life-course perspective, such as psychology, much ground has been broken by examining childhood behaviors as indicators of deviance. Behavioral problems such as bullying, lying, impulsivity, and rage are thought to be the result of poor parenting practices, dysfunctional family settings, deviant parents and family members, and other issues relevant to the immediate home and surroundings where developmental processes are strongly related. They also bespeak future behaviors that may develop into criminality and heightened risk taking.

The life-course approach begins to overlap with a new tendency in the field—the analysis of risk and *risk factors,* a perspective we will examine in more detail presently. A large slice of life-course research focuses on risk and protective factors—factors that increase or decrease the risk of deviance—that indicate the extent to which deviant behaviors will develop. Risk factors may involve low parental monitoring, parental abusiveness and authoritarianism, family deviance and criminality, difficult temperament, a history of impulsive behavior or parental impulsive behavior, low parental educational achievement, having a single parent, and the like; protective factors may involve the opposite, such as strong family cohesion, no family deviance, low association with deviant peers, educated parents, and the like (DeLisi and Piquero 2011).

The developmental/life-course model's approach of examining trajectories of deviance has received praise and condemnation, applause and criticism. On one hand, it positively reinforces the notion that family structure and healthy parenting practices are fundamental elements of ensuring that deviance does not take shape. Placing the parents and families at the core of its analysis, it provides much proof that normative family composition and certain kinds of parenting styles are more conducive to stability in childhood and adulthood. On the other hand, it fuels neoconservative views by individualizing social problems, devaluing other family orientations, and eschewing structural explanations for social issues that tend to be widespread phenomena with social policy and social welfare implications.

Regardless of these contestations, studies within this paradigm have proven effective for interventions at the childhood and early-adolescent stages, and research in this vein does not appear to be slowing down. With respect to the sociological and criminological field of deviance, the developmental/life-course perspective holds much promise. However, many elements vary according to the disciplinary lens. For example, Sampson and Laub maintained a structural analysis and avoided an individual-trait perspective. In any case, developmental/life-course approaches are finding more popularity as social scientists come to terms with the need to understand crime and deviance as stemming from dynamic processes that reflect how individuals move through life.

(The reader should note that we return to life-course theories in Chapter 12, "Contemporary Theories of Family Life.")

A Divided Field

This brief overview of the trajectory of the field and some of its contemporary theories reveals its propensity for fostering contending paradigms championed by communities of scholars with very different agendas. The mainstream remains extremely powerful (though itself divided into many channels), and the critical approaches have not become the main current. The close proximity of the field to the practical problems of policing and social control—to criminal justice and corrections—creates divisions. The field is deeply divided between those whose sympathies lie with the transgressors and the punished (or those who at least try to "get into their heads," as in Jack Katz's [1988] phenomenological existential approach to crimes from shoplifting to serial murder) and those who seek to reduce crime rates and deviant behavior. Among the former one can find scholars influenced by Foucault, many interactionists and labeling theorists, and most Marxists. The latter (theorists whose main concern is crime reduction) include theorists working in a structural functionalist vein, many mid-range theorists exploring the sources of specific types of deviant behavior, and most policy- and practice-oriented sociologists. But these two broad ideological camps are further divided into theoretical clusters.

As in other areas of sociology, a mainstream exists that carries out empirical research with middle-range explanatory theories. Some of the work is designed to identify correlates or predictor variables of lawbreaking and deviant behavior among individuals, tracing the life-course and longitudinal data about individuals, and examining sentencing patterns among jurisdictions. Other approaches include qualitative analysis of law enforcement organizations or criminal groups. These studies generally eschew the broader paradigm labels.

We conclude the chapter by examining new issues for theorists beyond the issue of crime: the surge in incarceration in the United States, which is closely linked to racial disparities, and the convergence of *public safety and public health* in the area of high-risk behavior.

Punishment and Incarceration

Nowhere was the urgency of bringing the state back into theorizing more visible than in the expansion of punishment, surveillance, and incarceration in recent decades. Law enforcement and social control shifted markedly in the last decades of the twentieth century, turning away from the discourses of rehabilitation toward a get-tough-on-crime ideology and practice. For example, underage offenders were tried as adults and sent to adult institutions. In the United States, many nonviolent offenses, especially drug possession, received long, mandatory sentences. As the tenor of discussion shifted from rehabilitation to punishment, particularly in the United States, vulnerable populations were hard-hit by policies that appeared to be race and class neutral but impacted groups very differently (Western 2006). As crime rates leveled off and eventually dropped in the last years of the twentieth century, the rate of incarceration in the United States soared, and the proportion of African Americans among the incarcerated rose, even though the percentage of crimes committed by blacks did not increase (Wacquant 2009a, 2009b). By 2008, there were 2 million people behind bars in the United States; other societies did not have nearly as high a proportion of their populations in prisons and jails. Once again the theoretical question had to be raised: Is the high US incarceration rate yet one more instance of US exceptionalism, or is it a trend soon to be replicated in other societies?

Were tougher law enforcement tactics and mandatory sentences for drug-related offenses reducing crime? In other words, were high levels of incarceration a cause of lower crime rates? Theories of rational choice and deterrence, often favored by law enforcement professionals, suggested this order of cause and effect, but it was a very different point of view from that of critical and conflict theorists. Critical sociological theorists suggested that the power of the *penal state* is wielded when the social state of income support and social services is cut back as a result of neoliberal policies. As Loïc Wacquant (2009a, 2009b) says, when the "invisible hand of the market" is freed from regulation and redistributive interventions, the "iron fist" of the criminal justice system becomes more necessary. High incarceration rates are not a cause of lower crime rates but a substitute for social policies as a way to manage the poor and marginalized. Mike Davis (1992) chronicled the transformation of Los Angeles into a carceral city, showing these processes of surveillance, intense policing, and punishment at a mesolevel in a specific city.

The critical theorists also pointed to the increasing racialization of law enforcement and incarceration in the United States, and Angela Davis has argued that mass incarceration must be understood as a specifically racial practice, the latest in a series of measures to maintain white supremacy. Her *Are Prisons Obsolete?* (2003) captures her thoughts on the history of racial projects that necessitated an abolitionist stance. Tracing white supremacy from slavery to Jim Crow and onward to the US prison system, she articulates connections between the racial politics of prisons and past practices of racial dominance, crafting a cogent argument for the abolition of prisons. The "prison industrial complex," the term she and other abolitionists use to refer to the US prison system, is replete with racism, sexism, classism, unimaginable violence, and for-profit motives. To date, prison abolition is an increasingly national social movement lead by Critical Resistance (2008), INCITE (Women of Color against Violence), and other radical organizations located in California with the explicit agenda of making prisons obsolete. Angela Davis, Ruth Gilmore (2007), Dylan Rodriguez, Beth Richie, and other well-known scholars are founding members of the prison-abolition movement and their advocacy, with that of other scholars and grassroots leaders, forms its theoretical and strategic direction.

In contrast, Wacquant's analysis foregrounds the changing structure of capitalism (neoliberalism, globalization, and deindustrialization of cities) and connects a failed social welfare system with intense urban marginality (racialized ghettos). Hence, Wacquant suggests that prisons are "surrogate ghettos" because they form a symbiotic relationship with the segregation and exclusion of the urban poor and ultimately represent a "new peculiar institution," the fourth in the history of racism against blacks: slavery, Jim Crow, ghettoization, and now prisons. Unlike David Garland and other scholars of the mass-incarceration debate, Wacquant believes that mass incarceration is a misnomer and that the term "hyperincarceration" is more appropriate. This stance reflects his argument that the only kinds of people being incarcerated at a heightened and accelerated rate are poor blacks and Latinos; therefore, David Garland improperly used the word "mass" in *The Culture of Control* (2001).

Several other theorists have weighed in on the discussion of the punishment-and-control complex as well. Bruce Western, a sociologist at Harvard, developed one of the most rigorous studies demonstrating how mass incarceration functions not only as punitive carcerality but also as a stratification system that drastically diminishes the life chances of African American men. In *Punishment and Inequality in America* (2006), Western's analyses depict a bleak picture for prison releasees. His conclusion is straightforward: over the life course, an African American male's chance of incarceration is dramatically increased, and his chance of living in an equitable position compared to other men is drastically diminished after he has been incarcerated. The phenomenon of mass incarceration disrupts every sector of life and plays an intrinsic role in underestimating unemployment rates of African Americans and overestimating income growth.

Whether the term "hyperincarceration" or "mass incarceration" is employed, and whether or not prisons and punishment represent a continued racial project in the history of racism, all of these scholars agree that a racial dimension exists that demands critical and incisive analysis and radical transformation. Though many of these scholars differ with regard to each other's analyses—for instance, the work of Davis emphasizes racial dominance, an approach that intertwines the analysis of incarceration and social control with the analysis of racism and other forms of discrimination that call for prison abolition, whereas Wacquant does not subscribe to prison abolition or the thesis of the prison industrial complex—all theoretical positions and scholars argue that current punishment and social-control apparatuses are drastically racialized and problematic in contemporary US society.

New Boundaries: Risk Taking and the Public Health Paradigm

By the beginning of the twenty-first century, much of the field was deeply divided between theories associated with law enforcement and public safety and critical theories drawing on Foucault and conflict perspectives. Then an additional new perspective entered the fray. The field of sociology of deviance expanded in the direction of public health with the incursion in the past few decades of new ideas and concepts useful for understanding social ills, including risk and protective factors, as well as notions derived from Foucault's work on regimes of regulation. These have tended to dissolve deviance into high-risk behavior and to link public safety and public health. After 2000, converging conversations took place in the areas of public safety, public health, and population well-being. Public health eases its way into the study of culture (ethnoepidemiology), with federally funded epidemiological studies relying heavily on ethnographic work to better understand the distribution of disease and protective factors; iatrogenic effects of law enforcement were revealed in studies that demonstrated that law enforcement (i.e., public safety) tactics often generate unhealthy outcomes at the individual and community levels.

The framework of this field was jolted from many directions simultaneously, both in its conceptual foundations and in the real world. Foucault's work cast doubt on the naturalness of normative regulation; the normative order is deconstructed as a series of regulatory regimes created by discourses of power increasingly lodged in the "human sciences"—medicine, social work, psychology, education, sociology, and so on. In the real world, new kinds of problems emerged, especially HIV/AIDS among men who have sex with men and among injection drug users, as well as transnational drug traffic and associated drug gangs, not to mention an explosion of white-collar crime (for instance, mortgage fraud and Enron's fraudulent accounting).

These changes destabilized the field of deviance studies within sociology by effectively blurring the boundaries between public health and public safety. In turn, a new generation of scholars has begun to link large-scale statistically defined risk factors with intense *microethnographies* of the social, cultural, and physical environments that sustain risky behavior, such as illicit drug use, gang participation, and unprotected sex, injection-drug use, and other behaviors associated with HIV transmission (see, e.g., Hagan and McCarthy 1998). The Vancouver Injection Drug Users Study (VIDUS), for instance, underscores the complexity of drug-related deviance. This open cohort study began in 1996 and tracked drug users' behaviors with semiannual surveys, ultimately finding that drug use and its adverse outcomes, such as HIV and overdose fatality, result from a confluence of individual, ecological, and structural factors. Moreover, the study revealed multifarious influences on deviance, implicating both individual action/agency and institutional (e.g., law enforcement, health care, etc.) responses to deviance (UHRI n.d.; Small et al. 2005).

These new approaches that combined individual agency, community conditions, and institutional perspectives were buoyed by greater availability of data and statistical techniques that allowed researchers to identify predictor variables for adverse outcomes.

The analysis of large amounts of quantitative data allows us to identify what variables at multiple levels predict the incidence of crime, deviance, punishment, and long-term outcomes, as well as the categories of people who are overrepresented among the punished.

Conclusion

In the radical Durkheimian perspective and its elaboration by Foucault, deviance, punishment, and social control are the core practices of all societies. It is the task of sociologists to explain variation in these practices among societies. In many societies, especially in the United States, punishment and the workings of the criminal legal system (not the "criminal justice system," a term that presumes that justice can be attained within the present social order) must be seen as a product of a society structured in racial dominance, that is, in white supremacy, as well as in class inequality. This radical perspective is not so popular with functionalist and community-oriented theorists of deviance, even though these types of theories also have Durkheimian roots, as they are derived from a different reading of Durkheim. Law enforcement cadres prefer individual-level rational choice and deterrence models. Foucault-based theories and conflict theories are not embraced by scholars in the criminal justice field who see deviance and crime as problems to be solved. Meanwhile, sociology of deviance has an increasingly blurred boundary with public health. It is being redefined by epidemiological approaches to risk taking and adverse events. The field as a whole is deeply divided in theoretical contention over its definition and purpose.

SECTION 3

Paradigm Limited

Chapter Eleven

Social Class and Socioeconomic Inequality

Do you think of yourself as a member of a social *class,* such as the middle or working class, the rich or the poor? Are you satisfied with your income, assets, employment opportunities, and prospects for the future? Are you in the wealthiest "1 percent"? Have disparities in wealth and income increased in recent decades—and if so, why? Is the middle class shrinking, and does it need to be saved? If yes, who will save it and how?

The sociology of inequalities is a contentious and active area marked by the impact of external changes, growing amounts of data, and competing interpretations with roots in classical sociology. Prevailing perspectives are encountering a number of new and unsolved puzzles. Global and national patterns of inequality are undergoing marked shifts that pose challenges to the prevailing theories and paradigms. Despite the emergence of many new puzzles, classical approaches derived from the work of Karl Marx and Friedrich Engels, Max Weber, and Emile Durkheim retain their power. Conflict constructionism is not the leading theoretical contender in the explanation of class inequalities, but it does address major questions in the field. Its main contributions are in the analysis of macro/micro linkages in class formation (how classes get formed and how people develop class identities) and the exploration of *class reproduction* (why the same folks end up in pretty much the same class positions generation after generation—or do they?). It also offers an analysis of the ideologies and discourses that legitimate class inequality.

The terms "class structure" and "class system" are used less frequently than they were during the period of structural functional and conflict theories, so we can discern a concession to the conflict constructionist paradigm with its preference for fluidity, construction, and process over stability, fixity, and structure. But other elements of the paradigm have had only a moderate impact on this area of sociology where theories remain firmly connected to classical sociological perspectives on *socioeconomic stratification.* In the mainstream of sociology, concepts derived from Weber remain preeminent. Marxists rely on existing Marxist concepts of class. In this area, even the postmodernists are deeply influenced by classical sociology, specifically the work of Emile Durkheim.

Overview

Highlights of contemporary theories of class inequalities include the following developments:

- *Capitalism* continues to be the focus of contemporary discussion of class inequality and is not a concept confined to Marxist analysis. The concept of capitalism and a focus on the way market economies increase or decrease socioeconomic inequality are present in all of the theoretical paradigms.
- Weberians emphasize an open-ended struggle for *power* in which contending parties can be defined along status lines, such as religion and ethnicity, as well as by class divisions. Conflict is a constant, and power and *privilege* are omnipresent forces in stratification, but these struggles have no specific direction or outcome. Marxists reiterate the role of capitalist *relations of production* in the formation of classes and have not given up the hope that this objective force will come to be recognized and spark collective action. Postmodernists draw on Durkheim's emphasis on the complicated integrative forces within advanced capitalism, which they believe make *class consciousness* and class struggle unlikely in the contemporary world. Marxists and Weberians agree on the presence of conflict but interpret the origin and direction of conflicts differently, whereas Durkheim-inspired postmodernists are more likely to see contemporary capitalist society as highly ideologically integrated, regardless of the objective presence of class inequality in production and economic conditions.
- Ethnographic and observational research at the micro- and mesolevels casts light on processes of class formation and the creation of discourses, myths, ideologies, and identities associated with class inequality. Many of these studies are focused on schooling as a major site of class reproduction.
- New research focuses on the formation of dominant classes in advanced capitalism, especially in the financial sector. As the financial sector grew in most developed capitalist economies, a fascination with market risk emerged in culture and ideology, so theoretical and ethnographic work began to focus on this process.
- Despite new forms of inequality at the global and national levels, completely new paradigms are as yet difficult to discern, though the existing paradigms cannot encompass all of the new empirical phenomena. Many unsolved puzzles are emerging in this area of sociology.

Barriers and Facilitators

We can discern at least two major barriers to conflict constructionism in the analysis of class inequality. One is the persistence of classically inspired macrolevel theories of class, above all, Marxist and Weberian theories on the conflict side and Durkheimian ones on the integrationist side. These powerful new versions of classical theories can go a long way to explaining class inequalities, class formation, and the presence or absence of class-based collective action and therefore diminish the effort to invent new paradigms.

A second barrier to conflict constructionism is created by the presence of vast amounts of quantitative data about disparities on both national and global scales, which seem to call out for macrolevel analysis of trends in global and national economies. There is a disconnect between these bodies of data and the capillary and discursive approaches of conflict constructionism. So the conflict constructionist approaches have developed most readily in the analysis of social reproduction and socialization into social class in families and schools, as well as in the study of the formation of ideologies and myths that provide legitimating discourses for class inequality. Macro/micro linkages are being forged that connect this capillary research to the macroanalysis of political processes and data on disparities.

Trajectory

The analysis of class inequalities and socioeconomic stratification has been a central theme of sociology from the start. Contemporary theories of class and class inequality are in part extensions of the great classical theories, so the discussion must begin with the late nineteenth century.

- Much of the existing terminology among non-Marxist social scientists is ultimately derived from Weber's pioneering work in which *class* is a product of market position and can be contrasted with *status* (stratification related to honor and generally considered to be more traditional and more likely to be ascriptive).
- Inequality continues to be the subject of a mainstream analysis that uses concepts such as socioeconomic status, class, and stratification. These concepts are linked to education and occupation. Education can be used as a predictor of socioeconomic status, and occupation and property ownership are often used as operational indicators of class. An individual's class position is an abstraction from the more concrete information that we have about his or her occupation and assets.
- Similarly, among Marxists, the original Marxist concepts, and specifically the relations of production, continue to be central to the discussion of class inequality.

- Postmodernists have their own analysis of class and inequality, based on a sizable dose of the Durkheimian heritage with its focus on integration in the complex organic structure of advanced capitalism. But postmodernists inspired by Durkheim are probably less of a force in this field than the Weberians and Marxists.

Class and Classical Theories

Class has been a major category of social theory since the classical period when theorists began to look at capitalism as an essential element of the transition from traditional to modern societies. Traditional societies were largely agrarian and feudal, while modern societies are industrial and capitalist. Marx and Engels, Weber, and Durkheim all believed that groups based on economic position had become of central importance, not only objectively but subjectively as well. Economic stratification appeared in most societies, but capitalist societies are different from all previous stratified societies in their class structures and the resulting types of identities and action. The classical theorists elaborated this belief in different ways. It is essential to understand these original formulations, as well as the stratification theories of the mid-twentieth century, in order to understand contemporary interpretations of class in capitalist society.

Marxists

For Marx and Engels, class is constructed in the relations of production. Notice how the original theoretical formulation was already relational and interactive. Class is not something that individuals are or have; it is created in a relationship. In all but the simplest hunting-and-gathering societies, these relationships are unequal. Capitalist society differs markedly from previous class societies, such as slavery-based societies and feudalism, in its technological dynamism, the wage-labor form of the relations of production, and the growing scientific understanding of society itself. This objectively accurate understanding enables the proletariat—the subaltern and exploited class in the relations of production—to take collective action to bring capitalism to an end. Freeing themselves from confused religious, national, and ethnic identities, proletarians can come to comprise a class-for-itself (in contrast to a class-in-itself, one that is objectively present but without class consciousness). In other words, the subjective identity of proletarians comes to correspond to a scientific and objective understanding of the capitalist mode of production. The purpose of scientific analysis by revolutionary socialists is to contribute to the transformation of the consciousness of the proletariat from a confused, ideological one to an objectively accurate, scientific understanding of the role of the mode of production in historical change, and with it, of their own potential future as a hegemonic force.

The side of Marxism that focused on consciousness and purpose was developed by Antonio Gramsci, an Italian communist. Gramsci emphasized the need for hegemonic self-understanding in any class that seeks to rule a society, in contrast to merely benefiting from economic dominance. A hegemonic class understands the society as a whole, sees itself as the legitimate leading force of the society, and organizes the thought processes—the basic common sense—of others. While material factors, such as the relative power of the capitalist class and landed interests, influence whether the economically dominant classes develop this hegemonic view, the hegemonic view itself has a role in the history of the society.

Weber

Weber used the term "class" differently from Marx and Engels. He differentiated class (economic position) from status (ranked position based on honor and shared culture). Class inequalities are produced as different groups gain access to economically advantageous positions in society, and this process operates through power differences as well as through the inherent logic of the relations of production. Like the Marxists, Weber believed that class is a form of stratification characteristic of capitalist society, but unlike Marxists, he thought status stratification (e.g., along lines of ethnic or religious difference) might persist and become a basis of identity and *party* (by which he meant organized collective action). Class may be a more likely candidate than status as the basis for collective action in capitalist societies, but plenty of opportunity still exists for status-based action. Weber's conception of class is much closer than the Marxists' to everyday use of the term to mean simply difference in economic positions in markets; it includes inequality associated with the relations of production as well as other kinds of inequality in wealth and job access.

Weber's conception of class and stratification is closest to the contemporary theoretical mainstream in sociology and forms the explicit or implicit basis of much empirical work. Key in this mainstream preeminence of the Weberian approach to stratification is precisely the nuance in the difference with Marxism. Both approaches recognize the importance of power and political processes, and both recognize the importance of class in capitalist societies. But the Weberians are more inclined to believe that political processes can constitute or underpin economic differences. Power can come first in the chicken-or-egg debate about the relationship between economic inequality and political inequality. For Weberians, relations of production are not the bedrock determining force "in the last instance" of inequality in societies, and economic inequality can be produced by means of political power and privilege. Both Marxists and Weberians recognize the distinction between class and status, but Weberians are more likely to believe that status continues to be a social force, even though the capitalist mode of production tilts toward a class-based structure. Both have an interest in culture and cultural forces, but the Weberians are more prepared to see culture as a possible independent variable in stratification rather than as a superstructure, an ideology that emerges from the relations of production. (See Zeitlin 1997 for an excellent discussion of the considerable overlap as well as the key differences between Marx's and Weber's ideas.) The Weberian positions are on the whole closer to the mainstream of contemporary perspectives on class and stratification, at least among US sociologists.

Durkheim

Durkheim's perspective was more abstract and focused on cohesion and much less conflict oriented than that of the German theorists. He believed that in the past, in simpler, precapitalist societies, solidarity had been based on a sense of similarity and shared norms (mechanical solidarity), while in complex modern market societies, a more complicated kind of solidarity based on economic and occupational interdependence emerges. Organic solidarity based on complex economic interdependence enables persons who are different from each other in culture and religion nevertheless to participate in society and feel connected to each other. Thus capitalism, with its more complex division of labor, can actually generate larger, more stable, and more cohesive societies whose constituent groups are linked to each other through webs of economic interdependence in a way that clans, localities, and ethnic communities within archaic types of societies had never been connected (Pakulski 2005/2006).

Pressing a point, one might say that Durkheim's predictions were diametrically opposed to Marx and Engels's views; economic differentiation in capitalism would actually knit capitalist societies together more intricately than archaic segmented societies. To give one simple example of this integrative force of the advanced capitalist economy, we can see how people of many different occupations live together in modern communities. This interdependence and integration, which blurs all categorical distinctions, makes collective action of any kind much weaker. Not only is cultural, ethnic, and religious segregation diminishing, but occupational communities such as those of miners or factory workers in a company town or an industrial district are also disappearing. In the advanced modern society with its complex division of labor, strikes and other forms of collective action are dissipated in the diversity of communities and cities. Everybody in a mining town shared work experiences and supported each other in collective actions; in the modern city neighborhood, an intensely shared and physically separate collective life no longer exists. This analysis of advanced modern organic integration is very powerful and addresses puzzles in the Marxist analysis, especially the weak level of class identity, class formation, and class-based collective action in the contemporary capitalist world. But despite the sophistication of the Durkheimian approach, most contemporary non-Marxist theoretical and empirical work on stratification is guided by Weberian rather than Durkheimian theory.

Structural Functional Theories of Stratification

By the 1950s, a new approach to economic stratification had emerged in sociology, veering off from the classical legacies. *Structural functional theories of stratification* provided explanations for inequalities that brought together two approaches, functionalism and neoclassical economic theories (Davis and Moore 1945). The structural functionalists' first premise was that certain positions in societies are functionally important and have to be filled with qualified individuals. Their second premise, drawn from neoclassical economics, was a riff on the laws of supply and demand and the concept of human capital. If a position is functionally important, but only a limited number of people are qualified to fill it, it has to carry higher rewards than other positions in terms of income, perks and privileges, prestige, profits, and so on. People can invest in themselves—enlarge their own human capital—by committing themselves to education and other kinds of preparation for these important, lucrative positions. This premise connected the analysis of stratification to social psychology and individual motivation. For instance, on the demand side doctors are believed to be vital in a modern society, and on the supply side relatively few people spend the time and money required to become a doctor—and so doctors are well paid. Close scrutiny of this relatively straightforward market model reveals puzzles, and these puzzles seem to have multiplied in the closing decades of the twentieth century. For example, one has to ask why CEOs in the United States—but not Germany and Japan—have to be remunerated at over 1,000 times the pay of an average worker (*Economist* 2003) or why star athletes make millions of dollars.

Conflict Theories: Revisiting Weber and the Marxists

By the later 1960s and the 1970s, conflict theorists were attacking the functionalist model mercilessly, but from two distinct positions.

Varieties of Marxist Theories of Inequality

Marxists insisted that the relations of production are the basis of inequality. They articulated and elaborated the paradigm in a variety of ways. These approaches included relatively traditional approaches to class analysis, perspectives that emphasized the cultural and political superstructure associated with capitalism, and a new approach to global inequalities called *world-systems theory*. World-systems theorists (sparked by the work of Immanuel Wallerstein) examined how inequalities on a global scale were constituted by the development of capitalism. The capitalist core regions (in western Europe, North America, and Japan) dominated the global economy and political system. The nations of the semiperiphery were partially industrialized and dependent on the core regions, while the areas of the periphery had a history of colonization and were integrated into the world economy primarily as producers of raw materials and always on extremely unfavorable terms. A somewhat simpler but related set of theories of inequality in the global system was referred to as dependency theory; it too emphasized the dominance of the developed capitalist core nations over other regions of the world, regardless of whether the latter were colonies or nominally independent nations. Both world-systems theory and dependency theory gave attention to class relations within global regions as well; capitalist classes had emerged in the peripheral and dependent nations, but they were subordinate to the capitalist classes of the developed core regions.

Revisiting Weberian Theories: Power, Privilege, and Exclusion

Other conflict theorists, especially feminists and theorists of race and ethnicity, returned to Weberian conflict theory and incorporated Weberian insights on power, privilege, and exclusion. The Weberian attention to power and political action provided a foundation for theories that focused on the construction of gender and ethnoracial dominance, for example, glass ceilings that blocked upward mobility of women and minorities, old boy networks and old school ties that restricted access to wealth and power, mechanisms to limit enrollment in professional schools, and outright apartheid and discrimination. Those who are currently powerful—and that is not a color- or gender-neutral category—use their power to keep others out of the most lucrative and exciting professions and out of selective educational institutions.

This analysis of power and privilege is a major component of theories of social reproduction. Pierre Bourdieu pulled together the analysis into a general theory of reproduction, beyond the specific elements of racial and gender exclusion covered by US conflict theorists, as we already discussed in Chapter 4 on difference and dominance. Habitus, dominance in one or more fields, and control over one or more forms of capital (economic, cultural, social, and symbolic) enable dominant classes to maintain their position. Even supposedly meritocratic institutions are affected by power; for instance, the duller offspring of the wealthy can acquire college degrees (if not actual knowledge) at a higher rate than the brightest children of the poor as economic and social capital are transformed into cultural capital. As educational credentials become ever more important (e.g., the higher education premium in income for males in the United States went from 20 percent above the income of high school–educated workers in the 1970s to 42 percent by 2009 (US Bureau of Labor Statistics 2007; updated by Economic Policy Institute based on the Bureau of Labor Statistics; see Leonhardt 2010), the power to gain access to education is becoming increasingly important.

Differences between Marxist and Weberian Conflict Theories

Erik Olin Wright (2006) argues insightfully that these power, privilege, exclusion, and reproduction theories of social class are not Marxist theories. They can be traced back to a Weberian perspective on class and rest on the premise that exclusive control of a position, resource, or access route (such as education) allows some groups and individuals to obtain more wealth and power than others, often forming a vicious spiral of increasing inequality. One could see this control as a source of distortion in markets that would otherwise tend toward a more even distribution of rewards based on human capital and meritocratic principles. This perspective is distinct from the Marxist perspective, which argues that the source and central mechanism of inequality is the interaction of classes in an exploitative relationship of production (Wright 2006). As an example that is compatible with Weberian conflict theory, CEOs in the United States use their network ties, common social bonds, ideological influence, and manipulation of the CEO-selection process to limit access to these positions, exclude minority, female, and middle-class aspirants, and extract millions of dollars above and beyond their actual level of competence, talent, and functional importance (Khurana 2002). This type of analysis of inequality derives from the work of Weber, and it is different from a Marxist focus on corporations as capitalist enterprises that control productive property and hire labor.

Once again we see that the casual lumping together of Marxism with non-Marxist conflict theories has obscured our understanding of crucial distinctions in the ways theorists think about causes of inequalities. The views of the Weberian conflict theorists and Bourdieu's work were compatible with *postmodern theories of class* in capitalist societies that emphasized local processes and an ongoing play of differentiation and power. Marxist perspectives on inequality remained distinct and focused on the relations of production in a social formation as the underlying cause of class structure rather than on the full panorama of inequalities, disparities, exclusion, and power differences as a field of play with many players and many strategies of dominance.

Trends in Inequality

The single most important characteristic of inequality on a global scale is the presence of *between-nation inequality,* that is, enormous differences among nations in the purchasing power of their inhabitants. About 75 percent (or, more cautiously, somewhere between 60 and 90 percent) of the variation among human beings in individual purchasing power in the global economy can be explained or predicted based on the nation in which they live (Milanovic 2005a, 2005b, 2008). There are stark differences between the socioeconomic position of individuals in countries such as the United States, Sweden, Qatar, France, Germany, Canada, and Australia and the much larger numbers of people in places such as rural India and China, Pakistan and Indonesia, and most African nations. Income inequality among all human beings—in the entire global population—is greater than the level of income inequality in any one country, even those with very unequal distributions such as South Africa.

Within-nation inequality varies sharply from very high levels in countries such as South Africa and many Latin American nations to low levels in places such as Denmark, Sweden, France, Canada, Norway, and Japan. Generally places with higher per capita incomes also enjoy more income equality, but there are exceptions to this generalization. For a nation with a relatively high per capita income, the United States has a high and growing level of inequality, returning to pre–World War II levels in recent years (Piketty and Saez 2003; J. Bernstein 2013); in addition to a high level of overall inequality, it also has high levels of income inequality within occupations (Kim and Sakamoto 2008), as well as many other types of disparities in health coverage and schooling.

The neoliberal turn has produced inconsistent trends in class inequality. On the one hand, inequalities have grown in many countries such as the United States, and, globally, large populations live in absolute poverty. On the other hand, in a number of countries such as Brazil, India, and China, the middle classes have expanded, and larger proportions than in the past enjoy an affluent standard of living.

These trends in economic indicators of equality and inequality are linked with other social characteristics. In some societies, class inequality overlaps with ethnoracial stratification, a phenomenon especially prominent in "New World" societies in which the historical conquest and enslavement of Indians and Africans left persistent disparities among ethnoracial groups. It is also a new phenomenon in countries in which immigrants have become a stratum of low-wage workers in the "precariat"—the lowest and least secure tier of the labor force.

Globalization and transnational immigration have meant that flows of immigrants from poorer and postcolonial societies have entered wealthier nations, especially in Europe and North America. Historical processes have led to a sorting of individuals based on their ethnic and national origins. States have a major role in creating these complex stratification systems by the formulation of immigration laws and policies concerning citizenship rights (Cheng 2006; Chua 2002).

An additional trend is under way in many countries in the complex linkage of class and ethnoracial stratification: a dispersion across class lines of formerly highly concentrated ethnoracial groupings. For example, in postapartheid South Africa, the black middle class is growing, and in the United States, in the post–civil rights era, African Americans are increasingly distributed across a broad class spectrum ranging from affluent and middle-class locations to the most disadvantaged positions in the society. This dispersion of the class locations of ethnoracial categories has political implications for identity and collective action (Pattillo 2008; Soja 1996). The trend toward greater class diversity within ethnoracial status categories appears to be inconsistent with trends toward the increasing *racialization of economic inequality.* Is the significance of race as a predictor of economic position growing or declining (Wilson 1997)? The decline is certainly slow, and if we examine wealth rather than income as a marker of class, the disparities remain vast: the median wealth of a white household in the United States is twenty times that of an African American household.

A final challenge in the analysis of trends in inequality is the apparent weakness of working-class collective action in the neoliberal era. Until the Great Recession following the financial crash of 2008, class-based movements appeared weak in the neoliberal era compared to the strong union and socialist movements of the first part of the twentieth century. Religion and ethnicity—rather than social class and economic inequality—seemed to be at the center of movements and conflicts on a global scale.

Thus recent trends in class inequality and class formation have presented a series of theoretical puzzles: Has neoliberalism generated new middle classes or expanded poverty and inequality—or both at the same time? How tightly are ethnoracial and class stratification linked to each other? What accounts for the relatively weak formation of class-based movements in a world with huge objective inequalities?

Contemporary Theories of Inequality: Can Marx, Weber, and Durkheim Be Recycled?

These external conditions and their accompanying puzzles create a playground for a lively assortment of theories, with no distinct dominant paradigm or emergent new paradigm. Conflict constructionist formulations appear here and there, but the main lines of contention remain those between Marxists and non-Marxists, who in turn draw their concepts from the work of Weber and/or are postmodernists with a debt to Durkheim.

Let us focus on one of the puzzles we identified: the weak level of class identity and class formation within many developed capitalist nations, especially the United States. This puzzle is particularly challenging for Marxist theories.

Marxist Approaches

In a Marxist framework, one can argue that, objectively, class defined as inequality produced by the capitalist relations of production continues to be the key dynamic of the global system and national societies as well, even if it is not on the identity-formation agenda for many people. The disconnect between the objective conditions and the subjective responses can be explained by ideology, the role of corporate-controlled media, government policies, crosscutting cleavages of class and status in the developed nations, and various displacements of class consciousness into nationality, religion, ethnicity, and other bases of difference throughout the world.

Class fragmentation, competing identities, and state policies could be given a Marxist spin with the argument that these are indeed the trenches that protect the capitalist system; Ira Katznelson (1982) used this metaphor drawn from Antonio Gramsci in his analysis of local conflicts in New York City, a study that can be generalized to other advanced capitalist societies. Contention over local issues and racial-ethnic, regional, religious, and gender lines divides people with similar class interests. Furthermore, the state propagates powerful unifying ideologies of nationalism and national security that disrupt class-based identities.

A slightly different version of the Marxist perspective can be found in the work of Erik Olin Wright, who argues that advanced capitalism has an exceedingly complex class structure characterized by numerous intermediate and contradictory positions that impede polarization into a bourgeoisie and proletariat. Ownership and control of the means of production can be disconnected from control over workers; managers and small business owners form intermediate strata. New development of the forces of production has not uniformly lowered skill levels but has actually increased some workers' skill levels and autonomy, thereby slowing down class formation. Wright retains a Marxist definition of class based on relations of production but admits that polarization is difficult to discern.

Weberian Approaches: Where's the Party?

A Weberian might well point to the validation of Weber's analysis of political responses to status and class stratification, namely, that no single formula or inevitable process translates class and status positions into party, that is, into a specific form of political organization. As Weber argued, multiple power struggles along status lines disperse class divisions. In a Weberian perspective, power struggles persist, and the lines of conflict are often defined by religious and ethnoracial status rather than class. Class identities are dispelled by status identities. On a global scale, national and regional inequalities often lead to collective consciousness, identity, and action along national-populist and religious lines, and real class formation is unlikely in the near future.

Durkheimian Approaches

Alternatively, a Durkheim-inspired postclass and postmodern analysis suggests that inequalities persist, but advanced capitalist societies—rich or poor—are knitted together in extremely complex ways that preclude or undermine class formation. In this perspective, advanced capitalism generates enough equality and well-being diffused through a broad middle range of incomes within developed nations to successfully defuse within-nation class struggle. Furthermore, class identity is fragmented into multiple specializations and limited contention over fractions of the pie. The power of these Durkheimian and postmodern theories to explain the weakness of class conflict in advanced capitalist societies is highlighted in Jan Pakulski's contrast to Marxist theories, of which he states, "Their capacity to highlight the key aspects of social hierarchy, division and conflict has been declining. This is because 'class formation,' especially the social and political articulation of working classes, is in decline. Other aspects of social inequality and antagonism come to the fore, reflecting the divisions of race and gender, the impact of citizenship, the distribution of political power, and the actions of elites" (2005/2006, 1).

Who is right—the Marxists or the Weberians or the Durkheimian postmodernists? Pakulski believes "the jury is still out" on this question (2005/2006, 23). Marxists may well be right that objectively and in the final analysis, the capitalist mode of production is the fundamental and determining cause of the prevailing patterns of inequality, but the postmodernists can counter convincingly with revived and revitalized Durkheimian and Weberian views of class, an emphasis on local and micropatterns, attention to subjective factors in identity formation, the analysis of power and governmentality, and even the astonishing Durkheimian assertion that capitalism integrates rather than polarizes classes. The postmodernist analysis drawing on Weber and Durkheim may be more powerful than the Marxist one for a short-term understanding of current conditions.

What Does Conflict Constructionism Contribute to Understanding Class Inequality?

The explanatory power of the classical theories at the macrolevel has been a major barrier to the development of alternative paradigms for discussing class. But a few key elements of the conflict constructionist paradigm are being introduced into the older theories, though often not clearly connected to the quantitative macrolevel puzzles. They are seeping into cracks in the older frameworks, especially around the questions of new mechanisms of governing and managing a society, class reproduction, socialization into class positions, and the creation of myths and ideologies.

The Role of the State

A point on which Marxists, Weberians, and postmodern Durkheimian theorists agree is that the state has played a crucial role in both the development and perception of class inequalities. For Marxists, the period of embedded liberalism in the post–World War II era had the effect of diffusing class conflict, while the neoliberal shift gradually whittled away some of the protections, benefits, and organizational strength of the working class. Weberians would also emphasize the influence of the state in class-based politics. In this respect, interest in the state is not a new theme at all in theoretical approaches to class inequality. However, a new formulation of this issue is offered by Michel Foucault's concept of governmentality, practices of control that penetrate deeply into a society and fragment opposition. (See Bennett 2006 for a discussion of managerialism and political control of conflicts.)

Exploration of Macro/Micro Linkages

Both Marx and Weber posed puzzles that contemporary social scientists might reinterpret as questions about macro/micro linkages and social construction. Marx and Engels broached the question of how and when class-in-itself is transformed into class-for-itself. How are the objectively present categories generated by the relations of production transformed into categories of consciousness and collective action? In this question two contemporary concepts were already present. The first is the idea that class is not a fixed thing in a social structure or stratification system but a relationship, an interactive process in which the micro relations of production of employer to employee are the capillary level of the macro relationship of capital and labor. The second idea is that these relationships have a discursive side as well, their representation in consciousness (false or otherwise) and transformation from class-in-itself to class-for-itself. In Weberian terms, we ask how class (or, for that matter, status) gets translated into party—that is, collective action and organization. How do relational categories turn into actions?

On the Marxist side, E. P. Thompson took a big step forward in *The Making of the English Working Class* (1966). In his masterpiece, Thompson began to probe the cultural and discursive processes that produced the organizations and institutions of the working class. These processes were deeply influenced by the specifics of English history and culture, such as its early industrialization and the affinity among region, occupation, and religion—the way that workers were drawn to dissenting churches (and not to the Church of England). The process of class construction took place at the local level, though it was replicated throughout England.

Pierre Bourdieu on Habitus, Distinction, and Social Reproduction

A major effort to link class as a macrosocial phenomenon (as a "structure" or "system," although these terms are not universally favored) to capillary processes was offered by a big cluster of concepts in the work of Pierre Bourdieu. Much of this theorizing focuses on how social class is reproduced, a process that seemed especially puzzling in France, where education was supposedly universalistic and rigorous. Despite the best intentions of administrators and teachers in the national public education system, many children of working-class parents (and increasingly of immigrant parents) could not break out of their limited educational attainment. Bourdieu developed the concept of cultural capital, a set of luggage filled with knowledge that each child carries to school. The cultural capital of working-class and many immigrant children was incongruent with the cultural capital demanded in the French educational system, while the children of the bourgeoisie arrived in school with their satchels already loaded with a command of the language in both spoken and written forms (a challenge in French with its strange spellings), a rationalistic and scientific worldview, and many skills and capacities that enabled them to excel in the nominally egalitarian school system. In short, their habitus—their embodied knowledge—matched the expectations of the school system as an institution of class reproduction.

Bourdieu was also interested in the development of taste and the way class is expressed in taste. While the practices of taste are in themselves arbitrary, they are inextricably linked to social inequalities. Are leopard-print pants, bling, a drink of "7 and 7," and velvet paintings of Elvis inherently vulgar? Unless they are displayed ironically, they are markers of lower-class taste!

Socialization, Schooling, and Social Class

The interconnection of taste as a class phenomenon, child-raising practices, economic power, and social and cultural capital were further solidified by anthropologists and sociologists, such as by Beatrix Le Wita (1994) in her exploration of French bourgeois culture, a milieu in which she grew up. In the United States, Annette Lareau in *Unequal Childhoods: Class, Race, and Family Life* (2011) used ethnographic methods to examine differences in the lives of working-class, middle-class, and poor children in both white and African American families, teasing out the dimensions of child raising, family interaction, and the experiences of children that sustain class divisions. These studies reiterate earlier findings about differences in socialization, speech habits, and schooling that perpetuate class differences (B. Bernstein 1973).

A key work that examined the capillaries of class from a Marxist perspective was Paul Willis's *Learning to Labor: How Working Class Kids Get Working Class Jobs* (1977). Willis's ethnographic research in an English secondary school revealed the microprocesses of school failure among "the lads," young white men of working-class origin. Their constant pranks, horseplay, disrespect for authority, rebellion, and inattention to schoolwork were practices of resistance that ultimately condemned them to school failure and limited prospects in labor markets—to working-class jobs. But beyond this apparent self-relegation to an unfavorable individual class position, the lads were participating in and reinforcing a relegation of the class as a whole to a subaltern condition because they accepted and even celebrated the distinction between mental and manual labor. Rejecting mental labor, they accepted a subaltern position and gave up on hegemonic claims for the working class. The theoretical underpinnings here derived from Antonio Gramsci's concept of hegemony and even Lenin's reflections on how the proletariat can become a ruling class only through the development of a hegemonic understanding that replaces worker spontaneity and limited forms of opposition, though Willis's empirical design was ethnographic and rigorously focused on the microlevel and one school. The analysis included attention to discourses as Willis discusses how the lads' "partial penetrations" of capitalism, often learned from their fathers' experiences in factories, contributed to rebellion and an oppositional outlook but fell short of a full grasp of what working-class contention for hegemony entails. Willis's work remains one of the most complete and powerful efforts to link a macroanalysis of class (specifically a Marxist one) to a research design focused at the level of interaction, practices, and discourses in one local setting.

In the United States, this type of research was exemplified by Lois Weis's *Working Class without Work* (1990), a study of high school students in a community in which working-class jobs in manufacturing were disappearing, and it became difficult for young people to attain even the modest working-class jobs their parents had held. In this micro- and mesolevel study of deindustrialization in one community, Weis found that young women were more adaptable to the new demand for educational credentials than their male counterparts.

An important twist in this body of work was increased attention to the formation of ruling classes, such as Peter Cookson and Carolyn Hodges Persell's (1985) study of prep schools and Jean Anyon's (1980) brilliant observation of class construction in the classroom, in which she not only reports the stunting of intelligence in the schooling of the lower and upper working class but provides an account of the stimulation of mental abilities and nurturing of analytic talents enjoyed by the children of the business elite.

Class as Discourse, Ideology, and Embodiment

The 1980s saw a burst of micro- and meso- (or capillary) level analyses of class formation and more attention to discursive processes not necessarily influenced by Thompson's work but certainly consistent with it. One of these contributions was

Richard Sennett and Jonathan Cobb's *The Hidden Injuries of Class* (1972), in which they observed the way ideologies of equality and individualism in the United States create a painful dissonance with awareness of limited attainment among working-class individuals.

Most recently these studies of the construction of social class were joined by Karen Ho's *Liquidated: An Ethnography of Wall Street* (2009), a study of analysts in investment banks. Ho probes the venues in which individuals are shaped by and for the relations of financial production in a small number of Ivy League colleges and investment banks. She explores the intersectionality of class formation with race and gender; women and people of color remain at the margins. Above all, she dissects the creation of legitimating myths and ideologies, especially the myth of the supreme smartness of analysts and the myth of shareholder value, which she exposes as a patently inaccurate history of financial markets. Class identity is created and embodied in the formation of the analysts, who learn to work long hours for vast sums of money in jobs with no security. They begin to anticipate and celebrate this condition of extreme marketization in their education and then experience it at work; through this mental, emotional, and physical socialization, they come to envision their own condition as a utopian endpoint for humanity—as a limit condition of human perfection. Similar themes of experiencing class "in the flesh" appear in Richard Widick's (2003) carnal ethnography of options traders. Class is not simply a category in a structure or a relational category; it is an embodied condition, inscribed on the body and then expressed as an ideology of risk taking, smartness, aggression, individualism, and impermanence.

Mesolevel Analysis: The CEO

At a mesolevel, Rakesh Khurana (2002) examined the search for and appointment of CEOs; he gives the reader insight into the capillary level of selecting and "anointing" a CEO who closely resembles the directors in race, gender, education, and outlook. He traces the role of the search firm in orchestrating the process. Like Ho, Khurana exposes the way the market and talent function together as a legitimating myth that veils interactive and ascriptive selection, which contributes to social reproduction, glass ceilings, skyrocketing executive compensation, and exorbitant rewards for leadership even of failing companies and in situations of financial disaster.

These are examples of contemporary theoretically driven research that contribute to an understanding of how class is an interactive, discursive, and embodied meso- and microprocess—how it is inscribed on the body, acted out in organizations, and reflected into beliefs and myths.

Conclusion

The study of class inequalities remains a very lively field in which we see contending extensions and elaborations of the great classical paradigms as well as a range of more recent studies of the capillary and discursive levels of class formation and ideology. Large and growing gaps among and within nations in income and well-being pose immediate challenges to our future, and they also pose puzzles for theoretical understanding. The conflict constructionist paradigm is not a dominant one, but it can be discerned in research that sheds light on class formation through interaction, class as an embodied habitus, and ideological myth making in homes, schools, markets, and financial institutions.

Chapter Twelve

Contemporary Theories of Family Life

Tait Runnfeldt Medina and Julie E. Artis

What is a family? Is family defined by who lives in your household? By whom you depend on for emotional and financial support? By whom you are tied to through marriage or blood? Does family consist of your parents and siblings? Your spouse and children? Your grandparents and cousins? Would you consider an ex-stepsister a part of your family? If you and your spouse or you and your children lived in different countries, would you still be a family?

The question of how to define family has become more complex over the last several decades. In the United States and other developed countries, diverse family forms have become more acceptable. People are divorcing and remarrying, creating households that might include combinations of full siblings, half siblings, and step siblings—a very complicated *Brady Bunch* family. It has become more common for gay couples to adopt children or use technological advances in fertility treatments in order to create a family. Cohabitation is more common, even when there are children in the household. In the United States, over a third of never-married cohabitors have children in the household (Smock 2000). And similar patterns have been observed in European countries. In Norway, for example, 16 percent of all children live with parents who are cohabiting (Statistics Norway 2006). Marriage and heterosexual unions do not seem to be as important to family formation as they were several decades ago. So, while we may still cling to the notion of an "ideal" family—mom, dad, and two kids living in a pretty house with a white picket fence—our common understanding of family has become more broad and inclusive.

At the same time that our definition of family has changed, we have also changed our notions about the roles of individuals within families. For example, in the 1950s, mothers and fathers were confined to strict roles: mothers were to be caregivers, and fathers were to be breadwinners. However, women have entered the workforce in enormous numbers over the last several decades. In the United States about 60 percent of married mothers with children less than six years old work outside the home (Cohany and Sok 2007). Fathers are more involved with day-to-day child-rearing. So our expectations about what mothers do and what fathers do are different today.

Given these vast changes in family life since the 1970s, what new theories have emerged to help us understand family life? In this chapter, we first briefly explore the history of family sociology and family theory over the course of the twentieth century. Then, we offer a broad overview of five contemporary theoretical approaches that are commonly used by family sociologists: (1) exchange theory, (2) *life-course theory*, (3) feminist theories, (4) multiracial feminist theories, and (5) theories of social and cultural capital. None of these is the best way of approaching the understanding of family, but each illuminates a different aspect of family life. Also, even within these broad theoretical frameworks, there is not always consensus among scholars. For example, feminists do not have one view on the family. (See the "Reading Suggestions" chapter for work that will help you explore different theories in more depth.) After describing these theories, we turn to a discussion of two current issues about family life and illustrate how these theories can provide different perspectives on each issue.

Trajectory

Historical Trends in the Study of Family Life

Sociologists who study families document trends about family life and also develop theories that help to explain these trends. The roots of current-day family sociology can be traced back to the first few decades of the twentieth century. At that time, scientific approaches to understanding families began to emerge in sociological and psychological scholarship. Ernest Burgess (1926), a prominent sociologist at the University of Chicago, was one of the first sociologists to study the family, calling it a "unity of interacting personalities."

Structural Functional Theories

In the 1950s, scholars began to develop more systematic theories linking families to other social institutions. Talcott Parsons was in large part responsible for the systematic development of family theories in the 1950s, and his writings about family remain influential today. This perspective, elaborated in *Family Socialization and the Interaction Process* (Parsons and Bales 1955), drew on structural-functional explanations to understand how the institution of the family changed to fit changing needs of society. For example, the rise of industrialism led to a differentiation of social functions for many social institutions, including the family. Functions once performed by the family, such as production and education, have been taken over by other social institutions. The family adapted to these major societal shifts by becoming both smaller (the nuclear family) and more specialized. Instead of performing a wide range of functions, the modern family, Parsons argued, focuses its attention on only two main functions: (1) the socialization of children, and (2) the provision of emotional support and affection to its members. Parsons argued that the isolated nuclear family was an ideal fit for modern industrial society because the adult members had divided responsibility for family survival along gender lines. Because of the biological tie between mother and child (mothers both bear and nurse children), mothers took the expressive, caretaking role, while fathers fulfilled the instrumental role by working outside the home.

After Structural Functionalism: Conflict Theories and Demographic Data

In the 1960s and 1970s, challenges to a structural functionalist view of the family arose. Researchers argued against the assumption that the prevalence of the nuclear family and the gender division of labor in the home are indispensable in modern societies by showing that ties to kin are still important for many and that social roles are not always divided by gender (Goldthorpe 1987). In addition, scholars critiqued structural functionalism for ignoring the competing interests of individuals within families. A conflict perspective of the family emerged, particularly in research on domestic violence (Gelles 1974) and the division of household labor (Blood and Wolfe 1965). Relatedly, feminist scholarship began during this time, criticizing Parsons's notion that effective family functioning relies on expressive versus instrumental differentiation of gender roles in families. Differentiation, according to feminists, reinforces traditional gender roles and leads to inequality between men and women.

That these theories emerged in particular historical eras is not surprising. Historical shifts in family theory coincide with changes in family realities and social trends. For example, Parsons's structural functionalism, with its emphasis on traditional gender roles, developed during the golden age of the family, the 1950s, when marriage rates were high, divorce rates were low, and many middle-class women stayed out of the labor force to care for children in the home. The 1960s and 1970s, however, saw marked increases in divorce, remarriage, single-parent families, and the number of women entering the paid labor force. Conflict and feminist theories that came to prominence in this period emphasized the competing interests of individuals within families and the interplay of the family with other social institutions.

As we will see, demographic family realities also influence the contemporary theories we discuss in this chapter. Exchange theory, life-course theory, feminist theories, and theories of social and cultural capital conceptualize the family both as an institution and also as a group of individuals who may at times have divergent and conflicting interests. These theories use a broader and more fluid definition of family while acknowledging the influence of larger social forces on families and on individuals within families. In this way, contemporary family theories reflect the current complexity of family life discussed at the beginning of this chapter. The multiplicity of theories now used to understand family life reflects the multiplicity of definitions and conceptions we hold about what it means to be a family in contemporary society. Just as there is no longer one prevailing type of family, there is no longer one grand theory of family that dominates the sociological scene. Instead, scholars often engage multiple theories when trying to understand and describe the multifaceted experiences of contemporary families.

We now turn to a discussion of five theories commonly used in contemporary research on families.

Contemporary Theories

Exchange Theory

Introduction

One of the most widely used perspectives in the sociology of family is exchange theory (Bengston et al. 2004). Exchange theory views social relationships as sets of exchanges and draws on the principles of economic theory, namely, utility maximization and equilibrium (e.g., supply and demand), to explain family-related behavior such as marriage, divorce, fertility, housework, and the care of dependents. This economically grounded theory gained prominence in the realm of family studies in the 1960s and 1970s with the work of John Edwards, Stephen Richers, and John Scanzoni, among others. That a theory based on economic principles gained purchase in the United States in the 1970s is not surprising. This was a period of growing faith in the market, when neoliberal economic principals began to dominate US policy making. One could argue that the extension of market principles into the analysis of noneconomic areas of life—what some call economic imperialism—is a hallmark of neoliberal social thought.

There are three basic underlying assumptions of exchange theory. The first is that every interaction is characterized by the exchange of resources. The second is that individuals are forward-looking, rational actors who consider both benefits and costs before acting. And the third is that individuals choose to remain in exchanges that maximize their happiness. In this way the exchange perspective provides a model of human motivation. We interact because we need things—love, assistance, money, comfort, information—from one another, and our interactions are motivated by a desire to achieve happiness.

In the hands of sociologists, exchange theory often incorporates components of conflict theory, namely, a concern with unequal power relationships within families. Because individuals enter into exchanges with more or less power, exchanges tend to be asymmetrical. As a result, an individual with less power must exchange more resources than an individual with more power in order to maintain an exchange.

Application

Recent statistics show that although women throughout the industrialized world have increased the amount of time they spend in the paid labor market, the amount of time they spend on unpaid housework still remains higher than for their male counterparts. For example, a 2005 time-diary study of housework in Canada found that women spend an average of 4.3 hours a day on housework and child care, while men spend an average of 2.5 hours (Marshall 2006). What might exchange theory tell us about this phenomenon? The exchange perspective is used quite a bit by sociologists who study the division of housework between partners. In this application, housework and wages from paid work are conceptualized as resources that can be traded. Since wages have a higher market value than housework (it is easier to purchase a new car with cash than it is to convince the car dealer to trade you a car for a year's worth of housework), the spouse with higher wages is in a more powerful bargaining position. Exchange theory suggests, then, that the unequal division of housework between men and women is a result of an asymmetrical power relationship. Because women's wages lag behind men's (in the United States women earn about 77 cents for every dollar men receive), men are in a better position to bargain for a reduction in the amount of time they devote to housework. Exchange theory therefore predicts that, on average, the number of hours women spend doing housework will decrease as their relative income (compared to their husband's income) increases.

Sociologists have tested this theory and conclude that it holds, but only under certain conditions (Bittman et al. 2003; Brines 1994). Wives do reduce their housework as their relative incomes increase, which is in line with the exchange perspective. However, husbands actually reduce their housework when they make less money than their wives, which is counter to the prediction. What is going on here? When women deviate from traditional gender expectations by earning more money than their husbands, both men and women compensate by displaying traditional gender roles through either doing or not doing housework (Brines 1994). So women "do gender" by doing housework and men do gender by not doing housework in order to compensate for stepping outside traditional gender roles in terms of who brings home the bacon. These findings suggest, as far as explaining the unequal division of housework between men and women, that although the exchange perspective is consistent with some of the evidence, it might be leaving something out—namely, the influence of gender construction and gender-role expectations, which vary among cultures and nations.

Life-Course Theory

Introduction

The life-course perspective is concerned with how individual life paths are affected by historical change as well as how they are embedded in social institutions (such as families, work, and education). The first major work to articulate the life-course approach was Glen Elder's *Children of the Great Depression* (1974). By tracing the lives of a generation of children raised during the Great Depression, Elder explores how families adapted to economic hardship and, in turn, how family adaptations affected individual lives. Elder reported that these children, who faced such deprivation during their youth, managed to overcome these early experiences by entering the military (during World War II), finding a good job, and getting married.

The life-course perspective focuses on time and change over time. To look at change over time, it looks at transitions and trajectories. Transitions are discrete events, like a divorce or the death of a parent; sociologists study them to find out how certain transitions affect individuals. A trajectory looks at a series of years in a person's life, focusing, for example, on entries and exits from the labor force over a series of years or rises and falls in family income year after year.

Life-course scholars also separate out ideas of age, period, and cohort. A person's age has certain implications; for example, as people age they encounter more health problems. The historical period they live in has a large impact on their attitudes and beliefs, as Elder found in his study of children of the Great Depression. Finally, one's cohort includes the people who were born around the same time, or members of the same generation; for example, sociologists would call Generation X a cohort.

Focusing on time, history, and change has been a very important innovation in the study of family life over the last several years. For example, this perspective helps family scholars to focus more on child development over time in certain family types rather than comparing child achievement at one point in time. Major historical events, such as 9/11, can be analyzed for how they might affect fertility, marriage rates, and divorce rates. The life-course perspective is distinct from structural functional and symbolic interactionist approaches, which are more synchronic and less diachronic (attuned to historical change).

Application

Marina Adler (2002) has drawn on the life-course concepts of time, history, and change to understand the transformations that have taken place in the lives of East German women as a consequence of the unification of East and West Germany in 1989–1990. By examining the life-course trajectories of three cohorts of women who grew up in the former Socialist East Germany, or the German Democratic Republic (GDR), Adler illustrates that family life does not exist in a vacuum and that dramatic social events can have profound effects on a person's life course.

Through interviews with thirty-six East German women from three different cohorts, Adler finds what she calls a "standard biography of the GDR woman." The most prominent feature of this biography—which is provided by the oldest cohort of GDR women, who had completed their childbearing years at the time of unification—is the belief that one's life is not actively planned but predetermined. For the GDR woman, it was preordained that she would have children young and work full-time in the paid labor market throughout her life.

Adler argues that GDR social policies that provided universal child care, paid maternity leave, and guaranteed full-time employment, coupled with the socialist ideology of the worker state, helped to create this biography where family and employment are knit together without much planning, decision making, or internal conflict required from the individual. Unlike in the West, where work is often seen as a means to self-actualization and independence and often requires complicated planning and trade-offs with family (especially for middle-class women), in the East going to work was seen as a purely instrumental activity that was not diametrically opposed to family life. And because work was seen as purely instrumental, the standard biography privileges family over work in terms of providing both fulfillment and an identity to women, even though over 90 percent of GDR women worked full-time.

Since unification, the life trajectories of the youngest cohort of GDR women have dramatically diverged from this standard biography. These women were between the ages of eleven and nineteen at the time of unification. Adler finds that the life planning of these women, along with the economy within which they now navigate, has become more privatized. Instead of seeing their lives as preordained, members of the youngest cohort view their lives as full of choices and recognize the complicated relationship between work and family facing women living in a market economy. But rather than an adoption of the Western model, which fosters a dependence on male providers, Adler finds that the life patterns of the youngest cohort are influenced by their GDR experience in that they have a strong desire to be full-time workers. The youngest cohort views work as a means to self-actualization, and many plan to postpone motherhood until they have established themselves in a secure career.

The life-course perspective illustrates how turning points, which are often outside the individual's control, can have a profound effect on a person's life path. For the youngest cohort of women, the unification of Germany represents a turning point in their lives. This group of women entered into a unified Germany at the beginning of their childbearing years, and the changing social, economic, political, and ideological landscape had a profound effect on both their outlook and their behavior. As a result, their life trajectories will vary greatly from those of the women who came before them, as well as from those of their contemporaries in West Germany who did not begin their life course in the GDR.

Feminist Theories

Introduction

Feminist theories have also had a profound effect on the study of family life over the last several decades. Of the theories discussed thus far, the feminist perspective is the most internally varied. That is, there is not one feminist perspective. At the most basic level, feminist theories focus on gender inequalities. In terms of families, early feminists were very concerned with the division of household labor within families and domestic violence. Increasingly, family research has come to draw heavily on feminist theory and related theories of gender. According to a feminist perspective, our conceptions of gender fundamentally shape family experiences.

Role theory was one of the earliest ways that feminist scholars looked at how women and men act in families. This perspective focuses on gender-role attitudes and how women and men are socialized into different gendered identities that are opposite to each other. In research on housework, for example, scholars might examine the norm that housework and child care are women's labor. Why are women considered more suited to this kind of caregiving and housework? Understanding how young girls are socialized into a feminine role provides one answer. Young girls are given dolls, dollhouses, and Easy Bake Ovens; as a result, they learn that the appropriate way to be a girl is to care for others. In contrast, when boys are encouraged to play sports, they learn the competitiveness and aggression necessary for success in the paid labor force.

Some feminists have criticized role theory for conceiving of gender as an individual characteristic. An alternative way to think about gender is as a structural characteristic (see, e.g., Risman 1987). In this view, gender is a socially constructed phenomenon that is contingent on context (West and Zimmerman 1987): men and women are different because they encounter different structural limitations and cultural contexts on a day-to-day basis, not because their gender identity is inherent or fixed. This approach to gender is called the doing-gender perspective and was touched on briefly in the housework example above. Drawing on symbolic interactionism and Erving Goffman's dramaturgical approach, gender is conceptualized as a routine, everyday accomplishment that occurs when men and women interact with each other. Therefore, husbands and wives act in gendered ways in families in order to display their gendered identities.

Application

These feminist theories can be illustrated by research on motherhood and fatherhood. Since the 1950s, sociocultural beliefs surrounding motherhood and fatherhood have changed rapidly. The increasing number of women, especially mothers, entering the paid workforce over the past fifty years has resulted in major shifts in Americans' conceptions of both mothers' and fathers' roles. However, recent research on parenting suggests that while fathers have added to their responsibilities in the home, they do not typically do an equal share of day-to-day child-rearing activities. Women continue to be primarily responsible for household tasks and child care (Bianchi et al. 2000). While fathers are spending more time with children, they do not spend this time doing caretaking tasks (e.g., feeding the child, changing diapers). Rather, fathers tend to play with children during this time, while mothers retain the ultimate responsibility for child-rearing tasks (Hochschild with Machung 1989). Therefore, the evidence does not support the idealized image of the father who shares in day-to-day child-rearing activities (LaRossa 1988).

Feminist role theorists would explain these trends by exploring how men and women are socialized to be different in terms of the caregiving that they do. They would emphasize that because of the forces of socialization and the entrenched identities developed around gender roles, change will be slow.

However, other research on parenting using a doing-gender perspective gives us a different interpretation. Research done by Barbara Risman (1987) comparing single fathers with single mothers and with married mothers and fathers finds that the parental behavior of single fathers is more closely aligned with that of mothers rather than that of fathers. This lends support to the idea that family structure can influence behaviors that are thought to be connected to an individual's gender-role identity. Similarly, Douglas Downey, James Ainsworth-Darnell, and Mikaela Dufur (1998) compare the well-being of children who reside in single-mother and single-father households. Although much of the sociological and psychological literature assumes that mothers and fathers each make unique contributions to children's well-being, they find few notable differences between children who live with mothers and children who live with fathers. Again, this supports the notion that family structure (e.g., single-parent versus two-parent household) is more important in determining child well-being than the gender of the parent with whom the child resides.

Multiracial Feminist Theory

Introduction

Recent developments in feminist scholarship focus not just on gender inequalities but on how gender, together with race, class, nationality, and sexual orientation, leads to different experiences, challenges, and opportunities. Early feminist scholars have been criticized for focusing on issues of interest to white, middle-class women. In essence, multiracial and transnational feminist scholars argue that early feminists generalized from the experiences of white middle-class women in Western countries without recognizing that the experience of being female differs depending on race, class, nationality, and sexual orientation.

Multiracial *feminism* can be characterized by the following themes. First, gender is linked to race, class, sexuality, and nationality, and we must think of these together as interlocking inequalities (Baca Zinn and Dill 1996). Second, multiracial feminism does not just focus on women of color; it provides a way to think about many different systems of inequality in society and acknowledge how anyone may be given opportunities because of one characteristic but at the same time oppressed because of another. For example, a white, working-class man may experience some advantages due to his race and gender but some disadvantages because of his class. Finally, this perspective emphasizes the lived experiences of women and men as a way to generate new knowledge. For example, by studying a poor Mexican immigrant woman's standpoint within the system of interlocking inequalities, we gain fresh perspectives on the world that would not be evident from a more privileged position.

Application

One way that multiracial feminist theory has influenced family studies is through the conceptualization of diverse family forms and their impact on child development. A common theme in studies of minority families in the United States has been the idea that they rely more on extended kin networks than mainstream, white families. These extended family networks are thought to be beneficial to minority children in that they provide emotional support to the parent and child, as well as caregiving and monetary support. For the most part, the literature has characterized minority families as superintegrated and white families as disintegrated.

However, multiracial feminists have critiqued this line of research, arguing that many studies use problematic definitions of minority groups—for example, grouping several different ethnicities into the category of Hispanic. They also argue against the dichotomy of categories: generalizing that minority families are more integrated and white families are less integrated may miss important nuances and ignore variation across different minority groups, as well as conflate different dimensions of integration. Finally, much of the research on ethnic/minority families and integration has not examined how integration varies by gender. In giving help, monetary assistance, or social support, are there gender differences?

A recent study published in *Journal of Marriage and Family* uses a multiracial feminist theoretical framework to study differences in family integration among European and Mexican Americans (Sarkisian, Gerena, and Gerstel 2007). The authors find that Mexican Americans demonstrate higher levels of family integration than European Americans on dimensions like coresidence and proximity to family. Furthermore, Mexican American women are more likely than European American women to provide help with child care and housework. However, European Americans are more likely than Mexican Americans to provide monetary support. Many of these differences can be attributed to differences in social class across these groups. These findings, interpreted through the lens of a theoretical framework of multiracial feminism, highlight the importance of simultaneously examining how race-ethnicity, gender, and social class shape family life.

Theories of Social and Cultural Capital

Introduction

Family sociologists are also concerned with socialization processes within families—how parents shape children's understanding of the world around them. In particular, several recent studies have explored how parenting practices differ by social class and how these socialization processes can in turn reproduce class stratification across families generation after generation.

Sociologists often frame their discussions of inequality around various forms of capital, or resources, that individuals have. Some basic forms of capital include human capital (e.g., level of education, specialized training) and financial capital (e.g., income or wealth). Sociologists have identified and formulated theories of other forms of capital. The concepts of cultural capital (Bourdieu 1984) and social capital (Coleman 1988) help us to understand how and why inequalities persist.

Pierre Bourdieu's work focuses on the process of socialization—particularly, how individuals in different social locations are socialized in different ways. Bourdieu's concepts of habitus and capital are used to explain how socialization happens. Habitus is defined as a set of dispositions that include a wide range of preferences, for example, taste in music, food, or leisure activities. He argues that these dispositions become taken for granted and natural. As children grow into young adults, these dispositions can be translated into a form of value, or cultural capital. Family sociologists draw on Bourdieu's theory, particularly the idea of habitus, when conceptualizing the implications of different kinds of parenting practices for children's life chances.

James S. Coleman develops the notion of social capital, focusing on access to social networks. In terms of the family, he explicitly discusses how certain forms of social capital shape the creation of human capital. Specifically, although a parent's education is critical in determining educational attainment for children, human capital is transferred through the relationship between parent and child. Furthermore, other forms of social capital—for example, if parents know other parents of children at school—can be critical in understanding children's success (and may help to explain how and why students struggle if there are multiple residential moves in childhood).

Application

Family sociologists who draw on these theories of capital are primarily interested in the family as a site of the reproduction of inequality. Beginning with the work of Melvin Kohn (1977), sociologists have noted that child-rearing practices differ by social class. Kohn's study, for example, looked at styles of parenting communication and found that middle-class children learn autonomy, while working-class children learn to obey orders. The implications are that working-class children are socialized to take on more working-class jobs (e.g., factory work), whereas middle-class children learn communication styles that prepare them for professional careers.

More recent sociological work also focuses on families and social class. Annette Lareau's *Unequal Childhoods: Class, Race, and Family Life* (2011) is an ethnographic study of parenting differences across black and white working-class and middle-class families. Drawing on observations and interviews with eighty-eight families, Lareau argues that middle-class families and working-class families differ in important ways in how children's leisure time is used. Middle-class families use a strategy that Lareau calls "concerted cultivation." They schedule children for extracurricular activities such as sports or dance. They also frequently intervene with school authorities on their children's behalf. In contrast, working-class families are oriented more toward a natural growth model. Children in these families tend to be left to their own devices during leisure time. They are also not encouraged to speak out against adults, and their parents can be frustrated by their inability to successfully negotiate with school personnel.

These different socialization styles, Lareau argues, help us understand how inequality is reproduced in society. Drawing on Bourdieu's notion of habitus, Lareau sees her work as a "partial empirical application of Bourdieu's broader theoretical model" (2011, 276). The elements she identifies that constitute the daily lives of children—in particular their experiences at school and in activities outside school—shape their dispositions toward the world, or as Bourdieu would put it, their habitus. Because middle-class children are encouraged to negotiate and question authority, they are "naturally" more easily able to perform later in middle-class jobs. In contrast, because working-class children are encouraged to follow and trust people in positions of authority and do not learn to negotiate, they are prepared for jobs that are more working-class. In this way, the dispositions that children learn at a very young age can translate, as Bourdieu predicted, into more specific forms of capital as they grow into adulthood.

Current Issues

How can the theories described above help us to understand current debates and policies about family life?

The Opt-Out Revolution

"My mother's always told me you can't be the best career woman and the best mother at the same time.... You always have to choose one over the other."

This quote, published in a recent *New York Times* article, was taken from a very accomplished nineteen-year-old female student at Yale University who plans to become a lawyer but then stay home with her kids full-time. The article, "Many Women at Elite Colleges Set Career Path to Motherhood" (Story 2005), is the latest in a series of hotly debated news articles that point to highly educated, professional women leaving their professions and becoming stay-at-home mothers. An article published the previous year in the *New York Times Magazine,* "The Opt-Out Revolution," chronicled this pattern, reporting that only 38 percent of women with an MBA from Harvard in 1981, 1985, and 1991 continued to work full-time (Belkin 2003).

These articles received a great deal of media attention, spawning a series of television news reports about highly educated women not being able to find the right work-family balance. This is the modern-day return to the superwoman issue that was a popular debate in the 1980s: Can women have it all—a great job and a great family? According to these stories, it seems that the current answer, even for highly educated women, is no. The implication, of course, is that if these women can't manage to find the right balance, then how can anyone?

Do these media articles reflect what is truly going on in the job market? A 2005 study released by the Center for Economic and Policy Research finds little support for the idea that there is an opt-out revolution going on. Based on data analyses of the Current Population Survey from the Bureau of Labor Statistics, this study finds that women did not decrease their labor market participation between 2000 and 2004 and that there was no significant decline for mothers versus nonmothers or highly educated women versus women with less education.

Even women who work in professional and managerial jobs may not really be choosing to opt out. Sociologist Pamela Stone assessed the trend of mothers "opting out" of work in *Opting Out? Why Women Really Quit Careers and Head Home* (2007). Trends in women's labor force participation statistics, as well as statistics about women staying at home, suggest that the patterns have been quite stable—Stone calls this "the revolution that wasn't" (2007, 6). Through interviews with over fifty professional women who left careers to return home, Stone claims that for most of them, their decision to leave the workforce wasn't a choice at all. Instead, they describe professional workplaces that lacked flexibility. If they were able to make flexible arrangements, they found themselves marginalized and stigmatized—and facing a ceiling in terms of promotions. So, the story isn't one of a return to new traditionalism but instead a look at how professional careers can be inhospitable for mothers.

The theories we have discussed in this chapter would view this debate in different ways. Exchange theorists might emphasize the work-family trade-off that women make and how the power attached to wages influences negotiations with spouses and partners. Life-course theorists would draw attention to patterns of women's entry and exit from the labor force over time as these patterns are conditioned by historical shifts in the economy and public policy. They would also point out the potential income loss that women who opt out may face in retirement.

Feminists, as discussed earlier, would view the opt-out revolution in different ways. The process by which females are socialized to be caregivers, mothers, and family oriented, rather than successful professionals, would be the focus of feminist role theory. However, from a doing-gender perspective, women may exit high-paying, competitive careers in order to reaffirm and enact their feminine identity. Using the lens of cultural capital theory or social capital theory, one might focus on the implications of stay-at-home moms for the socialization of children and ask how having a parent at home might allow children different kinds of access to after-school activities.

Hidden from these debates about the opt-out revolution is the domestic help that upper-class women have even when they are not working. Most of these elite women who stay at home are not scrubbing the toilet or caring for their children 24/7. Instead, they hire domestic help to care for their home and help out with children, and their employees are almost always female and often immigrants or women of color. This issue is obscured in discussions about elite mothers staying at home, but multiracial feminist theories would point out that elite white women are complicit in the oppression of lower-income and minority women while at the same time being victims themselves of a gendered society that does not allow them flexible work or enough time home after the birth of a child. Of course, these dynamics may be most prevalent in the United States and other countries that have weakly developed social policies of gender equality and/or social support structures. Other countries—especially in Europe—with more extensive parental work-leave policies would present citizens with different sets of choices and opportunities. Governments have a major role in shaping gender practices, performances, and choices; their policies are rarely gender neutral, and these policies structure options in labor markets. Therefore sociologists use the term *gendering the state-market nexus.*

Transnational Families

In the era of globalization, where money, goods, services, information, and even people flow easily back and forth across national boundaries, a new type of family has emerged. The *transnational family,* which is a family that spans and is rooted in at least two nations, has grown in number over the last couple of decades. Although it is difficult to pinpoint exactly how many transnational families there are throughout the world, we do have information from a few sending countries. In the Philippines, for example, almost one-third of all children live in households where at least one parent has gone overseas to work (Hochschild 2002).

Although some families have been depending on the remittances of migrant workers since the late nineteenth century, researchers argue that the contemporary transnational family is quite different from the binational family of old in at least a couple of ways. First, because of technologies like the phone, fax, and instant messaging, members of transnational families are able to overcome great spatial barriers to maintain active, day-to-day connections. In this way, transnational families can be seen as inhabiting postmodern spaces—they are both here and there. For many of these families, time and space have literally become compressed (Parrenas 2005). Second, mothers are more likely now than ever before to be the ones leaving families behind to find work. For example, about two-thirds of Filipino migrant workers are women (Parrenas 2002).

Transnational families can occupy any social class, but many are poor. The economies of the developed world have come to depend on cheap labor, and workers from developing nations are relocating to wealthier ones to fill positions that native populations are unwilling to take. Some researchers who study transnational families have linked this phenomenon to what they call a "crisis of care" (Ehrenreich and Hochschild 2003). The confluence of below-replacement fertility rates and increased life expectancy has had a dramatic impact on the age structure throughout all industrialized countries. There are now many more elderly people than ever before in history. And because most women now work outside the home in the paid labor force, the pool of female family members available to care for these dependents has been depleted. All in all, there are simply not enough family members available to care for dependents, both young and old. As a result, the care industry has burgeoned throughout the industrialized world. About 20 percent of American jobs are in this sector (Hochschild 2002). Because the demand is now for "women's work"—taking care of the sick, the young, and the old—the gender structure of immigrant labor has shifted. At least half of workers who leave home to find a job are now women. And when these women leave their home countries they leave behind a care void. So while the care deficit in the developed world is eased with the transnational flow of female laborers, it is simultaneously created in the developing world.

The gender shift in the demand for immigrant labor has also challenged the traditional gender division of labor within families. Mothers are now the ones sending remittances home to their families, remittances that often keep their families out of dire poverty. But although mothers are now proximally separated from their families, they do not seem to be abandoning their previous role as nurturers. Instead, mothers continue to mother from afar, working hard to maintain intimate relationships with their families via the instant message and telephone (Schmalzbauer 2004). In this way, the experiences of transnational families both challenge and support traditional ideas of what it means to be a good mother. For poor women who live in developing countries, being a good mother means leaving home to find work while at the same time providing care from afar. Intimacy that spans national borders seems to be at the very core of what a transnational family is (Dreby 2010; Parrenas 2005).

The emergence of the contemporary transnational family raises many questions about what it means to be a family. The ideal family form that Parsons wrote about in the 1950s and the one that many Americans still cling to today is simply out of reach for these families. Structural inequalities throughout the world have made it impossible for some families to reside not only in the same household but in the same country. Families extend not only beyond the walls of households (think about stepfamilies) but also beyond the borders of nations. Contemporary families, it seems, are not easily defined by physical or national boundaries. Instead, they reside in a more fluid and symbolic space and are more transportable than ever before imagined.

The theories reviewed in this chapter generate different sets of questions about and ways to look at the transnational family. Using the exchange perspective, we see the decision to leave home for work as a rational strategy that families use to maximize benefits. Exchange theory might also cause us to focus on transnational exchanges between family members and the asymmetrical power relations that both stem from and are caused by these exchanges. For example, are expectations attached to the remittances that mothers send home? In addition to providing financial support, are remittances also a means for mothers to maintain some control over their families when they are so far away?

The life-course perspective might ask us to look at the life-course trajectories of women and how life patterns are altered when the decision to leave home to find work is enacted. Do women who migrate have fewer children? Do they marry later? Do they have more divorces? Do their ideals and aspirations change? This theory also requires that we link the decisions that people make to their social context. The question of whether to leave a family behind to find work is not answered in a vacuum. In fact, the very question is generated by a particular set of political and economic processes that are historically situated.

Theories of social and cultural capital might examine the transnational family from the perspective of social ties. How might cross-national connections facilitate opportunities for family members beyond financial support? How might the social ties for transnational families be weakened by the spread of family members all over the globe?

The feminist perspective generates a series of questions about the gender shift in migrant labor and how this is affecting the everyday lives of women and families. Migrant women often perform the dirty jobs—the washing of the sick, the cleaning of dirty diapers and dirty homes—from which men are usually exempt. Female migrant laborers are also in a more vulnerable position than their male counterparts. Some migrant women have their passports stolen and are forced to work in brothels or to provide sex while cleaning house and watching other people's children (Ehrenreich and Hochschild 2003). Although working provides independence and the ability to provide for their families, the potential for exploitation remains high.

Multiracial feminist theory asks us to look at the intersection of gender, class, and race-ethnicity. Migrant women are typically poor and rarely of western European descent. The dirty jobs these women do make it easier for middle- and upper-class white women to have it all, or at least to appear as if they do. The multiracial feminist perspective asks us to question the very nature of a society that would generate the need for one class and race of women to exploit another class and race of women in order to uphold an unrealistic ideal of the superwoman who can do it all.

Conclusion

There are many different ways to think about family, and each of the theories we have discussed takes a unique approach. The exchange perspective conceptualizes family as a series of exchanges that take place between people with varying degrees of power. The life-course perspective sees family as an institution that is intimately linked to history, as a place where a personal biography is created and enacted. While some feminists see family as a site of oppression, others see it as the place where gender roles are learned, and still others view the family as a social structure where gender is acted out. Those who use theories of social and cultural capital often focus on social ties and how those ties vary across different types of families. The theory that we choose to use to examine family life has a lot to do with how we conceptualize family.

The way we see family also drives the policy and legal solutions that we create to help families and the individuals in .them. For example, a recent controversial policy proposes funding to promote marriage in order to help families out of poverty. Depending on your theoretical frame, you would view this policy proposal in very different ways. From an exchange perspective, the long-term commitment implied by marriage should increase the incentive to pool resources, and this economy of scale could lift some individuals out of poverty. However, feminists frequently argue against this policy, citing negative outcomes for women within these marriages, like increased risk of domestic violence (Catlett and Artis 2004).

The contemporary family is very different from the family of just fifty years ago, and so are our ways of thinking about family life. The idea that there is one type of family—a nuclear, middle-class, heterosexual family—has been smashed by the reality around us. Definitions that rely on physical proximity or biological relatedness have lost their utility as families transcend both the walls of households and the borders of nations and as adopted and stepfamilies grow in number.

Family sociology has, in many ways, been resistant to contemporary postmodern developments in social theory. However, given recent rapid changes in family life, many family scholars have focused on exploring the making of meaning within families. This latter group of scholars may be more open to constructionist theories (see, e.g., Dreby 2010; Hansen 2004; Hays 1996; Pugh 2009; Stacey 1998). Annette Lareau's book, described earlier in this chapter, is one excellent example of this kind of work.

Even so, there remains a great deal of traditional, mainstream family research. However, interpretive theoretical frameworks are having an influence. As one example, sociologists Wendy Manning and Pamela Smock (2005) were concerned that recent large-scale surveys were not accurately capturing cohabiting families. Drawing on 115 in-depth interviews with cohabitors, they concluded that people may not necessarily use the term "cohabit" or "partner" to describe what they are doing—instead they used terms like "boyfriend," "girlfriend," or "fiancée." This study shows how more mainstream, demographic work on the family is being influenced by the shift to constructivist perspectives that focus on interrogating the very meaning of family.

Section 4

Paradigms Reconstituted in a Transdisciplinary Field

Chapter Thirteen

The Sociology of Health, Illness, and Medical Practice

Grace Budrys

Why are some people healthy and others often or chronically sick? Why do countries and social groups within each country have different health outcomes? What is the best explanation for these disparities? Is the *health-care system* of your country adequate to the task of keeping people healthy—and what do we mean by "adequate" and how can we measure it? How would you improve the system as a whole? Is your relationship with your doctors different from that of your parents and grandparents? How has the organization of health care changed over the last thirty years? Do we have to develop new theories to understand these rapid changes? As scholars from many different disciplines—biologists, economists, ethicists, policy analysts, epidemiologists, and anthropologists, as well as sociologists—examine health what types of theories and concepts are useful to them?

Introduction

Sociology of health represents an unusual and fascinating case of change in the concepts and perspectives of a field. At first glance, it appears to have moved through the usual sequence of theoretical paradigms from structural functionalism to micro and macro conflict theories and then unexpectedly shifted away from theory altogether. In our early formulations of this trajectory, we attached the label "paradigm lost" to the sociology of health, as it appeared to have abandoned theoretical formulations and any claims to having a coherent central paradigm because a dominant paradigm —or any trace of "too much theory"—would interfere with cross-disciplinary work and hamper applied and policy-related efforts. Practitioners and policy planners in *public health, epidemiology,* the economics of health care, and many other allied fields seemed to have decided that moving directly to findings rather than discussing theoretical implications not only saved a great deal of time but overcame the academic propensity to get bogged down in arguments about whose theories are most important and whose leading scholars are most widely known or highly regarded.

Yet a closer look at the field suggests that our initial use of the phrase "paradigm lost" too easily dismissed a more complex reality. The analysis of health (whether by sociologists or scholars in related disciplines) has become interdisciplinary and mirrors the concerns of theoretical thinking in the social sciences without specific reference to more traditional paradigms. It has absorbed the key concepts of these earlier paradigms and integrated them into new work without insisting on attaching labels of one type of theory or paradigm. The paradigms have not been lost but rather integrated as needed into a new field that is developing across traditional disciplines.

Trajectory

Origins of the Field

Although references to medical sociology appeared in the literature focusing on society's health during the first decade of the twentieth century, such references did not provide a foundation from which the field of medical sociology could or would emerge. According to Sam Bloom's account of the development of medical sociology in the United States, these early allusions to the field represent "a point of view and a moral disposition" rather than signify the emergence of a theoretical framework (2002, 12). Social workers and doctors dealing with the health problems experienced by the poor, not sociologists, were making allusions to medical sociological concerns.

Sporadic references to medical sociology continued to appear during the 1920s and 1930s in works authored by social historians and physicians concerned with distribution of disease. We first find specific mention of medical sociology by American sociologists in the 1930s, only in passing, in connection with assessment of the social impact of urbanization. Urban sociologists noted that there was a clear link between social deprivation and disease. Those who made reference to medical sociology during this time might be said to have been employing their respective "sociological imaginations." This is far from saying that these observers were beginning to connect what they were seeing to an emergent sociological analytical framework.

Medical sociology, as a clearly identifiable field of study firmly grounded in sociological theory, came into existence very suddenly with the publication of Talcott Parsons's *The Social System* (1951). Once this discussion appeared, medical sociology evolved at a remarkably rapid rate. By the end of the decade, the subfield was sufficiently well developed to establish itself as a section of the American Sociological Association (ASA), the second section to do so after social psychology. It quickly became the largest section, losing that position only when a faction of the membership interested in mental health issues moved to create its own section in 1991. A special issue of the *Journal of Health and Social Behavior* celebrating the fiftieth anniversary of the section appeared in 2010. An overview by Rosich and Hankin (2010, S1–S9) of contributions to the field introduces the volume.

By the end of the 1950s, there was clearly a great deal of momentum, as well as a large number of adherents willing to identify themselves as medical sociologists in North America, if not in Europe. Medical sociology has not evolved into a clearly identifiable, separate branch of sociology in other countries. Curiously, the enthusiasm with which medical sociology was embraced in the United States did not lead to its becoming a core concern within the discipline. Mainstream sociologists were far from ready to grant it legitimacy, arguing that it was an applied field lacking in theoretical substance—in short, that it was not true sociology. In retrospect, it is hard to explain why critics were so ready to dismiss it as "merely applied" and atheoretical given that Parsons was recognized to be the most prominent theoretician at the time.

That medical sociologists felt the need to respond to this criticism from their peers is clear from the presentation-of-self discussions that appeared in the introductory chapters of medical sociology texts published over the next couple of decades. The texts invariably began by noting the distinction between "sociology of medicine" and "sociology in medicine" (R. Strauss 1957). Sociology of medicine was said to be driven by questions grounded in sociological concerns. Sociology in medicine, by contrast, was said to be driven by questions of interest to medicine and described as applied research defined by physicians. Such discussions noted that while the sociologists involved may have been making an important scientific contribution, they were basically doing work in the service of medicine. More importantly, questions of interest to medicine were basically atheoretical and, accordingly, of less value from a sociological perspective. Sociology of medicine was presented as purer, therefore more significant and more legitimate. Such differentiations have received less attention from authors of medical sociological texts over the past couple of decades since the 1980s, even though this distinction may now reveal an even bigger chasm within the field than was the case when it was first articulated—as I will argue later in this discussion.

As an aside, it is worth noting that a couple of decades later, some North American medical sociologists would view the "medical sociology" label as objectionable. The faction objecting to the identifier sought to change the name of the ASA section from the Medical Sociology Section to the Sociology of Health and Illness Section. The vote was close but did not pass. Those who had argued for the change held that the "medical sociology" label suggested that sociologists were overly influenced by the values embraced by the medical profession, most notably medicine's focus on illness rather than health. Sociology, they argued, should focus on the whole person and the person's experience of illness and not just on objective indicators of disease used by physicians. In other words, they were opposed to employing what is generally known within the subfield as the medical model of disease as the basis for examining the impact of illness. The fact that so many college courses now carry the label "sociology of health and illness," or something that includes a reference to health, rather than the "medical sociology" label suggests that the matter of labeling and presentation of self by medical sociologists is not entirely settled.

Growth and Development of the Field

Clearly the lingering reservations regarding medical sociology's theoretical qualifications during its earliest stages did not prevent the subfield from expanding. The fact that it expanded to the extent that it did is attributable to both its theoretical and its methodological underpinnings. First, Parsons's fully articulated structural functional theoretical analysis of social roles inherent in health-care arrangements provided a framework from which research and course work could proceed; second, the ready availability of funding to support both pre- and postdoctoral research advanced methodological development. Let us first consider the effect of Parsons's assessment of the two basic roles involved in the delivery of health care, leaving the discussion of the impact of research funding until later.

The Parsonian Contribution

Parsons's work served to launch two bodies of medical sociological theoretical work grounded in role theory, or (1) the patient's role, and (2) the physician's role. Parsons's amazing insight with regard to the *sick role* played by patients was that we all learn the rules governing this role because everyone around us conspires to teach and reinforce the rules associated with it. Parsons outlined the sick role in the following four-part model:

1. The sick person is exempt from normal social-role responsibilities under three conditions:
2. The person is not responsible for his or her own condition and is not able to get well by an act of decision or will.
3. The person defines the state of being sick as undesirable and wants to get well.
4. The person seeks "technically competent help" from a physician and cooperates in the process of getting well.

Under such conditions, the illness episode constitutes a period of legitimated deviance. According to Parsons, persons who take advantage of the sick role when they are not truly ill are engaging in malingering. Parsons was firmly in favor of social sanctions to prevent such behavior. He argued that members of society must learn that they are expected to fulfill the social responsibilities associated with their status—to go to school in childhood and adolescence and fulfill work and other role responsibilities in adulthood. To do otherwise would be deviant. Parsons argued that nonperformance of an individual's respective role poses a threat to social stability, which was, in his view, crucial for the purpose of insuring social continuity.

Medical sociologists continued to build on Parsons's formulation of the sick role over the next couple of decades, even as his formulation of the sick role began to attract an increasing stream of criticism. His work laid the basis for research on illness behavior (Mechanic 1972, 1978), the illness experience (Roth 1973), labeling and mental illness (Scheff 1974), and steps leading to the decision to seek medical care (Suchman 1965). While researchers would continue to work on these topics, references to Parsons's contribution would fade over the next few decades.

Eliot Freidson (1961) was one of the first to point out the flaws in Parsons's formulation. He noted that the role, as depicted by Parsons, applied to sick-role performance in Western, urbanized societies; gave undue weight to medical definitions of illness; and applied to a limited range of sicknesses, namely, acute illness. The latter point initiated a new stream of work on the special case of disabled and chronically ill persons, who could not willingly leave the sick role and get back to their regular adult responsibilities (Zola 1972, 1982; Albrecht 1992). Given Parsons's depiction of the role, persons suffering such ailments would then have to be defined as permanently engaged in deviance and treated accordingly.

Parsons's other major contribution to the field focused on the social role played by physicians. Physicians, in his view, were charged with performing a vital social function and deserved to be highly rewarded for assuming this responsibility. They bore primary responsibility for insuring that individuals would not take unfair advantage of the privileges inherent in the sick role.

He characterized the physician's role using governing "pattern variables," which he listed in order of importance:

- Universalism: Modern medical practice is based on application of scientific knowledge (as opposed to particularism).
- Functional specificity: Modern medical practice is based on specialized expertise (as opposed to diffuseness).
- Affective neutrality: Physicians must avoid various emotional reactions that might interfere with professional decision making (in contrast to affectivity, or emotional attachment).
- Collectivity orientation: Because the sick person is "peculiarly vulnerable" and patients are not able to judge the physician's competence, the physician must be oriented toward the best interests of the patient. This is in sharp contrast to the orientation that is crucial to the businessperson's role in modern capitalistic society. The doctor-patient relationship should be based on mutual trust—the belief on the part of the patient that the physician is doing his best and belief on the part of the physician that the patient is cooperating to the best of his ability. (This is in opposition to self-orientation).

Parsons also noted that physicians achieved their social position through achievement as opposed to ascription. Accordingly, the high level of financial recompense and social prestige enjoyed by physicians was not only well deserved but socially functional.

Parsons's articulation of the unique characteristics associated with the physician's role contributed to what became a voluminous body of work on the professions building on the early work of A. M. Carr-Saunders (1933). Ernest Greenwood (1957) and William Goode (1957), who were interested in identifying the characteristics that distinguished professional occupations from other occupations, developed this body of literature further. The two core characteristics of a profession, according to Goode, are (1) prolonged specialized training, and (2) a collectivity or service orientation. Other characteristics include (1) the profession's ability to determine its own standards of education and training; (2) having students undergo further-reaching adult resocialization than other occupations; (3) legal recognition by licensure; (4) manning of licensing and admission boards by members of the profession; (5) shaping of most legislation concerned with the profession by the profession; (6) enhanced income, power, and prestige ranking and the ability to demand high-caliber students; (7) freedom of practitioners from lay evaluation and control; (8) enforcement by the profession of norms of practice that is more stringent than legal controls; (9) stronger identification and affiliation of members with the profession than is the case for other occupations; (10) status as a terminal occupation that a higher proportion of members assert they would choose again if given another chance.

This description led other sociologists to examine the characteristics of occupations that just missed being considered professions, sometimes referred to as the semiprofessions (Bucher and Strauss 1961; Etzioni 1969). One of the basic explanations for the inability of other occupations to attain full professional status, other than the obvious fact that they were largely female occupations, was that they could not claim to have a separate body of knowledge that they alone were responsible for developing.

The study of medical education and socialization into the medical profession constitutes another very large body of work that grew out of Parsons's initial analysis of the physician's role. Contributors include such eminent sociologists as Howard Becker, Blanche Geer, Everett Hughes, Anselm Strauss, Robert Merton, Leo Reeder, and Patricia Kendall. The overarching question that these researchers aimed to answer was why the medical educational process succeeded in producing a cadre of highly responsible, devoted practitioners. Another, more specific question driving this research grew out of the fact that so many physicians in training were seeking to become medical specialists. The researchers sought to find out whether medical students were motivated to specialize by the promise of increased income and prestige or if there were other explanations. They concluded that specialization allowed medical students to limit the scope of what they had to learn and afforded them the opportunity to develop a greater level of confidence in their ability to recognize and diagnose specific diseases within the range of their area of declared expertise (R. Fox 1957). Specialization served as a means to deal with medical uncertainty. The process responsible for the choice that medical students made regarding specialization was documented through analysis of the entire medical educational process.

The Shift from Structural Functional Theory
to Critical Theory and Conflict Theories

The critical reaction to Parsons's structural functionalist perspective took a decade to take hold, but once it did, any reference to the social benefits associated with the physician's role were dismissed as naïve and misled. Although Erving Goffman is not generally thought of as a medical sociologist, his book *Asylums* (1961) helped to lay the foundation for depicting medical practice as a value-laden instrument of social control rather than a purely objective science. Michel Foucault's work is also central to this argument. In *The Birth of the Clinic* (1973/1975), Foucault declared that medicine is not nearly as objective and scientific as the medical profession would have us believe. His observation that medicine was engaged in the process of socially constructing medical knowledge and diagnoses was to receive the most attention. He said that disease had become a biochemical event identified as a deviation from the statistical standard. Furthermore, medicine succeeded in shifting the focus away from a person's health to illness and, more specifically, to disease, which could only be confirmed by relying on laboratory tests. Patients' experience of their state of health was treated as secondary to the results of tests.

Although Michel Foucault's work made a major contribution to mainstream sociology, it never became well integrated into medical sociological discourse and texts in the United States. Sociologists addressing medical issues in countries outside the United States quickly embraced his observations. This stemmed in large part from the fact that American medical sociologists had been devoting more energy to empirical research, both field research and secondary analysis of data, since the 1970s rather than focusing on theoretical analysis and interpretation.

Rejection of the *functionalist* assessment of the social value of medical professionalism received a great deal of support from Eliot Freidson in *Profession of Medicine* and *Professional Dominance*, both of which appeared in 1970. That the professional dominance (specifically, *physician dominance*) concept received so much acclaim from medical sociologists may not be surprising. The fact that it attained a significant degree of recognition outside medical sociological circles is an indicator of how well it captured the spirit of the times. The essence of Freidson's criticism was that doctors were exerting dominance over both patients and other health-care workers, especially those whose status gave them less social power (i.e., women and minorities).

Feminists quickly embraced Freidson's assertion that physicians, who were predominantly male during that era, were acting in a dominant fashion (Ruzek 1979). Feminist sociologists went on to lend their support to the observation that physicians engaged in *medicalization,* that is, turning normal human conditions into medical problems, or "badness into sickness" (Conrad 1996; Conrad and Schneider 1992). Feminists pointed out that physicians were particularly interested in defining the conditions experienced by women as syndromes requiring medical treatment, most notably pregnancy, childbirth, menopause, and menstruation (S. Bell 2000). They said that women are more likely to be diagnosed with depression and anxiety and prescribed medications than men.

Other medical sociologists adopted the social constructionist perspective to explain the social meanings that society attaches to disability and various *stigmatized illnesses* (Zola 1972, 1982; Lorber 1997; Bury 1991). The emergence of the HIV/ AIDS epidemic provided fertile ground for applying a range of sociological concepts grounded in deviance theory. Studies of those afflicted with stigmatizing diseases generally begin with observations of how those afflicted feel they are perceived and go on to document their efforts to avoid a stigmatizing label (Brown 1995).

The charge that the medical profession was eager to medicalize a range of human conditions in an effort to increase its social influence by increasing its span of control and to benefit financially gained its greatest acceptance from the early 1970s through the mid-1980s. During this period the medical profession was especially highly regarded, as indicated by rankings of occupational prestige and trust in social institutions. This was when medical sociologists observed that surgeons were defining standards of beauty by performing cosmetic surgery to reshape faces and bodies. They pointed out that physicians were ready to diagnose persons having trouble sleeping, or who were tired or distraught, as requiring medications to help them sleep, have more energy, and achieve a sense of tranquility.

The one celebrated example of demedicalization is worth noting (Conrad and Schneider 1992). In 1973 the American Psychiatric Association (APA) Board of Trustees voted to drop homosexuality from the list of conditions requiring treatment. Only those homosexuals who were troubled by their homosexuality would be candidates for treatment for a condition labeled "homosexual-conflict disorder." Gays and lesbians cheered the shift. Critics pointed out that there was no counterpart for heterosexuals, as in "heterosexual-conflict disorder." Curiously, the question of whether the APA can be credited with having an impact on society's increasing acceptance of homosexuality, or whether it was the shift in thinking in society that caused psychiatrists to alter their position, has not received much attention.

Eventually a few sociologists began to register their objections to what they said amounted to "doctor bashing." They pointed out that it was the patients who were pressing to have behavior and particular life events viewed as medical problems rather than expressions of deviance, which were apt to be addressed by far harsher social-control methods. The attempt to define such problems as attention deficit disorder, alcoholism, and posttraumatic stress disorder as legitimate illnesses rather than conditions resulting from personal, moral failure is illustrative. More recently, the public health community, with some support from a few sociologists, has been active in trying to convince the public that drug abuse should be addressed as a health problem rather than one to be dealt with through legal intervention. That effort seems to have gained some public support. The public health agenda aimed at defining violence as a social problem that would benefit from a public health approach (i.e., better education, access to jobs, and so on), rather than legal intervention and punishment, has been less successful.

Paradoxically, while the term "medicalization" is now far less commonly invoked by sociologists, the medicalization process may be escalating. This is happening, in part, in response to the shift in the target audience pharmaceutical companies have decided to address. Direct-to-consumer advertising has been highly successful. It has increased drug company profits by encouraging patients to demand drugs that they have become convinced will relieve certain symptoms, even when the physician argues that they will not. More troubling is the increasing demand for drugs that patients believe will enhance performance rather than provide a cure for a real medical condition.

Deliberation regarding what constitutes disease and when prescribing medications is appropriate is now taking place within the ranks of the medical profession. For example, a faction of physicians has taken the stance that obesity is a disease and should be treated as such. The physicians who take this position say the disease label will make people take it more seriously. Another focus of debate is whether helping patients deal with their problems is the legitimate function of the physician. In other words, should physicians prescribe medicines used to enhance function? For example, should young, healthy persons be given Alzheimer's medicine to enhance memory if they request it? Should medicine encourage the development of vaccines to inoculate against unhealthy behaviors, such smoking, drug abuse, and alcoholism? The list of such debates is expanding, and there is little reason to expect that consensus with regard to any of these questions is on the horizon, either within the medical profession or outside it.

The locus of debate has clearly shifted. The topic of medicalization is not nearly as central to medical sociological discourse now that physicians' social prestige, income, and power are no longer as impressive as half a century ago. This suggests that medical sociologists have less reason to engage in "physician bashing." In effect, medical sociological interests and perspectives can be seen as following a pattern that reflects society's values and concerns. The fact that Foucault's assessment of physicians' ability to define illness continues to attract the interest of many European sociologists, but attracts somewhat less interest in the United States, may serve as a good indicator of the level of power physicians have in each respective society to exert social control over their work and the interactions that follow. In short, physicians' social control over their work has declined significantly over the last few decades in the United States. Let us next consider why that happened.

The Changing Health-Care System

The next milestone in the development of medical sociological theory occurred with the publication of Paul Starr's *The Social Transformation of American Medicine* (1982), which was awarded the Pulitzer Prize. As a result of that award, many people outside the discipline were exposed to Starr's analysis of medicine and related social institutions (i.e., hospitals, insurance companies, government agencies, organized medicine, and so on). While his detailed historical account of how the entire medical enterprise had come to look the way it did was impressive, his last chapter, titled "The Coming of the Corporation," was prophetic.

Medical sociologists had been observing the workings of hospitals and insurance companies, and everyone associated with both, for some time (H. Smith 1955; Perrow 1963; Anderson 1972). The enormous expansion of the health-care-delivery system after World War II in most countries had attracted the interest of an increasing number of researchers; however, the 1974 passage of *health maintenance organization*

(HMO) legislation in the United States in response to rising costs turned out to have the most dramatic and largely unanticipated long-term effect, stimulating a steady stream of empirical as well as ideologically grounded analyses.

The initial model for the new HMOs created in response to this legislation was the hugely successful, nonprofit Kaiser Permanente organization based in California. However, by the beginning of the next decade, health-care organizations—HMOs and hospitals alike—were beginning to reject their long-established roots as community-based nonprofits, opting to become for-profit, corporate enterprises operated in the interest of shareholders and corporate executives. The shift was inspired by the ideas promulgated during Ronald Reagan's presidential campaign, which promised a reduction in tax dollars being squandered on what Reagan claimed were inefficient, government-supported arrangements in favor of organizations operated by corporations relying on efficient business practices, primarily competition. There is no question that economists' interpretations of reality, especially those presented by classical economists, were enthusiastically embraced by the public and policy makers alike during this era, while sociological interpretations lost favor.

By the mid-1980s, Paul Starr's prediction—that all the problems inherent in the health-care arrangements that had evolved to date would pale in comparison to the problems that society would experience once the corporate sector took control—was turning into reality (Gray 1983). Managed care organizations (MCOs) came into existence in the Reagan era with the aim of consolidating, that is, buying up, the HMOs created during the 1970s. During the following decade, that trend took on the appearance of a survivor-take-all business plan. Not only did the constant changes in ownership and rules governing patient-care arrangements cause a great deal of disruption, but the newly reorganized entities were intent on reducing their costs. They accomplished this by imposing restrictions on the services available to patients. The public responded by demanding legislation limiting such restrictions, which resulted in state statutes throughout the country prohibiting certain restrictive practices. The two restrictions that seem to have inspired most public outcry were (1) the practice of discharging women from the hospital within twenty-four hours after giving birth, and (2) "drive-through" mastectomies.

In contrast to growing public dissatisfaction, the profitability of the MCOs was enthusiastically welcomed by investors, who liked seeing the organizations position themselves as integrated health-care systems—from doctor's office, to hospital, to nursing home. This rationalized approach enabling the companies to deliver an integrated line of health-care products and services became known as "managed competition," a label that developed negative connotations by being linked to all the practices that the public saw as objectionable and by being associated with the Clinton administration's failed health-care reform proposal of 1993. It was not long before the same organizations explained that they preferred the label *health plan*.

In retrospect, it is clear that a great deal more than labels had changed in the transition from HMO to MCO to health plan, which parallels the shift in theoretical perspectives embraced by medical sociologists. The most striking change was in the structure of health-care-delivery arrangements, which went from being comparatively small, nonprofit, independent, and community based to being delivered by highly competitive, for-profit, consolidated, national corporations. The long-standing, mutually gratifying doctor-patient relationship vanished. The new expectation that patients would see doctors on a rotating list was responsible for much of the public dissatisfaction. Patients blamed the corporations, not the doctors, for all the restrictions they now confronted.

For their part, doctors were left with little choice but to enter into contracts with the health plans, which had captured patients through employee-sponsored health insurance arrangements. The contracts they say they were forced to sign required them to see more patients for shorter periods, restricted referrals to specialists, and denied access to certain procedures—all of which made doctors very unhappy. They responded by organizing themselves into larger medical-practice groups and turning them into corporate entities. While this was happening, the managers of the health plans were actively recruiting younger and healthier enrollees to gain a greater share of the market and avoid being acquired by another organization. The fervor with which the health plans had been competing settled down by the beginning of the twenty-first century. By that time only a handful of health plans were left standing; by 2005 there were only four major plans, plus a few less-known plans, left (Budrys 2012, 124).

The fact that the post–World War II economy expanded in virtually all highly industrialized economies meant that citizens in all of these countries were demanding more from their health-care systems. Health-planning officials in other countries closely observed increasing participation of the corporate sector in health-care-delivery arrangements. Representatives of the health plans made presentations to any official who would listen in the hope of establishing their operations in other countries. Advanced industrialized countries did introduce some of the innovations outlined by the American corporate sector but adapted them to fit their own societal and cultural arrangements. As a result the adaptations do not resemble American arrangements very closely.

The degree to which people in a number of advanced societies were satisfied or dissatisfied with their health-care arrangements by the end of 1980s was captured in a comparative opinion poll by researchers associated with the Harvard School of Public Health (Blendon et al. 1990). Only 10 percent of Americans said they were satisfied, the lowest rate in comparison to the nine other highly advanced countries surveyed; the highest rate was among Canadians, with 56 percent saying they were satisfied. If we accept the idea that the functionalist position on social change requires that social institutions change and adapt to reflect society's preferences, then in this instance the theory clearly did not match reality.

The sociological lesson here is clear: social institutions do not change easily, and they certainly don't change as dramatically as the Clinton administration envisioned during the early 1990s, regardless of how dissatisfied Americans said they were about the workings of this social institution. Indeed, it would not be an exaggeration to say that there are no structural functionalists among medical sociologists anymore. The public has been demanding change, yet never seems to be satisfied with the changes that are introduced. The health-care system in the United States continues to be a source of public dissatisfaction in the wake of the far-reaching 2010 health-care reform legislation. The great divide in thinking that registered during the November 2010 midterm elections is clearly reflected in American public opinion regarding reform. Large majorities indicate approval of parts of the law, while registering dissatisfaction with the law as a whole.

Contemporary Developments

Disagreement within the Ranks

From a theoretical perspective, we see critical medical sociological theory moving toward a largely unacknowledged schism between scholars interested in studying the interactions between individual doctors and their patients or coworkers and those who take the position that recognizing that institutional arrangements have a far broader and more detrimental impact is far more important. One faction of sociologists continues to argue that the medical profession is engaged in the social construction of disease and acting in a dominant fashion in face-to-face encounters. This is more typical of European, rather than US, scholars. Indeed, a number of highly regarded medical sociologists in the United States have argued that physicians have become relatively powerless workers in a capitalist economy controlled by corporate owners and managers (Navarro 1976, 1986). Others have taken the position that it is time to reassess the social value of professional dominance and appreciate its value as a countervailing power to the growing control over health-care-delivery arrangements by corporations (Light and Levine 1988). Then there are those who maintain that physicians are far from dominant and can more accurately be described as proletarianized (McKinlay and Stoeckle 1988). The emergence of physicians' unions lends support to this observation (Budrys 1997).

To sum up, one branch of critical medical sociological theory is interested in addressing microlevel interactions, and the other is interested in addressing macrolevel social interactions. The effect on critical medical sociological theory is a split between scholars who focus on the interactions taking place between individual doctors and their patients or coworkers and those who focus on the interactions between the representatives of large-scale organizations. Both identify with a critical perspective even though they basically disagree with one another.

Medical Sociology and Health System Goals

Medical sociology's initial growth spurt during the early 1950s came at a time when increasing numbers of people were seeking medical care because it had become more effective than home remedies and potions obtained from the local apothecary. Moreover, medical care was relatively inexpensive during this era. Thus the problem was not so much availability of or access to medical care but concern about its quality.

This was when doctors identified themselves as general practitioners and worked out of one- or two-person offices located in the community. During this period, they enjoyed high prestige and earned a comparatively modest income, which was still seen as a good living.

Because communities were stable, people knew their doctors personally, and physicians' position in their communities meant that what they said and did was likely to be a topic of conversation among residents. In short, the fact that doctors practiced in isolated offices, behind closed doors, without much oversight from anyone could have easily led to deviance; however, that did not happen frequently. Parsons maintained that their role was not only clearly defined but socially enforced, though he did not spend much time explaining how. In retrospect, it is clear that doctors were highly respected and trusted during that era due to the control mechanisms that operated so effectively in stable, well-established communities, that is, communities where most people knew each other and discussed important personal events and encounters.

That changed with the trend toward suburbanization starting in the late 1950s. Members of the post–World War II generation moved away from the neighborhoods in which they had grown up. Doctors followed the same pattern. Patients were now in the position of seeing doctors with whom they had no established relationship, that is, strangers. Looking at reality and Parsons's assessment of it, it is reasonable to conclude that the structural functional perspective he outlined presented a fairly accurate picture of the doctor's role and society's view of it before suburbanization upset the familiar interactional patterns and the social-control mechanisms that had served society so well previously. To the extent that questions regarding improvements in the quality of medical care had come up, the medical profession was able to assure the public that any problems would be addressed through improvements in medical education. That seemed to serve as a satisfactory response to concerns about quality in the wake of the structural changes brought about by suburbanization.

There is no question that the steps that medicine took to achieve and maintain its privileged social position earlier in the twentieth century captured the attention of other occupational groups, which sought to gain the benefits society readily granted to professionals. The steps employed by medicine served as a model emulated by a wide range of occupational groups seeking professional status and social rewards over the next couple of decades.

A number of observers came up with lists of steps leading to professional occupational status (Wilensky 1964). The following is a combination of the lists: performance of tasks on a full-time basis; control over training and recruitment; creation of a professional organization; political agitation for legal restrictions on scope of work; and adherence to a code of ethics. Few occupational groups came close to meeting these standards, so medicine continued to stand as the model of professionalism until the label began losing social value in response to the health insurance organizations' active campaign to discredit physician professionalism during the 1980s.

While this description of the indicators of doctors' professionalism most closely applies to health-care-delivery arrangements in the United States, it also applies to the social position of doctors in most advanced societies. What varies is the extent to which changes in health-care-delivery arrangements altered the position of physicians in each respective society. The arrangements changed to a far greater extent in the United States than elsewhere. The increasing influence and power of for-profit health plans meant that patients were no longer in a position to see doctors of their choice, and physicians would have no patients unless they signed up with the insurance plans. Of course, the fact that employers gave employees a limited set of choices regarding which health insurance plans they could sign up with guaranteed that this would be the case. In order to gain greater social acceptance, the representatives of the plans made an effort to convince patients that doctors were in it for the money and were therefore providing more treatments than were really necessary. They could not be trusted. The health insurance organizations promised to monitor doctors' work and protect patients. The blow to medical professionalism was enormous.

The social climate of the time was also responsible for the rise in interest in social problems and social *inequality,* as illustrated by a number of movements that erupted during the 1960s and 1970s with regard to civil rights, women's liberation, and concern about economic inequality. In this period there was a shift in focus from quality of medical care to concern about access. A significant number of people were registering concern about the fact that some people—namely, the poor—could not afford to see a doctor. As a result, the two big public health insurance programs, Medicare and Medicaid, were legislated. Reports on the problems people were having getting medical care when they needed it continued to receive attention well into the next decade.

Sociologists were at the forefront of research on access to and utilization of health-care services. This body of work was grounded in quantitative methods of analysis and interpretation, rather than theoretical analysis. Work by LuAnn Aday and Ronald Andersen (1975) gave meaning to the concept of access by exploring all the factors that could interfere with it beyond the obvious inability to pay for care; factors like the time required to get to the doctor's office, waiting time in the doctor's office, language barriers, feeling of social discomfort, and so on. The researchers' other major contribution was to attend to demographic variables (e.g., income, poverty, age, and race) that identified those who were experiencing restricted access. This research lay at the heart of medical sociological concerns. However, it did more to advance data-collection methodology than sociological theory.

With the coming of the 1970s, Americans were beginning to register a rising level of concern about the increasing cost of care. While sociologists were also interested in the impact and consequences of rising health-care costs, cost containment was generally recognized to be the province of economists. At this point attention shifted from the findings that medical sociologists could present to those offered by medical economists.

Somewhere along the way, researchers and policy makers alike came to recognize that these topics—quality, access, and cost containment—constituted the three unstated, but widely accepted, goals embraced by the unorganized health system in the United States. There is also general consensus that thinking regarding which goal is most pressing shifts from time to time. The level of interest and social concern that any one of the three goals happens to inspire at a particular time determines which set of disciplinary skills and researchers is considered best suited to assess the problem and offer a solution. Since the need for cost containment has been inspiring more concern than the other two goals over the last few decades since the 1970s, when the Nixon administration introduced HMOs in an effort to control the rising cost of health care, medical economists have been playing a more prominent role in policy discussions than researchers associated with other disciplines.

Recognition of the significance of the three goals is reflected in the level of support for research aimed at addressing issues related to each. Research aimed at identifying factors leading to improvement in quality of care and, later, access to care has been supported by a number of important private foundations and government agencies. According to Sam Bloom (2002, 212, 252–267), most notable were the Russell Sage Foundation, the Commonwealth Fund, the Milbank Memorial Fund, and the National Institute of Mental Health. Other foundations and government agencies, most notably the National Institutes of Health, provided additional support. Funding for research problems identified by sociologists began to decline as of the 1980s, because cost containment renewed the Reagan administration's interest in market solutions offered by the corporate sector. That had an enormous impact. Medical sociology departments in major universities began to disappear as doctoral-training funds dried up. Funds to support training researchers who would seek practical solutions identified in applied settings became more available (Bloom 2002, 275). Interdisciplinary academic units committed to producing research results with policy implications rather than extending discussion of theoretical implications grew.

The Dissemination of Health-Care Statistics

The technological developments that occurred during the 1980s produced another, very different turning point in the development of medical sociology as well as virtually every other field of work. The sudden introduction and very rapid development of personal computers and information technology changed the way data are compiled, stored, and reported. The impact on medical sociology was interesting. The government had been systematically gathering health statistics since the late 1950s; however, it was taking a few years at best to organize the data and publish them. Researchers regularly bemoaned this state of affairs. Invariably, they ended their analyses of trends with the caveat that they could not predict future trends because they were looking at data that were already dated. Computers changed that. Health statistics became available to scholars, government-employed policy analysts, media representatives, and research units in interested organizations—basically anyone with access to a computer. Interpretation of the information would no longer be the exclusive domain of academics and analysts working in government agencies. Suddenly policy institutes supported by private foundations and research arms of interest group organizations were issuing reports. The analysts hired by these organizations to analyze the data and write reports came to this work from a wide range of disciplinary backgrounds. Because the organizations employing the analysts were committed to disseminating their position papers with the aim of influencing health-care policy, the papers had to be written in a style accessible to any educated reader. That meant that the position papers would have to be short, direct, and free of internecine scholarly argument.

The degree to which scholars from a range of disciplines are collaborating in the process of gathering health data, developing and analyzing statistics, and interpreting trends is unprecedented. The questions they address are designed to produce unambiguous results. It is not difficult to understand why theory might interfere with, rather than advance, interpretation of data when scholars with varying disciplinary backgrounds come together to analyze their findings. Relying on theory generated by any one discipline poses a threat to shared understandings and cooperation. If people from the same disciplinary background can argue about theoretical interpretations, then one can imagine why it might be far more difficult to come to any agreement if the parties involved bring very different perspectives and use separate disciplinary languages.

Theoretical interpretation of the volumes of health statistics that have been compiled is notably absent. At the same time, a common set of concepts is emerging. The fact that computers made it so much easier to access scholarly articles authored by researchers in other fields is undoubtedly responsible. It seems that scholars have been discovering and embracing particularly gripping concepts across disciplinary lines. Scholars from varying disciplinary backgrounds now utilize a number of shared concepts, many of which have sociological roots. The following, among others, are now part of the lexicon: social inequality, social class, social capital, social isolation, social disorganization, social trust, community, and medicalization.

Sociologists who are members of such teams generally do not identify themselves as medical sociologists. Since disciplinary affiliation is something that interdisciplinary teams strive to deemphasize, they needed another unifying label. Two especially large and productive interdisciplinary domains evolved during the 1990s, each with its own specific identity and designation. One focuses on health-care-delivery processes and organizations; it is known as health-services research. The other focuses on health disparities, that is, differences in mortality and morbidity rates in various populations; it is called social epidemiology or *population health*. Let us focus on the latter body of work first.

The Study of Population Health

Research on health became not only interdisciplinary but international during the 1980s. The credit for this goes to scholars in the United Kingdom. The fact that health statistics there had been collected on the basis of class rather than race since the first decade of the twentieth century helps to explain why sociologists would take notice. Early reports of differences in mortality rates by social status were regularly noted by medical sociologists in Britain, as well as in a number of other industrialized countries such as Canada, Sweden, and the Netherlands, between the 1950s and 1970s. These data were generally presented as an aside in discussing the fact that universal health-care coverage did not eliminate variations in life expectancy by social class. That changed dramatically during the 1980s.

What captured the attention of researchers in the United Kingdom was the shift in mortality trends: the life expectancy of persons in lower social classes had not just stopped increasing but was actually declining, while the life expectancy of those in higher classes continued to increase. The Thatcher government showed little interest and actually tried to suppress the findings. However, a 1976 newspaper editorial by Richard Wilkinson, a graduate student at the time, saying that this required "urgent inquiry" on the part of the government led to the formation of a committee to study the problem (Wilkinson 1996; Marmot 2004). The report that came out of this effort led to the Whitehall studies, whose impact has been enormous (Davey-Smith, Shipley, and Rose 1990).

A few factors came together over time to produce what can only be viewed as a mushrooming effect. The ready availability of research articles in electronic format rather than journals meant that the findings were more broadly available and being published shortly after the results were analyzed. Finally, the increasing use of English as an international language meant this body of research was being read by scholars across national boundaries, which stimulated comparative research in other countries. The results of those studies were also disseminated electronically. The literature initially inspired by the Whitehall studies has burgeoned. What accounts for the tremendous impact this research has had is worth considering because the findings are fundamentally sociological but have been largely ignored by mainstream sociology.

Whitehall, which employs government workers in the United Kingdom, became the site of studies aimed at identifying factors responsible for variation in life expectancy. The significance of using this population is that the position a person occupies at Whitehall reflects a combination of variables, namely, education, income, and occupation, which are social class indicators. Rank is a matter of official designation. This ranking leaves little room for the inaccuracy that comes from self-reports of social status. Since everyone in this population is employed, no one can be considered poor, and like all other UK citizens, this population receives free health care through the National Health Service. This eliminates two important variables traditionally used to explain the differential in life expectancy.

Two waves of Whitehall studies (1967–1970, 1985–1988) have produced momentous findings in that they have confirmed what could only be hypothesized and debated in the abstract before—and did so powerfully. Researchers have been following original study populations. New findings continue to appear.

The groundbreaking finding was that social hierarchy, together with all the advantages that go with higher-level occupational position, offers a far more powerful explanation for why some people live longer than others than previous research on lifestyle, genetic inheritance, and access to health care had been able to (Robert and House 2000). Review of the accumulating body of literature on spillover effects of inequality by state in the United States reveals that the level of violence directly relates to the level of inequality (Kawachi, Kennedy, and Wilkinson 1999; Kawachi and Kennedy 1997). The legal status and treatment of women is correlated with social inequality (Kawachi, Kennedy, and Wilkinson 1999). Voting rates are inversely related to inequality (Blakely, Kennedy, and Kawachi 2001).

Researchers who conducted comparable research in other countries were coming up with mixed results until recently. This was being interpreted to mean that inequality in the United States and United Kingdom is more extreme and therefore has more detrimental effects than it does elsewhere (Lynch 2000). Indeed, the most recent results indicate that Americans in the top third of the income distribution suffer worse health than UK residents in the bottom third (Banks et al. 2006). The researchers generally concluded that the circumstances in which Americans live and work account for these results, but the question of why high-status Americans are at a disadvantage requires further exploration. The compilation of comparative international trend data by Richard Wilkinson and Kate Pickett's *The Spirit Level* (2010), revealing the impact of inequality on morbidity and mortality as well as a range of other indicators of well-being, apparently captured the attention in 2011 of economists who come together every year in Davos, Switzerland, to discuss international economic policy. Attendees concluded that inequality increases the risk to national economic security and stability because a sickly population is simply not likely to be productive.

While the correlation between inequality and ill health, especially in the United States, had been convincingly documented, how socioeconomic inequality translates into physical health remained unclear. Social scientists may have been interested in finding the answer to this question but clearly did not have the skills to do so. Two sociologists, Bruce Link and Jo Phelan (1995), are credited with directing the attention of social scientists to the problem by introducing the concept of pathways between social inequality and objective indicators of health. Fortunately, researchers with backgrounds in medicine and the basic sciences who had been following the research on the relationship between social inequality and health became involved.

Scholars from a range of different disciplines have long suspected that stress had something to do with variation in mortality. Social psychologists had been studying stress and stress management for several decades (Thoits 1995). However, the results were consistently inconclusive, which is understandable given that there has never been much agreement on the validity and reliability of stress measures. Since inducing stress in human beings in order to measure it is clearly unacceptable, it is hard to see how such measures could be developed. Fortunately, a few neurophysiologists had been doing exactly that kind of research on rats (McKeown 1976) and primates (Sapolsky 1998). Moreover, some were prepared to argue that the results were clearly applicable to Homo sapiens. The work of Robert Sapolsky, whose findings have received a great deal of attention in the popular press, serves as an excellent example. His research reveals that high-status baboons enjoy an objectively measurable (i.e., physiological) health advantage. Their physiological (i.e., hormonal) response to stressful events differs from that of fellow baboons who occupy a lower status in the hierarchy. Furthermore, low-status baboons seem to experience low-level stress on a steady basis, which has the effect of releasing hormones that damage organs. High-status baboons do not exhibit signs of steady stress. One of the most interesting revelations is that a high-status baboon who (he gives them names and talks about their families) is removed from that position loses all the health advantages he enjoyed while occupying the high-status position. In short, the benefits are linked to the social position itself, not to the individual.

It does not take much of a stretch to see how these findings could apply to human beings. Research on the relationship between hypertension (high blood pressure) and social status reveals that poor people are at greater risk of hypertension, especially those who learn to accept the disrespect and discrimination they confront. That certainly should not be surprising because they do in fact experience a higher level of stress when they do not have sufficient funds to cover the needs that society says are basic. Obviously, counseling designed to develop better coping skills will not help them fully overcome this source of stress. Peggy Thoits (1995), in her extensive review of the literature on stress and coping, pointed out that it was curious that sociologists had not done more to acknowledge the importance of this basic fact, given the seemingly paramount significance of social support in all its forms. The sociological significance of this observation should be obvious; adapting the famous Clintonesque campaign phraseology, it's the group, stupid. Or as more sophisticated theorists who study health disparities would put it, it's social capital.

Reflecting on social inequality, which is clearly the central concept in this body of research, should remind us that sociologists produced a large body of research on the earlier version of this concept, that is, social stratification. However, we can see that sociologists did not, because they could not, move on to discuss the impact of status attainment beyond lifestyle indicators, such as how people decorated their living rooms—or beyond, as sociologist George Homans reportedly observed, discovering that "rich people live in big houses."

By contrast research currently being carried out by interdisciplinary teams shows that social inequality has life-and-death consequences. The challenge of capturing how perceptions about an abstract concept like social standing or social status translate into physical reality has attracted the interest of an enormous number and range of scholars. A Medline search in 1997 found that articles on the relationship between social class and health were appearing at the rate of 170 per month (Kaplan and Lynch 1997). The rate has probably increased since then. In other words, this makes clear that social inequality is far more significant than sociologists were in a position to establish. Yes, there was talk about life chances but not nearly enough convincing evidence to support the observation that social inequality determines life expectancy.

Moving from state-level analysis to that in the international arena, we turn to the lively scholarly debate launched by a Canadian sociologist, David Coburn (2000), when he proposed that neoliberalism is responsible for increasing economic inequality and a decline in social cohesion, which, he argued, leads to a decline in the health status of populations. The entire issue of *Social Science and Medicine* in which Coburn presented his thesis was devoted to his argument with little basic disagreement.

Others have argued that neoliberalism is the source of the decline in social trust, civic participation, and family integrity. That, they say, leads to an increase in the level of social disintegration, which ultimately threatens democracy. Indeed, Nobel Prize–winning economist Amartya Sen (1992) argues that mortality should be used as an international indicator of economic success and, by extension, an important marker for the risk of political instability. A report commissioned by the CIA's Directorate of Intelligence confirms the value of this suggestion. The report, which analyzed variables associated with state failure in 113 countries, in contrast to 339 control cases, concluded that infant mortality was the "single-most-efficient variable for reflecting a country's overall quality of material life" and political stability (Esty et al. 1998).

Research on the *relative-income hypothesis* is indicative of the role that sociological ideas play in this body of research (Kawachi, Kennedy, and Wilkinson 1999). This work is grounded in the idea that people's perception of their relative economic and social standing is based on the position of those to whom they are comparing themselves. The term "reference group" does not appear in this literature, but that is certainly the basic idea involved. Amartya Sen puts it this way: "*Relative* deprivation in terms of *incomes* can yield *absolute* deprivation in terms of *capabilities*. Being relatively poor in a rich country can be a great capability handicap, even when one's absolute income is high in terms of world standards. In a generally opulent country, more income is needed to buy enough commodities to achieve the *same social functioning*" (quoted in Kawachi, Kennedy, and Wilkinson 1999, 89; italics in the original).

Health-Services Research

The other major body of interdisciplinary work to which sociologists are contributing addresses health-service-delivery arrangements, generally referred to as health-services research. All advanced industrialized societies are experiencing similar pressures, namely, increasing demand for health-care services because of rising expectations regarding health status, aging populations requiring more health-care services, and a growing rate of national expenditures on health care. Thus, all are eager to learn about innovative health-care-delivery arrangements that will benefit society's health but not add to skyrocketing costs. Economists are of course taking the lead in this effort. Because health-services research invariably has policy implications, it is generally designed with this purpose in mind. Everyone involved is cognizant of the challenge—to contain costs while, ideally, maintaining increasing quality and at the same time extending access.

As mentioned earlier, sociologists' initial studies on the quality of and access to health-care services laid the groundwork for much of the work that has been done in the first decade of the twenty-first century in the United States and elsewhere. Quite a few sociologists have addressed these issues as independent analysts rather than as members of interdisciplinary teams. As there are too many names to list them all, the following includes only some of most recognized names not mentioned elsewhere in this discussion: Renee Anspach (1993), Charles Bosk (1979), William Cockerham (1999), Kathy Charmaz (1991), Frederic Hafferty (1991), Donald Light (1992), David Mechanic (2006), Leonard Pearlin et al. (1981), Bernice Pescosolido (1992), and Jill Quadagno (2004).

The volume of research on quality is enormous. A few questions that have recently been or are currently being addressed include whether specialists deliver a higher or lower quality of care than primary care practitioners; whether a higher ratio of doctors to patients lowers mortality and reduces morbidity; whether a higher ratio of nurses to hospitalized patients improves outcomes; whether surgeons do more surgery when the population in the area has better insurance coverage; whether doctors discriminate against certain categories of patients, namely, the poor, minorities, and women; whether care provided by for-profit hospitals is the same as care provided in nonprofit hospitals; whether for-profit HMOs provide the same quality of care as nonprofit HMOs; whether and to what extent being uninsured leads to poorer health outcomes; whether people are actually getting too much medical care because they demand attention and are in a position to pay for it; and so on. In short, scholars working in this area are addressing a very large and varied range of questions. Not only are many of these questions being addressed by interdisciplinary teams, but the researchers involved are participating with the support of funding from government and private foundations.

Conclusion

In the final analysis, it is difficult to assess the contribution of medical sociology to the discipline as a whole. Why that is the case becomes clearer when we look at what leading scholars in the field have to say when asked about the future of medical sociology. Some are very optimistic, some are very pessimistic, and others fall somewhere in between. To illustrate, Ray Elinson says that it is "alive and well ... and all about us"; Eliot Freidson has said that the field is "in decline and may even vanish"; Renee Fox's assessment is that it is "alive, even vital, but parochial" (Bloom 2002, 273). How different medical sociology is from other branches of the discipline is something readers of this volume will have to decide for themselves.

Based on the content of a significant proportion of medical sociology texts, it would not be unreasonable to conclude that the branch of medical sociology identified as sociology in medicine is now responsible for collecting more data, doing more analysis of those data, and reporting more findings, together with interpretation of those findings, than sociologists whose work lies more in the sociology-of-medicine branch. It is also true that many medical sociology texts continue to devote a much greater share of space to interactions between individuals than to all the other topics combined, reinforcing the idea that this is the core of what medical sociology is about.

It seems that medical sociology, as a subfield of the discipline, continues to struggle with the definition of its realm. Recall that the origins of medical sociology are grounded in role theory and the performance of both the doctor and patient roles by individuals. That is certainly what many of those who identify themselves as medical sociologists continue to study. Curiously, when authors of introductory sociology (as opposed to medical sociology) texts describe sociology as a discipline, they claim for it the distinction that it focuses on characteristics shared by groups of people; yet those who most closely self-identify with medical sociology rather than health-services research or social epidemiology seem to concentrate on interactions between individuals rather than the actions and attitudes of groups of people. This is not to say that the study of individual interactions is not central to sociological interests, given the work of some of the most eminent fathers of sociology—Georg Simmel, Charles Cooley, and George Herbert Mead. It is to say that medical sociology does not seem to have much to say, at the level of theory, about groups.

This is in sharp contrast to the contribution made by those whose work advances research methodology as opposed to theory, which by its nature addresses the behavior and attitudes of groups of people. Perhaps the answer lies in the fact that so many of the other disciplines also focus on the behavior and attitudes of groups that their sociological contribution appears to be less prominent—not because it is viewed as less important by the sociologists involved or anyone else but because it is less visible since it constitutes only one part of larger interdisciplinary efforts.

That applied research is far more likely to be funded certainly goes a long way in explaining why many sociologists who work on health-related issues identify themselves as members of teams dedicated to particular research concerns, primarily, health-services or population-health research, rather than as medical sociologists.

How one might assess the state of medical sociology is arguable. One might see it as ironic that the effort on the part of mainstream sociology to discredit sociology in medicine as atheoretical in preference for a sociology-of-medicine approach has left medical sociology with a far smaller range of legitimated research topics than it could have claimed. On the other hand, the fact that sociologists are members of interdisciplinary research teams means that the sociological perspective is gaining a far greater number of proponents than might otherwise have been the case. Some might argue that sociological ideas are being absorbed into the mainstream of health research without giving sufficient credit to their sociological origins. One could counter by saying that far more is being learned about the relationship between health and a wide range of social factors than has ever been understood before, and this is all to the good.

The contribution to understanding variation in life-expectancy rates—the difference between life and death chances—coming from economists rather than sociologists is especially provocative. Cross-national comparisons of the proportion of income received by the bottom 50 percent of the population reveal that a 7 percent increase in the share going to the bottom half increases life expectancy by two years (Gramlich, Kasten, and Sammartino 1993; Kunst and Mackenbach 1994). A comparative study of infant mortality in seventy countries indicates that the higher the share of income going to the top 5 percent of the population, the higher the infant-mortality rate (Waldman 1992).

Perhaps most surprising is the degree to which physicians, whom sociologists initially charged with distracting medical sociologists from doing "true" sociological research, are now taking the lead in creating sociological concepts to describe how social factors interact with health. Michael Marmot's introduction of the status syndrome concept makes the point eloquently: he simply says that "health follows a social gradient" and that the statement applies regardless of where a person finds him- or herself on that gradient (2004, 1). To illustrate, although the residents of Harlem are predominantly African American and many are poor, their health status varies; it follows a social gradient. Income and education of Harlem residents are inversely related to levels of hypertension, smoking, and physical inactivity, which are in turn related to the likelihood of mortality from heart disease (Diez-Roux et al. 1999). A great deal of effort has gone into explaining why a higher proportion of those at the lower end of the social hierarchy engage in such behaviors. Marmot makes the point that research aimed at understanding differences in lifestyle choice, important as that is, does not explain variation in health status. Referring to Robert Sapolsky's 1998 research on baboons, Marmot (2004, 82) notes that low-status baboons do not smoke, eat hamburgers, or fail to keep appointments with their doctors but still have higher rates of morbidity and mortality. As the always droll Canadian economist Robert Evans puts it, social inequality and the lifestyle choices associated with one's status reveal "a very systematic pattern with health implications. It cries out for explanation, rather than trivialization as 'personal choice'" (1994, 7).

After discussing how sociological work on health issues has evolved, we might want to consider whether the knowledge we have gained has any potential to translate into public sociology. It would seem that the findings have far-reaching practical ramifications and policy implications. This is especially important in light of the fact that, as Michael Burawoy (2005) points out, the world appears to be moving to the right. The problem that public sociology must overcome is that applied sociology, even when it results in dramatic findings, will not become public unless it is filtered through media outlets for public consumption. That is certainly not happening. People in most societies have no idea how their country ranks compared to other countries in terms of life expectancy, infant mortality, mortality rates, leading causes of death, and so on. Americans seem to be particularly unwilling to hear that they spend far more on health care than anyone else in the world and have a much lower life expectancy than people in twenty-six or thirty-seven other advanced societies, depending on which countries are included in the count. The commitment to individualism has allowed Americans to dismiss the evidence that America tolerates huge health disparities. The harsh realities are explained away as the consequence of individual choice to engage in risky behaviors, as well as the belief that it is, after all, ultimately a matter of genetics—despite all the scientific evidence to the contrary.

For public sociology or, as is more accurate in this case, public interdisciplinary discourse on the state of health to have a social impact, people need to be far better informed. A number of researchers have pointed to the sharply contrasting degree of attention devoted to economic indicators—which are examined in great detail during radio and television news reports, in newspapers and magazines, on dedicated television programs, and so forth—as opposed to social indicators. The Fordham Institute has compiled a list of indicators that might serve as a means to assess a nation's social performance in contrast to its economic performance: infant mortality, child abuse, child poverty, teenage suicide, teenage drug abuse, teenage birth rates, high school dropout rates, unemployment, wages, health-care coverage, poverty among those over age sixty-five, life expectancy of those over sixty-five, violent crime, alcohol-related traffic fatalities, affordable housing, and inequality. The idea is that members of each respective society would see where they stand on this list of indicators as compared to those living in other highly advanced societies.

An enticing idea, is it not, to see how much of the variation in life expectancy differences in social indicator rates can explain? Of course, there is no way to know exactly how such reports would be interpreted. Would people, helped along by those interested in maintaining the status quo, continue to find ways to explain away differences as the result of individual choice rather than social policy? One can hope that the graphic picture of variation in morbidity and mortality—life and death—would receive the attention it deserves. A place to start would be to encourage sociologists, including a number of medical sociologists, to develop much better command of and more interest in this material than they have exhibited to date. This is not to say that this would lead to the flowering of medical sociology theory. At the same time, there is reason to think that the recognition that theory matters on the part of some health researchers will result in a more comprehensive theoretical development than would be the case if sociologists were the only ones involved in creating it. Nancy Kreiger, a respected social epidemiologist, puts it this way: "Ultimately, it is theory which inspires our questions, which enables us to envision a far healthier world than the one in which we live, and which gives us the insight, responsibility, and accountability to translate this vision to a reality. Who shall create this theory? The task is ours" (2001, 674).

Conclusion

HAVE WE MADE PROGRESS?

The aim of our project has been to provide an overview or map of the complex territory of contemporary sociology. We have attempted to draw together the diverse threads of what we have labeled conflict constructionism and to compare its impact across areas of sociology, from full embrace to general indifference. We have come full circle in our project. At this point of return, we seek to look forward rather than to repeat what has already been covered. So we try to address a question about the discipline: Have we made progress? While no definitive response can be given to such a question, we offer the following speculations as points of future inquiry.

In the natural sciences, a paradigm represents progress over its predecessor when it explains more, offers a better match between concepts and empirical results, produces more accurate predictions, and solves unsolved puzzles. The social sciences do not have a clear progression of paradigms; yet some of these criteria are relevant as well. Although we promised in the introduction that we would not be advocates for the paradigm of conflict constructionism, we can point to various ways it offers progress or at least benefits that would not exist if it had not been developed.

Explaining New Phenomena

As we have seen, new paradigms are needed to give insight into new phenomena, and in this case conflict construction fulfilled these expectations. Social changes, such as the media explosion, globalization in the age of neoliberalism (so different from colonial-era globalization), race and ethnic relations in the post–civil rights era and the era of immigration, and the entry of women into the paid labor force, all called for a new paradigm. Since all theories are products of the historical conditions within which they are conceptualized, new events and shifts in social life will surely bring new ideas, puzzles, and problematics to the forefront of our attention, leaving less important ones on the periphery. It is this issue of change that should attract our utmost attention here, since it is the circumstances of social life themselves that truly matter most in speculating about what the future may hold for the relevance of conflict constructionism. In sociology and other social sciences, the subject matter changes on a human and historical scale, new paradigms are called for by new circumstances, and conflict constructionism addresses these changes.

Solving Old Puzzles

Conflict constructionism assembled a convergent set of heterogeneous concepts and provided new concepts that could encompass the puzzles that were not resolved by older paradigms and explain aspects of reality that the older paradigms failed to address. For example, the fluidity of social construction, macro/micro linkages, the play of conflict, and the role of frames and discourses are aspects of reality that are not new but that had not been captured well by previous paradigms. Structural functionalism had problems explaining patterns of conflict and change. On the other hand, conflict theories in many instances could not explain stability and tended to overestimate the frequency and effects of conflicts. Neither of these paradigms gave adequate attention to the body, and neither encompassed microlevel phenomena well. Microinteractionist perspectives did not deal well with macro phenomena, especially the state (with the partial exception of labeling theory). Conflict constructionist theory helps bridge the oppositional binaries such as subjective/objective, macro/micro, structure/agency, action/institutionalized order, and culture/interaction.

Acknowledging Postmodern Destabilization: The Advantages of Flexibility

The new paradigm is able to acknowledge the postmodern destabilization of the objective observer's position without a total rejection of the possibility of objective, scientific knowledge. It can include critical theories and offers a critical-reflexive research methodology. The new paradigm's loose structure, its tendency to offer a cluster of concepts or elements rather than a rigid framework, is an advantage, offering flexibility and allowing scholars in many different areas to absorb those elements and ideas that are most adapted to the puzzles of that specific area. As we shall argue in the last paragraphs, this seepage into the discipline can be both a strength and a weakness. It is altering work in many subfields, often gradually rather than suddenly, and has influenced theorists and researchers who may never have thought about it as a new paradigm at all, just a shift in terminology and a drift in the research questions that can be asked.

Building Bridges and Overcoming Fragmentation

The new paradigm builds bridges among theories and helps to overcome the fragmentation that began to appear in the entire structure of the discipline under the sign of the triad of the late 1960s and the split between quantitative and qualitative methodologies. The organization of the field that is usually considered the high point of American sociological hegemony—its division into a triad of structural functionalism, symbolic interaction, and conflict theories—actually fragmented sociology into subfields without an overall paradigm that united them in a common discourse. This theoretical fragmentation seeped into the logic of inquiry as well, opening a schism between qualitative and quantitative approaches. Conflict construction provides connective tissue among the fragments, and by its very flexibility and lack of monolithic rigidity, it has prevented further dissolution of the discipline. It is probably not a coincidence that the quantitative/qualitative fissure is gradually being healed.

A Generative Reading of Classical Sociology

Conflict constructionism offers a new, generative reading of classical sociology, a born-again version of classic sociological theory that allows the discipline to invigorate itself while remaining in touch with its traditions. For example, Max Weber's thinking can be assimilated with the work of Pierre Bourdieu, as we saw in Mayer Zald's explorations of social movement potentials of institutions, a blending of field and traditional concepts of organization, institutions, and political action. Emile Durkheim has been miniaturized in terms of microregulation (a new reading linked to Erving Goffman's work) as well as reread as offering clues to understanding class in postmodern societies (Pakulski 2005/2006). Karl Marx and Friedrich Engels have been read not only as contributors to an understanding of neoliberalism but as social constructionists for whom class is not something people "are" or "have" but something people do in relationships, and their thought has a central role in the work of Fredric Jameson and Jean Baudrillard.

Has the New Paradigm Already Run Its Course?

Some might argue that conflict constructionism has already reached the end of its shelf life without having a clearly defined impact—no heroes, no leaders, no martyrs, no narratives of intellectual struggles, at least for the time being. Conflict constructionism has seeped into the discipline and many of its subfields without a dramatic moment of penetration. This seepage gives it an abiding character but an uncertain story. Without the presence of new theoretical innovators, conflict constructionism may fall back on itself and become trapped in doing little more than fruitlessly mining itself for new ideas.

If we are coming to the end of conflict constructionism—now that we are all conflict constructionists—what lies beyond? We can only speculate about what new paradigm may emerge. Does sociology of health show the shape of things to come with its grounded concepts to expedite interdisciplinary collaboration, even along the contested border with neuroscience? Or, in response to global warming and the crash of 2008, will we see the reappearance of a harder-edge political economy approach driven by environmental problems, unemployment, and growing inequality?

Glossary and Concepts

Constructing Difference and Dominance

Glossary Terms

Race and Ethnicity

Construction and conflation of categories. These terms point to the way we confuse socially and historically constructed categories such as race (and the behaviors or cultures of races) with genetically determined phenotypical features such as skin tone.

Difference and the relational definition of difference. These terms refer to the understanding that race is a socially constructed category defined in social relationships rather than a fixed or essential trait of individuals.

Essentialism. This negative term refers to the erroneous belief that values and attributes we assign to ethnic groups, races, and men and women are natural and inherent qualities rather than social constructs specific to historical times and places.

Historical invention of race; of whiteness; of white supremacy. Race and ethnicity as systems of classification and construction of different groups are historical creations that became closely tied to the development of Western modernity and the establishment of societies structured on racial dominance around the institutions of European settlers and colonial forces.

Race is a floating signifier (Stuart Hall). Race is an impermanent category of identity, defined within a set of classifications, that is associated with a specific set of relationships at specific times and places in history.

Racial formation and racialization (Michael Omi and Howard Winant). Categories of race are created in specific historical contexts, and within these contexts, individuals and groups are defined, labeled, and treated as if race were a natural or essential characteristic. Entire societies are organized around the creation and imposition of racial difference.

Societies structured in racial dominance. Many societies have been or are organized around institutions and practices that are based on, promote, and reproduce racial inequality, so that race is a central dimension of stratification and disparities.

Whiteness. Whiteness is the invisible, underlying, normalized operation of the racial organization of society. Whiteness is not an individual phenomenon to be examined on an individual level; rather, it is the defining principle of social organization by which white values, ideas, aesthetics, preferences, and privileges are made to appear normal and as the basis of the social order.

Gender

Gender performance (Judith Butler). Gender is socially constructed through the reiterated acting that normalizes gender categories and makes them appear binary, essentialized, and natural.

Gender rituals. These are practices through which we produce and reproduce gender in terms of behaviors and identities. Closely related to gender performance, gender rituals are enacted and confirm, consecrate, and naturalize gender classifications.

Heteronormativity. This concept is a shorthand expression for the ways that heterosexuality structures social norms, behaviors, and identities, as well as feelings and desires, within a society or group and produces a definition of the normal.

State policies and gender construction. The state is always a major seen and unseen mechanism in the construction and legitimation of gender and gender hierarchy in terms of how policies and institutions are embedded with ideologies of gender in areas such as health-care policy and family law.

Transgression (Judith Butler). The intentional or unintentional violation of normalized gender performances disrupts the hegemonic status quo.

Related Concepts

Liberal, Marxist, and multicultural feminism. Feminism can best be understood as a collection of movements or orientations toward establishing and protecting the equal economic, political, and social rights of women by examining their structural positions and lived experiences in society, whether primarily as individuals (liberal), in opposition to capitalism (Marxist), or in the context of racial and ethnic identities that intersect gender (multicultural).

Culture in the Global Era

Glossary Terms

Borders. These are boundary lines between nations and do not always match cultural boundaries, especially when colonial powers have created arbitrary dividing lines. Borders may also separate and demarcate areas with very different types of economies and levels of purchasing power, creating discontinuities, flows of attempted migration, and tensions, as along the US-Mexican border.

Commodity circulation and global trade networks. These terms refer to global markets and flows of goods in a capitalist world economy, such as of sugar, slaves, furs, precious metals, and, more recently, financial derivatives and media products.

Cultural domination and the cultural dominant. The dominant culture is a way of life, values, norms, practices, knowledge, and so on, that is imposed on people through coercion or through market forces. The cultural dominant (Fredric Jameson) is a patterning of culture in a particular era that reappears across media and the arts.

Cultural dumping. This is the market-driven process of moving outdated and low-value cultural products of the center to buyers in the peripheral and semi-peripheral areas of the globe—for example, selling old Hollywood movies to television systems in developing nations.

Cultural policies of the state. These are government decisions about which cultures and which types of cultural products, such as movies or TV programs, to promote, prohibit, export, import, or ban in a society.

Deterritorialization and global social networks (Arjun Appadurai). These terms refer to people and activities that are no longer localized but scattered to many different areas or regions, yet remain in contact or connected with each other after a scattering (diaspora).

Global cultural flows, scapes, and disjuncture of flows (Arjun Appadurai). These terms refer to transnational movements of people, ideas, media, technology, and capital. These flows are not necessarily coordinated with each other, and the term "disjuncture" indicates the possibility that they occur at different rates or that some are blocked while others are open.

Hybridity, transculturation, creolization, and mestizaje. These terms refer to the ways virtually all cultures are blends of elements borrowed from or imposed by many cultures through colonial impact, immigration, markets, and voluntary borrowing, so that most cultures are the product of two-way or multiple flows of influences.

Peasants. This term refers to a large range of individuals engaged in agriculture, especially tenant farmers, sharecroppers, peons, owners of very tiny subsistence farms, and in some cases landless wage laborers in agriculture.

Postmodern culture. This refers to the culture associated with advanced capitalism and is characterized by the blurring of high, popular, and commercial culture, as well as by propagation through electronic media and a strong sense of irony and abandonment of the concept of human progress.

Syncretic cultures. These, like hybrid cultures, are formed by contribution and blending of beliefs and practices from more than one culture, as can be seen in the blend of Catholic and West African beliefs, practices, and imagery in Haitian vodun ("voodoo").

Related Concepts

Postcolonial nations and cultures. These are found in areas that went through a period of colonial rule by colonizing nations (usually European powers) that shaped the official language, borders, and political, educational, and economic institutions.

Media and Culture

Glossary Terms

Aura (Walter Benjamin). This is the mystique, intense emotion, and worshipful attitude traditionally associated with a unique work of art, often believed to be the creation of an individual genius. The aura is dispelled when art is produced as a commodity in capitalism.

Capitalist realism (Michael Schudson). This is applied to commercials because they are idealized representations of a world in which commodities magically solve all problems, a capitalist parallel to the idealized imagery of "socialist realism" imposed by Stalinists.

Colonization. A wide range of critical theorists use this term to describe the penetration of thought processes by the media and related ideological institutions, as the mind is "taken over" by pacifying, numbing, and manipulative commercial and political messages emanating from the media.

Common culture (Paul Willis). This posits that subaltern strata and classes (the English working class, ethnoracial minorities, unemployed youth, and other "ordinary people") fashion their own culture through practices such as "DIY" and musical experimentation and refuse to accept a ready-made commercial culture circulated by the mass media, instead refashioning the products of mass culture into their own irreverent creations.

Encoding and decoding (Stuart Hall). These are key processes in the circulation of ideology and ideas. Dominant or hegemonic messages are often encoded in capitalist media products (such as news shows or entertainment programs), but viewers may decode them in oppositional or "mixed" interpretations.

Frames (Erving Goffman). These are ways of expressing ideas that limit and structure our thinking, forcing us to "think inside the box." Although inherent in all human communication, in modern societies frames are increasingly formed and propagated by the media and thus have a political impact by narrowing our understanding of the world.

Global village (Marshall McLuhan). This term expresses the idea that the electronic media ushered in an age of shared experiences across the globe that linked everyone to everyone else in terms of views and topics of conversation, like the dense webs of gossip that link people in small communities.

Icon. Marshall McLuhan used this word, originally reserved for a sacred image, to mean an image, symbol, or logo that communicates a thought or slogan in a condensed, easy-to-grasp, and almost automatic way that can be shared by many viewers. McLuhan used the term "mosaic" to refer to an image or idea composed of multiple fragments that are glued together to give an appearance of coherence and connectedness.

Informationalism (Manuel Castells). This term summarizes a new configuration of culture, media, technology, and capitalist relations of production in which capitalism has entered a new phase with global media and new computer and network technologies.

Local interpretation (Ien Ang). This is the notion that global news and entertainment are in fact viewed differently by audiences in different nations and locations.

Mean-world syndrome (George Gerbner). This term summarizes the finding that individuals (especially children) who watch a lot of television become fearful and misperceive the world as much more violent, threatening, and dangerous than it really is.

Means of mental production (Karl Marx and Friedrich Engels). This term refers to the technology, infrastructure, and skills needed to create and disseminate ideology and ideas—for example, in publishing and broadcasting. In capitalist societies, these means of mental production are privately owned and operated for profit, just like manufacturing enterprises.

Media monopoly (Ben Bagdikian). This term refers to the position that ownership of newspapers and electronic media was becoming increasingly concentrated and that channels of news, information, and entertainment were rapidly falling under the control of a small number of large corporations.

New symbolic environment (Manuel Castells). This term describes the pervasive impact of the media, their ability to penetrate into even the remotest areas, and their commercial messages, which now reach everyone on the globe.

Objectivity. This contentious term has many meanings. In the context of the media, it came to mean adhering to procedures that insure that different sides of an issue are represented as fairly and accurately as possible and that journalists do not themselves take sides. But these routines can themselves act as barriers to questioning and deeper examination and analysis. In a broader, philosophical sense, objectivity refers to the belief that some accounts and narratives are better, truer, or more accurate representations of reality than others and that we must strive to create these narratives, even if we cannot completely succeed in doing so. These narratives are essentially the ones that would be created by beings who see things clearly and are not caught up in the interests and subjective understandings that motivate human actors.

Prime-time ideology (Todd Gitlin). This perspective holds that media propagate hegemonic messages that represent dominant classes and their worldviews even within entertainment programs, whose format is structured to foster conformity.

Receivers and senders of opinion (C. Wright Mills). This phrase is linked to the idea that by the middle of the twentieth century the media had become one-way channels through which elites shape the opinions of the masses—who no longer comprise an informed public that can initiate discussions and disseminate its own views.

Recuperation. In postmodern theory, this refers to the way oppositional discourses and practices of resistance and rebellion are reclaimed and reinstated in dominant or hegemonic discourse and used to sustain the dominant social order or promote commercial values.

Ruling ideas of an age are the ideas of the ruling class (Karl Marx and Friedrich Engels). This phrase summarizes how a dominant ideology accompanies political and economic power as values and perceptions are forced into categories and discourses that sustain class dominance. These discourses express the interests of the ruling class in universalized terms to make them generally appealing, as "honor" was in feudal societies and "freedom" is in capitalist societies.

Simulacrum (Plato, Jean Baudrillard). This refers to a perfect copy of a nonexistent original. The simulacrum sustains a confusion between the real and the imaginary that has become pervasive in a society saturated by media; the concept is closely related to Guy Debord's notion of pseudoworlds and spectacles.

Society of the spectacle (and separation and commodification) (Guy Debord). These terms summarize the condition of our society as one in which human beings are completely alienated from their own capacities, realities, and experiences. They inhabit a pseudoworld created by the dominant classes and live only through vicarious experiences conveyed by the media as commodities.

Stereotypes. These are clichéd, inaccurate, and overgeneralized images and representations of groups, demographic categories, and places; they are often negative or demeaning.

Surface intensity (Fredric Jameson). This term describes a feature of postmodern culture: images are exciting, but the thrill masks an emptiness of real feeling and reflection and is associated with a flattening of affect.

Two-step communication process. This is a premise and observation of postwar US sociologists who believed that most people do not consume or absorb media messages directly but instead are influenced by opinion leaders, who pass these messages along and interpret them for those with whom they interact personally.

"We are not living in a global village, but in customized cottages globally produced" (Manuel Castells). This phrase challenges the proposition that local cultures are being respected and preserved in the global media environment, because although cultural production appears to have local flavor or even to address local and multicultural themes, it is controlled by transnational corporations, and its products are basically the same everywhere, even if they are superficially decked with local touches.

Related Concepts

Media as reflectors versus media as shapers. This dichotomy summarizes the debate between those who believe that the media largely reflect or mirror public taste and opinion because market forces compel them to respond to "what people want to see" and those who argue that the media create and mold these views and choices.

Pseudoevent. This concept, introduced by media critics in the 1960s, refers to events that are staged for and by the media or that have no reality except that which is created in the media. The pseudoworld is the sum total of these false images of reality, the fake world that is created for us by the media as a commodity and that serves the purposes of pacification and generating compliance and consumption of commodities.

Self-censorship (Warren Breed). This emerges as a major mechanism of social control of journalists (and others in the media) in a nominally free and democratic society in which the state does not own, manage, or even censor the media. Instead, journalists limit what they say and are careful in their framing of news and analysis in order to smooth their career paths and avoid hassles with editors and corporate owners.

Work of art in an age of mechanical reproduction (Walter Benjamin). This concept suggests that the modern recording and film industries have transformed art from unique treasures with an aura into mass-marketed and mass-produced commodities such that they lose their mystique.

Self

Glossary Terms

Alienation (Karl Marx). This term refers to the way class-based societies, especially capitalist ones, estrange human beings from the full potential with which they are endowed by nature—their species being. This expression launches a critical social psychology in which human nature is not a fixed set of capacities but a historically situated project.

Authoritarian personality (Theodor Adorno). This applies to a type of person driven primarily by obedience to authority and the demand for obedience from those who have less authority and power. Historically it is associated with fascist movements and regimes.

Body modifications (postmodern theories). These are practices of tattooing, piercing, scarification, pinning, and transsexual surgical and hormonal alterations that transform the body from what is seen as a natural state to one that is actively constructed by human intervention.

Flexible capitalism and the corrosion of character (Richard Sennett). This phrase summarizes the argument that contemporary flexible capitalism, with its high-risk markets, complex technologies, uncertain career lines, concentrations of power, and low levels of loyalty between individuals and corporations, fosters a corroded character—that is, a self who is insecure, egocentric rather than socially and collectively oriented, focused on people skills rather than knowledge, and lacking in loyalty and commitment to others.

Habitus (Pierre Bourdieu). This term refers to the physical, mental, and emotional capacities and dispositions into which individuals are socialized. It is thus a theoretical construct to understand how "society gets into people" and includes knowledge, skills, habits of mind and body, deeply held values, and orientations toward the self, others, and the physical world.

Historically contingent self. This phrase implies that the structure, contents, and generating processes of selves are not uniform across historical periods and types of societies but change markedly.

Identity talk. This is similar to the idea of the self as narrative construct. A discourse establishes who we are and how we want others to see us.

Mental disorder and madness in historical context. This phrase emphasizes that social responses to unusual, disordered, and disruptive behaviors are not simple reactions to uniform physical conditions but complex social practices that vary with different societies. Even if they ultimately have genetic and physiological causes, conditions such as schizophrenia, autism, and bipolar disorder are not illnesses like measles, syphilis, or diabetes (with relatively uniform symptoms, identifiable causes, and predictable physiological trajectories); rather, they are configurations of behaviors and feelings that are socially defined as disordered with specific labels in different historical periods and societies.

Oedipus complex and gender identity. These concepts in psychoanalytic theories of the self address the construction of gender identity. The child grapples with intense attachment to the parent of the opposite sex and a feeling of distance, threat, and dislike regarding the same-sex parent (like Oedipus in Greek mythology, who, albeit unwittingly, killed his father and married his mother). The intense longing for the opposite-sex parent is eventually resolved and repressed, leaving an unconscious trace that influences the adult.

Other directed and inner directed (David Riesman). These labels refer to two successive historical character types. The *inner-directed* individual, characteristic of industrial capitalism, was guided by habits and values instilled by parents, whereas the other-directed type, found in advanced capitalist societies, constantly adjusts behavior to the expectations of others and to messages in the media, as if guided by radar.

Psychoanalysis (Sigmund Freud). This analytic method investigates how human beings are shaped by their infantile repressed desires and childhood experiences and largely motivated by unconscious or submerged parts of the personality. As individuals recognize this determining force, they can begin to free themselves from it and start to act with more awareness and rationality.

Rational choice theory (rational action theory). This paradigm explains human behavior as the reflection of reasoned calculation of means and ends, costs and benefits, whether material or not.

Self as a narrative (or text) (postmodernist theories). This is the notion that the self is a construct produced as an individual tells him- or herself and others a life story and performs according to scripts; these texts constitute the self, and we are the stories we tell about ourselves.

Unconscious (Sigmund Freud, Louis Althusser). This is an area of the self or the mind that is not accessible to awareness in ordinary waking life, yet has a determining power in the feelings and actions of individuals. It is composed of fragmentary narratives or fantasies formed by repressed traces of infantile desires and distorted memories of childhood experiences during the passage of each individual from infancy to adulthood.

Unconscious as a text (Louis Althusser, Jacques Lacan). This expression suggests a new, postmodern way of understanding the Freudian concept of the unconscious as a region of the mind and brain that contains infantile and socially unacceptable aggressive and sexual impulses and longings, and specifically as a distorted and fragmentary narrative about the universal transition from infancy to puberty and adulthood.

Virtual self. This term refers to the construction of the self in online media and social networks. This self is very fluid, guided by constant electronic feedback, and often no more than a performance, because the material self is invisible in electronically mediated interaction.

Political Sociology and the Study of Collective Action

Glossary Terms

Alternative globalization. This is an aim of activists and organizations such as the World Social Forum that envision peaceful, egalitarian relationships among nations and a more equitable distribution of global resources, in contrast to the current unequal, market-driven process of globalization in which relatively few countries, corporations, and individuals benefit.

Bowling alone. This term, invented by Robert Putnam, is shorthand for the decline of civic engagement in the United States and shrinking participation in voluntary associations, political organizations, and citizenship roles; not all political scientists agree with this thesis.

Civic engagement. This entails commitment to act as a citizen in order to improve society or a local community or to enhance the common good; it is seen as distinct from interest-group politics, in which immediate individual or group interests and advantages are the goals of action and participation.

Collective action. This very broad term is often associated with Marxist or Weberian conflict theories to refer to the entire spectrum of emergent and noninstitutionalized behaviors and practices, including civic engagement, voluntary association, and participation in social movements, as well as more ephemeral behavior such as crowd behavior.

Field versus apparatus. These contrasting terms correspond to the traditional sociological term "institution," meaning a regularly occurring, relatively stable set of behaviors, roles, and organizations. "Apparatus" (Marxist theories) refers to a concentration of power, strong regulation, and coercive integration, often associated with states. "Field" (Pierre Bourdieu) suggests a looser, weakly regulated, and relatively dispersed set of practices and organizations, some public and some private.

Global civil society (Saskia Sassen). This new expression refers to political engagement by individuals and groups on a transnational basis and independently of specific governments or nation-states.

Governmentality (Michel Foucault). This term combines "government" and "mentality" in order to suggest that in modern societies, social control is exercised through self-regulation, voluntary compliance, and what others might consider ideological manipulation.

Identity construction and identity formation. These are collective processes, often initiated by social movements, by which individuals define who they are, what their origins are, and what categories of belonging (e.g., gender, class, race-ethnicity, religion, sexual orientation) are most meaningful to them.

Ideology, culture, discourse, and frame. These terms refer to categories of language that participants in political action use to express their ideas and name the world. "Ideology" usually refers to a consistent or coherent system of ideas (and sometimes to one that is explicitly contrasted to both science and common sense). "Culture" is a very broad term that refers to all the ideas and "designs for living" of a group of people. "Discourse" is a term used by Michel Foucault to designate a cluster of speech acts (or written texts). "Frame" is a term introduced by Erving Goffman, then widely used by others, to designate a way of expressing ideas that constrain and guide our thought processes.

New social movements. These left-wing movements in western Europe between the late 1960s and 1980s were associated with the emergence of postindustrial economies and identities other than the class categories of communist and socialist movements (working class and proletariat) and included environmental activism, gay rights, gender equality, affordable housing, and peace movements.

Political practices and practices of power (Pierre Bourdieu). These terms suggest that power is exercised throughout society and imposed through a variety of means, including coercion, self-regulation, extension of privileges and advantages, and ideological persuasion.

Revolution. This is a generally violent, major transformation and discontinuity in a state, civil society, and class structure; not only are elites ousted but relationships throughout the society are markedly altered.

State and civil society. This pairing implies a division of societies into the state (an entity whose power is ultimately based on coercion or force) and all other relationships of a private and voluntary nature, which are grouped together as civil society.

State-identity-culture. This multifaceted new perspective in the social movement field (see, e.g., Meyer, Whittier, and Robnett 2002) brings the study of culture and identity formation together with the analysis of state (government) policies and actions as influences on and outcomes of collective action.

Cities and Urban Sociology

Glossary Terms

Affordable housing. This refers to a housing policy in which rentals (and, more rarely, purchase prices) are set and usually subsidized by government (state, national, or local) in order to ensure adequate housing for moderate- and low-income households that would otherwise not be able to live in communities in which market forces determine housing costs.

Arcades Project (Walter Benjamin). This project brought together literary materials and social-historical information to give a wide-ranging portrait of the Paris passages, "shopping mall–like" spaces created in nineteenth-century Paris that marked the beginning of consumer capitalism.

Banlieues. This French word refers to the peripheral areas of French cities with high concentrations of immigrants and working-class residents; they are suburbs with connotations of relegation and marginality.

Bowling-pin or hourglass shape of income distribution. These terms refer to the thesis that in recent decades, stratification in the United States and other developed economies has experienced a shrinking of the middle class, a small increase at the top among the upper ranks of managers, professionals, and financial analysts, and a substantial increase in the low-wage tiers.

Carceral city. This term suggests that contemporary cities are spaces of marginalization and coercive social control of poor populations believed to be threats to social order. Urban design, city management, and policing are used to segregate and control these populations through practices modeled on the prison system.

Chicago School. This school of urban theory and research had its heyday from the 1920s to the 1940s but continues to influence urban sociology. It emphasized lively ethnographic research designs (using observation, life narratives, and analysis of documents and cultures) and was strongly empiricist and rather micro oriented. It focused on neighborhoods, individuals, communities, and local conflicts rather than on larger socioeconomic and political forces.

City as growth machine. This phrase refers to efforts from the 1960s to the 1990s to transform industrial cities in the United States (and other advanced economies) into postindustrial spaces through policies of urban renewal and business-oriented economic development spearheaded by coalitions of government, downtown retail and financial interests, and construction firms.

Concentric zone theory (Robert Park and Ernest Burgess; Chicago School). This theory of urban spatial patterns and metro-area growth (loosely based on the configuration of Chicago in the first half of the twentieth century) posits that in most cities a central business district is surrounded by industry and by a seedy, marginal "zone of transition," then a zone of working-class housing, and finally successive rings of more attractive, upscale housing, with the entire configuration driven by market forces.

Consumer choice and the marketization of public services. These are associated with the privatization of services, a common policy of governments in the neoliberal era; for example, garbage pickup has been privatized, but even public services are increasingly organized on a market model, with consumers able—or compelled—to make complicated choices among competing options.

Deindustrialization. This refers to a shift in the economies of many large cities that, through the 1950s, had been manufacturing centers; after the 1950s, these functions declined and were moved to other areas of the country or to other countries, leaving cities as centers of postindustrial activities, such as finance, education, health care, retailing, entertainment, and advanced corporate services. These shifts were followed by shifts in occupational structure and land use, as well as high unemployment rates among the industrial labor force.

FIRE sector. This refers to financial institutions, insurance, and real estate, seen as a major growth sector in cities in the later decades of the twentieth century.

Gentrification and the revanchist city (Neil Smith). These terms refer to affluent strata moving into previously working-class neighborhoods, an "invasion" and "succession" in which poorer populations are displaced by more advantaged ones through market processes.

Geographies of urban restructuring (Edward Soja and the LA School). This term connects economic, political, demographic, cultural, and spatial processes that transformed Los Angeles (and other cities) between the 1960s and the 1990s.

Global cities. These cities are major nodes in transnational economic and financial networks, as well as key places where culture is produced. Tokyo, Paris, and New York are often cited as prime examples of global cities, which have more recently come to include Mumbai, Shanghai, Dubai, and Rio.

Global communication and transportation networks. This term indicates that these linkages are now global, decreasing the time it takes to move people or information between key nodes, while communities remote from the networks are "distant" in time, space, culture, and economic opportunities.

Hinterland. This word means "backcountry" in German and refers to regions that are not primary, and perhaps not even included, in the global networks. They furnish migrants and raw materials to the global economy but are disconnected culturally and are often even hard to reach, especially by global economic, cultural, and political elites.

Human ecology. This perspective in sociology analyzes human activities and relationships in terms of spatial patterning or territorial organization based on the premise that location is a key factor in human life and that activities and social relationships must be understood in their geographical context.

LA School. This critical approach to cities posits that Los Angeles is close to the "ideal type" of contemporary urban form, displaying features—such as suburban sprawl, automobile dependency, a weak center, and cultural/ethnic diversity— likely to appear in many cities in transition from the industrial to the postmodern (which can nevertheless still contain intense industrial activity).

Megacities. These are very large urbanized areas containing multiple centers, distinct government units, and diverse economic activities, which generally include financial centers, port facilities, airports, industrial zones, and cultural, residential, and entertainment districts. The United Nations uses a population threshold of 10 million for the term.

Multiple-nuclei model. This theory is based on the observation that many large metropolitan areas contain several economic centers and often several distinct municipalities.

Postmodern urbanization. This refers to the idea that the functions, spatial organization, and demographic characteristics of cities are different in the present era from their form during the period of "high modernity" and industrial development in the advanced capitalist economies (the late nineteenth century and first half of the twentieth century) and are becoming more specialized in the entertainment, tourism, FIRE, cultural, and corporate-service sectors.

Real estate markets. These are among the major forces shaping urban economies. They include both commercial and residential properties and spaces. In global cities, these markets are in large part global, which may cause a shortage of affordable housing for local residents.

Revalorization of the inner city (or central areas). This refers to increased land values and demand for residential and commercial space in the central areas of cities, reflecting the decline of manufacturing in central cities and associated with the displacement of poor residents through rising housing costs.

Segregation and exclusion. These are processes that separate populations in urban areas on the basis of class and/or ethnic-racial categories, making some areas into areas of racial isolation, ghettos, or zones of relegation.

Spatial analysis. This refers to the effort to understand social processes and relationships in terms of historically changing location and territorial patterning. Racial hierarchies, class inequalities, and differentiated functions are all marked by distinct location patterns of people and activities.

Themed urban spaces. This is a process of assigning a distinct character to parts of a city, largely in response to the entertainment and tourism functions of the city, in order to make these areas attractive, exotic, and amusing as tourist destinations. Theming is reinforced and promoted through naming ("Boys Town" for a gay neighborhood in Chicago or "the French Quarter" in New Orleans), street decorations, and special events.

Urban imaginary. This refers to the images and representations of cities and city life that people hold, images that do not always match economic, demographic, and cultural realities. These images form an "imaginary," a coherent but inaccurate and often stereotypical picture of the city—for example, of Chicago as "the city that works," New York as the financial center headquartered at Wall Street, and Los Angeles as synonymous with Hollywood, Malibu, freeways, and gangs.

Zone of transition. The concentric zone model of urban development designated this a "seedy" zone located around the central business district and containing light industry, warehouses, flophouses and shelters, brothels, and low-cost hotels.

Deviance and Public Safety

Glossary Terms

Broken window (George Kelling and James Wilson). This term refers to a premise in the law enforcement field that the smallest indication of illegal or antisocial behavior in an area needs to be addressed because it is a symptom and early warning sign and may become an entry point for more serious problems. A broken window signals a possible starting point of deterioration in civility, social control, and the quality of life in a community.

Community-level studies of crime and deviance. These adhere to the premise that crime and risky behavior are not only individual acts but emerge from the culture, practices, and social conditions of a neighborhood (or larger area). Understanding such behavior requires examining the situation of the whole community, and it follows that social policies to mitigate problems require a change in prevailing conditions, not only a focus on individuals.

Microethnography. Ethnography is a research design for understanding culture; it requires observation and total immersion in a setting. A microethnography focuses on a very small area or group. Once a high degree of risk has been found in that setting, the microethnographer tries to identify beliefs and practices that explain the higher incidence of risk exposure or risky behavior.

Penal state (Marxists, Michel Foucault, and critical theorists). Critical approaches to social control, punishment, and the criminal-legal system use this term to convey the concept that a key activity of government is exercising its punitive functions, usually through incarceration of poor people and minorities.

Public safety and public health. These areas are linked and overlapping; both examine factors that produce risk of death, injury, and illness. For example, gun violence, domestic violence, AIDS transmission, and substance abuse must be understood as both safety and health issues, not only for individuals but also for communities and societies.

Race and incarceration. Critical theorists of the criminal-legal system juxtapose these terms in order to highlight the disproportionately high incarceration rate of African Americans and other people of color in the United States and to emphasize the use of incarceration as part of a system of racial dominance.

Risk factors. These characteristics of individuals, households, areas, and groups are correlated with higher probabilities of a negative outcome such as death, crime, victimization, illness, and addiction. In many cases, the absolute risk is fairly low, and the focus is on a relatively higher rate. Risk factors contrast with protective factors—that is, characteristics correlated with positive outcomes or the absence of negative ones.

Routinization of deviance. In communities, groups, and organizations, deviant behavior—behavior that is illegal or violates regulations—can become informally acceptable and widely practiced. It is no longer seen as wrong but becomes a normal part of everyday life and may even be considered necessary for the smooth functioning of the institution.

Class

Glossary Terms

Between-nation inequality. These are differences in wealth, average income, average purchasing power, and quality of life that are discernible when we compare countries as the units of analysis (rather than individuals or groups within a single nation). Within-nation inequality is inequality among the residents or citizens of a specific country, comparing the individuals (or households) in that country, and much of it is related to social-class position among individuals in that country.

Capitalism. This refers to an economic system based on private ownership of the means of production, wage labor, and the market mechanism for the distribution of goods and services as commodities.

Class consciousness. This term, drawn from Marxist theory, implies that in the long run, subjective identity and cohesion can, will, or should align with one's objective position in the relations of production, such that an objectively existing "class-in-itself" becomes a "class-for-itself" engaged in collective action.

Class reproduction. This is a process of replicating class differences and inequalities from generation to generation so that the overall structure or shape of the stratification system remains more or less the same and most individuals end up in the same class position as their parents.

Classes. These are categories comprising individuals or households defined by wealth, income, ownership of productive assets, and market position. In Marxist theories, they are defined by their position in the relations of production. Classes are identified by economic characteristics that exist objectively, regardless of individuals' subjective identity or perceptions.

Postmodern theories of class. These theories question fundamental Marxist premises such as the primacy of class (the relations of production) over other bases of identity and action (such as ethnoracial or gender identities), the emergence of class consciousness, the basic antagonism between capitalists and proletarians, and the viability of a socialist alternative. Instead they posit the fragmentation of classes, disappearance of a distinct industrial proletariat, and absence of a clear shift toward class consciousness.

Racialization of economic inequality. This refers to the observation that economic or class inequality (as defined by Marxists or Weberians) aligns closely with ethnoracial dominance, especially of whites, in many societies in Europe and the Western Hemisphere.

Relations of production (Marxist theory). This refers to relationships created or entered into during the course of producing everything needed for a society's physical survival and well-being. When these relationships are unequal, they define different categories in society (classes in the Marxist sense), such as those found in feudalism, slavery-based societies, and capitalism.

Socioeconomic stratification. This refers to unequal positions based on income, wealth, ownership of productive assets, market position, position in the relations of production, or other characteristics related to production or consumption.

Structural functional theories of stratification. These are closely linked to market models of behavior. Inequality is believed to emerge through operation of supply and demand as functionally important positions, and those that require large amounts of self-investment in education (human capital), are rewarded more highly than positions that are easily filled or not so important.

World-systems theory (Immanuel Wallerstein). This theory of global inequality posits the emergence of three global zones with distinct class structures and institutions formed by the emergence of modern capitalism in Europe and European conquest and colonization. The zones include a dominant center of developed capitalist nations, as well as peripheral and semiperipheral areas that are disadvantaged, underdeveloped, and exploited by the core economies.

Related Concepts

Gini ratio (or coefficient). This measures the degree of inequality in the distribution of wealth, income, land ownership, or other good that exists in a limited amount in a specific country or other type of territorially defined unit. The Gini coefficient expresses the discrepancy between the actually existing distribution and a hypothetical distribution of complete equality. Values of the Gini coefficient can range from 0 to 100 (often alternatively expressed as 0 to 1), where low values (in the twenties) indicate a relatively equal distribution (e.g., in Finland and Norway), and high values, around 50 to 60, indicate a high level of inequality (e.g., in Paraguay). The Gini coefficient is one of the most widely used measures of inequality among economists and economic sociologists and has the advantage of summarizing inequality in a single number (rather than a percentile distribution).

Power, privilege, and "party" (Max Weber). These are major practices that sustain inequality and stratification, linked generally to class in market societies and to status distinctions in traditional societies; "party" refers to organizations that are formed in order to maintain power and privilege.

Families

Glossary Terms

Gendering the state-market nexus. This term implies recognition that economic and political arrangements, especially the relationship between government policies and market behaviors, are never gender neutral. The economic and political order is always also a gender order that regulates gender and defines and assigns appropriate gender roles, a process that has historically disadvantaged women and sexual minorities.

Life-course theory. This is both a theoretical and a research design approach that maps individual biographies and cohort experiences in the context of historical change.

Role theory. Generally considered part of structural functional theory, this refers to analysis of family behaviors and practices, focusing attention on functions of the family as an institution, roles associated with these functions, and the division of labor in families and households.

Transnational families. These formed with the accelerated pace of emigration and immigration in the late twentieth century so that individuals in nuclear and extended families ended up in different countries from other family members, thereby creating webs or networks of family ties across borders, a process supported by new means of communication.

Related Concepts

Evolutionary psychology. This perspective (sometimes referred to as sociobiology) argues that many characteristics of human societies (including both competition and altruism) are genetically based, reflecting biological evolution and not just historical conditions.

Liberal, conflict, and multicultural feminism. See the "Gender" glossary.

Welfare state. This term, which carries a more positive connotation in Europe than in the United States, refers to an advanced capitalist society with an extensive social safety net, as well as robust entitlements to assure a high and fairly egalitarian quality of life.

Health

Glossary Terms

Epidemiology. This is the study of the distribution of disease in a population. It relies on data collection and statistical analysis of data to document the prevalence of disease and related risk factors. It documents infectious-disease outbreaks, that is, epidemics, and tracks chronic-illness trends.

Functionalist theory. This explains how specific social arrangements and institutions contribute to maintaining the stability of the social order. Contrary to an erroneous view, functionalist theory does not argue that such arrangements are rational, humane, or desirable—only that they contribute to maintaining a social order.

Health maintenance organizations (HMOs) and health plans. These are programmatic arrangements to organize health care and reduce costs by standardizing payments to providers and limiting access to specialists. For example, HMOs control access to specialized care through a gatekeeper, the primary care physician. Costs may also be contained by specifying the rates at which insurers reimburse patients or providers for certain types of treatment.

Health-care system. This term implies that the way health care is provided in a society is institutionalized and has stable, recurrent features and an overall organization. For example, a health-care system could be a single-payer system (in which providers are paid directly by the government out of general revenue), a system of public or private insurers, or an entirely privately marketized and profit-oriented fee-for-service system. Systems differ in per-patient costs, the amount that individuals have to pay in premiums or fees, universality of coverage, ways of managing limited resources, the mix of public and private services, the level of preventive care, the percent of gross domestic product of a nation that goes to health care, and many other variables.

Inequality and the relative-income hypothesis. This refers to the empirical finding that high levels of inequality in income, wealth, or social status in a society are associated with poor health outcomes, even for individuals in the upper tiers of the stratification system (and obviously for those in the lower tiers). More egalitarian societies tend to have lower mortality and morbidity rates for the population as a whole.

Medicalization. This refers to the practice of defining deviant or socially unacceptable behavior as a biomedical problem. For example, homosexuality was medicalized until recently, and currently disruptive behavior among children is often classified as ADHD. The medicalization label justifies efforts to cure the stigmatized illness through use of medications or other therapies.

Physician dominance. This term in conflict theories of health and illness implies that physicians have (or had) power in health-related institutions. They set the conditions and behavioral expectations for all others in the system, including nurses, skilled and unskilled hospital workers, and patients. After the 1970s, this premise came to be questioned as hospital administrators, HMO managers, and corporations assumed much of the power previously ascribed to physicians. Physician dominance is a specific instance of professional dominance, the power of professionals to set conditions and expectations for all role occupants in a field or institution, such as health care or educational institutions.

Population health. This term focuses on the health status of a large number of people—for example, all of the residents of a country or a city. It is usually assessed by measures such as life expectancy, age-specific mortality rates, infant- and child-mortality rates, morbidity rates, and the incidence of various acute and chronic diseases.

Public health. This is a field of study and a view of social policy based on the idea that health in a society is more than the sum total of individuals' health statuses. It posits that the overall health and well-being of a population can be advanced by social policies. Historically, immunization, sanitation and waste disposal, a safe water supply, and inspection of food and agricultural products were introduced in order to enhance individual health by the development of infrastructure, regulation, and social services.

Sick roles. These are performed by individuals who see themselves, and are recognized by others, as sick. The individual may seek professional care, is excused for not working, and is socially accepted as a patient. The term was introduced by Talcott Parsons to emphasize that "being sick" is also a social condition and not simply a physical one.

Stigmatized illness. This is a disorder that carries a social stigma and may be associated with exclusion, segregation, and mistreatment of patients, who are believed to be unclean, highly contagious, personally responsible for their condition, or afflicted with illness as a punishment for moral transgressions. At various times, AIDS, leprosy, and even cancer have been socially stigmatized.

Related Concepts

Critical theory. This includes any perspective that questions the status quo or the dominant social arrangements and does so primarily by focusing on the discourses, assumptions, prejudices, stereotypes, and mistaken ideas that underpin these arrangements. Often the negative assessments based on critical theory are directed against other theories that justify inequality or social arrangements of dominance or exploitation.

References

Abu-Lughod, Janet. 2000. "Can Chicago Make It as a Global City?" A Great Cities Institute Working Paper, University of Illinois, Chicago.

Aday, LuAnn, and Ronald Andersen. 1975. *Development of Indices of Access to Medical Care.* Ann Arbor, MI: Health Administration Press.

Adler, Marina A. 2002. "German Unification as a Turning Point in East German Women's Life Course: Biographical Changes in Work and Family Roles." *Sex Roles* 47: 83–98.

Adler, Patricia, and Peter Adler. 2008. "Of Rhetoric and Representation: The Four Faces of Ethnography." *Sociological Quarterly* 49: 1–30.

Adorno, Theodor. 2001. *The Culture Industry.* New York: Routledge.

Adorno, Theodor, Else Frenkel-Brunswik, and Daniel Levinson. 1993. *The Authoritarian Personality.* New York: W. W. Norton.

Albrecht, Gary. 1992. *The Disability Business: Rehabilitation in the United States.* Newbury Park, CA: Sage.

Alexander, Jeffrey. 2006. *The Civil Sphere.* Oxford: Oxford University Press.

Allen, Theodore. 1997. *The Invention of the White Race.* London: Verso.

Althusser, Louis. 1971a. "Freud and Lacan." In *Lenin and Philosophy,* 189–220. New York: Monthly Review Press.

———. 1971b. "Ideology and the State." In *Lenin and Philosophy,* 127–186. New York: Monthly Review Press.

Alvesson, Mats. 2002. *Postmodernism and Social Research.* Buckingham, UK: Open University Press.

Anderson, Benedict. 1983. *Imagined Communities: Reflections on the Origins and the Spread of Nationalism.* London: Verso.

Anderson, Elijah. 1999. *Code of the Street: Decency, Violence, and the Moral Life of the Inner City.* New York: W. W. Norton.

Anderson, Odin. 1972. *Health Care: Can There Be Equity? The United States, Sweden and England.* New York: Wiley and Sons.

Ang, Ien. 1996. *Living Room Wars.* New York: Routledge.

Anspach, Renee. 1993. *Deciding Who Lives: Fateful Choices in the Intensive-Care Nursery.* Berkeley: University of California Press.

Anyon, Jean. 1980. "Social Class and the Hidden Curriculum of Work." *Journal of Education* 162, no. 1: 67–92.

Appadurai, Arjun. 1993. "Disjunction and Difference in the Global Cultural Economy." In *Global Culture: Nationalism, Globalization and Modernity,* edited by Mike Featherstone, 295–310. London: Sage.

Baca Zinn, Maxine, and Bonnie Thornton Dill. 1990. "Difference and Domination." In *Women of Color in U.S. Society,* edited by Maxine Baca Zinn and Bonnie Thornton Dill, 3–12. Philadelphia: Temple University Press.

———. 1996. "Theorizing Difference from Multiracial Feminism." *Feminist Studies* 22: 321–331.

Bagdikian, Ben. 1983. *The Media Monopoly.* Boston: Beacon Press.

Banks, James, et al. 2006. "Disease and Disadvantage in the United States and in England." *Journal of the American Medical Association* 295: 2037–2045.

Baudrillard, Jean. 1969/2000. "The Ideological Genesis of Needs." In *The Consumer Society Reader,* edited by Juliet Schor and Douglas B. Holt, 57–80. New York: Penguin.

———. 1970. *The Consumer Society.* Translated by Chris Turner. London: Sage Publications.

———. 1983. *Simulations.* Translated by Paul Foss, Paul Patton, and Philip Beitchman. New York: Semiotext[e].

Becker, Gary, with Kevin M. Murphy. 2000. *Social Economics.* Cambridge, MA: Harvard University Press.

Becker, Gary Stanley. 1991. *A Treatise on the Family.* Enl. ed. Cambridge, MA: Harvard University Press.

Becker, Howard. 1963. *Outsiders: Studies in the Sociology of Deviance.* New York: Free Press.

———. 1967. "Whose Side Are We On?" *Social Problems* 14: 249–247.

Becker, Howard, et al. 1961. *Boys in White.* Chicago: University of Chicago Press.

Belkin, Lisa. 2003. "The Opt-Out Revolution." *New York Times Magazine,* October 23.

Bell, Daniel. 1973. *The Coming of Post-Industrial Society.* New York: Basic Books.

Bell, Susan. 2000. "Experiencing Illness in/and Narrative." In *Handbook of Medical Sociology,* edited by Chloe Bird, Peter Conrad, and Allen Fremont, 184–199. Upper Saddle River, NJ: Prentice Hall.

Bengston, Vern L., et al., eds. 2004. *Sourcebook of Family Theory and Research.* Thousand Oaks, CA: Sage.

Benjamin, Walter. 1968. "The Work of Art in the Age of Mechanical Reproduction." In *Illuminations,* translated by Harry Zohn, 217–252. Orlando, FL: Harcourt Brace and Company.

———. 2002. *The Arcades Project.* Edited and translated by Rolf Tiedemann, Howard Eiland, and Kevin McLaughlin. Cambridge, MA: Belknap Press.

Bennett, M. 2006. "The Rebirth of Bronzeville." In *The New Chicago,* edited by John Koval et al., 213–220. Philadelphia: Temple University Press.

Bernstein, Basil. 1973. *Class, Codes, and Control.* London: Routledge and Kegan Paul.

Bernstein, Jared. 2013. "Updated CBO Data Reveal Unprecedented Increase in Inequality." Economic Policy Institute, www.epi.org/publication/ib239.

Bernstein, Mary. 2002. "The Contradictions of Gay Ethnicity: Forging Identity in Vermont." In *Social Movements: Identity, Culture, and the State,* edited by David Meyer, Nancy Whittier, and Belinda Robnett, 85–104. Oxford: Oxford University Press.

Best, Steven, and Douglas Kellner. 1991. *Postmodern Theory.* New York: Guilford Press.

Bianchi, S. M., et al. 2000. "Is Anyone Doing the Housework? Trends in the Gender Division of Household Labor." *Social Forces* 79: 191–228.

Birch, Eugenie. 2005. "Who Lives Downtown." Brookings, November, www.brookings.edu /research/reports/2005/11/downtownredevelopment-birch.

Bittman, Michael, et al. 2003. "When Does Gender Trump Money? Bargaining and Time in Household Work." *American Journal of Sociology* 109: 186–214.

Black, Donald. 1976. *The Behavior of Law.* New York: Academic Press.

Blakely, Tony, Bruce Kennedy, and Ichiro Kawachi. 2001. "Socioeconomic Inequality in Voting Participation and Self-Rated Health." *American Journal of Public Health* 91: 99–104.

Blau, Peter. 1964. *Exchange and Power in Social Life.* New York: Wiley.

Blauner, Robert. 1972. *Racial Oppression in America.* New York: Harper and Row.

Blendon, Robert, et al. 1990. "Satisfaction with Health Systems in Ten Nations." *Health Affairs* (Summer): 185–192.

Blood, Robert, and Donald Wolfe. 1965. *Husbands and Wives: The Dynamics of Married Living.* New York: Free Press.

Bloom, Samuel. 2002. *The Word as Scalpel.* New York: Oxford University Press.

Boddy, Janice. 1990. *Wombs and Alien Spirits: Women, Men, and the Zar Cult in Northern Sudan.* Madison: University of Wisconsin Press.

Bonilla-Silva, Eduardo, and Karen Glover. 2004. "We Are All Americans: The Latin Americanization of Race Relations in the U.S." In *The Changing Face of Race and Ethnicity,* edited by Maria Krysan and Amanda Lewis, 149–185. New York: Russell Sage.

Booth, A., K. Carver, and D. A. Granger. 2000. "Biosocial Perspectives on the Family." *Journal of Marriage and Family* 62: 1018–1034.

Bosk, Charles. 1979. *Forgive and Remember: Managing Medical Failure.* Chicago: University of Chicago Press.

Bourdieu, Pierre. 1984. *Distinction: A Social Critique of the Judgment of Taste.* Cambridge, MA: Harvard University Press.

———. 1988. *Homo Academics.* Translated by P. Collier. Stanford, CA: Stanford University Press.

———. 1989. "The Corporatism of the Universal: The Role of Intellectuals in the Modern World." Translated by C. Betensky. *Telos* 81: 99–110.

———. 1990. *The Logic of Practice.* Translated by R. Nice. Stanford, CA: Stanford University Press.

———. 1991. *Language and Symbolic Power.* Edited by J. B. Thompson. Translated by G. Raymond and M. Adamson. Cambridge, MA: Harvard University Press.

———. 1993a. *The Field of Cultural Production.* Edited by R. Johnson. New York: Columbia University Press.

———. 1993b. *Sociology in Question.* Translated by Richard Nice. London: Sage Publications.

———. 1996. *The State of Nobility: Elite Schools in the Field of Power.* Translated by L. C. Clough. Stanford, CA: Stanford University.

———. 2000. *Pascalian Meditations.* Translated by R. Nice. Stanford, CA: Stanford University Press.

———. 2001. *Masculine Domination.* Translated by R. Nice. Stanford, CA: Stanford University Press.

Bourdieu, Pierre, Jean-Claude Chamboredon, and Jean-Claude Passeron. 1991. *The Craft of Sociology.* Translated by R. Nice. Berlin: Walter de Gruyter and Company.

Bourdieu, Pierre, et al. 1999. *The Weight of the World.* Translated by P. P. Ferguson (translation editor) et al. Stanford, CA: Stanford University Press.

Bourdieu, Pierre, and Loïc Wacquant. 1992. *An Invitation to Reflexive Sociology.* Chicago: University of Chicago Press.

Bourdieu, Pierre, Loïc J. D. Wacquant, and Samar Farage. 1994. "Rethinking the State: Genesis and Structure of the Bureaucratic Field." *Sociological Theory* 12, no. 1 (March): 1–18. Retrieved August 7, 2004. Available from JSTOR at www.jstor.org/stable/202032.

Breed, Warren. 1954. "Social Control in the Newsroom: A Functional Analysis." *Social Forces* 33: 326.

Brines, Julie. 1994. "Economic Dependency, Gender, and the Division-of-Labor at Home." *American Journal of Sociology* 100: 652–688.

Brookings Institution Center on Urban and Metropolitan Policy. 2003. "Chicago in Focus: A Profile from Census 2000." Living Cities: The National Community Development Initiative, www.brookings.edu/~/media/Research/Files/Reports/2003/11/livingcities%20chicago/chicago.PDF.

Brown, Phil. 1995. "Naming and Framing: The Social Construction of Diagnosis and Illness." *Journal of Health and Social Behavior* 33: 267–281.

Bucher, Rue, and Anselm Strauss. 1961. "Professions in Process." *American Journal of Sociology* 46: 325–344.

Buck-Morss, Susan. 1989. *The Dialectics of Seeing: Walter Benjamin and the Arcades Project.* Cambridge, MA: MIT Press.

Budrys, Grace. 1997. *When Doctors Join Unions.* Ithaca, NY: Cornell University Press.

———. 2012. *Our Unsystematic Health Care System.* 3rd ed. Lanham, MD: Rowman and Littlefield.

Buechler, Steven. 2000. *Social Movements in Advanced Capitalism.* New York: Oxford University Press.

Burawoy, Michael. 2005. "For Public Sociology." *American Sociological Review* 70: 4–28.

Burawoy, Michael, et al. 1991. *Ethnography Unbound: Power and Resistance in the Modern Metropolis.* Berkeley: University of California Press.

Burchell, Graham, Colin Gordon, and Peter Miller. 1991. *The Foucault Effect: Studies in Governmentality.* Chicago: University of Chicago Press.

Burgess, E. W. 1926. "The Family as a Unity of Interacting Personalities." *Family* 7: 3–9.

Bury, Michael. 1991. "The Sociology of Chronic Illness: A Review of Research and Prospects." *Sociology of Health and Illness* 13: 451–467.

Butler, Judith. 1990. *Gender Trouble: Feminism and the Subversion of Identity.* New York: Routledge.

———. 1993. *Bodies That Matter: On the Discursive Limits of "Sex."* New York: Routledge.

———. 2004. *Undoing Gender.* New York: Routledge.

Camilleri, Kristian. 2009. *Heisenberg and the Interpretation of Quantum Mechanics: The Physicist as Philosopher.* Cambridge: Cambridge University Press.

Cankar, Louise. 2006. "Immigrants from the Arab World." In *The New Chicago,* edited by John Koval et al., 182–196. Philadelphia: Temple University Press.

Carr-Saunders, A. M. 1933. *The Professions.* Oxford: Clarendon Press.

Castells, Manuel. 1996. *The Rise of the Network Society.* Malden, MA: Blackwell Publishers.

Catlett, Beth Skilken, and Julie E. Artis. 2004. "Critiquing the Case for Marriage Promotion: How the Promarriage Movement Misrepresents Domestic Violence Research." *Violence against Women* 10: 1226–1244.

Caute, David. 1990. *The Year of the Barricades: A Journey through 1968.* New York: Harper Collins.

Chambliss, William T. 1973. "The Roughnecks and the Saints." *Society* (November–December): 24–31.

Charmaz, Kathy. 1991. *Good Days, Bad Days: The Self in Chronic Illness and Time.* New Brunswick, NJ: Rutgers University Press.

Cheng, Shu-Ju Ada. 2006. *Serving the Household and the Nation: Filipina Domestics and the Politics of Identity in Taiwan.* Lanham, MD: Rowman and Littlefield.

———. 2007. "Service, Servitude, and Identities: Subaltern Subjectivities in Transnational Care." In *Social Theory,* edited by Roberta Garner, 503–519. Peterborough, ON: Broadview Press.

Chodorow, Nancy. 1989. *Feminism and Psychoanalytic Theory.* New Haven, CT: Yale University Press.

Chua, Amy. 2002. *World on Fire: How Exporting Free Market Democracy Breeds Ethnic Hatred and Global Instability.* New York: Doubleday.

Clark, Terry Nichols. 2004. *The City as Entertainment Machine.* Bingley, UK: Elsevier/ Emerald Group Publishing.

Cloward, Richard, and Lloyd Ohlin. 1961. *Delinquency and Opportunity: A Theory of Delinquent Gangs.* Glencoe, IL: Free Press.

Coburn, David. 2000. "Income Inequality, Social Cohesion and Health Status of Populations: The Role of Neoliberalism." *Social Science and Medicine* 51: 139–150.

Cockerham, William. 1999. *Health and Social Change in Russia and Eastern Europe.* New York: Routledge.

Cohany, Sharon R., and Emy Sok. 2007. "Trends in Labor Force Participation of Married Mothers of Infants." *Monthly Labor Review* (February): 9–16.

Coleman, James S. 1988. "Social Capital in the Creation of Human Capital." *American Journal of Sociology* 94: S95–S120.

Collins, Patricia Hill. 2000. *Black Feminist Thought.* Rev. ed. New York: Routledge.

Collins, Randall. 1994. *Four Sociological Traditions.* New York: Oxford University Press.

Connell, R. W. 1995. *Masculinities.* Berkeley: University of California Press.

Conrad, Peter. 1996. "Medicalization and Social Control." In *Perspectives in Medical Sociology,* edited by Phil Brown, 137–162. Prospect Heights, IL: Waveland Press.

Conrad, Peter, and Joseph Schneider. 1992. *Deviance and Medicalization: From Badness to Sickness.* Philadelphia: Temple University Press.

Cook, Karen, ed. 1987. *Social Exchange Theory.* Newbury Park, CA: Sage.

Cookson, Peter, and Carolyn Hodges Persell. 1985. *Preparing for Power: America's Elite Boarding Schools.* New York: Basic Books.

Cooley, Charles. 1983. *Human Nature and the Social Order.* New Brunswick, NJ: Transaction University Press.

Crapanzano, Vincent. 2004. "Hermes' Dilemma: The Masking of Subversion in Ethnographic Description." In *Anthropological Theory: An Introductory History,* edited by Jon R. McGee and Richard L. Warms, 593–608. 3rd ed. New York: McGraw-Hill.

Critical Resistance. 2008. *Abolition Now! Ten Years of Strategy and Struggle against the Prison Industrial Complex.* Oakland, CA: AK Press.

D'Emilio, John. 1983. "Capitalism and Gay Identity." In *Powers of Desire: The Politics of Sexuality,* edited by Ann Snitow, Christine Stansell, and Sharon Thompson, 100–113. New York: Monthly Review Press.

Daly, Martin, and Margo Wilson. 1999. *The Truth about Cinderella: A Darwinian View of Parental Love.* New Haven, CT: Yale University Press.

Daly, Mary, and Jane Lewis. 2000. "The Concept of Social Care and the Analysis of Contemporary Welfare States." *British Journal of Sociology* 51: 281–298.

Davey-Smith, G. M., J. Shipley, and G. Rose. 1990. "Magnitude and Causes of Socioeconomic Differentials in Mortality: Further Evidence from the Whitehall Studies." *Journal of Epidemiology and Community Health* 44: 265–270.

Davis, Angela. 1984/1990. *Women, Culture, and Politics.* New York: Random House/Vintage.

———. 2003. *Are Prisons Obsolete?* New York: Seven Stories Press.

Davis, Kingsley. 1959. "The Myth of Functional Analysis as a Special Method in Sociology and Anthropology." *American Sociological Review* 24, no. 6: 757–772.

Davis, Kingsley, and Wilbert E. Moore. 1945. "Some Principles of Stratification." *American Sociological Review* 10 (April): 242–249.

Davis, Mike. 1992. *City of Quartz.* New York: Vintage Books.

———. 2004. "Planet of Slums." *New Left Review* 26 (March–April): 5–34.

Dear, Michael J. 2002. *From Chicago to L.A.: Making Sense of Urban Theory.* Thousand Oaks, CA: Sage Publications.

Debord, Guy. 1967/1995. *The Society of the Spectacle.* New York: Zone Books.

Debray, Regis. 1979. "A Modest Contribution to the Rite and Ceremonies of the Tenth Anniversary." *New Left Review* 115: 45–65.

DeLisi, Matt, and Alex R. Piquero. 2011. "New Frontiers in Criminal Careers Research, 2000–2011: A State-of-the-Art Review." *Journal of Criminal Justice* 39: 289–301.

Denzin, Norman. 1993. *The Alcoholic Society: Addiction and Recovery of the Self.* New Brunswick, NJ: Transaction Books.

Derrida, Jacques. 1994. "Spectres of Marx." *New Left Review* 1, no. 205 (May–June): 31–59.

Desai, Manisha. 2002. "Multiple Mediations: The State and Women's Movements in India." In *Social Movements: Identity, Culture, and the State,* edited by David Meyer, Nancy Whittier, and Belinda Robnett, 66–84. Oxford: Oxford University Press.

Diez-Roux, Ana, et al. 1999. "Prevalence and Social Correlations of Cardiovascular Disease Risk Factors in Harlem." *American Journal of Public Health* 89: 302–307.

Downey, Douglas B., James W. Ainsworth-Darnell, and Mikaela J. Dufur. 1998. "Sex of Parent and Children's Well-Being in Single-Parent Households." *Journal of Marriage and Family* 60: 878–993.

Downey, Douglas B., and Brian Powell. 1993. "Do Children in Single-Parent Households Fare Better Living with Same-Sex Parents?" *Journal of Marriage and the Family* 55: 55–71.

Dreby, Joanna. 2010. *Divided by Borders: Mexican Migrants and Their Children.* Berkeley: University of California Press.

DuBois, W. E. B. 1970. "Souls of White Folk." In *The Selected Writings of W. E. B. DuBois,* edited by Walter Wilson. New York: Penguin Putnam.

Duneier, Mitchell. 1994. *Slim's Table: Race, Respectability, and Masculinity.* Chicago: University of Chicago Press.

During, Simon. 1999. *The Cultural Studies Reader.* London: Routledge.

Durkheim, Emile. 1893/1964. *The Division of Labor in Society.* New York: Free Press.

———. 1897/1951. *Suicide.* New York: Free Press.

———. 1912/1965. *The Elementary Forms of Religious Life.* New York: Free Press.

Economist. 2003. "CEO Compensation." June 23.

Ehrenreich, Barbara. 2001. *Nickel and Dimed: On (Not) Getting By in America.* New York: Metropolitan Books.

Ehrenreich, Barbara, and Arlie Russell Hochschild. 2003. *Global Woman: Nannies, Maids, and Sex Workers in the New Economy.* New York: Metropolitan Books.

Elder, Glen. 1974. *Children of the Great Depression.* Chicago: University of Chicago Press.

Engels, F. 1884/1970. *The Origin of the Family, Private Property, and the State.* New York: International Publishers.

———. 1968. *The Condition of the Working Class in England.* Stanford, CA: Stanford University Press.

Esping-Andersen, Gøsta. 1990. *The Three Worlds of Welfare Capitalism.* Princeton, NJ: Princeton University Press.

Esty, Daniel, et al. 1998. *State Failure Task Force Report: Phase II Findings.* McLean, VA: Science Applications International Corporation.

Etzioni, Amitai. 1969. *The Semi-Professions and Their Organization.* New York: Free Press.

Evans, Robert. 1994. "Introduction." In *Why Are Some People Healthy and Others Not?* edited by Robert Evans, Morris Barer, and Theodore Marmor, 3–26. New York: Aldine.

Ewen, Stuart, and Elizabeth Ewen. 1982. *Channels of Desire.* New York: McGraw-Hill.

Fainstein, Susan. 1999. *The Tourist City.* New Haven, CT: Yale University Press.

———. 2001. *The City Builders: Property Development in New York and London.* Lawrence: University Press of Kansas.

Fanon, Frantz. 1965. *The Wretched of the Earth.* New York: Grove Press.

Feyerabend, P. 1975. *Against Method.* London: New Left Books.

Fields, Barbara Jeanne. 1990. "Slavery, Race, and Ideology in the United States of America." *New Left Review* 1, no. 181 (May–June): 95–118.

Foner, Eric. 1999. *The Story of American Freedom.* New York: W. W. Norton.

Ford, Kenneth. 2011. *101 Quantum Questions.* Cambridge, MA: Harvard University Press.

Foucault, Michel. 1965. *Madness and Civilization: A History of Insanity in the Age of Reason.* New York: Vintage.

———. 1966. *The Order of Things: An Archaeology of the Human Sciences.* New York: Vintage.

———. 1969. *The Archaeology of Knowledge and the Discourse of Language.* New York: Harper Collophon.

———. 1973/1975. *The Birth of the Clinic: An Archaeology of Medical Perception.* New York: Vintage.

———. 1979. *Discipline and Punish: The Birth of the Prison.* New York: Vintage.

———. 1980. *The History of Sexuality.* Vol. 1: *An Introduction.* New York: Vintage.

Fox, Kathryn. 2001. "Self-Change and Resistance in Prison." In *Institutional Selves: Troubled Identities in a Postmodern World,* edited by J. F. Gubrium and J. A. Holstein. New York: Oxford University Press.

Fox, Renee. 1957. "Training for Uncertainty." In *The Student Physician,* edited by Robert Merton, George Reeder, and Patricia Kendall, 207–241. Cambridge, MA: Harvard University Press.

Freeman, Jo. 1982. *Movements of the Sixties and Seventies.* New York and London: Longman.

Freese, J., J. C. A. Li, and L. D. Wade. 2003. "The Potential Relevance of Biology to Social Inquiry." *Annual Review of Sociology* 29: 233–256.

Freidson, Eliot. 1961. *Patients' Views of Medical Practice.* New York: Russell Sage Foundation.

———. 1970a. *Profession of Medicine.* New York: Dodd, Mead.

———. 1970b. *Professional Dominance.* New York: Atherton Press.

Freud, Sigmund. 1920/1966. *Introductory Lectures on Psycho-Analysis.* New York: W. W. Norton and Company.

———. 1958. *Civilization and Its Discontents.* New York: Doubleday Anchor.

———. 1960. *The Ego and the Id.* New York: W. W. Norton.

Frey, William H. 2005. "Metro America in the New Century: Metropolitan and Central City Demographic Shifts since 2000." Brookings Institution, Living Cities Census Series, September. Reprint No. 612.

Friedman, John. 2002. *The Prospect of Cities.* Minneapolis: University of Minnesota Press.

Gans, Herbert. 2005. *Deciding What's News.* Evanston, IL: Northwestern University Press.

Garcia Canclini, Nestor. 2003. *Culturas hibridas: estrategias para entrar y salir de la modernidad* [*Hybrid Cultures: Strategies for Entering and Leaving Modernity*]. Mexico: Editorial Grijalbo.

Garland, David. 2001. *The Culture of Control: Crime and Social Order in Contemporary Society.* Chicago: University of Chicago Press.

Garner, Roberta. 1996. "Fifty Years of Social Movement Theory: An Interpretation." In *Social Movement Theory and Research: An Annotated Bibliographical Guide,* edited by Roberta Garner and John Tenuto, 1–58. Magill Bibliographies. Lanham, MD, and London: Scarecrow Press.

———. 2001. *Social Theory, Continuity and Confrontation.* Peterborough, ON: Broadview Press.

———. 2007. *Social Theory: Continuity and Confrontation.* 2nd ed. Peterborough, ON: Canada: Broadview Press.

———. 2006. "Learning from Chicago." In *The New Chicago,* edited by John Koval et al., 305–318. Philadelphia: Temple University Press.

Garner, Roberta, Black Hawk Hancock, and Kiljoong Kim. 2007. "Segregation in Chicago." *The Tocqueville Review* 28, no. 1: 41–74.

Gelles, Richard J. 1974. *The Violent Home: A Study of Physical Aggression between Husbands and Wives.* Beverly Hills, CA: Sage.

Georgakis, Dan. 1998. *Detroit: I Do Mind Dying: A Study in Urban Revolution.* Boston: South End Press.

Gerbner, George. 1981. "George Gerbner Archive: House Subcommittee on Telecommunications, 1981." Annenberg School of Communications, www.asc.upenn.edu/gerbner/archive.aspx?sectionID=158&packageID=212.

———. 2002. *Against the Mainstream: The Selected Works of George Gerbner.* New York: Peter Lang Publishers.

Gergen, Kenneth. 1991. *The Saturated Self.* New York: HarperCollins (Basic Books).

Gerth, Hans, and C. Wright Mills. 1953. *Character and Social Structure.* Boston: Beacon Press.

Gilmore, David. 1991. *Manhood in the Making: Cultural Concepts of Masculinity.* New Haven, CT: Yale University Press.

Gilmore, Ruth Wilson. 2007. *Golden Gulag: Prisons, Surplus, Crisis, and Opposition in Globalizing California.* Berkeley: University of California Press.

Gilroy, Paul. 1993. *The Black Atlantic: Modernity and Double-Consciousness.* Cambridge, MA: Harvard University Press.

———. 1994. *Small Acts: Thoughts on the Politics of Black Cultures.* London: Serpent's Tail.

Gitlin, Todd. 1983. *Inside Prime Time.* New York: Pantheon Books.

———. 2003. *The Whole World Is Watching.* Berkeley: University of California Press.

Goffman, Erving. 1959. *The Presentation of Self in Everyday Life.* Garden City, NY: Anchor Books.

———. 1961. *Asylums: Essays on the Social Situation of Mental Patients and Other Inmates.* Garden City, NY: Anchor Books.

———. 1963a. *Behavior in Public Places: Notes on the Social Organization of Gatherings.* New York: Free Press.

———. 1963b. *Stigma: Notes on the Management of Spoiled Identity.* Englewood Cliffs, NJ: Prentice Hall.

———. 1967. *Interaction Ritual: Essays on Face-to-Face Behavior.* Garden City, NY: Anchor Books.

————. 1971. *Relations in Public: Microstudies of the Public Order.* New York: Basic Books.

————. 1974. *Frame Analysis: An Essay on the Organization of Experience.* New York: Harper and Row.

————. 1988. *Gender Advertisements.* Rev. ed. New York: HarperCollins.

Goldthorpe, J. E. 1987. *Family Life in Western Societies: A Historical Sociology of Family Relationships in Britain and North America.* Cambridge: Cambridge University Press.

Goode, William. 1957. "Community within a Community: The Professions." *American Sociological Review* 25: 483–496.

Goodman, Paul. 1962. *Growing Up Absurd.* New York: Vintage.

Goodwin, Jeff, and Theda Skocpol. 1989. "Explaining Revolutions in the Third World." *Politics and Society* 174 (December): 489–509.

Gottfredson, Michael R., and Travis Hirschi. 1990. *A General Theory of Crime.* Stanford, CA: Stanford University Press.

Gramlich, Edward, Richard Kasten, and Frank Sammartino. 1993. "Growing Inequality in the 1980s: The Role of Federal Taxes and Cash Transfers." In *Uneven Tides: Rising Inequality in America,* edited by Sheldon Danziger and Peter Gottschalk, 225–249. New York: Russell Sage Foundation.

Gramsci, Antonio. 1971. *The Prison Notebooks of Antonio Gramsci.* Edited and translated by Quentin Hoare and Geoffrey Nowell Smith. New York: International Publishers.

Gray, Bradford. 1983. *The New Health Care for Profit.* Washington, DC: National Academy Press.

————. 1991. *The Profit Motive and Patient Care.* Cambridge, MA: Harvard University Press.

Greenwood, Ernest. 1957. "Attributes of a Profession." *Social Work* 2: 44–45.

Grometstein, Alan A. 1999. *The Roots of Things: Topics in Quantum Mechanics.* New York: Kluwer Academic/Plenum Publishers.

Gunder Frank, Andre. 1971. *Capitalism and Underdevelopment in Latin America.* London: Penguin Books.

Hacking, Ian. 2002. *Mad Travelers: Reflections on the Reality of Transient Mental Illnesses.* Cambridge, MA: Harvard University Press.

————. 2003. *Rewriting the Soul: Multiple Personality and the Sciences of Memory.* Darby, PA: Diane Publishing Company.

Hafferty, Frederic. 1991. *Into the Valley of Death.* New Haven, CT: Yale University Press.

Hafferty, Frederic, and John McKinlay. 1993. *The Changing Medical Profession: An International Perspective.* New York: Oxford University Press.

Hagan, John, and Bill McCarthy. 1998. *Mean Streets: Youth Crime and Homelessness.* Cambridge: Cambridge University Press.

Hall, Stuart. 1980a. "Cultural Studies: Two Paradigms." *Media, Culture and Society* 2: 57–72.

————. 1980b. "Encoding/Decoding." In *Culture, Media, Language: Papers in Cultural Studies,* edited by D. Hobson, A. Lowe, and P. Willis, 128–138. London: Hutchinson.

————. 1980c. "Race, Articulation and Societies Structured in Dominance." In *Sociological Theories: Race and Colonialism,* 305–345. Paris: UNESCO.

————. 1981. "The Whites of Their Eyes: Racist Ideologies and the Media." In *Silver Linings: Some Strategies for the Eighties,* edited by G. Bridges and R. Brunt, 28–52. London: Lawrence and Wishart.

————. 1982. "The Rediscovery of 'Ideology': Return of the Repressed in Media Studies." In *Culture, Society and the Media,* edited by M. Gurevitch et al., 56–90. London: Methuen.

————. 1986. "Gramsci's Relevance for the Study of Race and Ethnicity." *Journal of Communication Inquiry* 10, no. 5: 5–27.

———. 1987. "Minimal Selves." In *Identity: The Real Me*, 44–46. ICA Documents 6. London: Institute of Contemporary Arts.

———. 1991a. "The Local and the Global: Globalization and Ethnicity." In *Culture, Globalization and the World-System: Contemporary Conditions for the Representation of Identity*, edited by A. King, 19–39. Basingstoke, UK: Macmillan.

———. 1991b. "Old and New Identities, Old and New Ethnicities." In *Culture, Globalization and the World-System: Contemporary Conditions for the Representation of Identity*, edited by A. King, 41–68. Basingstoke, UK: Macmillan.

———. 1992. "What Is This 'Black' in Black Popular Culture?" In *Black Popular Culture*, edited by Gina Dent, 21–33. Seattle: Bay Press.

———. 1996/1988. "New Ethnicities." In *Stuart Hall: Critical Dialogues in Cultural Studies*, edited by D. Morley and K. Chen, 441–449. London: Routledge.

Hall, Stuart, et al. 1978. *Policing the Crisis.* London: Macmillan Press.

Hall, Stuart, and T. Jefferson, eds. 1976. *Resistance through Rituals: Youth Subcultures in Postwar Britain.* London: Hutchinson.

Hamilton, L., S. Cheng, and B. Powell. 2007. "Adoptive Parents, Adaptive Parents: Evaluating the Importance of Biological Ties for Parental Investment." *American Sociological Review* 72: 95–116.

Hancock, Black Hawk. 2005. "Steppin' Out of Whiteness." *Ethnography* 6, no. 4: 481–515.

Hannerz, Ulf. 1992. *Cultural Complexity: Studies in the Social Organization of Meaning.* New York: Columbia University Press.

Hansen, Karen V. 2004. *Not-So-Nuclear Families: Class, Gender, and Networks of Care.* New Brunswick, NJ: Rutgers University Press.

Hartigan, John, Jr. 1999. *Racial Situations.* Princeton, NJ: Princeton University Press.

Harvey, David. 1990. *The Condition of Postmodernity.* Cambridge: Blackwell Publishers.

———. 2007. *A Brief History of Neoliberalism.* Oxford: Oxford University Press.

Hays, Sharon. 1996. *The Cultural Constructions of Motherhood.* New Haven, CT: Yale University Press.

Hebdige, Dick. 1981. *Subculture: The Meaning of Style.* London: Routledge.

Herdt, Gilbert. 1987. *The Sambia: Ritual and Gender in New Guinea.* Orlando, FL: Holt, Rinehart and Winston.

Herman, Edward S., and Noam Chomsky. 1988. *Manufacturing Consent.* New York: Pantheon Books.

Hertsgaard, Mark. 1989. *On Bended Knee: The Press and the Reagan Presidency.* New York: Schocken Books.

Hirschi, Travis. 1969/2002. *Causes of Delinquency.* New Brunswick, NJ: Transaction Books.

Ho, Karen. 2009. *Liquidated: An Ethnography of Wall Street.* Durham, NC: Duke University Press.

Hobsbawm, Eric, and Terence Ranger, eds. 1992. *The Invention of Tradition.* Cambridge: Cambridge University Press.

Hochschild, Arlie, with Anne Machung. 1989. *The Second Shift: Working Parents and the Revolution at Home.* New York: Viking.

Hochschild, Arlie Russell. 2002. "Love and Gold." In *Global Woman: Nannies, Maids, and Sex Workers in the New Economy*, edited by Barbara Ehrenreich and Arlie Russell Hochschild, 15–30. New York: Metropolitan Books.

hooks, bell. 1990. *Yearning: Race, Gender, and Cultural Politics.* Boston: South End Press.

Iceland, John, and Rima Wilkes. 2006. "Does Socioeconomic Status Matter? Race, Class, and Residential Segregation." *Social Problems* 53, no. 2: 248–273.

Ignatiev, Noel. 1996. *How the Irish Became White*. New York: Routledge.

Irvine, Leslie. 2000. "Even Better Than the Real Thing: Narratives of Self in Codependency." *Qualitative Sociology* 23: 9–28.

Jacoby, Russell. 1986. *The Repression of Psychoanalysis: Otto Fenichel and the Freudians*. Chicago: University of Chicago Press.

Jameson, Fredric. 1972. *The Prison-House of Language*. Princeton, NJ: Princeton University Press.

———. 1981. *The Political Unconscious*. Ithaca, NY: Cornell University Press.

———. 1988. *The Ideology of Theory: Essays 1971–1986*. 2 vols. Minneapolis: University of Minnesota Press.

———. 1990/1996. *Late Marxism*. London: Verso.

———. 1991/2005. *Postmodernism, or the Cultural Logic of Late Capitalism*. Durham, NC: Duke University Press.

———. 1998. *The Cultural Turn*. London: Verso.

———. 2007. *Jameson on Jameson*. Durham, NC: Duke University Press.

———. 2011. *Representing Capital: A Reading of Volume One*. London: Verso.

Jaskot, Paul. 2000. *The Architecture of Oppression*. New York: Routledge.

Jay, Martin. 1996. *The Dialectical Imagination: A History of the Frankfurt School and the Institute of Social Research, 1923–1950*. Berkeley: University of California Press.

Kakpo, Nathalie. 2007. *L'islam, un recours pour les jeunes* [*Islam: A Recourse for Youth*]. Paris: Presses de Sciences Po.

Kaplan, George, and John Lynch. 1997. "Editorial: Whither Studies on the Socioeconomic Foundations of Population Health?" *American Journal of Public Health* 87: 409–411.

Katz, Elihu. 1957. "The Two-Step Flow of Communication: An Up-to-Date Report on a Hypothesis." *Public Opinion Quarterly* 21, no. 1 (Spring): 61–78.

Katz, Elihu, and Paul Lazarsfeldt. 2005. *Personal Influence: The Part Played by People in the Flow of Mass Communication*. New Brunswick, NJ: Transaction Books.

Katz, Jack. 1988. *Seductions of Crime: Moral and Sensual Attractions in Doing Evil*. New York: Basic Books.

Katznelson, Ira. 1982. *City Trenches: Urban Politics and the Patterning of Class in America*. Chicago: University of Chicago Press.

———. 2006. *When Affirmative Action Was White: An Untold History of Racial Inequality in America*. New York: W. W. Norton.

Kawachi, Ichiro, and Bruce Kennedy. 1997. "Health and Social Cohesion: Why Care about Income Inequality?" *British Medical Journal* 314: 1037–1040.

Kawachi, Ichiro, Bruce Kennedy, and Richard Wilkinson. 1999. *The Society and Population Health Reader*. Vol. 1. New York: The New Press.

Kelling, George, and James Q. Wilson. 1982. "Broken Windows: The Police and Neighborhood Safety." *Atlantic Monthly* 249, no. 3 (March): 29–38.

Kerr, Peter. 2001. *Postwar British Politics: From Conflict to Consensus*. London: Taylor and Francis/Routledge.

Khurana, Rakesh. 2002. *Searching for a Corporate Savior: The Irrational Quest for Charismatic CEOs*. Princeton, NJ: Princeton University Press.

Kim, Chang Hwan, and Arthur Sakamoto. 2008. "The Rise of Intra-Occupational Wage Inequality in the U.S., 1983–2002." *American Sociological Review* 73: 129–157.

King, Deborah. 1988. "Multiple Jeopardy, Multiple Consciousness: The Context of a Black Feminist Ideology." *Signs* 14, no. 1: 42–72.

Klatch, Rebecca. 1999. *A Generation Divided: The New Left, the New Right, and the 1960s.* Berkeley: University of California Press.

———. 2002. "The Development of Individual Identity and Consciousness among the Movements of the Left and Right." In *Social Movements: Identity, Culture, and the State,* edited by David Meyer, Nancy Whittier, and Belinda Robnett, 185–204. Oxford: Oxford University Press.

Klinenberg, Eric. 2002. *Heat Wave.* Chicago: University of Chicago Press.

Koch, Andrew, and Rick Elmore. 2006. "Simulation and Symbolic Exchange: Jean Baudrillard's Augmentation of Marx's Theory of Value." *Politics and Policy* 34, no. 3: 556–575.

Kohn, Melvin. 1977. *Class and Conformity: A Study in Values.* Chicago: University of Chicago Press.

Koval, John, et al. 2006. *The New Chicago.* Philadelphia: Temple University Press.

Kreiger, Nancy. 2001. "Theories for Social Epidemiology in the 21st Century: An Ecosocial Perspective." *International Journal of Epidemiology* 30: 668–677.

Kriesi, Hanspeter. 1996. "The Organizational Structure of New Social Movements in a Political Context." In *Comparative Perspectives on Social Movements,* edited by Doug McAdam, John McCarthy, and Mayer N. Zald, 152–184. Cambridge: Cambridge University Press.

Kubrin, Charis E., and Eric A. Stewart. 2006. "Predicting Who Reoffends: The Neglected Role of Neighborhood Context in Recidivism Studies." *Criminology* 44, no. 1: 165–197.

Kuhn, Thomas. 1962. *The Structure of Scientific Revolutions.* Chicago: University of Chicago Press.

Kunst, Anton, and Johan Mackenbach. 1994. "The Size of Mortality Differences Associated with Educational Level in Nine Industrialized Countries." *American Journal of Public Health* 84: 32–37.

Ladanyi, J., and I. Szelenyi. 2006. *Patterns of Exclusion: Constructing Gypsy Ethnicity and the Making of an Underclass in Transitional Societies of Europe.* East European Monographs. New York: Columbia University.

Lagrange, Hugues, and Marco Oberti. 2006. *Émeutes urbaines et protestations* [*Urban Riots and Protests*]. Paris: Presse de Sciences Po.

Lareau, Annette. 2011. *Unequal Childhoods: Class, Race, and Family Life.* 2nd ed. Berkeley: University of California Press.

LaRossa, Ralph. 1988. "Fatherhood and Social Change." *Family Relations* 37: 451–457.

———. 1997. *The Modernization of Fatherhood: A Social and Political History.* Chicago: University of Chicago Press.

Le Wita, Beatrix. 1994. *French Bourgeois Culture.* Translated by J. A. Underwood. Cambridge: Cambridge University Press.

Leggett, John. 1968. *Class, Race, and Labor: Working Class Consciousness in Detroit.* Oxford: Oxford University Press.

Leonhardt, David. 2010. "The Value of College." *New York Times, Business Day,* May 17, http://economix.blogs.nytimes.com/2010/05/17/the-value-of-college-2.

Lerner, Daniel. 1958. *The Passing of Traditional Society: Modernizing the Middle East.* New York: Macmillan Company.

Light, Donald. 1992. "The Practice and Ethics of Risk-Rated Health Insurance." *Journal of Health and Social Behavior* 29: 307–322.

———. 2004. "Cost Containment and the Backdraft of Competition Politics." In *Political and Economic Determinants of Population Health and Well-Being: Controversies and Developments,* edited by Vicente Navarro and Carles Muntaner, 173–200. Amityville, NY: Baywood Publishing Company.

Light, Donald, and Sol Levine. 1988. "The Changing Character of the Medical Profession: A Theoretical Overview." *Milbank Quarterly* 66: 10–32.

Lindesmith, Alfred, and Anselm Strauss. 1956. *Social Psychology,* 2nd ed. New York: Henry Holt.

Link, Bruce, and Jo Phelan. 1995. "Social Conditions as Fundamental Causes of Disease." *Journal of Health and Social Behavior* (extra issue): 90–94.

Lipman, Pauline. 2006. "Chicago School Reform: Advancing the Global City Agenda." In *The New Chicago,* edited by John Koval et al., 248–258. Philadelphia: Temple University Press.

Lorber, Judith. 1997. *Gender and the Social Construction of Illness.* Thousand Oaks, CA: Sage.

Lorde, Audre. 2004. *Conversations with Audre Lorde.* Oxford: University of Mississippi Press.

Loseke, Donileen. 1992. *The Battered Woman and Shelter: The Social Construction of Wife Abuse.* Albany: State University of New York Press.

Lowenthal, Leo. 1984. *Literature and Mass Culture.* New Brunswick, NJ: Transaction Books.

Lynch, John. 2000. "Income Inequality and Health: Expanding the Debate." *Social Science and Medicine* 51: 1001–1005.

Maloutas, Thomas. 2007. "Middle Class Education Strategies and Residential Segregation in Athens." *Journal of Education Policy* 22, no. 1 (January): 49–68.

Mandel, Ernest. 1978. *Late Capitalism.* London: Verso.

Manning, Wendy D., and Pamela J. Smock. 2005. "Measuring and Modeling Cohabitation: New Perspectives from Qualitative Data." *Journal of Marriage and Family* 67: 989–1002.

Mansbridge, Jane, and Aldon Morris, eds. 2001. *Oppositional Consciousness: The Subjective Roots of Social Protest.* Chicago: University of Chicago Press.

Marcuse, Herbert. 1955. *Eros and Civilization.* Boston: Beacon Press.

Marmot, Michael. 2004. *The Status Syndrome.* New York: Henry Holt and Company.

Marshall, Katherine. 2006. "Converging Gender Roles" *Perspectives on Labor and Income* 7, no. 7: 5–17. Available from Statistics Canada at www.statcan.gc.ca/pub/75-001 -x/10706/9268-eng.htm.

Marty, Martin, and Scott Appleby. 1992. *The Glory and the Power: The Fundamentalist Challenge to the Modern World.* Boston: Beacon Press.

Marx, Gary T. 1984. "Role Models and Role Distance: A Remembrance of Erving Goffman." *Theory and Society* 13: 649–662.

Marx, Karl, and Friedrich Engels. 1960. *The German Ideology.* New York: International Publishers.

———. 1969. *The Communist Manifesto.* In *Selected Works, Volume One,* translated by F. Engels (1888) and Samuel Moore, 98–137. Moscow: Progress Publishers.

Mason-Schrock, Douglas. 1996. "Transsexuals' Narrative Construction of the 'True Self.'" *Social Psychology Quarterly* 59, no. 3: 176–192.

Massey, Douglas, and Mary Denton. 1993. *American Apartheid: Segregation and the Making of the Underclass.* Cambridge, MA: Harvard University Press.

Matza, David. 1961. "Subterranean Traditions of Youth." *Annals of the American Academy of Political and Social Science* 338, no. 1: 102–118.

McAdam, Doug, John McCarthy, and Mayer N. Zald. 1996. *Comparative Perspectives on Social Movements.* Cambridge: Cambridge University Press.

McAdam, Doug, Sidney Tarrow, and Charles Tilly. 2001/2003. *Dynamics of Contention.* Cambridge: Cambridge University Press.

McCall, Leslie. 2000. *Complex Inequality: Gender, Class, and Race in the New Economy.* New York: Routledge.

McKeown, Thomas. 1976. *The Role of Medicine.* London: The Nuffield Provincial Hospitals Trust.

McKinlay, John. 1986. "The Case for Refocusing Upstream: The Political Economy of Illness." In *The Sociology of Health and Illness: Critical Perspectives,* edited by Peter Conrad and Rochelle Kern, 484–498. 2nd ed. New York: St. Martin's Press.

McKinlay, John, and John Stoeckle. 1988. "Corporatization and the Social Transformation of Doctoring." *International Journal of Health Services* 18: 191–205.

McLuhan, Marshall. 1964. *Understanding Media: The Extensions of Man.* New York: McGraw-Hill.

Mead, George Herbert. 1932. *Mind, Self, and Society.* Chicago: University of Chicago Press.

Mechanic, David. 1972. *Public Expectations and Health Care.* New York: Wiley-Interscience.

———. 1978. *Medical Sociology.* New York: Free Press.

———. 2006. *The Truth about Health Care.* Piscataway, NJ: Rutgers University Press.

Melucci, Alberto. 1989. *Nomads of the Present: Social Movements and Individual Needs in Contemporary Society.* Philadelphia: Temple University Press.

Merton, Robert. 1938. "Social Structure and Anomie." *American Sociological Review* 3, no. 1: 672–682.

Merton, Robert, George Reeder, and Patricia Kendall. 1957. *The Student Physician.* Cambridge, MA: Harvard University Press.

Messerschmidt, James. 1993. *Masculinities and Crime.* New York: Rowman and Littlefield.

Meyer, David, Nancy Whittier, and Belinda Robnett. 2002. *Social Movements: Identity, Culture, and the State.* Oxford: Oxford University Press.

Milanovic, Branko. 2005a. "Global Income Inequality: What It Is and Why It Matters." Carnegie Endowment, www.carnegieendowment.org/2005/12/01/global-income-inequality-what-it-is-and-why-it-matters/bn33.

———. 2005b. *Worlds Apart: Measuring International and Global Inequality.* Princeton, NJ: Princeton University Press.

———. 2008. "Where in the World Are You? Assessing the Importance of Circumstances and Effort in a World of Different Mean Country Incomes and (Almost) No Migration." World Bank, February, http://elibrary.worldbank.org/content/workingpaper/10.1596/1813-9450-4493.

Miles, Malcolm. 2007. *Cities and Cultures.* London: Routledge.

Mills, C. Wright. 1940. "Situated Actions and Vocabularies of Motives." *American Sociological Review* 5: 904–913.

———. 1954/1963. "Mass Society and Liberal Education." In *Power, Politics and People,* 353–373. New York: Ballantine Books.

———. 1959/2000. *The Sociological Imagination.* New York: Oxford University Press.

Mitchell, Juliet. 1975. *Psychoanalysis and Feminism: Freud, Reich, Laing and Women.* New York: Vintage Books.

Mollenkopf, John. 1983. *The Contested City.* Princeton, NJ: Princeton University Press.

Molm, Linda, and Karen Cook. 1995. "Social Exchange and Exchange Networks." In *Sociological Perspectives on Social Psychology,* edited by Karen Cook, Gary Fine, and James House, 209–235. Needham Heights, MA: Allyn and Bacon.

Molotch, Harvey, and Marilyn Lester. 1974. "Accidents, Scandals, and Routines: Resources for Insurgent Methodology." In *The TV Establishment,* edited by Gaye Tuchman, 53–65. Englewood Cliffs, NJ: Prentice Hall.

Navarro, Vincente. 1976. *Medicine under Capitalism.* New York: Prodist.

———. 1986. *Crisis, Health and Medicine: A Social Critique.* New York: Tavistock.

Navarro, Vicente, and Carles Muntaner. 2004. *Political and Economic Determinants of Population Health and Well-Being: Controversies and Developments.* Amityville, NY: Baywood Publishing Company.

O'Connor, Julia S., Ann Shola Orloff, and Sheila Shaver. 1999. *States, Markets, Families: Gender, Liberalism and Social Policy in Australia, Canada, Great Britain and the United States.* Cambridge: Cambridge University Press.

Oberti, Marco. 2005. "School Choice in Paris." Paper given at the Conference on Comparative Perspectives on Urban Segregation: Chicago, Paris, Rio de Janeiro, DePaul University, Chicago, June 3–4.

Omi, Michael, and Howard Winant. 1994. *Racial Formation in the United States: From the 1960s to the 1980s.* New York: Routledge.

Orloff, A. S. 1993. "Gender and the Social Rights of Citizenship: The Comparative-Analysis of Gender Relations and Welfare States." *American Sociological Review* 58: 303–328.

Pakulski, Jan. 2005/2006. "Foundations of a Post-Class Analysis." In *Approaches to Class Analysis,* edited by Erik Olin Wright, 152–179. New York: Cambridge University Press (2005 for online; 2006 for print).

Parenti, Michael. 1986. *Inventing Reality: The Politics of the Mass Media.* New York: St. Martin's Press.

Park, Robert, and Ernest Burgess. 1925. *The City.* Chicago: University of Chicago Press.

Parrenas, Rhacel. 2005. "Long Distance Intimacy: Class, Gender and Intergenerational Relations between Mothers and Children in Filipino Transnational Families." *Global Networks* 5: 317–336.

Parrenas, Rhacel Salazar. 2002. "The Care Crisis in the Philippines: Children and Transnational Families in the New Global Economy." In *Global Woman: Nannies, Maids, and Sex Workers in the New Economy,* edited by B. Ehrenreich and A. R. Hochschild, 39–54. New York: Metropolitan Books.

Parsons, Talcott. 1937/1961. *The Structure of Social Action.* Glencoe, IL: Free Press.

———. 1951. *The Social System.* Glencoe, IL: Free Press.

Parsons, Talcott, and Robert F. Bales. 1955. *Family Socialization and the Interaction Process.* New York: Free Press.

Pattillo, Mary. 1999. *Black Picket Fences: Privilege and Peril among the Black Middle Class.* Chicago: University of Chicago Press.

———. 2008. *Black on the Block.* Chicago: University of Chicago Press.

Pearlin, Leonard, et al. 1981. "The Stress Process." *Journal of Health and Social Behavior* 22: 337–356.

Perrow, Charles. 1963. "Goals and Power Structures: A Historical Case Study." In *The Hospital in Modern Society,* edited by Eliot Freidson, 112–146. New York: Free Press.

———. 1999. *Normal Accidents.* Princeton, NJ: Princeton University Press.

Pescosolido, B. A. 1992. "Beyond Rational Choice: The Social Dynamics of How People Seek Help." *American Journal of Sociology* 97: 1096–1138.

Pescosolido, Bernice, Jane McLeod, and Margarita Alegria. 2000. "Confronting the Second Social Contract: The Place of Medical Sociology in Research and Policy for the

Twenty-First Century." In *Handbook of Medical Sociology,* edited by Chloe Bird, Peter Conrad, and Allen Fremont, 411–426. Upper Saddle River, NJ: Prentice Hall.

Petersilia, Joan. 2003. *When Prisoners Come Home?: Parole and Prisoner Reentry.* Oxford: Oxford University Press.

Piketty, Thomas, and Emmanuel Saez. 2003. "Income Inequality in the United States, 1913–1998." *Quarterly Journal of Economics* 118, no. 1: 1–39.

Pitts, Victoria. 2003. *In the Flesh: The Cultural Politics of Body Modification.* New York: Palgrave Macmillan.

Pleck, Joseph H. 1987. "American Fathering in Historical Perspective." In *Changing Men: New Directions in Research on Men and Masculinity,* edited by M. S. Kimmel, 83–97. Beverly Hills, CA: Sage.

Popenoe, David. 1993. "American Family Decline, 1960–1990: A Review and Appraisal." *Journal of Marriage and Family* 55: 527–542.

Powdermaker, Hortense. 1950. *Hollywood: The Dream Factory.* Boston: Little, Brown and Company.

Powell, Brian, and Douglas B. Downey. 1997. "Living in Single-Parent Households: An Investigation of the Same-Sex Hypothesis." *American Sociological Review* 62: 521–539.

Przeworski, Adam. 1991. *Democracy and the Market.* Cambridge: Cambridge University Press.

Puentes, Robert, and David Warren. 2006. "One-Fifth of America: A Comprehensive Guide to America's First Suburbs." Brookings, February, www.brookings.edu/research/reports/2006/02/metropolitanpolicy-puentes.

Pugh, Allison J. 2009. *Longing and Belonging: Parents, Children, and Consumer Culture.* Berkeley: University of California Press.

Putnam, Robert. 2001. *Bowling Alone: The Collapse and Revival of American Community.* New York: Simon and Schuster.

Quadagno, Jill. 2004. *One Nation, Uninsured.* New York: Oxford.

Quinney, Richard. 1974. *Critique of Legal Order: Crime Control in Capitalist Society.* Boston: Little, Brown and Company.

Rangaswamy, Padma. 2006a. "Asian Indians in Chicago" In *The New Chicago,* edited by John Koval et al., 128–140. Philadelphia: Temple University Press.

———. 2006b. "Devon Avenue: A World Market." In *The New Chicago,* edited by John Koval et al., 221–230. Philadelphia: Temple University Press.

Reich, Robert. 1991. *The Work of Nations.* New York: Alfred A. Knopf.

Riesebrodt, Martin. 1993/1998. *Pious Passion: The Emergence of Modern Fundamentalism in the United States and Iran.* Berkeley: University of California Press.

Riesman, David, Nathan Glazer, and Reuel Denney. 1961. *The Lonely Crowd.* New Haven, CT: Yale University Press.

Risman, Barbara J. 1987. "Intimate Relationships from a Microstructural Perspective: Men Who Mother." *Gender and Society* 1: 6–32.

Ritzer, George. 1996a. *Sociological Theory.* New York: McGraw-Hill.

———. 1996b. *The McDonaldization of Society.* Thousand Oaks, CA: Pine Forge Press.

Robert, Stephanie, and James House. 2002. "Socioeconomic Inequalities in Health: An Enduring Sociological Problem." In *Handbook of Medical Sociology*, edited by Chloe Bird, Peter Conrad, and Allen Fremont, 79–97. 5th ed. Upper Saddle River, NJ: Prentice Hall.

Roberts, Kenneth. 1999. *Deepening Democracy: The Modern Left and Social Movements in Chile and Peru.* Stanford, CA: Stanford University Press.

Roediger, David. 1999. *The Wages of Whiteness: Race and the Making of the American Working Class.* Rev. ed. London: Verso.

Rosaldo, Renato. 2004. "Grief and a Headhunter's Rage." In *Anthropological Theory: An Introductory History,* edited by Jon R. McGee and Richard L. Warms, 579–593. 3rd ed. New York: McGraw-Hill.

Rosich, Katherine, and Janet Hankin. 2010. "Executive Summary: What Do We Know? Key Findings from 50 Years of Medical Sociology." *Journal of Health and Social Behavior* 51, no. 1: Supplement 1–59.

Roth, Julius. 1973. *Timetables.* Indianapolis: Bobbs-Merrill.

Ruzek, Sheryl. 1979. *The Women's Health Movement.* New York: Praeger.

Said, Edward. 1979. *Orientalism.* New York: Vintage.

Sainsbury, Diane. 1996. *Gender, Equality, and Welfare States.* Cambridge: Cambridge University Press.

Sampson, Robert. 2011. *Great American City.* Chicago: University of Chicago Press.

Sampson, Robert, and John H. Laub. 1995. *Crime in the Making: Pathways and Turning Points through Life,* 1st ed. Cambridge, MA: Harvard University Press.

———. 2005. "A Life-Course View of the Development of Crime." *The Annals of the American Academy of Political and Social Science* 602, no. 1: 12–45.

Sampson, Robert, and Stephen Raudenbush. 1999. "Systematic Social Observation of Public Spaces: A New Look at Disorder in Urban Neighborhoods." *American Journal of Sociology* 105: 603–651.

Sapolsky, Robert. 1998. *Why Zebras Don't Get Ulcers.* New York: W. H. Freeman.

Sarkisian, Natalia, Mariana Gerena, and Naomi Gerstel. 2007. "Extended Family Integration among Euro and Mexican Americans: Ethnicity, Gender, and Class." *Journal of Marriage and Family* 69: 40–54.

Sassen, Saskia. 2000. "The Global City: Strategic Site/New Frontier." *American Studies* 41, no. 2–3 (Summer/Fall): 79–95.

———. 2001. *The Global City: New York, London, Tokyo.* Rev. ed. Princeton, NJ: Princeton University Press.

Scheff, Thomas. 1974. "The Labeling Theory of Mental Illness." *American Sociological Review* 39: 444–452.

Schmalzbauer, Leah. 2004. "Searching for Wages and Mothering from Afar: The Case of Honduran Transnational Families." *Journal of Marriage and Family* 66: 1317–1331.

Schudson, Michael. 1981. *Discovering the News. A Social History of American Newspapers.* New York: Basic Books.

———. 1986. *Advertising: The Uneasy Persuasion.* New York: Basic Books.

Scott, James. 1987. *Weapons of the Weak: Everyday Forms of Peasant Resistance.* New Haven, CT: Yale University Press.

Sen, Amartya. 1992. *Inequality Reexamined.* Cambridge, MA: Harvard University Press.

Sennett, Richard. 1998. *The Corrosion of Character: The Personal Consequences of Work in the New Capitalism.* New York: W. W. Norton.

Sennett, Richard, and Jonathan Cobb. 1972. *The Hidden Injuries of Class.* New York: W. W. Norton.

Simmel, Georg. 1950/1978. "The Metropolis and Mental Life." In *The Sociology of Georg Simmel.* Translated and edited by Kurt H. Wolff, 409–424. New York: Simon and Schuster/The Free Press.

Skocpol, Theda. 1979. *States and Social Revolutions: A Comparative Analysis of France, Russia, and China.* Cambridge: Cambridge University Press.

———. 2002. "Will 9/11 and the War on Terror Revitalize American Civic Democracy?" *PS: Political Science and Politics* 35, no. 3: 537–540.

————. 2004. *Diminished Democracy: From Membership to Management in American Civic Life.* Norman: University of Oklahoma Press.

Skocpol, Theda, and Vanessa Williamson. 2012. *The Tea Party and the Remaking of Republican Conservatism.* Oxford: Oxford University Press.

Small, Will, Evan Wood, Ralf Jürgens, and Thomas Kerr. 2005. "Injection Drug Use, HIV/AIDS and Incarceration." *Canadian HIV/AIDS Legal Network: HIV/AIDS Policy and Law Review* 10, no. 3 (December): 1–10.

Smelser, Neil. 1963. *The Theory of Collective Behavior.* New York: Free Press.

Smith, Dorothy E. 1990. *The Conceptual Practices of Power: A Feminist Sociology of Knowledge.* Lebanon, NH: University Press of New England.

Smith, Harry. 1955. "Two Lines of Authority Are One Too Many." *Modern Hospital* 84: 59–64.

Smith, Neil. 1996. *The New Urban Frontier: Gentrification and the Revanchist City.* New York: Routledge.

Smock, Pamela J. 2000. "Cohabitation in the United States: An Appraisal of Research Themes, Findings, and Implications." *Annual Review of Sociology* 26: 1–20.

Snow, David, and Leon Anderson. 1993. *Down on Their Luck: A Study of Homeless Street People.* Berkeley: University of California Press.

Snow, David, and Robert Benford. 1988. "Ideology, Frame Resonance and Participant Mobilization." In *From Structure to Action: Comparing Social Movements across Cultures,* edited by Bert Klandermans, Hanspeter Kriesi, and Sidney Tarrow, 197–217. Greenwich, CT: JAI Press.

Soja, Edward. 1996. "Los Angeles 1965–1992: From Crisis-Generated Restructuring to Restructuring-Generated Crisis." In *The City: Los Angeles and Urban Theory at the End of the Twentieth Century,* edited by A. J. Scott and E. W. Soja, 426–462. Berkeley: University of California Press.

Sorkin, M. 1992. *See You in Disneyland.* Cambridge, MA: MIT Press.

Spirou, Costas, and Larry Bennett. 2003. *It's Hardly Sporting: Stadiums, Neighborhoods, and the New Chicago.* DeKalb: Northern Illinois University Press.

Stacey, Judith. 1998. *Brave New Families: Stories of Domestic Upheaval in Late-Twentieth-Century America.* Berkeley: University of California Press.

Starr, Paul. 1982. *The Social Transformation of American Medicine.* New York: Basic Books.

Statistics Norway. 2006. "Fewer Children Live with Both Parents." June 20, www.ssb.no/english/subjects/02/01/20/barn_en/arkiv/art-2007-01-26-01-en.html.

Stone, Pamela. 2007. *Opting Out? Why Women Really Quit Careers and Head Home.* Berkeley: University of California Press.

Story, Louise. 2005. "Many Women at Elite Colleges Set Career Path to Motherhood." *New York Times.* September 20, www.nytimes.com/2005/09/20/national/20women.html?pagewanted=all&_r=0.

Strauss, Anselm. 1959. *Mirrors and Masks: The Search for Identity.* Glencoe, IL: Free Press.

Strauss, Robert. 1957. "The Nature and Status of Medical Sociology." *American Sociological Review* 22: 200–204.

Suchman, Edward. 1965. "Social Patterns of Illness and Medical Care." *Journal of Health and Human Behavior* 6: 2–16.

Sullivan, Maureen. 1996. "Rozzie and Harriet? Gender and Family Patterns of Lesbian Coparents." *Gender and Society* 10: 747–767.

Sutherland, Edwin. 1949. *White Collar Crime.* New York: Dryden Press.

Szelenyi, Ivan, and Janos Ladanyi. 2006. *Patterns of Exclusion: Constructing Gypsy Ethnicity and the Making of an Underclass in Transitional Societies of Europe.* East European Monographs. New York: Columbia University Press.

Takaki, Ronald. 1994. *A Different Mirror: A History of Multicultural America.* Boston: Back Bay Books.

Tarrow, Sidney. 1998. *Power in Movement.* Cambridge: Cambridge University Press.

Taussig, Michael. 1985. *The Devil and Commodity Fetishism in South America.* Chapel Hill: University of North Carolina Press.

Thoits, Peggy. 1995. "Stress, Cooing, and Social Support Processes: Where Are We? What Next?" *Journal of Health and Social Behavior* (extra issue): 53–79.

Thompson, E. P. 1966. *The Making of the English Working Class.* New York: Vintage.

Thorne, Barrie. 1993. *Gender Play: Girls and Boys in School.* New Brunswick, NJ: Rutgers University Press.

Tilly, Charles. 1978. *From Mobilization to Revolution.* Reading, MA: Addison-Wesley.

———. 1992. "How to Detect, Describe and Explain Repertoires of Contention." Unpublished paper, New School for Social Research, New York.

Tilly, Charles, Louise Tilly, and Richard Tilly. 1975. *The Rebellious Century, 1830–1930.* Cambridge, MA: Harvard University Press.

Travis, Jeremy, and Christy Ann Visher. 2005. *Prisoner Reentry and Crime in America.* Cambridge: Cambridge University Press.

Tuchman, Gaye. 1980. *Making News: A Study in the Construction of Reality.* New York: Free Press.

Turkle, Sherry. 1997. *Identity in the Age of the Internet.* New York: Simon and Schuster.

Urban Health Research Initiative (UHRI). n.d. "VIDUS [Vancouver Injection Drug Users Study]." UHRI, http://uhri.cfenet.ubc.ca/content/view/35/57.

US Bureau of Labor Statistics. 2007. "Charting the U.S. Labor Market in 2006." US Bureau of Labor Statistics, www.bls.gov/cps/labor2006/home.htm.

Vaughan, Diane. 1990. *Uncoupling: Turning Points in Intimate Relationships.* New York: Vintage.

———. 1996. *The Challenger Launch Decision: Risky Technology, Culture, and Deviance at NASA.* Chicago: University of Chicago Press.

Venkatesh, Sudhir. 2002. *American Project: The Rise and Fall of a Modern Ghetto.* Cambridge, MA: Harvard University Press.

———. 2006. *Off the Books: The Underground Economy of the Urban Poor.* Cambridge, MA: Harvard University Press.

Verhoeven, Jef C. 1993. "An Interview with Erving Goffman." *Research on Language and Social Interaction* 26, no. 3: 307–315.

Visher, Christy A., and Jeremy Travis. 2003. "Transitions from Prison to Community: Understanding Individual Pathways." *Annual Review of Sociology* 29: 89–113.

Wacquant, Loïc J. D. 2000. "The New 'Peculiar Institution': On the Prison as Surrogate Ghetto." *Theoretical Criminology* 4, no. 3: 377–389.

———. 2002. "Scrutinizing the Street: Poverty, Morality, and the Pitfalls of Urban Ethnography." *American Journal of Sociology* 107, no. 6 (May): 1468–1532.

———. 2004. *Body and Soul: Notebooks of an Apprentice Boxer.* New York: Oxford University Press.

———. 2005. "Urban Outcasts: Stigma and Division in the Black American Ghetto and the French Urban Periphery." In *The Urban Sociology Reader,* edited by Jan Lin and Christopher Mele, 144–151. London: Routledge.

———. 2007. *Urban Outcasts: A Comparative Sociology of Advanced Marginality.* Cambridge, UK: Polity Press.

———. 2008. *Deadly Symbiosis: Race and the Rise of the Penal State.* Cambridge, UK: Polity Press.

———. 2009a. *Punishing the Poor: The Neoliberal Government of Social Insecurity.* Durham, NC: Duke University Press.

———. 2009b. "The Body, the Ghetto, and the Penal State." *Qualitative Sociology* 32, no. 1: 101–129.

Waldman, R. J. 1992. "Income Distribution and Infant Mortality." *Quarterly Journal of Economics* 107: 1283–1302.

Wallerstein, Immanuel. 1974. *The Modern World-System.* Vol. 1: *Capitalist Agriculture and the Origins of the European World-Economy in the Sixteenth Century.* New York: Academic Press.

Warr, Mark. 2001. "The Social Origins of Crime: Edwin Sutherland and the Theory of Differential Association." In *Explaining Criminals and Crime: Essays in Contemporary Criminological Theory,* edited by Raymond Paternoster and Ronet Bachman, 182–191. Los Angeles: Roxbury Publishing Company.

Weber, Max. 1946/1958. "Class, Status, and Party." In *From Max Weber: Essays in Sociology,* edited by H. H. Gerth and C. W. Mills, 180–195. Oxford: Oxford University Press.

Weis, Lois. 1990. *Working Class without Work: High School Students in a De-Industrializing Economy.* New York: Routledge.

West, Candace, and Don H. Zimmerman. 1987. "Doing Gender." *Gender and Society* 1, no. 2: 125–151.

Western, Bruce. 2006. *Punishment and Inequality in America.* New York: Russell Sage.

Western, Bruce, and Becky Pettit. 2010. "Incarceration and Social Inequality." *Daedalus* 139, no. 3 (Summer): 9–19.

Whyte, William H. 2002. *The Organization Man.* Philadelphia: University of Pennsylvania Press.

Widick, Richard. 2003. "Flesh and the Free Market: (On Taking Bourdieu to the Options Exchange)." *Theory and Society* 32: 679–723.

Wilensky, Harold. 1964. "The Professionalization of Everyone?" *American Journal of Sociology* 70: 137–158.

Wilkinson, Richard. 1996. *Unhealthy Societies: The Afflictions of Inequality.* London: Routledge.

Wilkinson, Richard, and Kate Pickett. 2010. *The Spirit Level.* New York: Bloomsbury Press.

Williams, Gareth. 2002. *The Other Side of the Popular: Neo-Liberalism and Subalternity in Latin America.* Durham, NC: Duke University Press.

Williams, Rhys. 2002. "From the 'Beloved Community' to 'Family Values' Religious Language, Symbolic Repertoire and Democratic Culture." In *Social Movements: Identity, Culture, and the State,* edited by David Meyer, Nancy Whittier, and Belinda Robnett, 247–265. Oxford: Oxford University Press.

Willis, Paul. 1977. *Learning to Labor: How Working Class Kids Get Working Class Jobs.* New York: Columbia University Press.

———. 1990. *The Ethnographic Imagination.* New York: Polity Press.

Willis, Paul, et al. 1990. *Common Culture: Symbolic Work at Play in the Everyday Cultures of the Young.* Berkshire, UK: Open University Press.

Wilson, Elizabeth. 1992. "The Invisible Flaneur." *New Left Review* 191 (January–February): 95.

Wilson, William Julius. 1987. *The Truly Disadvantaged.* Chicago: University of Chicago Press.

———. 1997. *When Work Disappears: The World of the New Urban Poor.* Reprint. New York: Random House.

Winant, Howard. 2004. *The New Politics of Race: Globalization, Difference, Justice.* Minneapolis: University of Minnesota Press.

Wolf, Eric R. 1982. *Europe and the People without History.* Berkeley: University of California Press.

———. 1990/1999. *Peasant Wars of the Twentieth Century.* Oklahoma: University of Oklahoma Press.

Wolfgang, Marvin E., and Franco Ferracuti. 1967. *The Subculture of Violence: Towards an Integrated Theory in Criminology.* London: Tavistock.

Wolinsky, Frederic. 1980. *The Sociology of Health.* Boston: Little, Brown and Company.

Wright, Erik Olin. 2006. "Foundations of a Neo-Marxist Class Analysis." In *Approaches to Class Analysis,* edited by Erik Olin Wright, 4–30. New York: Cambridge University Press.

Yanow, Dvora. 2003. *Constructing "Race" and "Ethnicity" in America: Category-Making in Public Policy and Administration.* Armonk, NY: M. E. Sharpe.

Zald, Mayer N. 2009. "Looking Back on Collaborations, Looking Forward on Movements and Institutional Analysis." John McCarthy Award Address, Center for the Study of Social Movements and Social Change, Notre Dame University, April 17.

Zald, Mayer, and Roberta Ash. 1966. "Social Movement Organizations: Growth, Decay, and Change." *Social Forces* 44: 327–341.

Zald, Mayer, and John McCarthy. 1977. "Resource Mobilization and Social Movements: A Partial Theory." *American Sociological Review* 61: 478–499.

Zeitlin, Irving. 1997. *Ideology and the Development of Sociological Theory.* Toronto: University of Toronto Press.

Zerubavel, Eviatar. 1999. *Social Mindscapes: An Invitation to Cognitive Sociology.* Cambridge, MA: Harvard University Press.

Zola, Irving. 1972. "Medicine as an Institution of Social Control." *Sociological Review* 20: 487–504.

———. 1982. *Missing Pieces: A Chronicle of Living with a Disability.* Philadelphia: Temple University Press.

Zukin, Sharon. 1991. *Landscapes of Power: From Detroit to Disneyland.* Berkeley: University of California Press.

Suggested Readings

Theory: General

Benjamin, Walter. 1968. "The Work of Art in the Age of Mechanical Reproduction." In *Illuminations*. Translated by Harry Zohn, 217–252. Orlando, FL: Harcourt Brace and Company. Benjamin, Walter. 1968.

Best, Steven, and Douglas Kellner. 1991. *Postmodern Theory*. New York: Guilford Press.

Gramsci, Antonio. 1971. *The Prison Notebooks of Antonio Gramsci*. Edited and translated by Quentin Hoare and Geoffrey Nowell Smith. New York: International Publishers.

Jay, Martin. 1996. *The Dialectical Imagination: A History of the Frankfurt School and the Institute of Social Research, 1923–1950*. Berkeley: University of California Press.

Zeitlin, Irving. 1997. *Ideology and the Development of Sociological Theory*. Toronto: University of Toronto Press.

Science and Method

Camilleri, Kristian. 2009. *Heisenberg and the Interpretation of Quantum Mechanics: The Physicist as Philosopher*. Cambridge: Cambridge University Press.

Feyerabend, P. 1975. *Against Method*. London: New Left Books.

Kuhn, Thomas. 1962. *The Structure of Scientific Revolutions*. Chicago: University of Chicago Press.

Theoretical Innovators

Boucher, Geoff. 2006. "The Politics of Performativity: A Critique of Judith Butler." *Parrhesia* 1, no. 1: 112–141.

Butler, Judith, and Bronwyn Davies. 2007. *Judith Butler in Conversation: Analyzing the Texts and Talk of Everyday Life*. London: Routledge.

Butler, Judith, and Joan W. Scott, eds. 1992. *Feminists Theorize the Political*. London: Routledge.

Carver, Terrell, and Samuel Chambers, eds. 2008. *Judith Butler's Precarious Politics: Critical Encounters*. London: Routledge.

Chambers, Samuel, and Terrell Carver. 2008. *Judith Butler and Political Theory: Troubling Politics.* London: Routledge.

Davies, Bronwyn, ed. 2007. *Judith Butler in Conversation: Analyzing the Texts and Talk of Everyday Life.* London: Routledge.

Dreyfus, Hubert, and Paul Rabinow. 1982. *Michel Foucault: Beyond Structuralism and Hermeneutics.* Chicago: University of Chicago Press.

Goffman, Erving. 1959. *The Presentation of Self in Everyday Life.* Garden City, NY: Anchor Books.

———. 1961. *Asylums: Essays on the Social Situation of Mental Patients and Other Inmates.* Garden City, NY: Anchor Books.

———. 1963. *Stigma: Notes on the Management of Spoiled Identity.* Englewood Cliffs, NJ: Prentice Hall.

———. 1974. *Frame Analysis: An Essay on the Organization of Experience.* New York: Harper and Row.

———. 1988. *Gender Advertisements.* Rev. ed. New York: HarperCollins.

Gutting, Gary. 1994. *The Cambridge Companion to Foucault.* Cambridge: Cambridge University Press.

Homer, Sean. 1998. *Fredric Jameson: Marxism, Hermeneutics, Postmodernism.* New York: Routledge.

Jagger, Gill. 2004. *Judith Butler: Sexual Politics, Social Change and the Power of the Performative.* London: Routledge.

Jameson, Fredric. 1991. *Postmodernism, or The Cultural Logic of Late Capitalism.* Durham, NC: Duke University Press.

Kellner, Douglas, ed. 1989. *Jameson/Postmodernism/Critique.* Washington, DC: Maisonneuve Press.

Kellner, Douglas, and Sean Homer, eds. 2004. *Fredric Jameson: A Critical Reader.* New York: Palgrave Macmillan.

La sociologie est un sport de combat [Sociology Is a Martial Art]. 2001. Directed by Pierre Carles and Pierre Bourdieu. Video cassette. First Run Icarus Films.

Lloyd, Moya. 2007. *Judith Butler: From Norms to Politics.* Cambridge, UK: Polity.

Macey, David. 1993. *The Lives of Michel Foucault.* New York: Random House.

Rojek, Chris. 2003. *Stuart Hall.* Cambridge, UK: Polity Press.

Culture

Adamson, Glenn, and Jane Pavitt. 2011. *Postmodernism: Style and Subversion.* London: V and A Publishing.

Adler, Patricia, and Peter Adler. 2008. "Of Rhetoric and Representation: The Four Faces of Ethnography." *Sociological Quarterly* 49: 1–30.

Anderson, Benedict. 1983. *Imagined Communities: Reflections on the Origins and the Spread of Nationalism.* London: Verso.

Appadurai, Arjun. 1996. *Modernity at Large: Cultural Dimensions of Globalization.* Minneapolis: University of Minnesota Press.

Butler, Christopher. 2003. *Postmodernism: A Very Short Introduction.* Oxford: Oxford University Press.

Castells, Manuel. 2009. *Communication Power.* New York: Oxford University Press.

During, Simon. 1999. *The Cultural Studies Reader.* London: Routledge.

Eagleton, Terry. 1996. *The Illusions of Postmodernism.* Oxford, UK: Blackwell.

Frank, Thomas. 1997. *The Conquest of Cool: Business Culture, Counter-Culture, and the Rise of Hip Consumerism.* Chicago: University of Chicago Press.

Gellner, Ernest. 1992. *Postmodernism, Reason and Religion.* New York: Routledge.

Giddens, A. 1990. *The Consequences of Modernity.* Stanford, CA: Stanford University Press.

Grenz, Stanley J. 1996. *A Primer on Postmodernism.* 2nd prt. ed. Grand Rapids, MI: William B. Eerdmans.

Hardt, Michael, and Antonio Negri. 2000. *Empire.* Cambridge, MA: Harvard University Press.

Harvey, David. 2007. *A Brief History of Neoliberalism.* Oxford: Oxford University Press.

————. 2007. *The Limits to Capital.* Upd. ed. London: Verso.

————. 2011. *The Enigma of Capital and the Crisis of Capitalism.* 2nd ed. Oxford: Oxford University Press.

Hebdige, Dick. 1981. *Subculture: The Meaning of Style.* London: Routledge.

Hicks, Stephen R. C. 2011. *Explaining Postmodernism: Skepticism and Socialism from Rousseau to Foucault.* Exp. ed. Roscoe IL: Ockham's Razor.

Jameson, Fredric. 1991. *Postmodernism, or The Cultural Logic of Late Capitalism.* Durham, NC: Duke University Press.

Jameson, Fredric, and Masao Miyoshi, eds. *The Cultures of Globalization.* Durham, NC: Duke University Press.

Lyotard, Jean-Francois, et al. 1984. *The Postmodern Condition: A Report on Knowledge.* Minneapolis: University of Minnesota Press.

Robertson, Roland. 1992. *Globalization: Social Theory and Global Culture.* London: Sage.

Sassen, Saskia. 2001. *The Global City: New York, London, Tokyo.* Rev. ed. Princeton, NJ: Princeton University Press.

Smith, James K. A. 2006. *Who's Afraid of Postmodernism? Taking Derrida, Lyotard, and Foucault to Church: The Church and Postmodern Culture.* 2nd ed. Grand Rapids, MI: Baker Academic.

Tomlinson, John. 1999. *Globalization and Culture.* Chicago: University of Chicago Press.

Wallerstein, Immanuel Maurice. 1991. *Geopolitics and Geoculture: Essays on the Changing World-System.* Cambridge: Cambridge University Press.

Willis, Paul, et al. 1990. *Common Culture: Symbolic Work at Play in the Everyday Cultures of the Young.* Berkshire, UK: Open University Press.

Wolf, Eric R. 1982. *Europe and the People without History.* Berkeley: University of California Press.

Difference and Dominance: General Concepts

Butler, Judith. 1990. *Gender Trouble: Feminism and the Subversion of Identity.* New York: Routledge.

————. 1993. *Bodies That Matter: On the Discursive Limits of "Sex."* New York: Routledge.

————. 2004. *Undoing Gender.* New York: Routledge.

Collins, Patricia Hill. 2000. *Black Feminist Thought.* Rev. ed. New York: Routledge.

Katznelson, Ira. 2006. *When Affirmative Action Was White: An Untold History of Racial Inequality in America.* New York: W. W. Norton.

Race and Ethnicity

Baker, Lee D. 1998. *From Savage to Negro: Anthropology and the Construction of Race, 1896–1954.* Berkeley: University of California Press.

Gilroy, Paul. 1993. *The Black Atlantic: Modernity and Double-Consciousness.* Cambridge, MA: Harvard University Press.

Morley, David, and Kuan-Hsing Chen, eds. 1996. *Stuart Hall: Critical Dialogues in Cultural Studies.* Comedia. New York: Routledge.

Omi, Michael, and Howard Winant. 1994. *Racial Formation in the United States: From the 1960s to the 1980s.* New York: Routledge.

Pattillo-McCoy, Mary. 2000. *Black Picket Fences: Privilege and Peril among the Black Middle Class.* Chicago: University of Chicago Press.

Roediger, David. 1999. *The Wages of Whiteness: Race and the Making of the American Working Class.* Rev. ed. London: Verso.

Wacquant, Loïc J. D. 1997. "Towards an Analytic of Racial Domination." *Political Power and Social Theory* 11: 221–234.

———. 2004. *Body and Soul: Notebooks of an Apprentice Boxer.* New York: Oxford University Press.

Wilson, William Julius. 1980. *The Declining Significance of Race.* Chicago: University of Chicago Press.

———. 1997. *When Work Disappears: The World of the New Urban Poor.* Reprint. New York: Vintage Books.

Gender and Sexuality

Butler, Judith. 1990. *Gender Trouble: Feminism and the Subversion of Identity.* London: Routledge.

———. 1993. *Bodies That Matter: On the Discursive Limits of "Sex."* New York: Routledge.

Chodorow, Nancy. 1978. *The Reproduction of Mothering.* Berkeley: University of California Press.

Connell, R. W. 2005. *Masculinities.* 2nd ed. Berkeley: University of California Press.

Fausto-Sterling, Anne. 2000. *Sexing the Body: Gender Politics and the Construction of Sexuality.* New York: Basic Books.

Grosz, Elizabeth. 1994. *Volatile Bodies: Toward a Corporeal Feminism.* Bloomington: Indiana University Press.

Hill Collins, Patricia. 2000. *Black Feminist Thought.* 2nd ed. London: Routledge.

hooks, bell. 2000. *Feminism Is for Everybody.* Cambridge, MA: South End Press.

West, Candace, and Don H. Zimmerman. 1987. "Doing Gender." *Gender and Society* 1, no. 2: 125–151.

Media (See Also Suggested Readings for Culture)

Castells, Manuel. 1996. *The Rise of the Network Society.* Malden, MA: Blackwell Publishers.

Debord, Guy. 1995. *The Society of the Spectacle.* New York: Zone Books.

Gerbner, George. 2002. *Against the Mainstream: The Selected Works of George Gerbner*. New York: Peter Lang Publishers.

Self

Adorno, Theodor, Else Frenkel-Brunswik, and Daniel Levinson. 1993. *The Authoritarian Personality*. New York: W. W. Norton.

Chodorow, Nancy. 1989. *Feminism and Psychoanalytic Theory*. New Haven, CT: Yale University Press.

Denzin, Norman. 1993. *The Alcoholic Society: Addiction and Recovery of the Self*. New Brunswick, NJ: Transaction Books.

Pitts, Victoria. 2003. *In the Flesh: The Cultural Politics of Body Modification*. New York: Palgrave Macmillan.

Sennett, Richard. 1998. *The Corrosion of Character: The Personal Consequences of Work in the New Capitalism*. New York: W. W. Norton.

Zerubavel, Eviatar. 1999. *Social Mindscapes: An Invitation to Cognitive Sociology*. Cambridge, MA: Harvard University Press.

Political Sociology

Alexander, Jeffrey. 2006. *The Civil Sphere*. Oxford: Oxford University Press.

Anderson, Benedict. 1983. *Imagined Communities: Reflections on the Origins and the Spread of Nationalism*. London: Verso.

Castells, Manuel. 1996. *Power and Identity*. Malden, MA: Blackwell Publishers.

Mansbridge, Jane, and Aldon Morris, eds. 2001. *Oppositional Consciousness: The Subjective Roots of Social Protest*. Chicago: University of Chicago Press.

McAdam, Doug, Sidney Tarrow, and Charles Tilly. 2001/2003. *Dynamics of Contention*. Cambridge: Cambridge University Press.

Meyer, David, Nancy Whittier, and Belinda Robnett. 2002. *Social Movements: Identity, Culture, and the State*. Oxford: Oxford University Press.

Putnam, Robert. 2001. *Bowling Alone: The Collapse and Revival of American Community*. New York: Simon and Schuster.

Skocpol, Theda. 1979. *States and Social Revolutions: A Comparative Analysis of France, Russia, and China*. Cambridge: Cambridge University Press.

Urban Sociology

Clark, Terry Nichols. 2004. *The City as Entertainment Machine*. Bingley, UK: Elsevier/Emerald Group Publishing.

Davis, Mike. 1992. *City of Quartz*. New York: Vintage Books.

———. 2004. "Planet of Slums." *New Left Review* 26 (March–April): 5–34.

Klinenberg, Eric. 2002. *Heat Wave*. Chicago: University of Chicago Press.

Miles, Malcolm. 2007. *Cities and Cultures*. London: Routledge.

Sassen, Saskia. 2001. *The Global City: New York, London, Tokyo.* Rev. ed. Princeton, NJ: Princeton University Press.

Deviance

Anderson, Elijah. 1999. *Code of the Street: Decency, Violence, and the Moral Life of the Inner City.* New York: W. W. Norton.

Becker, Howard. 1963. *Outsiders: Studies in the Sociology of Deviance.* New York: Free Press.

Bogira, Steve. 2005. *Courtroom 302: A Year Behind the Scenes in an American Criminal Courthouse.* New York: Knopf.

Davis, Angela Y. 2003. *Are Prisons Obsolete?* New York: Seven Stories Press.

Katz, Jack. 1988. *Seductions of Crime: Moral and Sensual Attractions in Doing Evil.* New York: Basic Books.

Sampson, Robert, and John H. Laub. 1995. *Crime in the Making: Pathways and Turning Points through Life.* 1st ed. Cambridge, MA: Harvard University Press.

Travis, Jeremy, and Christy Ann Visher. 2005. *Prisoner Reentry and Crime in America.* Cambridge: Cambridge University Press.

Wacquant, Loïc J. D. 2007. *Urban Outcasts: A Comparative Sociology of Advanced Marginality.* Cambridge: Polity.

———. 2008. *Deadly Symbiosis: Race and the Rise of the Penal State.* Cambridge, UK: Polity Press.

Western, Bruce. 2006. *Imprisonment and Inequality in America.* New York: Russell Sage Foundation.

Class and Social Inequalities

Khurana, Rakesh. 2002. *Searching for a Corporate Savior: The Irrational Quest for Charismatic CEOs.* Princeton, NJ: Princeton University Press.

Lareau, Annette. 2011. *Unequal Childhoods: Class, Race, and Family Life.* 2nd ed. Berkeley: University of California Press.

Milanovic, Branko. 2005. *Worlds Apart: Measuring International and Global Inequality.* Princeton, NJ: Princeton University Press.

Sennett, Richard. 1998. *The Corrosion of Character: The Personal Consequences of Work in the New Capitalism.* New York: W. W. Norton.

Wacquant, Loïc J. D. 2007. *Urban Outcasts: A Comparative Sociology of Advanced Marginality.* Cambridge, UK: Polity Press.

———. 2009. *Punishing the Poor: The Neoliberal Government of Social Insecurity.* Durham, NC: Duke University Press.

Willis, Paul. 1977. *Learning to Labor: How Working Class Kids Get Working Class Jobs.* New York: Columbia University Press.

Wright, Erik Olin. 2006. "Foundations of a Neo-Marxist Class Analysis." In *Approaches to Class Analysis,* edited by Erik Olin Wright, 4–30. New York: Cambridge University Press.

Families

Dreby, Joanna. 2010. *Divided by Borders: Mexican Migrants and Their Children.* Berkeley: University of California Press.

Ehrenreich, Barbara, and Arlie Russell Hochschild. 2003. *Global Woman: Nannies, Maids, and Sex Workers in the New Economy.* New York: Metropolitan Books.

Hansen, Karen V. 2004. *Not-So-Nuclear Families: Class, Gender, and Networks of Care.* New Brunswick, NJ: Rutgers University Press.

Lareau, Annette. 2011. *Unequal Childhoods: Class, Race, and Family Life.* 2nd ed. Berkeley: University of California Press.

Manning, Wendy D., and Pamela J. Smock. 2005. "Measuring and Modeling Cohabitation: New Perspectives from Qualitative Data." *Journal of Marriage and Family* 67: 989–1002.

Pugh, Allison J. 2009. *Longing and Belonging: Parents, Children, and Consumer Culture.* Berkeley: University of California Press.

Risman, Barbara J. 1987. "Intimate Relationships from a Microstructural Perspective: Men Who Mother." *Gender and Society* 1: 6–32.

Stone, Pamela. 2008. *Opting Out? Why Women Really Quit Careers and Head Home.* Berkeley: University of California Press.

West, Candace, and Don H. Zimmerman. 1987. "Doing Gender." *Gender and Society* 1, no. 2: 125–151.

Sociology of Health, Illness, and Medicine

Angell, Marcia. 2004. *The Truth about the Drug Companies: How They Deceive Us and What to Do about It.* New York: Random House.

Bird, Chloe, et al., eds. 2010. *Handbook of Medical Sociology.* Nashville, TN: Vanderbilt Press.

Budrys, Grace. 2012. *Our Unsystematic Health Care System.* Lanham, MD: Rowman and Littlefield.

Institute of Medicine. 2002. *Care without Coverage: Too Little Too Late.* Washington, DC: National Academy Press.

McKinlay, John. 1986. "The Case for Refocusing Upstream: The Political Economy of Illness." In *The Sociology of Health and Illness: Critical Perspectives,* edited by Peter Conrad and Rochelle Kern, 484–498. 2nd ed. New York: St. Martin's Press.

Phelan, Jo, et al. 2004. "'Fundamental Causes' of Social Inequality in Mortality: A Test of the Theory." *Journal of Health and Social Behavior* 45: 265–285.

Physicians' Working Group for Single-Payer National Health Insurance. 2011. "Proposal of the Physicians' Working Group for Single-Payer National Health Insurance." *Journal of the American Medical Association* 290: 798–805.

Sered, Susan, and Rushika Fernandopulle. 2005. *Uninsured in America: Life and Death in the Land of Opportunity.* Berkeley: University of California Press.

Wennberg, John. 2010. *Tracking Medicine: A Researcher's Quest to Understand Health Care.* New York: Oxford University Press.

Wilkinson, Richard, and Kate Pickett. 2010. *The Spirit Level: Why Greater Equality Makes Societies Stronger.* New York: Bloomsbury Press.

Index

About the Authors and Contributors

Julie E. Artis is associate professor and chair of the Department of Sociology at DePaul University. She received her PhD from Indiana University in 1999. Her recent work on family and child well-being has been published in *Journal of Marriage and Family* and *Contexts*. She is currently engaged in a longitudinal study of judges, tracing changes in accounts of child custody decision making from the late 1990s to the present.

Grace Budrys is interested in health occupations and organizations, a focus that has led to a number of publications, including *How Nonprofits Work* (2013), *Our Unsystematic Health Care System* (third edition 2012), and *When Doctors Join Unions* (1997). She has also examined the factors that are related to the tremendous variation in this country's morbidity and mortality rates in *Unequal Health* (second edition 2003). She is currently affiliated with the Sociology and Master of Public Health Departments at DePaul University. She received her doctorate in sociology from the University of Chicago.

Roberta Garner received a PhD from the University of Chicago, where she was a student of Morris Janowitz. She is a professor of sociology at DePaul University. She has published in the area of social movements and collective behavior, most recently "Now We Are Almost Fifty! Reflections on a Theory of the Transformation of Social Movement Organizations," with Mayer N. Zald in *Social Forces*. Her current interests include the relationship between theory and quantitative and qualitative methods, presented in books such as *Changing Theories* (coauthored with Black Hawk Hancock), *Social Theory: Continuity and Confrontation* (third edition forthcoming, coedited with Black Hawk Hancock), and *Doing Qualitative Research* (coauthored with Greg Scott).

Black Hawk Hancock is an associate professor of sociology at DePaul University. He is the author of *American Allegory: Lindy Hop and the Racial Imagination* (forthcoming), as well as coauthor of *Changing Theories: New Direction in Sociology* with Roberta Garner. His main research interests are in ethnography, race and ethnicity, and social theory. His work has appeared in *Ethnography, Journal of Contemporary Ethnography, Qualitative Sociology,* and *Sociological Perspectives.*

Tait Runnfeldt Medina is a doctoral candidate in sociology at Indiana University–Bloomington. Her current research interests include the stigma of mental illness; lay and professional conceptualizations of health, illness, and healing; and cross-national research methods. She is currently involved in a seventeen-country study of public prejudice associated with mental illness. Her research on stigma and mental illness has appeared in the *American Journal of Public Health* and the *American Journal of Psychiatry* and her methodological work has appeared in the *International Journal of Public Opinion Research.* Tait has also taught quantitative methods at the Inter-University Consortium for Political and Social Research (ICPSR) Summer Program at the University of Michigan.

Greg Scott, associate professor of sociology and director of the Social Science Research Center (SSRC) at DePaul University in Chicago, Illinois, received his doctorate in sociology in 1998 from the University of California at Santa Barbara. Greg conducts quantitative, qualitative, and ethnographic research on drug-dealing street gangs and illicit drug users, mainly heroin injectors and crack smokers. He's also an independent documentary filmmaker, concentrating most of his efforts on urban street drug scenes. His most recent film, *Hurricane Blow* (National Geographic Channel, Drugs Inc.), chronicles the redevelopment of illicit drug markets in the years since Hurricane Katrina devastated the city of New Orleans.

José Soltero (PhD, University of Arizona) is associate professor of sociology at DePaul University. He works on topics related to Mexicans migrants in the US and has published *Inequality in the Workplace: Underemployment among Mexicans, African Americans, and Whites; A New Economics of Labor Migration: Analysis of Remittances to Mexico from Mexican Immigrants in Chicago;* and *Educational Achievement and Residential Distribution of Latinos in the Chicago Metropolitan Area,* among other works.

Julian Thompson is a current doctoral student at the School of Social Service Administration at the University of Chicago. His interests are the sociology of punishment, critical criminology, the intersection of the criminal justice system and the mental health system, race and ethnicity, and critical social policy. His research addresses the tensions and contradictions between the therapeutic and the punitive that emerge when the criminal justice system interfaces with the mental health system; he is examining how the attendant processes, experiences, and relationships are negotiated, mediated, and transformed.

Dan Causton, who designed the chart and table for this book, graduated from DePaul with a BA in sociology in 2011 and has a wide range of interests in race, culture, social theory, and medical sociology. He looks forward to continuing his education as a doctoral student in sociology and developing his work on Michel Foucault, care of the self, and the pharmaceutical industry.